Anne of Tim Hortons

Herb Wyile

Anne of Tim Hortons

Globalization and
the Reshaping of
Atlantic-Canadian
Literature

WILFRID LAURIER
UNIVERSITY PRESS

This book has been published with the help of a grant from the Canadian Federation for the Humanities and Social Sciences, through the Aid to Scholarly Publications Programme, using funds provided by the Social Sciences and Humanities Research Council of Canada. Wilfrid Laurier University Press acknowledges the support of the Canada Council for the Arts for our publishing program. We acknowledge the financial support of the Government of Canada through the Canada Book Fund for our publishing activities.

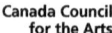  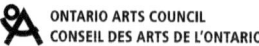

Library and Archives Canada Cataloguing in Publication

Wyile, Herb, 1961–
    Anne of Tim Hortons : globalization and the reshaping of Atlantic-Canadian literature / Herb Wyile.

Includes bibliographical references and index.
Issued also in electronic formats.
ISBN 978-1-55458-326-3

    1. Canadian literature (English)—Atlantic Provinces—History and criticism. 2. Atlantic Provinces—In literature. 3. Literature and globalization—Atlantic Provinces. I. Title.

PS8131.A8W95 2011   C810.9'9715   C2011-902268-0

Electronic formats.
ISBN 978-1-55458-370-6 (PDF), ISBN 978-1-55458-351-5 (EPUB)

    1. Canadian literature (English) —Atlantic Provinces—History and criticism. 2. Atlantic Provinces—In literature. 3. Literature and globalization—Atlantic Provinces. I. Title.

PS8131.A8W95 2011a   C810.9'9715   C2011-902269-9

Cover design by David Drummond using an image from Shutterstock. Text design by Kathe Gray.

© 2011 Wilfrid Laurier University Press
Waterloo, Ontario, Canada
www.wlupress.wlu.ca

Every reasonable effort has been made to acquire permission for copyright material used in this text, and to acknowledge all such indebtedness accurately. Any errors or omissions called to the publisher's attention will be corrected in future printings.

No part of this publication may be reproduced, stored in a retrieval system or transmitted, in any form or by any means, without the prior written consent of the publisher or a licence from The Canadian Copyright Licensing Agency (Access Copyright). For an Access Copyright licence, visit www.accesscopyright.ca or call toll free to 1–800–893–5777.

Contents

	List of Illustrations	vii
	Acknowledgements	ix
1	Introduction: "Now Our Masters Have No Borders"	1
	Section One | I'se the B'y That Leaves the Boats: The Changing World of Work	29
2	Sucking the Mother Dry: The Fisheries	33
3	"Acceptable Levels of Risk": Mining and Offshore Oil	55
4	Uncivil Servitude: The Service Sector	87
	Conclusion to Section One	99
	Section Two | "About as Far from Disneyland as You Can Possibly Get": The Reshaping of Culture	101
5	"The Simpler and More Colourful Way of Life"	105
6	Rebuffing the Gaze	137
	Conclusion to Section Two	167
	Section Three | The Age of Sale: History, Globalization, and Commodification	169
7	"A 'Sea-Change' of Sorts": Newfoundland and Labrador	173
8	"A Place That Didn't Count Any More": The Maritimes	217
	Conclusion to Section Three	233

Conclusion: Speculative Fiction for the Rest of the Country?	237
Notes	249
Works Cited	255
Photo Credits	269
Index	271

List of Illustrations

1. House of Mr. Malcolm Rogers being towed by a 40-hp motorboat during relocation — 39
2. Federal Fisheries Minister John Crosbie after announcing the 1992 cod moratorium — 42
3. "Damage to portal at No. 1 Main" — 68
4. Drill platform of *Ocean Ranger,* lost 15 February 1988 — 76
5. Donald Marshall after his acquittal in May 1983 — 109
6. Africville houses on either side of a hillside lane, seen from across the railroad tracks — 116
7. Two Halifax city officials walking up an Africville path — 119
8. Sheree Fitch, "Filling Out the Form" — 128
9. "The McGarritys watching TV." Scene from the 1997 Live Bait premiere of *The Maritime Way of Life* — 145
10. "Poor Donnie." Scene from the 1999 Live Bait Theatre/Mulgrave Road Theatre co-production — 147
11. Daniel Woodley Prowse, ca. 1900 — 180
12. J.R. Smallwood campaigning for Confederation — 185
13. John Peyton Jr., Justice of the Peace, Twillingate — 189
14. Artist's rendering of the murder of Nonosabusut and the capture of Demasduit — 191
15. Rockwell Kent in Studio — 205
16. Kent dressed as a German spy — 208
17. Captain Bob Bartlett using a sextant — 211
18. *Portrait of the MIC MAC*, 1853, painted by John O'Brien — 221
19. Police photo of George Hamilton — 225
20. Police photo of Rufus Hamilton — 225

Acknowledgements

Although my interest in Atlantic-Canadian literature goes back to my graduate work at McGill University in the mid-1980s, this present study was truly galvanized by a conference I co-organized with Jeanette Lynes at Acadia University in the fall of 2004 titled "Surf's Up! The Rising Tide of Atlantic-Canadian Literature." This installment of the Department of English's ongoing Raddall Symposium series was a vigorous, intimate, and apparently contagious gathering of established and emerging scholars and graduate students busily engaged in revitalizing the field (many of the papers from the conference appeared in a revised form in *Surf's Up! The Rising Tide of Atlantic-Canadian Literature,* a special issue of *Studies in Literature* published in 2008). David Creelman had recently published *Setting in the East: Maritime Realist Fiction* (2003), the first book-length monograph on East Coast writing in nearly twenty years, and at the conference we had the opportunity to celebrate the publication of Danielle Fuller's *Writing the Everyday: Women's Textual Communities in Atlantic Canada* (2004), a sophisticated cultural materialist investigation of the writing of women in the region. *Anne of Tim Hortons* owes much to David and Danielle's work, as well as to the contributions, collaborations, collegiality, feedback, and friendship of others working in the area, particularly the indefatigable Tony Tremblay (especially his invaluable scholarship on David Adams Richards), Jeanette Lynes, Cynthia Sugars, Chris Armstrong, Christian Riegel, Tracy Whalen, Jennifer Andrews, Bill Parenteau, and Paul Chafe (to whom go special thanks for putting me on to Frank Barry's *Wreckhouse*). Parts of this book were presented at various conferences, particularly of the Association of Canadian College and University Teachers of English and the Atlantic Canada Studies association, and I am indebted to the valuable feedback

Acknowledgements

from various colleagues at these gatherings. The book also obviously owes a huge debt to Ian McKay's *The Quest of the Folk: Antimodernism and Cultural Selection in Twentieth-Century Nova Scotia*, which has had a profound influence on Atlantic Canada studies since its publication in 1994. I am grateful to McGill-Queen's University Press for permission to quote from McKay's book in numerous instances in the following study.

Portions of this book were previously published in the form of articles. The segments on Lynn Coady's *Strange Heaven* appeared in integrated form as "As for Me and Me Arse: Strategic Regionalism and the Home Place in Lynn Coady's *Strange Heaven*" in *Canadian Literature* 189 (2006). The chapter on tourism was published in slightly different form in *English Studies in Canada* 34.2–3 (2008) as "Going Out of Their Way: Tourism, Authenticity, and Resistance in Contemporary Atlantic-Canadian Literature." Finally, my discussion of Lisa Moore's *February* appeared as "February Is the Cruelest Month: Neoliberalism and the Economy of Mourning in Lisa Moore's *February*" in *Newfoundland and Labrador Studies* 25.1 (2010). I am grateful to the editors of these three journals for granting me permission to reprint that material here. Some of the ideas in this study, furthermore, were first developed in different contexts in earlier publications. My discussion of George Elliott Clarke's *George & Rue* here owes a debt to an article I wrote on Clarke and Michael Crummey, "Making a Mess of Things: Postcolonialism, Canadian Literature, and the Ethical Turn" in *University of Toronto Quarterly* 76.3 (2007). The groundwork for the discussion of Michael Crummey's novel *River Thieves* was laid in a reading of the Gothic motifs in the novel, "Beothuk Gothic: Michael Crummey's *River Thieves*," published in *Australasian Canadian Studies* 24.2 (2006). Finally, the section on Wayne Johnston's work reframes my treatment of Johnston in an earlier article, "Historical Strip-Tease: Revelation and the *Bildungsroman* in Wayne Johnston's Writing," which appeared in *The Antigonish Review* 141/142 (2005), and in *Speculative Fictions: Contemporary Canadian Novelists and the Writing of History* (Montreal: McGill-Queen's University Press, 2002).

I am also grateful for permission to quote from a number of poems in the study. "Civil Servant," "What Rhoda Remembers about the First Five Minutes," "The Fashion Show," "If I do say so myself," "Marie's Lullaby," "Jane's Observation Notes," "Barbara," and "Filling Out the Form" were originally published in *In This House Are Many Women and Other Poems* by Sheree Fitch.[1] "Filling Out the Form" and excerpts from the other poems are reprinted by permission of Goose Lane Editions. I am also grateful to Jeanette Lynes for permission to quote from her poem "Markings," to Brent MacLaine for permission to use material from his poem "North Shore Park," to Harry Thurston for permission to quote from *A Ship Portrait*, and to George Elliott

Clarke and Gaspereau Press for permission to quote from *Saltwater Spiritual and Deeper Blues*, *Whylah Falls*, and *Execution Poems*.

During the writing of this book I interviewed a number of the writers who are the subject of this study for a website on contemporary Atlantic-Canadian literature, *Waterfront Views: Contemporary Writing of Atlantic Canada*; I'd like to thank them—namely, George Elliott Clarke, Leo McKay Jr., Lisa Moore, Edward Riche, Harry Thurston, and Michael Winter—once again, not only for participating in the project but also because those conversations helped to inform my perspective on the writing of the region in this study. Both the book and the website were funded by a Standard Research Grant from the Social Sciences and Humanities Research Council of Canada, and I would like to thank SSHRC for providing such invaluable support. I would also like to acknowledge the efforts of the student assistants who worked on *Waterfront Views*, especially Jordan MacDonald, who really helped me to get the project off the ground. Lisa Quinn and the staff at Wilfrid Laurier University Press were behind this book from early on, and I am very grateful to them, especially Leslie Macredie, Clare Hitchens, and Rob Kohlmeier, for their support and their work in getting *Anne of Tim Hortons* into print. A debt is owed, too, to the press's two anonymous readers for their supportive responses but also for some extremely constructive suggestions that prompted me to take this back to the anvil and hammer it into a more refined shape (a tip of the hat, too, to the reader who suggested that *Anne of Tim Hortons*—a phrase I use in discussing Lynn Coady's *Strange Heaven*—was a good candidate for a title). Thanks to Karen Valanne of Live Bait Theatre for her help in providing photos of productions of Charlie Rhindress's *The Maritime Way of Life* and for permission to use those photos, as well as to numerous archivists—especially Mark Ferguson and the staff at The Rooms and Cecilia Esposito at Plattsburgh State Art Museum—for their help in tracking down some of the other illustrations for the book.

For their more crucial support, eternal gratitude goes to my family: Andrea, Hannah, and Anikó, thanks for understanding that the absent-minded professor comes by it honestly. Finally, I'd like to express my deep gratitude to Alexander MacLeod, who, along with dispensing sundry sage advice, valiantly agreed to read the book-in-progress and gave the steering wheel the solid nudge it needed to get the thing back off the shoulder of the road. This book is especially for him.

1

Introduction:
Now Our Masters Have No Borders

> There's an island where
> lives, much of the world believes, an orphan
> with red hair. She has never been home. (Lynes 2001, 68)

Thus writes Jeanette Lynes in her poem "Markings," gesturing to the international appeal of the plucky heroine of Lucy Maud Montgomery's 1908 classic *Anne of Green Gables*. Such is the power of Montgomery's fictional world, Lynes sardonically conveys, that tourists come to Montgomery's home province of Prince Edward Island from all over the globe, expecting to encounter the idyllic, pastoral society that Anne inhabits. But Anne is not there. As suggested by the title of this book, *Anne of Tim Hortons: Globalization and the Reshaping of Atlantic-Canadian Literature*, in the early twenty-first century, a young girl in Eastern Canada is less likely to be found in a quaint, gabled farmhouse than in an internationally successful chain doughnut store that is a ubiquitous presence throughout the region and indeed serves, in so many towns and villages, as the de facto community centre.

Lynes's gesture to *Anne of Green Gables* is part of a broader trend in recent Atlantic-Canadian literature of writers highlighting the disparity between outsiders' expectations about life in the region and the more complicated and less idyllic lived realities of Atlantic Canadians. Where visitors so often expect a laid-back, unchanging rural existence, the Atlantic Canada of today is very much caught up in the profound economic, political, cultural, and social shifts that have come to be described by the term "globalization." Rather than a haven from the consumerism, corporatization, and global competition that characterize our current milieu, Atlantic Canada has been palpably affected by these very trends, as recent writing in the region has underscored. Hence, *Anne of Tim Hortons* it is.

Introduction

Recognizing that life in the East is not as slow-paced and unchanging as to defy the force of time is especially important because of the profound transformation the region is currently undergoing. On the one hand, there is a widespread sense that the Atlantic provinces have reached a kind of threshold, even a state of crisis,[1] marked by demographic decline, increasing out-migration (especially from rural areas), major shifts in the resource industries, and intensified debate about the region's place in the rest of the country. On the other hand, there is also a more invigorating sense of regional redefinition and cultural vitality. The resulting ambivalence about the future extends even to one arena in which there is much to be cheered by: the literature of Atlantic Canada. The last twenty years have been marked by a proliferation of sophisticated writing, helping to make the region a greater cultural force within the country than it arguably ever has been. Times of social, political, and cultural crisis, though, are often marked by cultural and artistic ferment, and it is hard not to see the proliferation and sophistication of recent Atlantic-Canadian literature in English as at least in part a consequence of the charged milieu that informs it. Atlantic Canada, many feel, is at a turning point in its fortunes, and the challenges and promise that its future offers have clearly shaped the current generation of writers in the region.[2]

Not least of all of those challenges is the regard in which Atlantic Canada is held by much, indeed most of the rest of the country, which tends to view the region with a mixture of patronizing acceptance and growing impatience. It is seen alternately as an inconvenient vestige of Confederation, as a fiscal drain on the rest of the country, and as leisure space—Canada's "ocean playground" (an official motto of the province of Nova Scotia that serves nicely as a metaphor for the region as a whole). At first glance these perspectives may seem to be conflicting, even contradictory, but on closer inspection they are not so far apart, and, indeed, can be seen as structurally related. In the touristic version, Atlantic Canadians are seen as proud, stoic, independent, communal, and culturally vibrant, providing a welcome antidote to the alienating, consumerist modernity that characterizes life in the ostensibly more prosperous and cosmopolitan parts of the country. Furthermore, in many respects Atlantic Canada has been turned into a kind of park, as the region's continuing economic challenges (the promise of offshore gas and oil aside) have made it highly reliant on tourism and thus on the characterization of itself as recreational space.

The comparative lack of industrialization and development, the low population density, and the relative absence of the trappings of modern consumer society in Atlantic Canada, however, are not signs of some blessed Edenic state but the results of an economic and political history that has seen a previously thriving region decline relative to (and to the advantage of) other parts of the country. Unfortunately, complaints directed toward Atlantic Canada tend to be conveniently uninformed, assessing the region's fortunes primarily in fiscal terms and not bothering to ask the question of how this state of affairs came to be. The stereotype of an impoverished East Coast, Ursula Kelly maintains, is a good example of how regionalism tends to be "approached ahistorically and with little regard for the ways in which regions have been constructed, historically, into the social and economic positions which they now hold" (1993, 19). At the same time, in the Maritimes and Newfoundland there is still a strong sense that joining the federation might have been a mistake. Such a stance no doubt perplexes Canadians outside the region who focus primarily on how Atlantic Canadians are net beneficiaries of the nation's fiscal redistribution policies and consequently see Atlantic Canadians as the sort of dogs that bite the hand that feeds. Such perplexity is usually grounded in the belief that it is Ontario and, increasingly, the richer Western provinces of Alberta and British Columbia who pick up the tab, and it would no doubt intensify in the face of arguments that the continued grumbling over Confederation on the East Coast is not just envious resentment of the strong by the weak but, indeed, a residual sense that the federation's gain has been the region's loss. Canadians' perceptions of that redistributive apparatus routinely overlook its grounding in particular historical circumstances and, more importantly, particular political agreements. The prosperous provinces tend to believe that they reached such a position by virtue of their own hard work, but as scholars in Atlantic Canada have argued, the reality is much more complex and much less flattering.

Such an ambivalent attitude toward the East Coast, of course, is not the product of a stark, monolithic dichotomy of outsider/insider; there are many outside the region with a deep, genuine knowledge of and affection for Atlantic Canada, just as there are many in the region who happily participate in disparaging it. Nor is it a recent phenomenon, extending back at least to the early twentieth century. However, the tensions between these contrasting images of the region arguably have intensified with the increasing sway of neo-liberal ideology, a belief in the power of the market and in the limited role of government that has been the driving force of economic globalization over the last thirty years. As David Harvey characterizes it, neo-liberalism is "a theory of political economic practices that proposes that human well-being can best be advanced by liberating individual entrepreneurial freedoms and skills within an institutional framework characterized by strong private property rights, free markets, and free trade"

Introduction

(2005, 2). Summarizing the development of neo-liberalism, Jamie Peck and Adam Tickell describe how, from its roots in the Chicago School of Economics, "[w]hat began as a starkly utopian intellectual movement was aggressively politicized by Reagan and Thatcher in the 1980s before acquiring a more technocratic form in the self-styled 'Washington consensus' of the 1990s" (2002, 380). While globalization and neo-liberalism are far from synonymous, Alejandro Colas argues, neo-liberal advocates have effectively hijacked the idea of globalization, appropriating it "as a process denoting the universal, boundless and irreversible spread of market imperatives in the reproduction of states and societies across the world" (2005, 70). Although some have begun to suggest "that, as a concept, neo-liberalism is now 'entirely overworked' and even a 'cliché'" (Dobrowolsky 2009, 2), in the view of many, neo-liberalism has become the prevailing default thinking, "incorporated into the common-sense way many of us interpret, live in, and understand the world" (D. Harvey 2005, 3).

In Canada, as elsewhere, neo-liberals' critique of the welfare state model and their promotion of an unbridled international *laissez faire* economy have frayed the national commitment to a system of fiscal redistribution that developed over the course of the twentieth century to ensure relative parity of benefits and quality of life for Canadians in different regions of the country. In conjunction with the continuing decline of the resource sectors in Atlantic Canada—especially the crisis in the fisheries, but also the impact of corporate practices in the mining, lumber, and agricultural industries—this ideological sea change has put a heavy burden on the region that is likely at best to be only temporarily offset by the exploitation of offshore energy resources. Given this rather dire set of circumstances, all four provinces have increasingly relied on tourism to pick up the slack, eagerly promoting their constituencies as leisure, cultural, and recreational destinations. This promotion has often taken the form of casting New Brunswick, Nova Scotia, Prince Edward Island, and Newfoundland and Labrador as repositories of natural wonders. But they are also often depicted as the locus of thriving Folk cultures—the home of vibrant, communal, and hospitable denizens whose lives represent a refreshing throwback from the competitive, individualistic modernity of Canada's urban centres. Although this strategy has not proven to be the economic panacea that governments hoped it would be, tourist promotion of the region nonetheless has had a pronounced impact on how the region is seen from outside and, indeed, how it sees itself.

If this set of economic and political challenges suggests that Atlantic Canada has reached a daunting threshold in its history, beyond which lies an uncertain future that provides little reason for optimism, the literature of the region in English is, by contrast, a going concern. For much of the twentieth century, writers from the region (with some exceptions, such as Hugh MacLennan, Milton Acorn, and Alden Nowlan) were a marginal presence on the Canadian literary scene. Over the 1980s and 1990s, though, writers such as Alistair MacLeod, David Adams Richards, George Elliott Clarke, and Wayne Johnston made the region much more visible on the national stage. Over the last twenty years we have witnessed a veritable explosion of writers from all four provinces, including Lisa Moore, Michael Winter, Lynn Coady, Daniel MacIvor, Anne Simpson, Anne Compton, Michael Crummey, and many others. For this generation of writers, however, the stereotypes by which the region is framed have presented a substantial challenge. While these stereotypes are a key source of the region's appeal, they also constitute a complex of misconceptions with which writers from the East Coast routinely have been compelled to contend.

Indeed, the career of New Brunswick's David Adams Richards provides a perfect illustration of the tide against which writers from the East have had to swim. Richards has been pigeonholed from early on as a gritty regionalist, disdained for the dour, brutish, impoverished lives of his characters, and chastised for not reinforcing expectations of a more pleasantly pastoral Maritimes. In response, Richards has resolutely persisted in his artistic vision while happily tipping the sacred cows of what he sees as a self-righteously progressive, middle-class academic and literary establishment. As Tony Tremblay has astutely argued, the substantially hostile critical reception of Richards's work is fuelled by critics' and readers' desire for the "heart-rending nostalgia for the old world, the agrarian ethos, and the triumphs, not humiliations, of poverty." As a logical consequence, his characters are dismissed as "untypical Maritimers," "rubes who live outside of what has been consigned as *natural* in Canadian/Maritime fiction." Thus, Tremblay concludes, "readers' opprobria about coarseness and violence in Richards's work masks a habit for censure that ... tells us very little about Richards and a great deal about these readers, the most vocal of whom have come from outside the region" (2008, 35). In contrast to the sweeping dismissal of Richards's world as a hardscrabble, benighted demimonde, his fictional universe, modelled on his home region of the Miramichi, is a complex, highly political, highly economic, and very socially stratified one. It is populated by mill workers, drug dealers, and bootleggers, but also—contrary to caricatures of his work as uniformly populated by the working class or underclass—millionaires, politicians, social workers, academics, and so on.

More importantly, what particularly distances it from "nostalgia for the old world" and "the agrarian ethos" is the thorough implication of Richards's

Introduction

fictional world in the structures of continental and even global capitalism, the global media village, and contemporary commodity culture. Richards's 1981 novel *Lives of Short Duration* to my mind serves as a kind of annunciation of the cosmopolitan, global sensibility of contemporary Atlantic-Canadian literature that this study describes. The novel provides a dense, genealogical vision of a region increasingly implicated in the continental web of capitalism and consumer culture and in the process of being transformed into the commodified and despoiled "Atlantic Salmon Centre of the World." It is a world in which "the modern efficiencies that together promise to make life happier, faster, easier, safer, and wealthier actually quash human potencies of various types" (Tremblay 2010, 232). As Richards's protagonist Patrick Terri muses, "we too ... have joined, and bragged about having and wanting, the great unwholesome anonymity of North America" (1981, 254), and *Lives of Short Duration* chronicles that process of absorption in fine, historicized detail. In other words, visions of the Maritimes as an "ocean playground" are hard to sustain, but Richards also refuses to accept and reinforce the condescending image of the region as backward and dependent. Instead, *Lives* is characterized by a resolute resistance to such expedient stereotyping and firmly adopts a complex, contrarian tone that has been sustained throughout Richards's career.

Although *Anne of Tim Hortons* occupies itself for the most part with the generation of writers who have followed in Richards's wake, his fictional world reflects many of the concerns articulated in the following chapters. He is, in a way, the book's *éminence grise*. At the same time, Richards hovers at the edges of this book somewhat uneasily. He has been vocal in emphasizing the primacy of moral and spiritual concerns in his writing, and, indeed, his work does not fit that readily with the kinds of political, social, and economic considerations driving this study, nor is Richards particularly receptive to the interpretation of his work in these terms. Atlantic-Canadian literature in English, this study seeks to argue, is characterized by a sophisticated response to the double-edged and profoundly disempowering vision of the region outlined above. Many of the new writers who have appeared on the East Coast both stage a resistance to idyllic constructions of the region as a leisure space and exhibit an acute consciousness of the degree to which the region is shaped by past and present economic, political, and social developments, rather than being hermetically sealed in the nineteenth century. Although it would be a disservice to these writers to suggest that their work is part of a unified project, in many ways it can be seen as constituting a kind of collective re-characterization of the region in a fashion that highlights rather than obscures the very contemporary challenges it faces. Before exploring that re-characterization, though, it is necessary to understand just what those challenges are and, indeed, what it even means to address Atlantic Canada as a region.

Atlantic Canada: The Making of a Region

One reason to hesitate in seeing the work of Atlantic-Canadian writers as part of a collective redefinition of the region is that the very notion of "Atlantic Canada" is a novel and contested one, especially because of the difference in the histories of the Maritimes and Newfoundland. First of all, as Margaret Conrad and James Hiller note, the term "Atlantic Canada" only came into being in 1949 and many "have trouble imagining such a community" (2001, 1). While the Maritimes can hardly be considered a homogeneous entity, Newfoundland and Labrador's much longer history as a colony of England, its existence (however brief) as a quasi-independent country, and its much later entry into Confederation constitute a profound dividing line that imparts to the notion of Atlantic Canada a slightly provisional quality. At the same time, as Conrad and Hiller contend, there is in the region a "deep sense of place that sets Atlantic Canadians apart from many other North Americans" (1), and Atlantic Canadians "have increasingly come to share an angle of vision on the world they inhabit" (6) because of a common sense of political and economic marginality relative to the rest of the country. Robert Finbow likewise stresses the "similarities among these provinces, notably proximity to the sea and the maritime orientation to economic activity"; "a population with fewer recent immigrants, mostly old-stock British and Acadian, with First Nations and African-Canadian minorities"; as well as "marginal resources, limited economic prospects, and regional disparities, marked by high unemployment and reliance on federal transfers for provincial and individual incomes" (2004, 149). Furthermore, part of what unites the two entities is the shared experience of a wary, divided entry into Confederation, a legacy that continues to shape the attitudes of inhabitants of the region toward the rest of the country. Given the historical differences between the four provinces and their shared contemporary experiences, there is much to be gained from putting the notion of "Atlantic Canada" into both theoretical and historical perspective, to consider not so much whether Atlantic Canada is a region but how, and in what terms, it is seen as one.

It is a commonplace idea that Canada as a federation is a kind of mosaic of regions, differentiated along economic, political, historical, social, cultural, and geographical lines. This diversity has been burned into the brains of most Canadians through the stereotypical coast-to-coast-to-coast iconography of

Introduction

innumerable documentaries, commercials, and sundry political propaganda: the majestic mountains of the West Coast, the wheat fields of the Prairies, the Laurentian landscape and thriving metropolises of Central Canada, the fishing sheds of the East Coast and the dogsleds of the North. Such an inventory is a shorthand version of an essentialist view of a federation made up of static, cohesive pieces, "a symbiotic union of regions, as organic as a coral reef" (Woodcock 1981, 22). The mosaic metaphor, however, has for some time been troubled by various tensions within and across the pieces of the mosaic that challenge the supposed cohesion of the very concept of region. In other words, what seem from the outside to be distinct and cohesive regions on closer scrutiny prove to be heterogeneous, unstable, even internally divided.

In more recent theorizing about the concept in various disciplines from geography to political science to literary criticism, region is increasingly being viewed not as a geographical/cultural/political given but as a construct, a kind of imagined and at times strategic sense of cohesion and community, projected usually from without but also from within. The concept of region can be seen as an assumed or imposed homogeneity and/or unity. It is, to use French theorist Henri Lefebvre's phrase, a particular "production of space" inseparable from, rather than existing outside of the political, cultural, and disciplinary discourses in which its existence is posited ([1974] 1991, 26–27). Lefebvre's conceptualization of the production of space has been extended by American geographer Edward Soja, who underscores how the power relations within capitalism are simultaneously reliant on space and make their mark on it, reshape it to the needs of capital. Indeed, according to Soja, uneven development (the geographical or territorial imbalances in economic activity and material wealth) is a necessary part of the operation of capital. Capitalism "intrinsically builds upon regional or spatial inequalities as a necessary means for its continued survival" (1989, 107). Thus, Soja contends, regionalism must be understood within the larger context of the spatial dimensions and effects of the relations of production under capitalism.

In this light, then, a region in a number of ways can be considered a "produced space": it can be seen as a geography formed to and inscribed by the requirements and activities of capital, and as a kind of imagined community (to use Benedict Anderson's phrase) or projected unity, with the interplay between the two being fluid and not necessarily controlled by people in the region itself. Regions, of course, can comprise clusters of entire nation-states, but more pertinent to understanding a region like Atlantic Canada is Soja's description of subnational regions, which are the product of uneven development within the nation-state, reflecting a "subnational spatial division of labour" (1989, 163) that arises "from competitive struggles and particular conjunctures, filled with tensions, politics, ideology, and power" (163–64).

David Harvey describes this differentiation as a reflection of "the 'self-organizing' dynamics of concentration and centralization of capital in space" in which "capital rich regions tend to grow richer while poor regions grow poorer" (2006, 98).

Such an analytical framework, emphasizing the relations between economics, politics, and space, is crucial for understanding the current situation of Atlantic Canada within the larger Canadian federation. During the last thirty years of economic globalization, the region has undergone a substantial restructuring of capital that is part of a broader reshaping of traditional spatial boundaries, driven in large measure by neo-liberal thinking. What Soja's insights suggest, though, is that this restructuring is part of a longer history of the spatial effects of the uneven development characteristic of capitalism. To appreciate Atlantic Canada's particular vulnerability within this neo-liberal restructuring, therefore, requires a foray back into the longer history of its tenuous place in the federation—a preoccupation that can be seen in the work of writers such as Newfoundland's Wayne Johnston and Nova Scotia's Harry Thurston.

One of the effects of nationalism, of course, is to give a corporate identity and purpose to what is invariably a diverse constituency with different and often competing interests. Thus phrases such as "Canadian identity," "Canada's destiny," and "Canada's interests" are at best selectively representative and more typically evocative of the priorities of a select economic and political elite—an elite concentrated, for most of the country's history, in Central Canada. Highly pertinent to the case of Canada in this respect is Soja's broader observation that regionalism in the nineteenth century developed in part "to resist the particular spatial division of labour being imposed by expansive market integration and the equally expansive national state" (1989, 165), as part of a larger process of centralization at the turn of the century. In the process "the centres of monopoly control ... tended to grow much more rapidly than those which may have formerly been at similar levels of industrial development" (166), as were the Maritimes and, to a lesser degree, Newfoundland at the time of Confederation in 1867. Perhaps the crucial insight Soja's analysis suggests (one echoed by various "regional" scholars in Canada) is that such centralization tends to be naturalized as the "national interest," usually to the detriment of other parts of the country.

Although very different in political temperament from Soja's Marxist critique of capitalism, economist Donald Savoie's recent study *Visiting Grandchildren: Economic Development in the Maritimes* charts the dynamics of political and economic concentration that Soja describes. Drawing on the work of a range of Maritime historians, Savoie underlines the orientation of "national" policy in Canada toward the interests of Central Canada and the

Introduction

attendant tendency to dismiss Atlantic Canada's interests as regional and marginal. This double standard, Savoie argues, is a dynamic extending back to Confederation, a time in which the colonies on the East Coast were enjoying a much greater level of prosperity relative to the rest of the nation than they do today. The Maritimes, David Alexander observes, "possessed one of the world's foremost shipbuilding industries, the third or fourth largest merchant marine, financial institutions which were the core of many of the present Canadian giants, and an industrial structure growing as fast as that of central Canada" (1983, 4). Newfoundland was relatively prosperous and very much oriented eastward rather than toward the continent to its west. F.L. Jackson describes nineteenth-century Newfoundland as "a lively and optimistic society" and contends that historians see the first half of the century "as a golden age of modest proportions; an age when Newfoundland seemed to leap from forgotten, downtrodden territory to thriving colony, as if at a single bound" (1986, 66). Although there was support for Confederation with Canada in some quarters, for the most part on the East Coast there was little interest in and much active opposition to the prospect. Conrad and Hiller observe that "[m]ost Newfoundlanders, it seems, were convinced that their country had the resources to support an independent future" (2001, 133). In the Maritimes there was substantial opposition to Confederation, amid fears of central Canadian domination.

Most Maritime historians, to be sure, readily concede the mitigating factors that made entering into Confederation a necessary compromise. Philip Buckner, for one, argues that in agreeing to Confederation, the colonial elites of the Maritimes were making a pragmatic choice in a difficult situation: "they saw no other option if the Maritimes were to avoid annexation to the United States, to retain their traditional ties with Britain, and to develop a more diversified economy less vulnerable to the whims of external markets" (1994, 386). Although he stresses that "no external pressures could have compelled the Maritimes to join Confederation if ultimately they had not been convinced that it was in their interests to do so" (Buckner 1990, 386–87), Buckner observes nonetheless that there was little enthusiasm for "a scheme of union that seemed primarily designed to benefit the United Province of Canada" (1994, 360).

The fate of the Maritimes over the ensuing decades suggests that these fears were well justified. The system of protective tariffs reinforcing the east–west continental integration of John A. Macdonald's National Policy, Savoie argues, strengthened Central Canada as the base of industry and manufacturing at the expense of Maritimers, who "concluded that under the National Policy they were compelled to buy what they consumed in a substantially protected home market but had to sell their products in a virtually unprotected one" (2006, 28). Federal economic policies from then on favoured Ontario and Quebec, leading to a concentration of economic and political power in Central Canada, a situation exacerbated by out-migration from the Maritimes and a consequent decline in parliamentary seats and therefore in political influence (27–30). As T.W. Acheson argues, the National Policy initially stimulated the development of manufacturing in the Maritimes, cultivating a sense of optimism about the economic prospects of the region ([1972] 1985, 4). However, after this initial flourishing of manufacturing in the region ebbed, local bankers and entrepreneurs were compelled to "re-orient themselves in the light of the new geographic scope and economic opportunities of the Dominion" (Clow 2005, 43), and many did so by consolidating with Central Canadian interests, moving to Central Canada, or both. This exodus of capital has had long-standing and detrimental effects on the region as a whole—a long decline reflected in Thurston's 2005 verse novella, *A Ship Portrait*.

Contributing to the lingering sense of grievance over Confederation were various aspects of federal transportation policy that discriminated against the Maritimes and amounted to a violation of the spirit and the letter of Confederation as a political and economic arrangement. As E.R. Forbes contends, a key factor in the economic decline of the Maritimes at the turn of the century was the erosion of federal commitment to the Intercolonial, a railway designed to compensate for the shift in economic activity to Central Canada and, as Forbes describes it, "the *sine qua non* of [Maritime politicians'] entry into Confederation" (1989, 114). More importantly, the demise of the Intercolonial was part of a long-term trend of Central Canadian politicians sacrificing Maritime interests to suit their own economic and political purposes (172–99). Such policy decisions have had a multiplying effect, contributing not only to the decline of industry and manufacturing in the Maritimes but also to waning political influence, leaving the region further vulnerable to policy changes that run counter to its interests.

As reflected in Johnston's writing, Newfoundland's much later entry into Confederation —after the divisive 1948 referendum on the island's future— was even more profoundly ambivalent and conducive to a lingering sense of grievance about the province's place in the federation. The crucial consideration, of course, is Newfoundland's prior status as a self-governing colony since 1855. This status was ultimately surrendered in 1933, with Newfoundland on the brink of defaulting on its debt payments due to a combination of political corruption, "[c]rises in the fishing economy, the heavy burden of debt left after World War I, and largely unsuccessful attempts at bringing industrial development to Newfoundland through railway ventures" (Wright 2003, 93). What complicated the still-debated decision to join Canada for many was the

Introduction

questionable role of Canada and the United Kingdom in encouraging, perhaps even orchestrating, the outcome during the referendum over Newfoundland's future. Consequently, many Newfoundlanders "then and now—have felt that morally, at least, they were ill-treated by a British government which bent the rules of the game to suit its needs" (Baker 2003, 64). This history, Melvin Baker stresses, explains in part why "Newfoundlanders and Labradorians still have a strong sense of political grievance over their place in the Canadian nation and why the people of the province feel a need to 'renew and strengthen' their place in Canada" (65–66).[3] Other historians, however, have questioned what they see as neo-nationalist reappraisals of Newfoundland history and particularly of the referendum. Jeff Webb argues that the effect of suggestions of a conspiracy is to question the very legitimacy of the decision itself: "The implication is that ... most Newfoundlanders did not choose union with Canada. Alternately, if a majority did vote for Confederation, then the British and Canadians manipulated Newfoundlanders into doing so. Thus Newfoundlanders did not give informed consent to join Canada" (1998, 171). Webb ultimately sees the lamenting of Newfoundland's lost independence as romantic, "counterfactual," and discrediting the legitimacy of a democratic decision (179).

As important as the historical context of the political and economic accommodations that accompanied Confederation—in the second half of the nineteenth century for the Maritimes and nearly a century later for Newfoundland—is the historical context for the redistributive arrangements that are the cornerstone of so many Canadians' disparaging views of the East Coast. Regionalism, for Soja, can be seen as a response to geographically uneven development (1989, 164), and the reaction of Maritimers as the inequity of the economic and constitutional arrangements of Confederation became increasingly clear certainly can be viewed in this light. As Savoie observes, continued concern about the Maritime provinces' plight within Confederation led to increasing pressure for federal solutions, which took the shape of various regional development programs. What Savoie emphasizes in exploring the history of postwar economic development programs in the Maritimes is that such programs did little to improve long-term economic prospects because they did not lead to the region's integration into "national" economic policy, according to which "political cohesion ... would be maintained by instituting a system of transfer payments designed to underwrite the cost of uneven economic development but leaving intact the economic relationships that gave rise to uneven development" (2006, 306). Thus the region suffered and still suffers from a double standard in economic policy: what's good for Central Canada is "national," and what's good for Atlantic Canada is "regional." "Big dogs," as Savoie puts it, "not only eat first, they also have a large appetite to satisfy when it comes to national economic development policies, federal investment, and the location of federal government activities" (304–5).

Because of the tendency to construe Central Canada's interests as those of the nation, the assumption forms "that strong economic regions in Canada became strong on their own merit, with little government intervention," and that "market forces and their own abilities explain their economic success" (Savoie 2006, 229). Like various Maritime historians, Savoie counters this widespread sentiment that the ensuing shape of the country was a natural adjustment to market factors. Nonetheless, the blinkered view "has become embedded in the national media and the Ottawa bureaucracy that Maritimers are considered less entrepreneurial and less productive than Ontarians" (229), an insight that readily applies to Newfoundlanders as well. In a similar if more polemical vein, in *Surviving Confederation* Jackson argues that Newfoundland is "caught up in an economic bind whereby we depend on a system to which we contribute but in whose benefits and strength we but miserably share" (1986, 50). Furthermore, where collective identification by Newfoundlanders "is called regionalism," he complains, "in Ontario it is called National Unity" (31). The picture of the Atlantic provinces as victims of an inequitable federation, to be sure, is increasingly being questioned by scholars, both inside and outside the region, as simplistic and romanticized. Kris E. Inwood, for instance, rejects the characterization of Confederation as a turning point in the economic fortunes of the Maritimes, arguing that the industrial decline of the region was already underway (1993, 160) and that "the well-documented capital outflow simply reflects a dearth of good investment opportunities within the region" (161). Sean T. Cadigan underscores how, "[s]ince Confederation, politicians have used a particular form of neo-nationalist Ottawa-bashing to distract the people of Newfoundland and Labrador from the failures of provincial policies and to co-op their support" (2009, 296); Maritime politicians, although not as prone to such expedient confrontation, have been far from immune to it. Nonetheless, the regional challenge to the Central Canadian biases of standard versions of the nation's history has firmly established the importance of a much more nuanced understanding of the historical roots of Atlantic Canada's present subordinate status within Confederation.

Neo-liberalism, Globalization, and Restructuring

While these political, economic, and cultural dynamics have a long history, their significance has been particularly underscored over the last couple of decades, during which, in conjunction with Canada's incorporation into a

Introduction

global economy, the "constitutional accommodation," to use Forbes's phrase, has come under increasing attack. As Robert Finbow summarizes, the history of uneven development on the East Coast provides crucial perspective on redistributive arrangements such as equalization payments: "For regional analysts, later redistributive policies are merely compensation for this discrimination." Furthermore, "revenues from transfers have largely circulated back to the centre in the form of purchases of goods and services from central Canadian enterprises, corporate taxes on company profits derived in part from the region, and exports of skilled labour" (1995, 64). However, such arrangements are increasingly viewed with a jaundiced eye in the prevailing neo-liberal order, in which the need to be globally competitive has become the new mantra, and around it has developed a new commitment to austerity, productivity, economic fitness, et cetera.

This increasingly dominant neo-liberal sensibility and the broader trend of economic globalization are defining features of our times. Unsurprisingly, they have had a considerable impact on contemporary Atlantic-Canadian literature and thus warrant some consideration prior to a more detailed study of that literature. The three decades after the Second World War, as historian Bryan D. Palmer notes, were characterized by "the full-blown arrival of Fordism, a larger regime of accumulation premised on the stabilizing impact of social security, high wages, placid and predictable class relations, and general corporate/trade union agreement on the parameters of industrial discipline" (1992, 283). Neo-liberalism emerged as an ideological force as this postwar "Fordist" contract between capital and labour—which involved an exchange of labour peace for shared prosperity—began to fray amid declining profits in the recessionary atmosphere of the 1970s (D. Harvey 2005, 12). Neo-liberals then put their stamp forcefully on Western governments in the 1980s, particularly the United States under Ronald Reagan and Britain under Margaret Thatcher. Peck and Tickell describe how the combative implementation of neo-liberal principles of the "Thatcher/Reagan era of assault and retrenchment" has since given way to a more naturalized, entrenched, and assertive neo-liberalism, characterized by "the technocratic embedding of routines of neoliberal governance" (2002, 384). Following on attempts in Britain and the U.S. to modify the impact of neo-liberal policies in the 1990s, in Canada "changing ideas, representations, and policy instruments ... introduced discourses that reflected something more than 'pure' unadulterated neo-liberalism" (Dobrowolksy 2009, 4). The social investment model Alexandra Dobrowolsky describes entails a more activist state intervening to modify the economic and social impact of neo-liberal policies: "Investments in education, innovation, healthcare, and children (particularly, children *at risk*) would 'pay off' later by producing skilled, productive workers and preventing a host of expensive social ills" (10; italics in original). However, the social investment perspective largely retains neo-liberalism's market-oriented ideology and instrumentalist approach (12). Neo-liberalism in its various permutations has profoundly reshaped not only the terms of public debate but also the quality of life around the world, not least in Canada. As Thom Workman argues, neo-liberalism has become

> the everyday wisdom that guides most discussions about public policy across the country. Its alluring language of efficiency, responsible state spending, flexibility and free markets has been absorbed effortlessly into the intellectual horizons of politicians, journalists, academics, bureaucrats and, indeed, even many on the left. (2003, 138)

A key dimension of economic globalization reflecting neo-liberal ideology has been the liberalization of finance, which has had a profound impact on the ability of governments to set their own fiscal and even political policies. "Controls over banking, currency exchange, and capital movement," Raewyn Connell notes, "were all loosened or abolished, as one country after another came under neoliberal control from the late 1970s on." What gradually emerged was "a fast-moving global arena of financial transactions, consisting of a network of national and international markets in shares, bonds, financial derivatives, and currency." According to Connell, "[t]his arena is the core of what corporate executives and financial journalists (as opposed to cultural analysts) mean by 'globalization'" (2010, 23). As Thomas Friedman describes in his popular (if overly sanguine) *The Olive and the Lexus Tree*, this diverse consortium of investors large and small, facilitated by improvements in information and communication technologies, effectively votes on the performance of countries, moving money across national borders on a daily basis and consequently wielding substantial economic and political clout without any accompanying accountability to the citizens of those countries. The effect of these myriad decisions, Friedman argues, is the creation of an implicit set of fiscal and political principles and practices to ensure investor confidence, principles and practices that usually constrain governments' room to manoeuvre: deregulation, removing capital controls, stressing balanced budgets, privatizing state institutions, reducing tariffs, shrinking the size of governments, and opening up economies to private investment ([1999] 2000, 103).

Responses to this international, neo-liberal economic regime—like responses to globalization generally—are highly divided. As Robert Holton observes, "[w]hile many are incensed at global inequality, poverty and deprivation, others take pride in the unprecedented post-war expansion of

Introduction

economic growth, technological dynamism and very recent revolutions in communication" (2005, 3). For many—whether supporters of the neo-liberal consensus or not—such an internationalized economic regime is a given, and those economies that ignore it are doomed to impoverished isolation. Others, however, see globalization as "a justificatory myth" (Bourdieu 1998, 38) that provides the pretext for an increasingly international concentration of wealth, intensifying the gap between the rich and the poor and progressively eradicating the middle class (largely in a downward direction).

While there is some justification for the argument that businesses must streamline and reduce costs (including labour costs) to compete in an open and international market, at the same time critics are also right to point out, as does Pierre Bourdieu, that these are familiar and old arguments, often pitting workers in the developed world against workers in the developing world. "In a general way," Bourdieu argues, "neo-liberalism is a very smart and very modern repackaging of the oldest ideas of the oldest capitalists" (1998, 34). Globalization, Alfredo Saad-Filho and Deborah Johnston contend, has been strategically characterized "as an inescapable, inexorable and benevolent process leading to greater competition, welfare improvements and the spread of democracy around the world" (2005, 2). In this view, the promotion of globalization is, at least in part, a narrative of convenience for an increasingly interrelated cadre of business and political leaders. It serves as an expedient myth about keeping up with the global Joneses, providing covering fire for rampant privatization, cutbacks in government services and in equalization payments, and dwindling concessions to labour and other groups disadvantaged in the new global order.

For others, however, seeing globalization as a worldwide capitalist juggernaut, a "race to the bottom," runs the risk of effacing the real possibility that at least some of these economic, technological, and political developments may also be providing greater opportunity and an overall alleviation of poverty in the developing world. Jay Mandle, for one, argues that although globalization needs regulation and reform, it nonetheless "contributes to development and ... development and the integration of global markets have a substantial impact on poverty reduction" (2003, 23). The lifting of barriers to international trade is seen by many to be a welcome free market corrective, providing a more level playing field for the innovative and the entrepreneurial, but also subjecting less competitive and productive businesses to the disciplinary pressures of a truly open market. Citing economist Joseph Schumpeter, Friedman describes this as "the process of 'creative destruction'—the perpetual cycle of destroying the old and less efficient product or service and replacing it with new, more efficient ones" ([1999] 2000, 10). Globalization thus intensifies how what Marshall Berman describes as the "innate dynamism of the modern economy, and of the culture that grows from this economy, annihilates everything that it creates—physical environments, social institutions, metaphysical ideas, artistic visions, moral values—in order to create more, to go on endlessly creating the world anew" (1982, 288). However, the recurring contention that the shift to economic competition on a global scale will ultimately drive up labour standards internationally seems to be at the very least prematurely hopeful. Friedman, for one, adopts the sunny view that globalization is a rising tide that will eventually lift all boats ([1999] 2000, 347). Instead, Stephen McBride observes, various studies suggest that "the closer economic integration globalization produces is zero-sum in its effect" and that "[t]here is ample evidence to challenge the mainstream view that globalization is a benign and progressive force" ([2001] 2004, 77). Rather than a benignly rising tide, in other words, globalization is closer to a powerful wave on top of which a privileged few comfortably ride while many others—as Newfoundland writer Edward Riche's 2004 novel *The Nine Planets* underscores—are vigorously rocked or even swamped.

The jury will be out for some time on the benefits of globalization, especially because of the reverberations of the recent global financial crisis and its dramatization of the shortcomings of neo-liberal ideology. What does seem to be clear in the short run is that one of the immediate effects of economic globalization has been increased pressure on workers and governments in the so-called developed world—including in Canada's resource and manufacturing sectors. It has also led to much more vigorous and vocal pressure to cut back on the size of government, particularly on the scope of social programs in the welfare states of the developed world (the impact of which is explored in Nova Scotian Wendy Lill's 1998 play *Corker*). Whether sympathetic to this pressure or not, politicians have much less leeway than heretofore, leading many to argue that the nation-state as once we knew it has ceased to exist, its authority increasingly superseded by international institutions like the International Monetary Fund, the World Bank, and the World Trade Organization. Many see the power of these bodies as an expropriation of democratic decision-making, arguing that "they represent *only* multinational capital ... and governments whose leaders and functionaries now act almost exclusively in the interests of transnational capital" (Clow 2005, 38; italics in original). As William Watson among others rightly stresses, though, rumours of the demise of the nation-state are highly exaggerated. Approaching the issue from a small-government perspective, Watson maintains that nation-states are by no means neutered in adapting to these pressures, and citizens are by no means deprived of their ability to influence the kind and size of state they would like to live in (1998, 13). At the same time, the room to manoeuvre has arguably been severely circumscribed, and as a result, "[t]he nation-state may not literally disappear, but in a globalized world all nation-states will look more and more alike" (9). McBride, though, provides an important qualifier in recognizing that the cession of many powers of the state in responding to the dictates of these powerful and largely undemocratic international trade bodies "was a political strategy that found favour with some domestic interests, notably capital" ([2001] 2004, 186). David Harvey goes so far as to argue that "the state functions more clearly now as an 'executive committee of capitalist class interests' than at any other time in history" (2006, 106).

One consequence of the neo-liberal reconfiguring of established political and economic relationships in Canada is that the redistributive arrangements that developed over the course of the last half-century as a response to, among other pressures, recognition of the justice of Atlantic Canada's complaints about the inequity of the federal system, have come under increasing attack as a competitive disadvantage in an era of global competition. The east–west economic orientation on which the nation was built, conservative economist Thomas Courchene points out, is increasingly being questioned in an era of continental free trade; "the three building blocks of the National Policy—high tariffs, transportation subsidies, settlement of the West—are no longer in play" and "in economic terms much of our east-west economic infrastructure is fast becoming a 'stranded asset'" (2001, 71). "This shift," McBride warns,

> weakens the already fragile unity of the Canadian state and thereby decentralizes the federation. In that sense, the impact of globalization on Canada's political system has been to increase the constitutional strains generated by Canada's internal and idiosyncratic cleavages based on nations, language, and region. ([2001] 2004, 180)

In such a global economic atmosphere, Canadian public discourse has been increasingly dominated by a neo-liberal bottom-line mentality promoting greater government austerity (if not when it comes to supporting the private sector, at least when it comes to social services and cultural programs). The growing sense of economic anxiety in Ontario as a result of deindustrialization and the decline of manufacturing is a prime example, leading as it has to calls for reform to the structure of equalization payments. The ensuing "deep societal division between the emerging requisites of north–south competitiveness versus the traditional requisites of east–west solidarity" (2001, 73) that Courchene sees spells a lot of trouble for Atlantic Canada. For better or worse, its economy has taken shape within this east–west framework of redistributive federalism, with a high degree of government involvement in and subsidization of the economy. This makes the region a ready target for neo-liberal hostility and contempt, exemplified by Watson, who points to its "long and inglorious history of sycophancy and supplication" as the most egregious example of a larger problem: "The clearest lesson that it teaches is that success is achieved not by being inventive, innovative, or imaginative, but by successfully petitioning government. What counts is not what you know but whom you know, a principle that has governed life in the Atlantic provinces for several generations now" (1998, 201). Presumably, in Ontario this is simply known as "networking." The result of such "neo-liberal concerns about deficits and debts," James Kenny notes, "has been the steady dismantling of Canada's welfare state, such that it was, in the name of economy," to the particular detriment of Atlantic Canada, "where federal transfers have long played an important role in the regional economy and individual survival more specifically" (1999, 133). In Atlantic Canada there are thus substantial

> fears that restructuring would change the rules of the political game, weaken the tradition of redistributing wealth, subsidizing old provincial cultures, boundaries, and institutions. Even though there is support for increasing economic innovation, there are also concerns that the Atlantic region would not benefit as much as the rich provinces if the national system of equalization and income transfers were suddenly abandoned and replaced with new structures. (Tomblin 2004, 20)

As a result, Atlantic Canada looks to be particularly vulnerable to the current neo-liberal assault on working conditions, welfare infrastructure, and social programs. As Workman sardonically observes, "the glamorous dimension of globalization is not as obvious in the region as it is elsewhere" (2003, 6). Rather, Atlantic Canadians are much more likely to experience the downside of globalization, which "tends to unfold in the region in a more pedestrian fashion, with unnumbered employers of all sizes taking advantage of working people in a climate of austerity and a downshift in wages" (Workman 2003, 6). The region is arguably ill-poised to adapt to a regime in which government involvement is (selectively) seen as a competitive disadvantage. These political tensions reflect how neo-liberalism plays "a decisive role in constructing the 'rules' of interlocal competition by shaping the very metrics by which regional competitiveness, public policy, corporate performance, or social productivity are measured—value for money, the bottom line, flexibility, shareholder value, performance rating, social capital,

Introduction

and so on" (Peck and Tickell 2002, 387). What this means for provincial and municipal governments in the region is a pronounced economic and political squeeze, as federal support becomes increasingly difficult to obtain and domestic political pressure to create jobs and sustain regionally beneficial social programs intensifies. The result is that the pressure to make concessions to business in order to attract investment in the region—already "notorious as a breeding ground for 'white elephants'" (Conrad and Hiller 2001, 194–95)—has been redoubled.

This is not to suggest, either, that neo-liberal prescriptions are embraced as a necessary evil, benefitting as they do members of the political and economic elite alike. Rather than turning "their backs on the governance paradigm of our day," Jennifer Smith asserts, governments in the Atlantic provinces "have adopted it and found ways to execute it. They have downsized, privatized, contracted-out delivery of various goods and services, and introduced market-style incentives within the organization of the public service" (2002, 157). The Liberal government of former New Brunswick premier Frank McKenna is a case in point, as its transformation of New Brunswick in the late 1980s and 1990s to meet the needs of the new "knowledge economy" involved substantial concessions to capital and McKenna's touting of the province "*as a business solution rather than a location*" (DeLottinville 1994, 42; italics in original). This semantic shift speaks volumes about the realignment of priorities and the reconfiguration of space under neo-liberalism, suggesting as it does that amenability to capital trumps a geographical and social sense of identity and belonging.

Indeed, in a fleet-footed, ostensibly boundaryless economic regime, mobility is the watchword and stability a thing of the past. Capital "must always be ready to abandon strategies, products, people and even customers in order to move into a more lucrative market or adopt a more efficient and profitable way of doing business" (Friedman 2000, 406), and workers likewise need to be ready to move to where the work is. This mobility, however, is highly asymmetrical. "Firms," Mandle observes, "can take their production facilities and jobs wherever they choose, but labor is restricted in its ability to exercise a comparable mobility in seeking employment" (2003, 116). The ability of capital to migrate gives it far more leverage than does that of workers, except perhaps for the most skilled. Indeed, for Zygmunt Bauman, such asymmetrical mobility is a defining structural feature of global culture: "Mobility climbs to the rank of the uppermost among the coveted values—and the freedom to move, perpetually a scarce and unequally distributed commodity, fast becomes the main stratifying factor of our late-modern or postmodern times" (1998, 2). This imbalance has particularly troubling implications for a region such as Atlantic Canada with a long history of occupation, a resource-based economy, and a concomitantly stronger attachment to place. With the ability to pick up and move—even to the other side of the world—capital has less and less need to demonstrate a commitment to place. Indeed, the tables are very much turned: place needs more and more to demonstrate a commitment to capital, even to the degree of renaming itself "a business solution." The result is that communities, municipalities and whole provinces are more and more vulnerable to the demands of capital. To borrow a phrase from Thurston's *A Ship Portrait*, "Now our masters / have no borders" (2005, 61).

This profound readjustment of priorities can have a deleterious impact on people's sense of community, identity, and belonging. As Conrad and Hiller conclude, the current neo-liberal restructuring poses a profound challenge to Atlantic Canadians' traditional sense of well-being and community:

> Toll highways, home-based health care, food banks, call centres, and corporate sponsorship of education and research may represent a brave new world to those converted to the religion of the marketplace, but many Atlantic Canadians regret the abandonment of the noble dream that made human welfare rather than corporate profits the measure of a civil society. (2001, 212)

Thus, for all its "newness," globalization asks a fairly old question: to what degree should capital be free to generate wealth and employment, and what are reasonable concessions to make to it in the pursuit of those goals? What social toll, in other words, is reasonable to endure? At least for the time being, as much of the literature in this study reflects, capital is in a particularly advantageous position to dictate the terms on which those questions are answered.

Atlantic-Canadian Literature and the Paradigm of the Folk

If we can see region, then, as a socially produced space, this largely externally imposed neo-liberal ideology has had a profound influence in reinforcing the image of Atlantic Canada as politically, culturally, and economically parochial. "Backward, conservative, and juiced up on handouts," writes Conrad, "we are widely perceived as a region blighted by location, culture, and identity" (2002, 162). The concept of Atlantic Canada certainly may be resisted internally, particularly because of the cultural and historical differences between Newfoundland and the rest of the region. Nonetheless, such a monolithic stereotype has been dominant on the national stage for the last three decades and intensified by neo-liberal thinking, reflecting the broader way in which economic and business considerations have come to hold sway over public discourse and so many other sectors in Canada.

How curious, amid all this, then, is the persistent view of the region as a seaside respite populated by cheery, hospitable, rubber-booted denizens figuratively laying out the welcome mat for weary urban visitors. Given the prevailing ideological mood in Canada, the pastoral and idyllic maritime scenes that pervade touristic images of the region seem particularly ironic. In this scenario, the region's inability to keep up with the times seems salutary, the relative lack of development and industrialization on the East Coast viewed more positively as part of the region's charm. Here, the Atlantic provinces come across as the preserve of an unspoiled, authentic, pre-modern culture. They present a therapeutic sanctuary from the alienating, competitive individualism associated with the more prosperous regions of the country—an appeal which the tourism industry in the region has effectively retailed.

In a number of ways, however, this construction of the Atlantic provinces as a quaint pastoral retreat is intimately related to the more derogatory view of the region and is ultimately likewise the product of the troubled history of the region in Confederation. The manufacturing and promotion of such an image, it can be argued, amounts to making a virtue of necessity. Indeed, it can be seen as commodifying and retailing the region's underdevelopment. As conveyed with particular force by Ian McKay in his influential study of Nova Scotia, *The Quest of the Folk: Antimodernism and Cultural Selection in Twentieth-Century Nova Scotia* (1994)[4] and James Overton in his essays on culture and tourism in Newfoundland in *Making a World of Difference: Essays on Tourism, Culture, and Development in Newfoundland* (1996), the paradox of tourist development in Atlantic Canada is that the region has promoted itself as an enclave of unspoiled nature and authentic culture as part of a thoroughly *modern* campaign to diversify economically and generate revenue. As these studies illustrate, the prevailing impression of culture in the Maritimes and Newfoundland is that it is pre-modern, rural, and small-m maritime, thoroughly associated with a life of resource extraction and proximity to the natural elements. The irony of this association, McKay and Overton highlight, is that it has promoted a way of life that is increasingly unrepresentative of the Atlantic provinces, as those resource industries decline and the region becomes more reliant on a service economy or on other conspicuously modern occupations. Paradoxically, in other words, much tourism celebrates a way of life whose waning has intensified the need for tourism to provide compensatory revenue. The further irony is that the romanticized pre-modernism in which tourism on the East Coast traffics is highly illusory. It masks the degree to which the region was and is industrialized and how thoroughly it is bound up in an increasingly global, modern, capitalist economy (including the very tourist industry promoting such a stereotype). In terms of the double standard that Savoie and others highlight, this can be seen as the region reduced to selling back to the rest of the country a very stylized and romanticized version of the underdevelopment in which those more powerful regions have played a large part. The increasing need to retail such images is compelled by the shift from seeming independence to seeming dependence, particularly because of the waning of those sectors around which much of the region's sense of community, identity, and culture has developed.

This stereotyping of the East Coast as quaint, conservative, backward, but still enjoying an enviable pre-modern sense of authenticity and community has implications for the culture of the region that extend beyond tourism as a kind of industrial packaging of such images. These assumptions, some literary critics have argued, have a bearing on how writing in Atlantic Canada is perceived as well. Janice Kulyk Keefer, for one, argues that it is possible to see operating in Canadian literary criticism a kind of cultural variant of the frontier thesis (1985, 25), in which the East is seen as culturally conservative, staid, and unexperimental, in contrast to the more vibrant and experimental literature of the West. David Creelman contends that critical reception of Maritime literature is distorted by stereotypical assumptions about Maritime culture and therefore about what qualifies as Maritime literature, a manoeuvre that has the effect of reinforcing images of Maritime conservatism. Creelman maintains that "artists in other regions are offered more varied possibilities, more widely defined constructions within which to work," whereas—given the limited options offered for the Maritimes—"a text does not have to stray too far to find itself outside the known boundaries and swimming hard against the stream" (2008, 77). Tony Tremblay has argued powerfully that reception of Maritime literature outside the region is often coloured by touristic assumptions that amount to a kind of internal cultural colonialism. As Tremblay puts it, regional cultural distinctiveness, like regional political autonomy, is highly circumscribed within "the quasi-imperial condition that the heart of our little Empire remains fixed in the centre," and thus "the regions produce narrative in a wider context of pre-existing myths that have already in large part defined them" (2008, 29). In effect, what these critics describe is the cultural analogue to the picture regional scholars paint of the economic position of Atlantic Canada, in which the region's subordinate position is in large part the outcome of structural relations with the more dominant regions and particularly with Central Canada, where the publishing industry, cultural funding, and the culturally influential have been no less concentrated than has industrial, financial, and political power.

Introduction

Indeed, at a time when Atlantic-Canadian literature is very much in vogue, it is crucial not to lose sight of this larger context. Certainly most of the credit for the proliferation and popularity of writing on the East Coast goes to the quality of the writing and the development of a much more sustaining and nurturing cultural community inside and outside the region. There are also grounds for suspicion, though, that these developments are in part due to a more transitory and capricious trend in publishing. Indeed, some writers and critics in the East point to the success of American Annie Proulx's depiction of Newfoundland in her Pulitzer Prize–winning *The Shipping News* (1993) as having drawn international attention to Newfoundland writing in particular and the writing of Atlantic Canada in general. As Danielle Fuller argues, this attention may well be a temporary manifestation of the culture of the bestseller and an example of the publishing industry's perpetual search for literary exoticism—that in Atlantic Canada is to be found a unique, unspoiled, even eccentric remedy for the blandness and monotony of modern consumer culture. The popularity of realistic fiction about Atlantic Canada in the 1990s, Fuller considers, may well reflect "the attraction of cultural difference, particularly that apparently offered by geo-politically marginalized communities, to those inhabiting urban sites in northern industrialized countries that increasingly look the same" (2008, 53). As Graham Huggan contends in *The Postcolonial Exotic*, the "fetishised otherness and sympathetic identification" (2001, 14) with the exotic other which characterizes exoticism mask an imbalance of power, "allowing the dominant culture to attribute value to the margins while continuing to define them in its own self-privileging terms" (24). Furthermore, particularly in the form of tourism, the experience of the exotic "proceeds according to an inexorably capitalist logic: once tourism has made the other accessible, other others must emerge to take its place" (178). It is important not to downplay the genuine interest of readers around the world, as well as the investment of publishers both large and small, in the work of Atlantic-Canadian writers. However, it would also be naive to dismiss the possibility that, at least to some degree, the present popularity of literature in Atlantic Canada may be yet another instance of the "creative destruction" of capitalism's voracious appetite for new products and markets—that the region's distinctiveness is just one more resource to be mined and left behind.

This framing of the region as exotic and marginal is crucial for understanding the proliferation and reception of writing on the East Coast. Writers in Atlantic Canada, as Fuller asserts, have long had to contend with the "risk of reinforcing sentimental, nostalgic, or romantic notions of particular places, thereby masking regional inequalities and/or having [their] work dismissed as unsophisticated" (2004a, 25). While some writers can be seen as catering to the desire for a homogeneous, exotic Folk culture, much recent Atlantic-Canadian writing offers more nuanced visions of the region or actively counters and subverts Folk archetypes. Instead, Atlantic-Canadian writing is becoming more inclined to reflect the distinctions and hierarchies of geography, class, gender, ethnicity, and culture that characterize life in the region. Rather than sustaining the illusion that life goes on much as it did in the nineteenth century, much of that writing foregrounds the degree to which the region is thoroughly situated within—rather than sealed off from—continental and global economic and political relations. Many of the writers in this study have contracts with major international publishers (and thus write for an audience principally outside the region), and at least some of them have resided for long periods outside of the region (Clarke, MacLeod, Johnston, and Coady, for instance). These external connections do not necessarily preclude the reinforcement of Folk stereotypes, and may indeed work to encourage it, but they nonetheless further underscore how the current generation of writers in Atlantic Canada is wired into an international culture and economy. The image of the isolated, self-contained Folk, as Ian McKay underscores at the end of *The Quest of the Folk*, is impossible to sustain in the palpable presence of the trappings of postmodern consumer culture,

> in a fully wired society, much of it tuned in, via cable television, directly to Detroit. The romance of the rural Folk has run aground on the shoals of its own implausibility. In the context of a countryside that bristles with satellite dishes and shopping-malls, populated with people who often work at urban jobs to support rural homes, and that is in a hundred other ways so evidently *not* a haven set apart from late twentieth-century capitalism, the notion of the "simple life" of the Folk can only be ironic. (1994, 308)

One of the dangers of McKay's sustained critique of the Folk paradigm, though, is its tendency to make out those activities associated with the Folk—fishing, fiddling, farming—to be naive or disingenuous, ironic or even cynical, leaving little space for a more genuine engagement with the place of such activities in life on the East Coast. Indeed, what contemporary Atlantic-Canadian literature makes clear is that fiddles and shopping malls, lobster boats, and satellite dishes can and do happily and unselfconsciously coexist. McKay's concern, though, seems to be more with how such activities are framed within a larger ideological perspective that sees them as incompatible. That is, while Atlantic-Canadian writing shares a cosmopolitan, contemporary sensibility with Canadian literature as a whole, what is distinctive

Introduction

about this sensibility in the East is the degree to which it must be developed in relation to expectations to the contrary. That the cosmopolitanism of Atlantic-Canadian writing should come as a surprise, in other words, reflects the extent to which the region has been constructed as insular, primitive, effectively lost in time.

What is arguably also distinctive about recent Atlantic-Canadian writing is that much of it reflects the sense of the region having reached a threshold, that a way of life grounded in the extraction of natural resources has been palpably and irrevocably transformed, if not eclipsed. The metaphor of threshold, of course, is a dramatic one, and subject to rejoinders that the region has long been struggling with its structural dependency within Confederation and problems with the resource sectors. While that may be true, these considerations have become intensified within the neo-liberal climate of globalization. Consequently, what we see in contemporary Atlantic-Canadian literature is a pronounced, if sometimes ambivalent, engagement with the Folk iconography that has had such a defining influence on the image of the region. We see this, for instance, through writing that marks the passing of traditional rural culture or writing that questions the very integrity and accuracy of such iconography in the first place. Contemporary Atlantic-Canadian literature palpably registers the profound changes in the region and in its fortunes, evoking not only a sense of a largely bygone way of life but also a vulnerability to the political and economic imperatives of the prevailing neo-liberal consensus.

The central contention of Creelman's *Setting in the East* is that Maritime fiction reflects a profound ambivalence, characterized by an awareness of the eclipse of the region's storied past and an unease about a future that looks less than prosperous:

> Just as Maritimers share a common *memory* of a lost community, so they share a distinctive fear or hesitation about their tenuous future. These forces of memory and hesitation form the central cultural boundaries of the region. The Maritimes no longer fit the image of a slow, stable, "folksy" society. The region is distinguished by its balance between hesitation about the future and its memory of the past and this fragile equilibrium is at the root of its distinct style of realist fiction. (2003, 14; italics in original)

What distinguishes contemporary Atlantic-Canadian literature, I would argue, is a more sophisticated understanding of the ambivalence of the storied pasts of both the Maritimes and Newfoundland, and a more sophisticated understanding of the economic, political, and cultural dynamics that shape the region's tenuous position within the present neo-liberal order. This dual consciousness imparts to that writing a greater sense of vitality and subversion, suggestive of a more general resistance to the subordination and passivity routinely imposed on people in the East, a readiness to contest the conventional national wisdom and seize back a degree of agency. The increasing untenability of the Folk paradigm, McKay concludes, provides the grounds for resistance: "In the dissolution of one powerful form of hegemonic ideology, there is perhaps a moment of opportunity for creative cultural opposition" (1994, 308). While writers in the Atlantic provinces have always to some degree reflected the socio-economic and political dynamics of their time—think of Thomas Chandler Haliburton's prescriptions for the economic success of Nova Scotia or Ernest Buckler's registering of the decline of small-scale agriculture— contemporary writing in the region is arguably much more consciously situated and engaged. In Nova Scotia, McKay saw a new generation of writers and artists emerging, "people whose work has undercut such images at every turn" and exposed them as "a thinly spread rhetoric, vulnerable to articulate and subtle moral critiques, including those of people who were brought up in the rural areas it romanticizes" (1994, 310). His prescient insight can indeed be extended to the Atlantic region as a whole, particularly to the literature of Newfoundland and Labrador. This shared combative spirit makes it both compelling and imperative to view contemporary writing in the four provinces together.

The purpose of this study, then, is to examine some of the more significant fronts on which contemporary writing in Atlantic Canada reflects and engages with various dimensions of the region's shifting fortunes within this neo-liberal regime, including the changing nature of centre–periphery relations, the continuing influence of Folk stereotypes, and the impact of economic restructuring. The next section, "I'se the B'y that Leaves the Boats: The Changing Nature of Work," will explore the reshaping of work in the region, particularly the demythologizing of the culture of the petty producer in which Folk stereotypes of the region are rooted, and depictions of the economic and occupational vicissitudes of working people, especially in an era of neo-liberal restructuring and economic globalization. The second section, "'About as Far from Disneyland as You Can Possibly Get': The Reshaping of Culture," will examine challenges to the hegemonic Folk image of the region on two fronts—challenges to the homogeneity and exclusivity of such a cultural construction and the increasing preoccupation with and critique of cultural stereotypes of the region, especially as reflected in depictions of the role of tourism in the region. Finally, the last section, "The Age of Sale: History, Globalization, and Commodification," will explore the ambivalence of the growing body of literary representations of the region's past, which not only commemorate ways of life that have profoundly shaped the culture of the region but also reflect a wariness of such commemoration and anachronistically comment, through the vehicle of historical fiction, on the region's conflicted present.

The contention that contemporary Atlantic-Canadian literature paints a very different picture from the Folk archetypes through which the region tends to be seen is not particularly surprising, perhaps even banal. However prevalent, seductive, and influential such Folk iconography has been, even the most naive and blinkered of visitors might expect to discover that life in the region is far more complicated and progressive than the kitschy, barnacle-encrusted postcard version would suggest. Furthermore, while many Atlantic-Canadian writers distance themselves from, or even diametrically oppose, the Folk archetypes that inform many people's idea of the Atlantic provinces, a palpable appreciation of and attachment to the "folk" themselves continues to run through the literature of the region. Certainly some Atlantic-Canadian writers reinforce, even cater to, these archetypes, where others merely appreciate those qualities—independence, cultural vitality, communal cohesion, and so on—that have been transformed into a kind of standard image of the region. In that sense, the issue is not so much that such stereotypes are unfounded but that they have been reified and even commodified in troubling ways. But much contemporary writing in the region stresses factors running counter to those archetypes: the presence of industrialism, the role of capital, the reshaping of the resource sectors, the staging of culture, the prevalence of neo-liberal austerity, and so on. Thus a crucial part of this book is its investigation of how recent Atlantic-Canadian literature engages and subverts Folk stereotypes, highlighting the degree to which powerful interests—from colonial authorities to corporate leaders to tourist promoters—have propagated such reductive and homogeneous views of the region to further their own ends. Nor is the intent of the study to suggest that the literature of the region is just an epiphenomenon of this globalized, neo-liberal context. The writers addressed in this book have their own individual concerns and contexts, and the work of many writers in the region does not really reflect these circumstances. What this study does stress, though, is that looking at the writing of the region against this backdrop provides valuable insights both about writing in Atlantic Canada and about the larger context of neo-liberalism and globalization.

| Section One

I'se the B'y That Leaves the Boats: The Changing World of Work

In contemporary Atlantic-Canadian literature, work is a conspicuous preoccupation: the availability of work, the conditions of work, the changing nature of work, and the larger context in which that work does or not does not take place. That larger context, of course, for the last three or four decades has been shaped by economic globalization and the implementation of neo-liberal policies, which have had a profound effect on what people in Atlantic Canada, as elsewhere, do for a living. In popular images of the Maritimes and Newfoundland, however, that bigger picture is often obscured. As Ian McKay's *The Quest of the Folk* and James Overton's *Making a World of Difference* have underscored, the dominant stereotypical images of Maritimers and Newfoundlanders have been those of independent producers leading simple lives close to the elements and reliant on the bounty of land and sea. Writing of the picture of the Folk cultivated by middle-class intellectuals and cultural producers in Nova Scotia in the middle of the twentieth century, McKay describes a highly idealized and romanticized iconography that to some degree still informs the way the whole Atlantic region is seen:

> They lived, generally, in fishing and farming communities, supposedly far removed from capitalist social relations and the stresses of modernity. The Folk did not work in factories, coal mines, lobster

canneries, or domestic service: they were rooted to the soil and to the rockbound coast, and lived lives of self-sufficiency close to nature. (1994, 26)

Overton describes the operation of a similar paradigm in Newfoundland, in which it is "the way of life and the attitudes and experiences of the rural small producer that form the core of a distinctive Newfoundland culture" (1996, 52). The defining milieu is the outport, "the seat of home-grown Newfoundland culture, authentic and popular. It is a culture that has developed organically in isolation and it is the environment (especially the sea) that has been one of the key forces which has moulded the Newfoundland character" (52). Such idealized visions of life in the region involve, as Raymond Williams argues of the pastoral in his landmark study *The Country and the City*, "the suppression of work in the countryside, and of the property relations through which this work is organised" (1973, 46).

In contrast, much recent writing on the East Coast offers very different views of how Atlantic Canadians occupy themselves and highlights the presence of "capitalist social relations and the stresses of modernity," including the impact of globalization. If Folk imagery promotes a vision of Maritimers and Newfoundlanders engaged in hardy, independent, elemental, and timeless toil, contemporary Atlantic-Canadian literature provides a very different picture. First of all, while the traditional resource sectors typically reflected in Folk iconography continue to be a significant part of the regional economy, the percentage of the overall population employed in those sectors is shrinking. Those occupations traditionally associated with the image of the Folk living close to land and sea and around which the economy of the Atlantic provinces developed—fishing, farming, and forestry—have all been characterized over the course of the twentieth century by the diminishing role of the independent petty producer, through declining participation and/or increasing mechanization and corporatization (Conrad and Hiller 2001, 197–99). Instead, a growing proportion of people in Atlantic Canada, as elsewhere, are engaged in various service industries from education to retail to tourism. Furthermore, the corporatization, mechanization, and computerization of work have reshaped the occupations of most Atlantic Canadians, in terms of both the availability and quality of work.

The changing nature of work in the region in turn has had a profound social and cultural impact, and many of the region's writers have concerned themselves with the reverberations of changing occupational patterns, changing work conditions, and even at times with the broader ideological culture within which these changes are taking place. This is not to suggest that such an awareness is an entirely novel phenomenon in Atlantic-Canadian literature; a major focus of Thomas Chandler Haliburton's early nineteenth-century *Clockmaker* series was the economic position and future health of Nova Scotia, Norman Duncan's collection of stories *The Way of the Sea* (1903) reflected the central role of the fishing merchant in Newfoundland outport culture, and in the iconic text of Maritime literature—L.M. Montgomery's *Anne of Green Gables* (1908)—the bank is poised to repossess Matthew Cuthbert's farm. What I am suggesting, though, is that in the contemporary writing of Atlantic Canada work and the broader economic conditions in which it takes place are a principal preoccupation, and that preoccupation says much about the region's position—historically, nationally, and globally.

2 |

Sucking the Mother Dry: The Fisheries

As a whole generation of Atlantic-Canadian historians have illustrated, one of the main problems with mythologizing the life of the independent petty producer is that it tends to obscure a much more complicated economic and social reality. Writing of the reliance on wage labour of agricultural workers in the nineteenth-century Maritimes, for instance, Rusty Bitterman concedes that, "[l]ike any powerful and pervasive mythology, the image of the independent yeoman is partly rooted in a reality," but points to the problems that develop "when a fragment of the rural experience becomes a characterization of the whole" (1994, 35). Bill Parenteau and Richard W. Judd examine how the rural working class in the Maritimes and New England were idealized as "friendly uncomplicated folk" (2005, 233) populating a pastoral landscape at the same time as governments and members of the elite collaborated to establish fish and game laws that criminalized traditional foraging practices often crucial to the survival of said folk. They argue that "[t]he rural areas of the region were, of course, much more complicated than the static portrait of rustic contentment presented in the tourist literature" (233) and instead offer a picture of sustained class conflict over the freedom to hunt and fish.

Perhaps the best illustrations of the shortcomings of idealizing life in the resource sectors are offered by the fishing industry, particularly in its present state. There is perhaps no more central a symbol of the Atlantic provinces than the hardy fisherman and the quaint fishing village that is his milieu. The staple maritime iconography of the region, however, tends to be resolutely anti-modern, seeking to preserve the romance of the era of "wood, wind, and sail," and, as Ian McKay powerfully argues, seeking to avoid the taint of modernization and capitalist relations. The illusion of maritime romance, though, is at present even more tenuous, especially given the increasing visibility of the crisis in the fisheries, most particularly the 1992 moratorium on the northern cod so vital to the economy and culture of Newfoundland and Labrador. Atlantic-Canadian literature of the past—works such as Frank Parker Day's *Rockbound*, Norman Duncan's depictions of outport life in Newfoundland, and the maritime adventures of Thomas Head Raddall—to some degree romanticized the ocean-going life. Contemporary Atlantic-Canadian literature, though, has a much more postlapsarian tone and furthermore emphasizes the extent to which life in the fisheries is shaped by larger networks of governmental oversight and global economic competition. The result is a more complex and much less idealized vision of hardship. What we see are not so much the elemental rigours of eking out a living in an often unforgiving environment, but the less tangible and less predictable struggle to survive in the face of rapacious modernization, governmental intervention, corporate domination, and dwindling resources.

"Everybody Knew": Donna Morrissey's *Sylvanus Now*

Underpinning essentialist Folk representations of the fishing life is the implicit presumption of the unlimited bounty of the sea. That is, if the Folk are engaged in a timeless relationship with the sea, the sea (however perilous and capricious) perforce will forever provide. A central aspect of the Atlantic provinces' current economic and cultural plight, however, is the demolition of that belief by the exhaustion of groundfish and other stocks and the consequent dilemma of what to do in the wake of recognizing this reality. Newfoundland writer Donna Morrissey's third novel, *Sylvanus Now* (2005), is set against the backdrop of the dawning of that realization. It focuses on an outport Newfoundland fisherman engaged in an occupation—the inshore fishery—that is in the process of being rendered obsolete. *Sylvanus Now* is an interesting book, because Morrissey's sympathies for Sylvanus are often expressed in the idealized, anti-modernist tones associated with the discourse of the Folk, but at the same time her portrait of life in an outport community in the mid-twentieth century disrupts the sense of timelessness characteristic of Folk portrayals of the fishing life. Although these tendencies are sometimes at war with each other in the novel, ultimately *Sylvanus Now* deflates the image of the fishing life on the East Coast as insulated from progress and, to the contrary, dramatizes the degree to which it has been victimized by it.

Sylvanus Now is a good example of how recent Atlantic-Canadian literature often both exploits and subverts the mythological aura of the Folk. Indeed, the hero of the novel, which chronicles the turbulent marriage of Sylvanus Now and his wife Adelaide from 1949 to 1960, is a man who has a near-mystical bond with the elements and articulates for much of the novel a profoundly anti-modernist resistance to change. Although Sylvanus does have a motor on his boat, he clings to the rudimentary technology of jigging and persists in the increasingly obsolete salt fish trade. He is also resolute in his resistance to his brothers' entreaties to go in with them and purchase a longliner to keep up with progress, and give up salt fish for the trade in fresh fish that improvements in technology have made possible. Sylvanus's commitment to the traditional life of the petty producer is motivated by a desire for independence but also by his family history and by a numinous bond with the sea. That is, Sylvanus is resistant to improvement and change to a great degree based on what can be seen as an ecological ethic. In this sense, Morrissey strikes an uneasy balance between a potentially romantic anti-modernism and a somewhat anachronistic conservationism. Looking back from a time in which the crisis in the fisheries has reached alarming proportions, Morrissey makes Sylvanus the voice of responsible resource management, struggling to survive but also to sustain his respect for that which makes survival possible: the sea.[1]

Morrissey's portrait of Sylvanus is consciously idealized. As his Latinate moniker suggests, Morrissey sees him as a mythological figure, closely linked to nature. The Folk are often depicted as atavistic, pre-modern beings living close to the physical elements and removed from the constraints of civilized, technological society, and Sylvanus fits the bill, as he has been physically shaped by the rigours of his occupation and is most at peace in the solitary pursuit of cod. At the same time, his participation in a way of life built around the extraction of resources is made to seem respectful, almost mystical, and even symbiotic. These overtones are particularly evident in Sylvanus's ruminations on the mother cod, those fish that he diligently returns to the deep to spawn, thus ensuring the future bounty of his maritime harvest. In this, Sylvanus is depicted as continuing in the way of his predecessors, and his role as a kind of repository of maritime heritage again has Folk overtones:

> he was more than the land and the sea. He was an accumulation of all that had come before him—his father, his grandfather, his great-great-grandfathers who had coddled and had been coddled by these waters since time began. A repository, that's what he was, a casket into which the old put themselves. No, not a casket, a sieve whereby they continued to flow through him, and those others who, God willing, would come from him. (Morrissey 2005, 269)

If Sylvanus in that sense is the novel's still centre, the rest of the book depicts a turning world, a way of life that is being profoundly reshaped by modernization and global competition, both of which pose an enormous threat to the lower-impact inshore fishery. The fate of the fisheries in the Atlantic provinces (and, indeed worldwide), Kent Blades contends, provides a classic example of the cumulative effect of capitalist competition for natural resources, with large corporations and individual fishers racing to develop ever more effective but capital-intensive ways to catch more fish, continuing to believe in the endless bounty of the sea even in the face of declining catches. Blades describes the devastating impact of technological innovation, global competition, and political (mis)management on fish stocks, in light of which the romantic image of the independent fisherman is impossible to sustain:

> In an attempt to curb fishing effort and protect marine resources, management schemes applied by coastal nations, including Canada, have failed miserably to account for the increased capacity of modern fleets to locate, chase, and kill. What has happened to fish stocks around the world, and specifically to the Atlantic groundfishery, must be recognized as the inevitable result of an exploitative mind-set—the belief that what is modern, more efficient, and faster is also better. And to be better is a necessity if exploiters of resources are to compete in a fast-moving global economy. (1995, 17)

Sylvanus fits the profile of the traditional, independent, inshore fisherman as he tenaciously adheres to the selective and less intrusive technology of the time-tried salt fish trade. However, as his efforts yield decreasing returns over the course of the novel, through Sylvanus and Adelaide Morrissey articulates concern about the destructive impact of technological innovations in the fishery. Both frown on the use of gill nets, for instance, which tend to be cut loose and drift, "filling up with fish till their weight sank them to the bottom" and then, "when all the fish rotted or were eaten by other fish, they rose again, fishing themselves full" (2005, 190) again and again. And Sylvanus objects to signing on to a trawler not just because of the loss of independence it represents but also because of the trawlers' indiscriminate efficiency and their damaging effects on the ocean floor, including the precious spawning grounds. While Sylvanus's brothers Jake and Ambrose stress the need to keep up with technological change in order to survive in a competitive industry, the novel makes clear the degree to which the prosperity ensuing from increasing efficiency in the fishery comes at the cost of the sustainability of the stocks. This is particularly the case with factory trawlers, which are depicted as industrial leviathans, "a plant and freezer all in one, filleting and freezing thirty tons of fish a day" (121), impressing on Sylvanus the enormity of their ability to deplete the ocean of cod. In *Lament for an Ocean*, Michael Harris likens the impact of these huge ocean-going trawlers to clear-cutting (1998, 63), and in *Sylvanus Now*, as more countries descend on the fishing grounds, Sylvanus pictures their impact in similar apocalyptic terms, "all the rest of them, the Spanish, the Portuguese, the French, and half the bloody globe were hunkering in colossal ships over the fishing grounds two hundred miles from shore, the sea lit up like a starry sky; spring, summer, winter, and fall, sucking, sucking, sucking the mother dry" (2005, 207).

Sylvanus Now also stresses the politicization of these changes in the industry. While the novel does not exactly absolve the domestic industry from complicity in the depletion of fish stocks, the principal culprits in *Sylvanus Now* are foreign overfishing and inadequate government oversight. This sense of the global context of the problem is developed particularly through Sylvanus's exchanges with his brothers, who take greater pains to monitor developments in the industry. They express concern over increasing foreign presence and encroachment and the decline in catches, sentiments that are received by government officials initially with patronizing, blithe assurances that there are plenty of fish to go around. Later, the authorities refuse to make much of the decline in catches, infuriating domestic fishers by cooperating with their foreign competitors. When the evidence of depleted stocks becomes too hard to ignore, they are slow to establish boundaries and quick to respond with diversionary finger-pointing at other factors, compounding the problem by encouraging fishers to invest in better technology such as gill nets. Only once the exhaustion of the stocks is palpable does the government impose an international boundary, a gesture that does too little, too late. A key part of the crisis in the fisheries, Blades argues, was a close collaboration, even collusion, between government and big business (1995, 121–22). Morrissey similarly depicts the government's involvement not simply as neglectful and counterproductive, contributing to overfishing and destructive practices, but wilfully, consciously so. In one of the novel's key moments, Sylvanus has an epiphany, coming to the realization that such practices are not the product of ignorance or neglect but indeed a conscious course of action spurred by greed: "They knew. Of course they knew. Everybody knew. Governments. Corporations. Merchants. Even the fishers working the big boats knew. But they would keep doing it anyway" (2005, 219).

Also contributing to the historicization of the setting of the novel is the background of the Household Resettlement Program, an extension of the forces of modernization and government involvement in the lives of rural Newfoundlanders. "The Smallwood government," Ursula Kelly recounts, "'resettled' thousands of people by dissolving smaller, more isolated, communities and relocating the inhabitants to 'growth centres'—towns where industries would be established, services centralized and people regulated" (1993, 22). According to Miriam Wright, the program was seen as an intrusive extension of the Smallwood government's commitment to an industrial vision of the fisheries. "Although many inshore fishers wanted some aspects of the industrial vision" and benefited from financial support offered through the program, Wright observes, "having the government tell them where they could live was another matter entirely. In trying to solve the economic and social problems of the Newfoundland fishery, the state crossed a barrier that many fishing people were not willing to accept" (2001, 149). In *Sylvanus Now*, the program is depicted in similar terms. "The government's paying a good penny, maid," Adelaide's friend Suze observes. "And like they says, they can't be building roads and light poles to every cove and cranny on the island— and they're promising lots more work for bigger places" (Morrissey 2005, 186). The results, however, are dubious and even destructive. Morrissey's three central characters (Sylvanus, Adelaide, and Sylvanus's mother Eva) are all resistant to resettlement and view it as tearing people from a nurturing, natural, and communal environment. Sylvanus imagines the abandonment of their community, Cooney Arm, with anthropomorphic romanticism:

> Now she, too, was threatened with death, her homes mutilated to stumps, her wells parched, and the wharves and flakes left to rot. For without the breath of her homesteaders sweeping through her grass, without their blood trumpeting down her hillside, carousing across her meadow, without their hands moulding her seedlings and touching their tongues to her fruit, she, too, would die. (268–69)

Both Sylvanus and Adelaide's father, furthermore, view the program as ill-considered, because it involves the relocation of fishers to fishing grounds that have been long claimed by others. Sylvanus also later responds to his brothers' enticing him to resettle—to accept the inevitability of modernization—with an anti-modernist rant, emphasizing that the terminus of all this change, progress, and modernization is the extinction of the fisherman: "next thing you'll be all nice and modern on the deck of a freezer, doing to us what the rest of the bastards have been doing for years now—wiping us out" (265).

Against this background of turmoil and change, however, Sylvanus and Adelaide at the end of the novel opt for stability. Initially, Sylvanus accepts that he has no right to tie Adelaide to the circumscribed life of the inshore fishery, which she so loathed when they were first married. Adelaide,

FIGURE 1 An iconic picture from the Household Resettlement Program. House of Mr. Malcolm Rogers being towed by a 40 hp motor boat during relocation from Fox Island to Flat Island, Dover, NL, August 1961.

however, resists his initiative to move and insists that they stay, galvanized in part by Eva's confession that she watched her husband and son drown nearby and therefore rejects moving in part because her husband's "haunt" or spirit needs a home to come back to. This arguably anti-modernist ending, though, is tempered by Adelaide's gift to Sylvanus of a pair of gill nets, a concession to the need to move—if not so rapidly—with the times. Although *Sylvanus Now*'s portrait of a bygone, sustainable inshore fishery has more than a whiff of nostalgic celebration, Morrissey stops short of implicitly criticizing any concessions to technological progress as an ecological violation. Instead, she dramatizes the tenuous position of the independent fisherman, faced with a Hobson's choice between short-term survival and long-term ecological sustainability, and sets her sights on a monopolistic industrial vision of the fisheries that, Wright contends, has proven calamitous:

> We can no longer afford to view the fisheries resources as "property" of the state and industry, to do with it as they choose. That path has led only to devastation of the resource, economic instability, and great social upheaval. Instead, we need to find a way to use and look after the fishery that provides economic and social benefits, and allows more equitable access to the resource without destroying it or the delicate ecosystem of which it is a part. (2001, 156)

Section 1: I'se the B'y That Leaves the Boats

Oceans 2000: Bernice Morgan's *Waiting for Time*

If *Sylvanus Now* punctures the myth of the independent fisherman with its emphasis on the progressive impact of technology, modernization, and global competition, that myth has been much more substantially discredited by the 1992 moratorium on the northern cod fishery, the official recognition of the exhaustion of groundfish stocks that Morrissey's mid-century milieu anticipates. As Harris describes it, the "collapse of the northern cod stock is one of the most spectacular failures in the history of Canadian government and an ecological disaster of worldwide significance," one which "devastated communities where fishing was not just an occupation but a way of life for hundreds of years" (1998, 307). Blades stresses that the crisis in the fisheries has had such a momentous impact across the region particularly because the evidence suggests that the decline is not a temporary one:

> Scores of people were thrown out of work as plants closed and millions of dollars worth of fishing boats and gear remained tied up at the docks. Those who have traditionally made their living from the sea are used to cycles of boom and bust, but this crisis is much more serious than its predecessors. This time it is not only the economic viability of industry players that is in question but the long-term survival of the resource itself, while a time-honoured way of life hangs in the balance. (1995, iv)

The 1992 moratorium thus represents a watershed moment for the Atlantic region, and particularly for Newfoundland, and novels by two Newfoundland writers, Bernice Morgan and Kenneth J. Harvey, in very divergent ways, address the reverberations of the moratorium in rural Newfoundland.

Published shortly after the moratorium, Morgan's *Waiting for Time* (1994) represents a more direct engagement than Morrissey's novel with the historical, economic, and political circumstances that led to the demise of a resource around which the life of the province had been built. The novel is a sequel to Morgan's celebrated historical romance, *Random Passage* (1992), which chronicles the intertwined lives of two families of impoverished immigrants from England struggling to survive after being deposited on Newfoundland's bleak French Shore in the first half of the nineteenth century. Although the novel highlights the class dynamics behind the populating of Newfoundland and the complicated gender and class relations within the cod fishery, the narrative of *Random Passage* is preoccupied with the romantic intrigue between the characters, particularly Lavinia Andrews, the merchant Thomas Hutchings, and Mary Bundle, who jumps ship with her newborn baby at Cape Random. *Waiting for Time* revisits the events of *Random Passage*, but it does so within a contemporary frame story of another Lavinia Andrews, an Ottawa-based fisheries researcher who travels to Newfoundland to oversee a major project out of St. John's. Having recently parted ways with her husband, the middle-aged Lavinia is at a crossroads. In returning to Newfoundland, her birthplace, Lavinia is coming to a place that is itself at a crossroads, on the cusp of a profoundly transformative catastrophe. Morgan's reframing of the earlier history within the contemporary context of the crisis in the fisheries sustains the focus on the class tensions at the foundation of Newfoundland culture and the hierarchical and subordinating nature of the fishery as an occupation. But it also situates that perspective within a potentially less romantic critique of the collusion between the political and economic elites in the management of the fisheries.

Lavinia arrives in St. John's determined to prove her capabilities in spearheading Oceans 2000. This objective, however, is torpedoed by her graduate student assistant, Mark Rodway, who surreptitiously faxes to Ottawa an interim report that contradicts the blithe optimism of the Department of Fisheries and Oceans' assessments. The fax amounts to an apocalyptic warning that the northern cod stocks are in danger of collapsing due to an array of dubious practices in the fisheries. In response, head office goes into full-court press mode, blunting the message of the report and dispatching to St. John's a posse of damage control experts headed by Wayne Drover, the point man for Fisheries Minister Timothy Drew. Concerned only with defusing the report and providing more palatable fodder for his boss, Drover effectively hijacks the Oceans 2000 project, his team of tactical researchers and public relations cosmeticians pushing Lavinia and Mark to the side.

Although Drew is seen only at a distance in the novel, his profile nonetheless draws attention to the questionable links between government and business, and situates the politics around the report within the global context of corporate involvement in the fisheries. Drew, crows Wayne, belongs to a wealthy and influential local family with diversified interests, including involvement in the fishing industry, and a virtual dominance of St. John's: "they owned half the town, rows of houses, shops, newspapers, factories and fish plants" (Morgan 1994, 61). Drew is clearly modelled on John Crosbie, the former Conservative MP and member of the prominent Crosbie family, active not only in the fisheries but also in "construction, manufacturing, transportation, shipping, communications, insurance, foreign exchange and real estate" (Harris 1993, 296). Crosbie presided over the announcement of the moratorium as the minister of Fisheries and Oceans in the federal government of Brian Mulroney, even though "a year earlier, Crosbie had

Section 1: I'se the B'y That Leaves the Boats

FIGURE 2 Federal Fisheries Minister John Crosbie leaving the press conference after announcing the 1992 cod moratorium.

discounted scientific evidence that the stocks were in serious trouble and refused to make dramatic cuts in the quota" (Harris 1993, 384).

According to Blades, the fisheries have been dominated in the second half of the twentieth century by large companies controlling the offshore industry as well as the fish-packing business, whose international reach allowed them to weather the restructuring in the fisheries. Adjusting to the reality of declining stocks, they "have closed plant after plant in an effort to rationalize their operations and have moved to purchase raw product on the world market" (1995, 173). In *Waiting for Time*, Wayne confides to Lavinia that Drew, with a new company based in Tennessee, is considering revitalizing a Southside plant—"Perhaps we can put a package together—you know, government backing, draggers, fish quotas, export licences, all that stuff!" (Morgan 1994, 56)—even though, as Wayne's mother Verna reveals, it has been "refinanced more times than poor Patsy Carey down behind the post office" (74). The manoeuvrings of the Drew empire exemplify what Blades describes as the unequal mobility of workers and capital within the fisheries. Whereas fish plant workers and inshore fishers, who bore the brunt of the crisis in the fisheries, are constrained by their limited mobility, Blades argues, "[c]orporate capital … is very mobile, shifting to wherever there is a profit to be made. The fortunes of the large company sector are therefore loosened from the constraints of sustainable development and are free to pursue profit at any cost" (1995, 172).

If the operations of the Drew family highlight the collusion of the financial and political elite, Morgan's portrait of Wayne emphasizes the political expediency at the heart of the crisis of the fisheries. Rather than a moustache-twirling Machiavellian, though, Wayne is a pork-barrel pragmatist, a charismatic populist ostensibly trying to do his best for his boss's constituents. With an election looming, the kind of bad news contained in Mark's fax just won't do; his boss's electoral fortunes are concomitant, Wayne suggests, with the province's: "if Timothy Drew goes, half the transfer payments coming down here goes with him—a dozen federal projects" (1994, 53). Conservation is just not an option, because it is not politically viable. Facilitating the continued prosecution of the fisheries, in contrast, is. Thus Wayne and his coterie set about massaging Lavinia's project, sacrificing scientific timelines to the interest of political deadlines and orchestrating the desired result, which will intensify rather than alleviate the pressure on the stocks. Suppressing the forecasted absence of fish, Wayne emphasizes how the province will be swimming in largesse:

> this incentive will bring big federal grants, funding for research on production, on marketing, funding for a five-million-dollar study on the feasibility of that international landing and distribution port we've been talking about for years—funding for fisherman, for factories, for longliners, for marine-related courses at the university. (64)

Such short-term economic alleviation, however, comes at the cost of Newfoundland's long-term interests, as Lavinia comes to realize. Having reacted to the invasion of her project by retreating to the basement of the provincial archives, Lavinia discovers the Ellsworth Ledger, which contains accounts by her namesake and Thomas Hutchings of the history of Cape Random. As she becomes preoccupied with the past, she increasingly removes herself from the present and lets Wayne have his way with her project—and, in a moment of vulnerability, with her. The spell is broken the next day, however, when she discovers that Mark has been arrested for breaking into the office to find a copy of the suppressed report.

As Lavinia reacts to the co-optation of her project by retreating into the Ellsworth Ledger, what she reads there clearly has a profound impact on her sense of self and her perspective of the fishery. Mary Bundle's version of the settlement of Cape Random (told in third-person omniscient) raises important questions about historical gender and class dynamics in the fisheries but also galvanizes Lavinia to reconnect with her Newfoundland relatives. Mary's narrative, written in the margins of the ledger and running against the grain of Lavinia's more romantic version, emphasizes the obstacles she must overcome to reach her place as the matriarch of Cape Random. Mary and her sister Tessa escape a life of brutal poverty in Dorset only to find themselves subjected to the arbitrary cruelty of members of the colonial elite in St. John's. Mary is forced to flee in the company of her friend the thief Tim Toop after Tessa is raped by their master and flogged at the command of their jealous mistress, and the two retaliate by ransacking the master's house. After Mary has a child, however, Tim arranges work for her as a cook on a ship bound for Labrador, but Mary gets off in Cape Random, where she ends up living the rest of her life. Mary's version of life on the cape emphasizes the political dynamics of the fishery, particularly through her struggle for power with Thomas Hutchings. Mary fails to improve her position by seducing Thomas, instead marrying the happy-go-lucky but impecunious Ned Andrews. After Ned's death, though, Mary stages a coup in Cape Random, having discovered the enigmatic Thomas's secret, that he is a former Catholic priest wanted in the capital for the murder of an Englishman. When Mary's daughter Fanny becomes pregnant (even though the paternity of the child is ambiguous), Mary threatens to reveal Thomas's past unless he marries the girl. After Fanny's death in childbirth, Hutchings departs from Cape Random, leaving Mary to take the reins of the community until his surprise return three years later. Throughout the novel, power politics intersects with romantic intrigue in this fashion, stressing the crucial interplay between sexual and marital relations and social and economic relations.

The circumstances of Thomas's return serve as a kind of preface to the contemporary frame of *Waiting for Time*. Thomas brings with him the news that the community is about to fall victim to what amounts to a restructuring of the fishery. The new owner of the firm to which the community sells its fish, Timothy Drew, is about to cut loose all the small communities along the shore: "he's worked out that he'll make more money if he keeps stores only in the bigger places" (Morgan 1994, 172). However, when Drew makes a visit to Cape Random, he turns out to be none other than Tim Toop, who has leveraged an advantageous marriage into a transatlantic financial empire over which his contemporary namesake continues to preside:

> In a thousand coves and bays, on a hundred tiny islands, thousands of fishermen and their families worked for the Drew empire and depended on Drew vessels for every mouthful of food, every item of clothing. Timothy's descendants became manufacturers, bankers, lawyers and, of course, politicians. In Newfoundland they were considered only a little lower than the angels and a good bit higher than royalty. (179)

Mary, however, shrewdly coerces Tim into sparing Cape Random and signing over ownership of the store to her and her descendents in perpetuity. The residents react to this reversal of fortune with subservient gratitude to Drew, illustrating a passive deferral to authority that Mary elsewhere diagnoses as a chronic condition of Newfoundland: "Always in need of savin' and never saved, this place is. Waitin' for time, Ned used ta call it—'we'um just waitin' for time, maid. Just waitin' 'til our ship comes in,' he'd say. Well, I allow our ship got sunk off the Funks" (Morgan 1994, 84).

Mary's narrative provides Lavinia with an object lesson in the hierarchical politics of the fishery—the degree to which ordinary people are at the mercy of the powerful. More specifically, it reveals the dubious origins of an enterprise that continues to dominate the province and whose interests Lavinia's project has been hijacked to support. Lavinia's reaction is to attempt to disrupt the latter-day Timothy Drew's press conference by releasing copies of Mark's report to the media. This act of defiance, however, is swiftly defused; the alternative report is suppressed, and Lavinia is fired for her insubordination. Mary's story also prods Lavinia out of her passivity and marks the beginning of her recovery of a sense of identity and belonging. After her dismissal, Lavinia travels to Davisporte on the French Shore hoping to meet Rachel, Mary's great-granddaughter and amanuensis, only to arrive in time for her funeral. As a middle-class come-from-away, Lavinia is initially an anxious outsider in Davisporte, "as apprehensive as if she were entering an African village to observe some unknown ritual" (195). Her sense of alienation from her origins is subsequently allayed somewhat when she discovers from Rachel's gruff grandson Alf that her own father (contrary to her mother's account that he died in the war) had returned to Cape Random a simpleton and was cared for by the rest of the family until his death in 1975. After returning to Ottawa, Lavinia discovers that Wayne Drover has made her pregnant, and returns to Cape Random to bring up her son. She moves in with Alf and takes over the house that her namesake and Thomas Hutchings used to live in, which had been floated up from Cape Random.

Lavinia's personal renaissance takes place against a backdrop that emphasizes the profound impact of the collapse of the groundfish stocks on rural Newfoundland. Lavinia watches as Mark's apocalyptic predictions come to pass and the implications of the mismanagement of the fisheries take palpable shape. The bitter divisions caused by such mismanagement are exemplified by the debate between Alf, who runs a motel, and his brother Ned, who has been encouraged by government programs to invest in improved technology for his boat. Even as apocalyptic predictions start to leak out,

Section 1: I'se the B'y That Leaves the Boats

"the crowd in St. John's keeps tellin' us everthin's all right" (Morgan 1994, 219), even increasing quotas for foreign trawlers fishing in Canadian waters, but rumours that the fishery is to be closed turn out to be true. In Alf's motel, Lavinia watches a news conference at which Timothy Drew, flanked by Wayne Drover, announces the closing of the fishery, and the press conference is disrupted by a group of fishers (including Ned, who is half a million dollars in debt), some of whom are frog-marched out by police.[2]

What the moratorium amounts to, *Waiting for Time* emphasizes, is the betrayal and abjection of rural Newfoundland. Initially, there is a wave of concern, as a bevy of government types, scientific experts, and representatives of the media descend on the coast, "people who ask endless, intrusive questions" (224). Morgan depicts their concern as shallow and transient, emphasizing the social divide between them and those with whose plight they seem so concerned: "Hearing one say he is about to give displaced fish plant workers a series of workshops on managing a small business and another ask Doris if the level of violence has increased in her family—Lav is enraged" (224). However, Alf's prediction that the "novelty'll soon wear off" proves to be true, and by October, "[t]here is not an expert to be found in Davisporte" (224). The banks, unfortunately, have a longer attention span, and start to lay claim to the property of fishers with loans. As Blades observes, many fishers made "heavy investments near the end of the boom years, when they upgraded to new and larger boats, often borrowing large sums and posting homes and vehicles as collateral" (1995, 160), and in *Waiting for Time*, this is the fate of Ned, who is forced to pile his family into a car and take them off to British Columbia. Thus, while Lavinia resolves to stay, she is clearly swimming against the tide of the depopulation of rural Newfoundland. In her study of two Newfoundland fishing communities, Nicole Power links restructuring in the fisheries to globalization and a neo-liberal emphasis on "restricting and regulating perceived state-dependents and containing 'traditional' orientations to the fishery"; government initiatives "have thus focused on reducing debt and social spending, expanding export production, increasing regulation of access and entry, and encouraging withdrawal from the fishery with financial assistance" (2005, 9). In a similar vein, Morgan explicitly frames the emptying out of rural Newfoundland as an outcome orchestrated by the elite:

> She can see, of course, that roads are deteriorating, that repairs are no longer made to the water and telephone systems, that every year more and more houses are boarded up, that more and more young people leave as soon as they finish school. She knows that Davisporte,

like a hundred other small places around the coast, is doomed—for
although they dare not utter the word "resettlement," government
policy is to relocate everyone, if not to Upper Canada, then to
those towns they have designated as "economically advantaged
communities." (1994, 226)

While Morgan provides a palpable critique of the economic and political manipulation attending the collapse of the cod stocks and the ensuing moratorium, however, the romantic overtones of her portrait of Lavinia arguably serve to defuse the power of this critique. Lavinia's return to the family fold is pervaded by quasi-mystical resonances. Before she even travels to St. John's to oversee Oceans 2000, she has a recurring dream of a female salmon, driving "herself to premature senility in frantic determination to lay eggs on the same bit of sand where she had been spawned" (35), a foreshadowing of her return to Newfoundland to give birth to her son David Saul. Her increasing preoccupation with her family history is depicted as an almost atavistic gravitation toward the past. While planning to steal the ledger from the archives, she falls asleep to the allure of the foghorn and realizes afterward that "she had merged into Lavinia's skin, known Lavinia's body and Lavinia's longing as her own" (63). This romantic essentialism is particularly marked in the epilogue, which chronicles Lavinia's endurance in the midst of the decline of rural Newfoundland. She becomes a kind of eccentric folk artist, painting garish sea creatures on any surface, arguably compensating through art for what time and human rapacity have taken away. However, out of a future time in which "*only the old, the hunted and the maimed live along this coast*" (230) comes hope, as the novel ends first with the return of Alf's departed daughter Rachel Jane, with her own daughter in tow, and then years later with the return of the caplin (suggesting, implicitly, the return of the cod that rely on them for food). That this heralds the renewal of things, the beginning of a cycle rather than the apocalyptic terminus of a road of no return, is signalled by the fact that the novel ends with the opening sentence of the prologue to *Random Passage*: "*She will write, 'It is spring and in the great pit at the centre of the sacred hill a fire burns as it has for a thousand springs'*" (1994, 230). The problems of such apparent romantic optimism—the sense that the disruption of an entire way of life built around the fisheries may be just temporary—are compounded by the way in which the ending seems to affirm a passive stance that had been critiqued earlier in the novel. The ravaging of a resource through the wilful mismanagement and collusion of the political establishment and corporate economic interests, Morgan seems to suggest, can ultimately be overcome by "waiting for time."

Section 1: I'se the B'y That Leaves the Boats

"No urgency to draw another breath": Kenneth J. Harvey's *The Town That Forgot How to Breathe*

Like *Waiting for Time*, Kenneth J. Harvey's *The Town That Forgot How to Breathe* (2003) also focuses on the aftermath of the moratorium in Newfoundland, but Harvey's approach to the impact of the moratorium on the lives of Newfoundlanders is a more inventive and less mimetic one. Where *Sylvanus Now* and *Waiting for Time* are fairly traditional realistic fictions, Harvey's novel is a Gothic, magical realist tale about the loss of purpose and identity in a Newfoundland outport community in the wake of the collapse of the cod fishery. Employing allegorical strategies characteristic of magical realism, mixing the empirical and realistic with the supernatural and the uncanny, Harvey creatively dramatizes the psychological and existential crisis that the moratorium constitutes for rural Newfoundland.

In many magical realist texts, plagues serve as allegorical devices for exploring societies undergoing profound social and cultural changes, and such is the premise underpinning *The Town That Forgot How to Breathe*. The outport town of Bareneed reflects the broader, fallen state of rural Newfoundland after the closure of the cod fishery. As one resident reflects, "Bareneed, once a lively and warm place, now stank of drabness and heartbreak" (K. Harvey 2003, 18). Dr. Thompson, the local physician who struggles to counter the plague that besets the community, reflects upon the prevailing sense of crisis:

> People moving away to the mainland, others becoming bitter or passive about the grave injustice the government had perpetrated against them, cutting off their livelihoods. Many residents still retained the fiery Newfoundland spirit and the ingenuity of true islanders, but a lifestyle had been destroyed for approximately half the community, and the despair was palpable. (140)

Amid this economic and psychological crisis, numerous residents of the community start to develop a mysterious complex of symptoms. Previously healthy and peaceful people find themselves becoming increasingly bitter and volatile, inexplicably lashing out at those around them. Blades describes the increase in social tension and domestic violence ensuing "when unemployed fishermen and fish plant workers find themselves spending increasing amounts of time at home" and stressed "by drastic cuts to the region's fishery and the loss of income" (1995, 161). In a similar fashion, in Harvey's novel RCMP sergeant Brian Chase attributes the increasing violence in the community to the atmosphere of economic crisis: "Job loss created idleness and all that went with it: shifts in morals, alcohol becoming solace, abuses born of frustration and powerlessness, and suffering turning so severe it manifests itself as rage" (K. Harvey 2003, 62). The allegorical nature of the plague is signalled by the fact that all who fall victim to it were previously employed in the fisheries but are now unemployed. Furthermore, the afflicted experience a disorienting loss of identity; as one baffled victim, Darry Potter, confesses to Dr. Thompson, "I'm not myself" (195). The culmination of these strange symptoms is an inability to breathe without making a conscious effort to do so, with victims lapsing into a comatose state, followed by death—one of many links, as Cynthia Sugars points out, between the residents and the vanishing cod (2010, 19–22). As another resident, Donna Drover, starts to succumb, there is "[n]o pressure to exhale" and "[n]o urgency to draw another breath" (K. Harvey 2003, 20), signalling the loss of purpose and vitality. Through this series of symptoms, Harvey creatively allegorizes the social consequences and the crisis of identity precipitated by the eclipse of a long-standing way of life, underscoring the degree to which people's identity and dignity are bound up with the centuries-long heritage of working in the fisheries. "Forgetting how to breathe" serves as a succinct metaphor both for the fundamental existential crisis Harvey chronicles and for the shift from an independent way of life to a humiliating dependence on and subordination to outsiders. In effect, the afflicted must be kept on artificial life support while the authorities struggle to remedy their condition—physiologically paralleling the social and economic plight of rural Newfoundlanders in the wake of the moratorium.

If the symptoms of the plague appear somewhat uncanny, subsequent developments in Bareneed destabilize the boundaries between the real and the supernatural or mystical in a more fundamental way, serving to develop Harvey's vision of the social and psychological transformation of rural Newfoundland. Bareneed becomes the locus of a series of supernatural phenomena: sightings of mermaids, landings of unusual fish, and particularly the appearance in the ocean of a series of bodies, corpses of members of the community lost at sea anywhere from a few years ago to centuries before, uncannily preserved from the ravages of time. A journal found on a fresh-looking corpse dates to the mid-1700s, a conclusion that Dr. Thompson resists, because, as Chase observes, "There shouldn't be anything left of him" (K. Harvey 2003, 221).

In *Waiting for Time*, the post-moratorium sense of crisis in rural Newfoundland prompted an onslaught of attention, concern, and proposed remedy. In the hyperbolic world of Harvey's novel, that unwelcome intrusion is given the proportions of an occupation. The military takes charge of the scene, cordoning off the beach and denying access to the community, and the media hordes descend, "sucking every bit of tragedy out of the proceedings" (239). Through this scenario Harvey explores the sense in post-moratorium Newfoundland of external forces being responsible for, and subsequently feeding off, the plight of the residents. The people of Bareneed bristle at the encroachment of outsiders (tourists, the police, the army, the media) and, fuelled by the plague, their hostility increasingly takes on a menacing and violent edge. At the same time, Harvey engages in some lively satire of these quasi-colonial forces, particularly through the character of Doug Blackwood, an inshore fisherman and folk artist infuriated by the moratorium, which he sees as an authoritarian intrusion by a "bunch of pasty-faced bureaucrats" (151). Through Doug, Harvey gestures to federally funded attempts to subsidize adjustment to the moratorium, including The Atlantic Groundfish Strategy, "the purpose of which was to direct recipients into alternative careers, to retire people from the fishery, and to provide temporary income support" (Power 2005, 42). As Power observes, however, such policies were grounded in the mistaken assumptions that people would be willing to be retrained and that there would be jobs available that they would be willing to take, even if it required relocating (2005, 63). With a finely attuned sense of contempt for outsiders meddling with his way of life, Doug scoffs at such patronizing, naive, and inept intervention: "Tie up your boats. Simple as that. Stay on land and learn a new trade. Train in Technology. Train in Business Administration. Train in Pet Grooming. He could see himself styling the fur on a poodle. He'd sooner shave it bald and give it a swift boot in the hole" (K. Harvey 2003, 151).

The occupation of Bareneed, furthermore, is marked by an opposition between the forces of rationalist modernity and the quasi-mystical, intuitive insight of traditional outport culture. While the invading authorities struggle to understand and contain the growing confluence of paranormal activity, including evidence of a tsunami building far out at sea, two elderly residents, Eileen Laracy and Tommy Quilty, are able to diagnose the problem and foresee its unfolding in the future of Bareneed. In many magical realist texts, the anachronistic eruption of the past in the present (in the form of revenants, ghosts, the impossibly old, and so on) is often a manifestation of the return of the repressed, the neglected, or the actively concealed past erupting unbidden in transmogrified form. In *The Town That Forgot How to Breathe*, Eileen, who is blessed with second sight, realizes early on that the bodies that have turned up (which are being kept, symbolically, in the community's moribund fish plant) are all related to those who have lost the ability to breathe. When she enters the plant, she sees the "disjointed," ethereal spirits of the dead forlornly hovering over their bodies, "as though barred from entering" (K. Harvey 2003, 327). Eileen recognizes these vexed spirits as a sign of a disruption of historical lineage, an allegorical expression, characteristic of magical realism, of a break in cultural continuity and a loss of traditional belief. The cause of the plague, and ultimately of the tsunami to which the confluence of energy of the alienated spirits leads, is the forgetting of the past. As Eileen reflects early on, the living are "filled with the blaze of their ancestors, lineage that trailed after them like a stream of unbroken dusty amber" (10). With the collapse of the fishery, though, the living have become detached from their predecessors. Eileen sets herself to discovering "what spell needed to be undone to deliver them, set them free to seek out and reenter their living loved ones" (377). Tommy, who was taken by the fairies as a child and returned as a changeling, laments that the community has also been alienated from the traditional oral culture of rural Newfoundland, particularly the belief in spirits. Considered "retarded" by the rest of the community, Tommy has been able to perceive coloured auras around others, although "those who were concerned only with their own gains devoured even their most basic light" (129–30). From the age of eight, though, Tommy has witnessed the disappearance of the fairies and the decline of belief in the community. As Eileen explains, "It be da dyin' belief in da fantastic dat cheats a person o' dere colours" (130). The plague, in other words, is due to the erosion of traditional belief and of communal solidarity and selflessness by materialistic individualism. The remedy is a reconnection to history: Tommy resuscitates the afflicted by telling them stories about their family's past, allowing the troubled spirits to return to their proper "hosts" and revivifying the victims by implicitly restoring their sense of identity.

In *Strange Terrain: The Fairy World in Newfoundland*, Barbara Rieti describes how belief in fairies in the province has "gone from ubiquity to obsolescence in one generation" (1991, 53), part of a broader "decline in oral tradition" (2). Reflecting on the findings of her oral social history, Rieti observes that the disappearance of fairies is the result of cultural and technological change associated with the coming of electricity, television, radio, cars, lights, and noise—fairy lore having much to do with the darkness and quiet of pre-electrical culture, fostering both belief and the social context for the narrative conveyance of those tales (210). This sense that modernity is the culprit in the decline of belief is central to Harvey's novel. The present calamity, Eileen understands, has had repeated precedents, and what shreds the spirits is electricity. She connects the disappearance of the spirits to the appearance of television, implicitly linking the erosion of oral culture to the advent of the technology facilitating the dissemination of mass culture. As she berates a military officer who tries to conscript her help, she is the voice of anti-modernism: "Ye'll kill us all widt yer high-tech gizmos. Nuttin' been da same since da snowmobiles 'n da chainsaws 'n all dat jewellery. Where be

Section 1: I'se the B'y That Leaves the Boats

da horses 'n da dog sleds 'n da healthy men who could clear a forest widt a bucksaw?" (K. Harvey 2003, 297).

Writing of magical realism in the fiction of West Africa, Brenda Cooper observes that "[m]agical realism arises out of particular societies—postcolonial, unevenly developed places where old and new, modern and ancient, the scientific and the magical views of the world co-exist" (1998, 216). In the novels she examines, "Western scientific and technological developments are contested ... and characterized as in cahoots with colonizing advances, which seek to obliterate indigenous ways of seeing, with the blinding light of so-called progress" (1998, 218). In a similar vein, in Harvey's novel the authority of empirical science and rationalist skepticism is repeatedly undercut. Whereas those who have the second sight are unconcerned because they foresee that everything will come out right, others struggle to contain the welter of fantastic phenomena within the realm of science. Despite his own susceptibility to mystical phenomena, the head of the military occupation, Commander French, strives to pass things off as the product of overactive imaginations. "From what I've read, ... these sort of attacks of outrageous fancy happen when a people's identity is threatened. Vast leaps and bounds of imagination and invention take place" (K. Harvey 2003, 358). He also links it to the larger process of the loss of independence: "It's not only about having your lifestyle threatened, it's about losing your place, your sense of self, if you will. A civilization that has been occupied or overthrown by an invading force has seen their storytelling capabilities peak to the point where visions are commonly recorded" (358).

Thus the cataclysm that besets Bareneed is a literalization of the existential and cultural severing of rural Newfoundland from its distinctive heritage and its absorption into an alienating, technological society. This somewhat troubling anti-modernist tone is particularly pronounced in the fabular epilogue to the novel, after the tsunami has washed away the fish plant, knocked out the power in the community, and restored the afflicted to their former selves, "as if the coming water had somehow absolved them of their ills" (K. Harvey 2003, 469). Before electricity is restored, the community is forced to resort to traditional methods of subsistence, leading ultimately to a complete reversion to the community's pre-modern conditions:

> In the days to come, many in Bareneed switched off their lights and reverted to lamplight and wood stove. Stories were told of hardships overcome while children sat around and listened in wide-eyed wonder. The residents of Bareneed returned to the sea as the fish were gradually replenished. In time, every last person reverted to lamplight and

wood stove, and a special sitting of council was convened to order the removal of the new power lines and poles from the community. (470)

It is tempting to dismiss the ending of *The Town That Forgot How to Breathe*—which, like the ending of *Waiting for Time*, opts for a post-apocalyptic vision of renewal and cyclical restoration—as an exercise in sentimental anti-modernism. "Contemporary Newfoundlanders, the novel suggests, are waiting to be saved from the condition of modernity through a reinvestment in romantic myths of inheritance, authenticity, and origin," Sugars persuasively contends. "Ancestral inheritance becomes the missing link that connects a people to an immemorial past located in place and time" (2010, 22). Still, while Harvey's representation of modernity as the source of the community's ills can be seen as romanticizing the pre-modern past, *The Town That Forgot How to Breathe* rightly suggests that modernization, for all its merits, has had some detrimental implications for the traditional oral culture that was an integral part of life in the inshore fishery. Indeed, the utopian thrust of Harvey's ending can be linked to the tendency in magical realist texts to reverse the verdict of colonization. As Jean-Pierre Durix argues, in order "to repossess their alienated reality, magic realistic writers frequently go back to the origins of their cultures; echoing the post-colonial desire to start with a clean slate, they set their novels in communities which are just coming into existence and whose foundation becomes a replaying of genesis" (1998, 121). Harvey's ending, then, can be seen as a drive to get back to the garden, as it were, to return to a Newfoundland before the fall, precipitated by the colonizing forces of modernity and federalist intervention. By giving allegorical substance to the cultural fissure and the loss of identity that the moratorium represents, Harvey suggests that at least some measure of remedy can be found in holding on to that maritime legacy.

THE DIFFERENCES BETWEEN THE MARITIMES AND NEWFOUNDLAND, OF COURSE, are considerable and not to be downplayed, and the focus in this chapter on the crisis in the cod fishery certainly highlights the shortcomings of studying the literature of the two under the unifying rubric "Atlantic Canada." Still, while the moratorium represents a singularly profound historical and cultural threshold for Newfoundland and Labrador, the crisis in the fisheries certainly implicates the region as a whole, if not to the same extent. Moreover, the concerns reflected in these three novels with changes in the conditions of work in the fisheries run through the literature of Atlantic Canada as a whole. One thing that *Sylvanus Now*, *Waiting for Time*, and *The*

Town That Forgot How to Breathe have in common is a preoccupation with a loss of independence—whether of the individual or the entire province. The solitary, undaunted figure of yore has in these books been swamped by the tide of technological progress, corporate concentration, global competition, and political machination, concerns that can be seen, for instance, in Catherine Banks's *Bone Cage* and in the fiction of Alistair MacLeod. Thus while the moratorium represents an unprecedented watershed moment in the region's history, the complex political, economic, and social dynamics that it represents run through depictions of work in other resource sectors as well.

3 |

"Acceptable Levels of Risk": Mining and Offshore Oil

The fishing industry, like the two other staple industries with which the history of Atlantic Canada is associated (farming and lumbering) readily lends itself to the kind of Folk iconography that Ian McKay and James Overton, among others, have highlighted and critiqued, especially because of the capitalist and class relations that such iconography tends to suppress. Another resource industry that has been central to the economic history of the region, however, particularly in Nova Scotia, is less amenable to the idealization of an open-air life on the sea, in the fields, or in the woods. The mining industry was central to the early twentieth-century prosperity of the Maritimes (and to a lesser degree in Newfoundland), but its history of labour turbulence, its much more palpable capitalist relations, and its much more obvious physical rigours present greater obstacles to the celebration of the figure of the independent petty producer of Folk mythology. What the history of mining in the region illustrates—as reflected in the work of early twentieth-century poets like Dawn Fraser and Joe Wallace, and more recently in the fiction of Sheldon Currie—is how the provision of the energy needs of the wider society, and the profit requirements of international capital, rely on the physical, social, and economic sacrifices of labour.

These tensions are in many ways being replicated a century later as the offshore oil and gas industry offers the potential of a similar industrial boom. With coal mining near the end of a long decline, the new frontier of offshore oil and gas has raised optimism about the future economic prospects of the region. For many decades, Maritimers and Newfoundlanders have migrated to the Alberta oil patch, lured by the promise of far higher wages than are attainable at home, a long-standing pattern that has had substantial social and economic implications for Atlantic Canada—not least of which is the consolidation of Atlantic Canada as a pool of reserve labour for other parts of the country.[1] In contrast, the growth of the offshore oil and gas industry on the East Coast not only offers the promise of economic revival for the region but also the prospect of greater economic autonomy and, especially for Newfoundland, the way out of being a have-not province. In the promotion of the prospect of autonomy, however, the impression is often given that offshore oil and gas are a kind of natural "windfall," obscuring not just the cost of exploration and extraction but their dangers as well. As with mining, for those engaged in the extraction of those resources, these dangers are considerable, and a growing number of Atlantic-Canadian writers are drawing attention to those perils and, more importantly, highlighting the larger economic and social circumstances that define such perilous work.

"I wende to be clad in clay": Alistair MacLeod

Without question, the most powerful images of mining in Atlantic-Canadian literature are to be found in the work of Alistair MacLeod. With its consistent focus on Cape Breton, on characters of Highland Scottish descent who live close to the elements, on Gaelic cultural and linguistic heritage, and on a quasi-mystical sense of collective tribal belonging, MacLeod's work certainly has affinities with the kind of elemental, ahistorical essentialism promoted in Folk discourse. But MacLeod in many ways challenges the central underlying assumptions of Folk ideology. Interviewed for the documentary *Reading Alistair MacLeod*, Lisa Moore rightly stresses of MacLeod's work that "he's documenting this very dynamic, dramatic, powerful change.... It's a very contemporary experience. These stories are sort of about globalization." MacLeod's workers, Moore points out, are "creating the capital that the people in New York are trading futures and options on. This is the work that makes that kind of life possible" (MacGillivray 2005). As Moore's comments suggest, far from being insulated from the presence of capitalism and industrialism, the occupational lives of MacLeod's characters are very much marked by time, by history, and by capital. Where the world of the Folk, in other words, is idyllic and halcyon, MacLeod's world is very much a historicized and fallen one.

MacLeod's fiction—the two short story collections *The Lost Salt Gift of Blood* (1976) and *As Birds Bring Forth the Sun* (1986),[2] and his novel *No Great Mischief* (1999)—is pervaded by what I would call a longing for belonging, both territorial and tribal. His characters, practically all of whom can be considered exiles of a sort, routinely pine for ancestral homelands (whether the Scottish Highlands or Cape Breton) and for a decaying or lost ancestral culture. As a consequence, many critics have pointed out, there is a prevailing sense of melancholy, nostalgia, grief, and mourning in MacLeod's writing. At the same time, one of the reasons MacLeod might be seen as promoting a more essentialist sense of culture is that his work is also pervaded by numinous moments of transcendence in which the alienating distances of time and space are eradicated. In *No Great Mischief*, for instance, the narrator's sister Catriona travels to Scotland, where she is recognized as a member of the *clann Chalum Ruaidh* as if her forebears had never left and the intervening centuries had never transpired. Catriona's brothers travel home to Cape Breton from northern Ontario and make a pilgrimage to a freshwater well at the sea's edge, which arguably serves as a symbol of the persistent and sustaining force of Gaelic identity. As these examples indicate, MacLeod's work is imbued with a melancholy longing, reflected in the recurrence of "archetypal motifs, widely available as cultural referents, of the wanderer's or voyager's departure from/return to the primal scene of affective ties" to "an originary community" (Hiscock 2000, 53). As a result, critics have seen in his work a "potentially Romantic nostalgia for a purer, more integrated pattern of existence (here of Old World clan social structures with their bodies of mythic knowledge) in opposition to the fractured identities necessitated by participation in a disorienting urbanized environment" (Hiscock 2000, 53). At the same time, however, there is a recognition in *No Great Mischief* that the well will eventually be permanently contaminated by the sea, and it is this consciousness of decline, I would argue, that is the more pronounced emphasis in MacLeod's work. That fortifying sense of collective heritage and belonging, of clan and regional identity, is both constrained and constraining, marked by a profound and double-edged sense of the dissolution of regional and cultural identity.

As Ian McKay observes, conceptions of the working lives of the Folk tended to efface both the industrial and capitalist contexts of labour in Nova Scotia, instead creating idealized images of independent, pre-modern toil close to the elements. While MacLeod's work has some affinities with such pastoral essentialism, in that some of his characters are farmers and fishers and most display an innate affinity with the natural elements, his work challenges such romanticizing conceptions. For one thing, many of MacLeod's characters are miners—particularly the members of the *clann Chalum Ruaidh* in *No Great Mischief*. For another, many of them are exiles, plying their trade outside of Cape Breton, where the mining industry has been in long-term decline, emphasizing the way in which shifts in the fortunes of resource industries have implications for those whose lives depend upon them. Furthermore, MacLeod underscores rather than obscures the way in which his characters' lives are inscribed by the larger context of consumer capitalism. Rather than depicting his characters as latter-day Highlanders protected

Section 1: I'se the B'y That Leaves the Boats

from the ravages of time, MacLeod's work provides a more nuanced and dialectical picture of the challenges of sustaining cultural identity in a socio-economic order that erodes the kind of collective tribal identity that his characters evince. Although MacLeod's work is pervaded by a sense of nostalgia that makes him vulnerable to charges of romanticizing Highland identity, that sense of loss is situated within a subtle socio-political critique that makes MacLeod's work more mordant, astute, and contemporary than he is usually given credit for.

Although these themes are given sustained treatment in *No Great Mischief*, an important precursor to be considered is the story "The Closing Down of Summer," which contemplates the seasonal rhythms and ambivalent lives of a group of nomadic, specialized miners as they prepare to leave Cape Breton at the end of their summer vacation. Narrated by one of the miners, "The Closing Down of Summer" conveys the collective, iterative, and cyclical nature of the miners' lives, as the narrator's tale modulates between first-person singular and plural and between past, present, and future tenses.[3] While the framework of the narrative is a projection of the miners' predictable movements once the decision is made to depart, the narrator also relates their often brutal past experiences as miners and tries to describe their alienated, ambivalent position as nomadic exiles on the verge of extinction. Like so much of MacLeod's work, "The Closing Down of Summer" oscillates between an archetypal atavism that defies the passage of time and a historicized contemporaneity that registers, however melancholically, time's inevitably corrosive effect.

The archetypal resonances in the story stem from the narrator's cultivation of the image of the miners as modern-day versions of their Highland warrior ancestors. First of all, the miners in their isolation are depicted as the inheritors and repositories of Gaelic culture. In what Ian McKay refers to as Folk Innocence, culture is depicted as both unconscious and immutable, and MacLeod's narrator depicts the miners' collective gravitation to Gaelic culture in similar terms. Oblivious to it while growing up, the narrator taps into a wellspring of Gaelic language and culture that has quietly abided inside him: "It was not until the isolation of the shafts started that it began to bubble up somehow within me" (Alistair MacLeod 2000, 194). In the isolation and collective rhythm of their work, the miners have reverted "to the Gaelic songs because they are so constant and unchanging and speak to us as the privately familiar" (194). This immutable, sustaining resource, furthermore, stands in contrast to the forced and artificial feel of the current renaissance of Gaelic back home in Cape Breton. Invited to sing at Celtic concerts as MacKinnon's Miners' Chorus, the miners appear to the narrator as "parodies of ourselves," and their music, sung to uncomprehending audiences and alienating tape recorders, "was as if it were everything that song should not be, contrived and artificial and non-spontaneous and lacking in communication" (195).

If the miners' shared cultural identity is a seemingly eternal and numinous one, it is also depicted as heroic, the contemporary equivalent to the martial accomplishments of their warrior predecessors: "We are big men engaged in perhaps the most violent of occupations and we have chosen as our adversary walls and faces of massive stone" (201). The parallel to their Highland forebears is made explicit in the narrator's description of how, after the miners leave Cape Breton, they will find small sprigs of spruce "wedged within the grillework of our cars or stuck beneath the headlight bulbs." They will carry these with them "to Africa as momentos or talismans or symbols of identity. Much as our Highland ancestors, for centuries, fashioned crude badges of heather or of whortleberries to accompany them on the battlefields of the world" (185). Finally, this connection is consolidated at the end of the story, as the narrator remembers an "anonymous lyric from the fifteenth century" (208) that he studied during his year at university, the speaker of which is a heralded knight: *Through fight in field I won the flower* (Alistair MacLeod 2000, 208).

At the same time as it cultivates this archetypal resonance, however, "The Closing Down of Summer," rather than effacing specific markers of time and place in order to fortify that resonance, instead is conspicuously historicized and contemporary. The story clearly situates the work of the miners in a globalized, capitalist economic context. Employees of a large corporation with a global reach, the miners are cosmopolitan nomads, witnessing the vicissitudes of different political climates from one continent to the next: "We have moved about the world, liberating resources, largely untouched by political uncertainties and upheavals, seldom harmed by the midnight plots, the surprising coups and the fast assassinations. We were in Haiti with Duvalier in 1960 and in Chile before Allende and in the Congo before it became associated with Zaire" (202). Uncharacteristic of the economy of the stable, waged work week—the so-called Fordist model which prevailed for the three decades after the Second World War—McKinnon's Miners are forerunners of the specialized contract workers of the post-Fordist global economy, prized for their sensory expertise: "what we know through eye and ear and touch is of a finer quality than any information garnered by the most sophisticated of mining engineers with all their elaborate equipment" (199). Because these abilities will translate into profit, the miners are granted a greater deal of latitude and flexibility than their less-specialized Fordist counterparts. Their Bay Street employer "will endure our summer on the beach and our lack of response to their seemingly urgent messages....

Section 1: I'se the B'y That Leaves the Boats

And when we go they will pay us thousands of dollars for our work, optimistically hoping that they may make millions in their turn" (202).

The miners, moreover, are not only within time (that is, the historical era of competitive, global capitalism) but are also subject to its ravages. Although "[t]he miners' working life seems to unroll in archaic time, free from the bonds of change or progress, or from the tyranny of the fleeting moment," Laurent Lepaludier observes, the story "conveys the sense of a coming end" (2002, 50). However heroic and prized their accomplishments, the miners are depicted as being in the twilight of their existence. The portrait of their lives is pervaded by a sense of their obsolescence and eclipse. As they leave Cape Breton, they pass "by the scarred and abandoned coal workings of [their] previous generations and drive swiftly westward into the declining day" (Alistair MacLeod 2000, 207), a harbinger of their own fate. They are like "Greek actors or mastodons of an earlier time. Soon to be replaced or else perhaps to be extinct" (206). This extinction is linked to the waning of the culture that sustains them: "For all of us know we will not last much longer and that it is unlikely we will be replaced in the shaft's bottom by members of our own flesh and bone. For such replacement, like our Gaelic, seems to be of the past and now largely over" (198).

The narrator's attitude toward this eclipse, though, is a complex one, and further reinforces the importance of historical progression in the story. On the one hand, the narrator laments that the miners' sons will not follow in their footsteps but instead "will go to the universities to study dentistry or law and to become fatly affluent before they are thirty" (198). The narrator seems to express the miners' collective disappointment that their heirs "will be far removed from the physical life and will seek it out only through jogging or golf or games of handball with friendly colleagues" (198). However, in pursuing such a course, "they will not die in falling stone or chilling water or thousands of miles from those they love" (198) precisely because "we have told them not to and have encouraged them to seek out other ways of life which lead, we hope, to gentler deaths" (198–99). The result is a profound sense of ambivalence: "because it seems they will follow our advice instead of our lives, we will experience, in any future that is ours, only an increased sense of anguished isolation and an ironic feeling of confused bereavement" (199).

Rather than evoking a particular iteration of a timeless archetype, then, "The Closing Down of Summer" is marked by a pronounced, if divided, sense of finality, the "closing down" of a whole way of life. This sense of finality, indeed, is consolidated by the narrator's evocation of the miners' medieval predecessors. As the miners prepare to leave, the narrator sees himself as "a figure in some mediaeval ballad who has completed his formal farewells and goes now to meet his fatalistic future" (207). Furthermore, the knight in the medieval lyric that he recalls at the end of the story is making his way toward death: "*Death is to man the final way— / I wende to be clad in clay*" (208). But if there is regret that their time-honoured example of physical strife against a formidable adversary is not to be emulated, there is also a sense in which this is (no irony intended) progress.

Although the main action of No Great Mischief takes place against the turbulent backdrop of the 1960s, the novel resonates with the same preoccupation with the global dynamics of contemporary consumer capitalism. It chronicles the rivalry between members of the *clann Chalum Ruaidh* and Fern Picard's Québécois miners, the suspicious death of Alexander MacDonald in a mineshaft accident, and the subsequent brawl in which Calum MacDonald kills his rival Picard and is sentenced to life in prison. These events are presented, though, within the contemporary frame of the narrative of Calum's younger brother Alexander, who travels through southern Ontario to visit Calum, living a life of alcoholic penury in Toronto after his release from Kingston Penitentiary. Alexander's narrative imparts to the novel a sophisticated, though divided, consciousness about the place of physical labour and cultural identity in the contemporary economic order.

Perhaps even more than McKinnon's Miners in "The Closing Down of Summer," the miners of the *clann Chalum Ruaidh* lead lives of ambivalent mobility. They are, first of all, economic exiles, forced by circumstance to work outside of the region they long for, Cape Breton. Furthermore, their movements as well as their labour are regulated and policed by capital. The uranium mine where they work in northern Ontario is gated and guarded. That their stay in the camp is akin to doing time in prison is reflected in the way the miners mark time on their calendars until the end of their stints, and also in the degree of animosity expressed toward their overseers. At the same time, however, as "specialized drift and development miners" (Alistair MacLeod 1999, 145), the MacDonalds are highly valuable workers and enjoy a greater degree of leeway and leverage with the company. When they leave en masse to attend the funeral of Alexander MacDonald, for instance, their boss calls Cape Breton to entreat them to come back, offering bonuses and apologizing for the behaviour of the shift supervisor who has alienated them.

Indeed, MacLeod's miners, working in the 1960s, anticipate the dynamics of a more global, post-Fordist regime. They work for a transnational corporation as part of an international workforce (including Irishmen and Portuguese as well as Québécois and Newfoundlanders) and they travel all over the world, the company easing their passage across political and monetary boundaries. Rather than the fixed-wage labourers of the Fordist era, they are more akin to the mobile, independent contractors of our current neo-liberal regime:

> Although we were paid a fixed hourly wage, the various bonus clauses were what really interested us financially. We were paid by our footage and by how rapidly we progressed to the black uranium ore which waited for Renco Development and for us behind and beyond the walls of stone. In some ways we were like sports teams buoyed forward and upward by private agreements and bonuses based upon our own production. (145–46)

Indeed, Alexander notes that the company flew Calum to British Columbia and "paid him upward of fifteen hundred dollars to set up a blast that lasted only seconds, but which was so fine and delicately expensive that it was felt that only he could engineer it" (146).

Such treatment, of course, is a reflection of the degree to which the miners' specialized abilities are profitable for the company. Indeed, that such mobility is highly asymmetrical and shaped by the dictates of capital in an increasingly global economic regime is highlighted in the frame story of *No Great Mischief*. While Alexander travels to Toronto, his reflections on the landscape around him reveal a melancholy skepticism about consumer capitalism that at first glance exudes a romantic anti-modernism. He takes "the longer but more scenic routes" (2) instead of the 401, "a highway built for the maximum movement of people and goods and ... flat and boring and as efficient as can be" (3). As he looks at the seasonal harvesters at work in the fields, he thinks of the distraught reaction that his grandmother had once "at the sight of the rejected and overripe tomatoes which were being ploughed under" (2) outside of Leamington. These insights suggest a consciousness of the shortcomings of a culture of efficiency and commodification, one that is particularly evident in Alexander's meditations on the migrant workers toiling in the fields. "Instead of a free labour market," Susan Braedley and Meg Luxton argue, "neoliberal policies exclude workers from many countries, while at the same time ensuring that labour market needs are met with the lowest waged workers possible"; they point to how "temporary migration programs bring foreign workers to countries with particular labour needs without offering them the labour protections or benefits accorded to permanent residents" (2010, 17). The Jamaican and Mexican immigrants Alexander sees among the locals and migrants from other parts of Canada are clearly the less fortunate counterparts to Calum's mining crew, their transience underscoring their comparative lack of leverage: "Some are on 'nine-month' contracts allowing them to stay in Canada for a maximum of nine continuous months. If they stay longer they become eligible for Canada's social assistance and health programs. No one wishes them to become eligible for such programs except themselves" (Alistair MacLeod 1999, 169). The message is clear: while their labour is desired, their presence is not. Indeed, some have cycled through so many such contracts in short succession that they find themselves in what amounts to a permanent state of exile, "following this pattern for decades while their children are continents and oceans away" (169).

Moreover, unlike Calum's crew, their movement across borders is not smooth, emphasizing how mobility in a global economy is profoundly hierarchical. The Mexican Mennonites, Alexander reflects, will have to travel back through two borders, vulnerable to the suspicions of the authorities policing, rather than easing, their movements:

> They may be herded into small overcrowded rooms, clutching their vehicle permits, their creased and tattered birth certificates, their yellowed work visas, and their passports containing the uncertain photographs. The children will clasp their parents' browned hands. They will be asked to take a number and later to answer the complicated question of exactly who they are. (197)

The contrast between these immigrants and MacLeod's mobile miners reflects how restrictions on immigration amid all the rhetoric praising mobility seem fundamentally hypocritical and cruel. As Zygmunt Bauman sardonically observes, "to deny the poor and hungry their right to go where food is more plentiful" entails a staggering ideological about-face: "one needs to deny the others the self-same right to freedom of movement which one eulogizes as the topmost achievement of the globalizing world and the warrant of its growing prosperity" (1998, 76). In contrast, Janice Kulyk Keefer astutely asserts, "MacLeod suggests that nations are not defined by arbitrary borders" and "insists upon a transnational and transcultural solidarity among those who perform authentic, necessary and demanding physical labour" (2001, 82).

The "question of exactly who they are," though, is also a complicated one for Alexander and his sister, who are likewise exiles, perhaps doubly so. They have left Cape Breton and also arguably have migrated from their working-class roots, through the mixed fortune of having been brought up by their grandparents after the death of their parents and their brother Colin. Catriona is an actress living in a "modernistic house" (Alistair MacLeod 1999, 93) in Calgary, and Alexander is an orthodontist who looks at his profession with a baleful if muted skepticism. He is "unsure of his role in the family genealogical line" because of his early separation from his brothers (Sugars 2008, 140). In pursuing his profession, Alexander has taken the advice of his mentor to migrate in search of greener pastures: "You are capable of making a lot of money in this field, but you will never do it in the Maritimes. There is not a population here which cares enough about its teeth" (103). "You've got to make teeth *better*," his professor exhorts him, "not just pull the fuckers out" (105; italics in original). Making teeth better, unfortunately, does not seem to have proved a source of fulfillment for Alexander, who, like his sister, comes across as a mournful, alienated exile, "haunted by a past that he never had, a nostalgia for what he has never known" (Sugars 2008, 140). His work is a kind of parodic parallel to the drilling of his miner kin, but his cosmetic surgery practice affiliates it more to his sister's world of role-playing. The one sibling takes on the personalities of others, something her grandparents look upon with perplexity: "Why would you want to spend your life trying to pretend you're somebody else? Wouldn't it be easier just to be yourself?" (Alistair MacLeod 1999, 239). The other helps people to look like somebody other than themselves. The cosmetic part of Alexander's practice effectively amounts to helping people revamp their identities and implicitly shuck off the past. "There are some who would wish to alter their jawlines so that they might look more like current pop stars. Sometimes they bring pictures of what they would hope to be along with them" (82).

Although Alexander's reservations about the "modernistic" world in which he lives at times suggests an anti-modernism leaning toward pastoral romanticism, the more pronounced tone is a concern with the gratuitous commodification and consumption of contemporary capitalism. This note is nicely captured when Alexander makes a trip to the liquor store to buy alcohol for Calum, as MacLeod engages in some quiet but withering satire of the giddy, cynical artifice of capitalism:

> The beer store is fashioned with items of commercial happiness. It seems at first glance like a cheery clothing store for those who are under the age of twenty-five. Brightly coloured shirts and caps and jackets and tank tops proclaim the jolly goodwill of their distant manufacturers. There are coolers and icepacks and thermoses; all of them dedicated to summer fun although it is already September. The companies are reluctant to relinquish the joy of summer... Everything in the beer store exudes happiness and goodwill. It is as if the store is imitating the relentless TV commercials, and obviously both the commercials and the store itself are born of similar agencies. I do not

think the agencies would recruit my blood-stained brother sitting on the edge of his bed in his underwear as an example of one of their happy consumers. (Alistair MacLeod 1999, 183)

Nonetheless, the fact that Alexander in all his middle-class affluence is alienated from his regional roots is suggested at the end of the novel when he visits his elderly grandmother, who is unable to recognize him, describing him as if he were absent and, moreover, in terms that stress the class divide between them, "He is a dentist and is a rich man. He and his wife have a lovely big house. They have a cleaning lady. Think of that! When I visited them I used to want to clean the house before the cleaning lady came" (267). When Alexander tries to convince her that he is the grandson she is describing, the *gille beag ruadh* or "little red-haired boy" (18), her response widens the divide: "The *gille beag ruadh* is thousands of miles from here. Yet I would know him if I met him anywhere in this whole wide world" (272).

Although Alexander's melancholy alienation suggests a longing for a lost sense of collective identity and cultural sustenance, rooted in a shared sense of geography and in collective physical labour, there is much in *No Great Mischief* that complicates such a celebratory interpretation of tribal belonging. While the shared physical work in the mines reinforces a sense of tribal cohesion, for instance, both the work itself and the collective identity it cultivates have their perils. In a double-edged fashion reminiscent of the narrator of "The Closing Down of Summer," Grandpa (his paternal grandfather) congratulates Alexander on his graduation by saying that "'[t]his means you will never have to work again.' What he meant was that I would not spend my life pulling the end of the bucksaw or pushing the boat off the *Calum Ruadh*'s point in freezing water up to my waist" (Alistair MacLeod 1999, 107). It also means that he will not die in a mine accident, as does his cousin and doppelganger, Alexander MacDonald, who is resentful of the opportunity Alexander and Catriona have in living with their grandparents.

The often atavistic celebration of tribal belonging and Highland clan heritage also does not go without challenge. The betrayal of the clan by the Alexander MacDonald from San Francisco (whose theft of the miners' belongings precipitates the fatal brawl) shows the shortcomings of tribal identification, as he effectively ruins Calum's life. More importantly, the resistance of Grandfather (his mother's father) to Grandpa's simplistic glorification of the past of *clann Chalum Ruaidh* shows how such instability has a long history. While Grandpa punctuates Grandfather's heroic account of the return of the MacDonalds from the Battle of Killiecrankie in the midseventeenth century with hyperbolic plaudits—"Loyal as hell" and "Never was a MacDonald afraid" (89)—Grandfather then considers the alternate possibility that their experience was much more divided, more compromised, and less glorious. Instead, he imagines the returning MacDonalds as maimed, destitute, and hesitant about their cause, a version that dampens Grandpa's enthusiasm and hastens his departure. Elsewhere, Grandfather corrects Grandpa's celebratory version of their ancestor's role as part of the vanguard that helped win Canada from the French at the Battle of the Plains of Abraham. Complicating the post-colonial reading of Highland history as a resistance to oppression by the English—evoked by Wolfe's dismissive comment about the Highlanders, "No great mischief if they fall" (109)—Grandfather reminds Grandpa that MacDonald and the Highlanders fought against Wolfe at Culloden and then fought for Wolfe at Quebec years later, after MacDonald was pardoned: "MacDonald died fighting *for* the British Army, not *against* it" (108; italics in original).

Thus Alistair MacLeod's novel becomes less about the atavistic persistence of clan identity across the centuries (a reading much more compatible with the ahistoricism of Folk discourse) than about the way in which cultural identity is impinged upon across the generations by a complex of economic and political forces and decisions. While MacLeod's portrayal of Gaelic culture suggests a belief in, and longing for, a numinous, essential, and transhistorical sense of cultural identity, that impression is mitigated by his acute awareness of the nuances and impact of historical developments. Perhaps the most crucial part of that awareness is MacLeod's sense of the economics and cultural politics of globalization, and its consequences for traditional cultural, occupational, and territorial identities. If, in short, MacLeod seems to be striving for an ahistorical, anti-modernist sense of *location*, what his fiction chronicles is a very historical and contemporary process of *dislocation*.

"Zellers has never blown up": Leo McKay Jr.'s *Twenty-Six*

Whereas in MacLeod's work miners are largely exiles, those who have had to migrate from Cape Breton to seek work elsewhere in the wake of the decline of the coal mining industry, Leo McKay Jr.'s *Twenty-Six* (2003) addresses the implications of trying to resuscitate the moribund industry on the Nova Scotia mainland. A thinly fictionalized portrait of the 1992 Westray disaster, in which twenty-six miners were killed in an explosion at the Westray mine in Plymouth, Pictou County, Nova Scotia, *Twenty-Six* dramatizes the human impact of such a calamity by focusing on the lives of the fictional family of one of the miners.[4] At the same time, the novel reflects Leo McKay's awareness of how the larger socio-economic context of the recession in the 1980s formed the backdrop to a situation in which safety concerns were egregiously eclipsed by political and economic considerations. As Dean Jobb observes in his account of the explosion, "the Westray disaster will stand as an indictment of a style of politics that puts more emphasis on economic development and job creation than the safety of employees" (1994, vii). *Twenty-Six* serves as a similar indictment and as a powerful tribute to those who died at Westray. The novel arguably goes farther, though, by situating the disaster within a larger economic and social restructuring that has had dramatic implications for working people.

As suggested by the title of his account, *Calculated Risk: Greed, Politics, and the Westray Tragedy,* Jobb presents the story of Westray as a foreseeable and thus preventable disaster, a needless and reprehensible loss of life brought about by a combination of political pressure and a rush to generate profits. Jobb describes the complicated manoeuvring on the part of provincial and federal Conservative politicians to provide funding for Westray, as well as the political haggling that led to delays in opening the mine and the decision to take a more dangerous route into the historically volatile Foord coal seam. Although some of the problems in the mine could thus be attributed to the political and economic machinations prior to its opening, "Westray is a stark example" as Chris McCormick puts it, "of an operation where production demands resulted in the violation of the basic and fundamental tenets of safe mining practice" (1999a, 18). The Westray mine was littered with volatile garbage, and unacceptable levels of methane gas and coal dust (a highly explosive combination) were allowed to accumulate in the mine shafts. The use of open combustion engines in such hazardous conditions exponentially increased the risk of explosion. Compounding the risk to the miners, methanometers (devices used to detect the level of methane in the mine and to shut off machinery when the gas reaches explosive levels) were occasionally tampered with in order to allow the machinery to keep running in areas where methane levels were dangerously high. In the words of Westray Inquiry commissioner Justice K. Peter Richard, such "deliberate interference with the methanometers makes it clear that production of coal was to be maintained at all costs, and with blatant disregard for safety" (*Westray Mine Inquiry* 1997, 1:292).

Miners' concerns about these hazardous conditions were routinely and contemptuously dismissed, particularly by the mine's belligerent general manager, Gerald Phillips, notorious for abusive and demeaning tirades against his employees.[5] The result was a censorious atmosphere in which workers had to choose between putting their lives on the line and losing their jobs (Comish 1993, 28). Furthermore, inspectors from the Department of Labour "tolerated hazardous conditions and illegal practices underground, apparently because of [their] unwillingness to confront Westray

Section 1: I'se the B'y That Leaves the Boats

FIGURE 3 The Westray Mine after the explosion. "Damage to portal at No. 1 Main."

management" (*Westray Mine Inquiry* 1997, 2:499). As McCormick succinctly puts it, "Day after day the danger became almost banal, as the workers anticipated they could be killed at any time" (1999a, 28). These conditions led to the predictable result, a massive explosion that took the lives of twenty-six miners, fifteen of whose bodies were never recovered. Thus the Westray disaster, among other things, "certainly is a story about the political economy of death and profit" (30).

Leo McKay's novel closely mirrors this history but locates the explosion four years earlier, in 1988, changing the name of the mine to Eastyard and renaming most of the principal figures involved in the disaster and its aftermath. Most of the power of the novel comes from McKay's ability to humanize the tragedy by setting the explosion within a web of specific relationships to highlight its emotional, psychological, and material impact. The novel also has a wider resonance, though, because of McKay's consciousness of how this particular episode was part of a larger socio-economic shift that had devastating effects on the lives of working people. McKay achieves these dual objectives by focusing on the generational conflict between Ennis Burrows and his two sons, Ziv and Arvel. Starting by introducing the ensemble cast *in medias res* on the eve of the explosion, *Twenty-Six* develops contrapuntally, as McKay switches from the narrative of the explosion and its aftermath to examining his characters' pasts—the complex of allegiances, conflicts, and misunderstandings that is so brutally rent asunder by the explosion, in which Arvel is killed. A storied union organizer with a long career in the nearby car works in Trenton, Ennis is vocal in his contempt for his sons, who are struggling to find work in a time of recession. Although he has completed two years of university, Ziv has a marginal job at Zellers, and Arvel has barely survived by cobbling together piecework, putting a great deal of pressure on his marriage as well as on his relationship with his father. Through the tensions between Ennis and his sons, who internalize their father's contempt, and through explicit recognition of the contrasting socio-economic conditions in which their working lives have unfolded, McKay draws attention to the reverberations in people's lives of the unforgiving recessionary conditions of the 1980s, what it means to scrabble for a decent job in a time and place of high unemployment.[6] What becomes clear is that the explosion is, at least in part, the result of capital's exploitation of the desperation of labour, its ability to maximize profit at the expense of safety because of the leverage provided by the wider recessionary context. In a climate in which "governments favour private economic activity over public enterprise as a means to create the welfare which tends to be maintained to legitimate them," Harry Glasbeek and Eric Tucker argue, "politicians who feel the need to demonstrate to their constituents that they are promoting economic prosperity, are willing, maybe even eager, to enter into cozy deals with private entrepreneurs who promise to create jobs if their conditions are met" (1995, 409).

At the heart of the conflict between Ennis and his sons is his inability to perceive the comparative advantage he has enjoyed coming of age as a worker during a postwar era of relative peace and prosperity, and his willingness, as a consequence, to hold his sons' lack of success against them. Ennis, reflects Arvel, landed his job at the car works after dropping out of junior high and, aside from the occasional temporary layoff, has been there ever since.

> In his father's mind, anyone without a full-time job for longer than a few months was lazy and shiftless, not trying hard enough to find steady work. He would see Arvel at the end of an especially hard day's work, covered in dirt and sawdust, or elbows deep in soot from mucking about in people's chimneys. He'd take a look at him and say, "Don't you have a job yet?" (L. McKay 2003, 244–45)

What Ennis fails to see, Arvel complains to Ziv, is that the difference between them is not one of effort but one of timing. Whereas Ennis "fucked up, dropped out, and the world put a forty-year job right in his lap," Arvel "followed all the steps, but nothing happened" (152).

In a similar manner, Ennis lionizes his efforts as a union organizer at the expense of his sons. He takes rightful pride in the gains brought to his own neighbourhood through his union work: improved wages, better living conditions, and health care for the residents of Red Row, a cluster of company houses built for workers during the heyday of the industry. Although he rightly credits the resolve and determination of the labour movement to wrest concessions from capital, he also suggests that his sons' employment woes are due to a lack of effort, brains, and commitment. "We organized and fought for what we wanted," he mercilessly berates them. "You think the company was tripping over itself to give us a seniority system, a decent wage, holidays? We got that stuff because we were smart enough to demand it. If young people today aren't happy, it's up to them to fix it" (263). Ennis's achievements, Arvel rightly concludes, were only made possible by a vibrant economy, low unemployment, and a more balanced, mutually beneficial relationship between labour and capital. "You can only make demands if you have an employer," Arvel complains. "Who are today's young people going to threaten with a strike? The unemployment office? Their social worker? The parents they're living off?" (264). What Arvel makes clear, in other words, is that Ennis's relative success was made possible by the broader context of economic prosperity and the Fordist trade-off of labour peace for stability of employment. Furthermore, he suggests that Ennis's passionate commitment to the cause of labour has been inversely proportional to his commitment to his family, who have been traumatized by his alcoholic tirades and his undisguised contempt: "You spent your whole life looking after workers' rights. Those people were strangers to you. What about your own sons?" (31).

In contrast, his sons struggle to find employment and dignity in a time of scarcity and economic decline. In Ennis's heyday, before the birth of his sons, "just about every adult male in the area, and many of the children, would have been employed at the pits in some capacity" (L. McKay 2003, 16). However, "by the late sixties and early seventies ... there were only one or two pits still running, and those at a capacity so small as to hardly compare with the glory days" (16–17). The sense of economic decline is not limited to the stagnating mining industry, either. At the mall in New Glasgow where Arvel's wife Jackie works at a high-end clothing store, "the early signs of decline were already setting in" even though the mall has "been open for less than two years.... There were empty shop stalls, their windows papered over with For Lease signs or the Coming Soon signs belonging to the next, lower-end businesses that would set up shop" (116). The "century-plus-old buildings" of "the commercial district of Albion Mines" (70) have largely been deserted by commerce. Amid them, the local Tim Hortons, "[w]ith its plate-glass windows, brick and steel construction, paved parking lot, and iridescent plastic and aluminum sign" is a conspicuous, "alien" presence, "the unmistakable stamp of the present on the main street of Albion Mines" (71).

McKay highlights the psychological and emotional implications of such a decline on the working people of the area. Ziv muses about how, in his father's time, one's identity was defined by where one worked, but in the present, there are an increasing number of people who were beyond unemployed, "because they weren't looking for work. Long past their eligibility for unemployment insurance, many of these people lived on welfare, the generosity of relatives, and whatever odd jobs they could do for the neighbours in exchange for a few dollars" (6). Although Ziv himself is employed at Zellers, the marginality and instability of his status puts him barely above such desperate circumstances. "Zellers classified him as *extra*, a category that all but a handful of the people who worked at the store fit into. He received no benefits, contributed to no pension, had no reliable schedule" (6). Ziv's marginal job reflects how neo-liberalism's "emphasis on labour market 'flexibility' produces a growing workforce of part-time, casual, and contract labour at the bottom of an organization" (Connell 2010, 26). Despite being "certified in electrical construction" (L. McKay 2003, 109) and having "tried everything" (110), Arvel is no better off. With no solid prospects, he is reduced to doing piecework in the woods, small electrical jobs, and servicing oil furnaces. "'Jobbing around' was what people called what he was doing, and although jobbing around kept him busy, and he sometimes earned a half-decent amount of money from it, it was no way to live for the long term" (244). Perhaps more importantly, Arvel recognizes "that the sort of work that had been sustaining him was economic table scraps, and when you are being thrown table scraps, you are no better than a dog whose owner doesn't even care enough to buy it its own food" (244). If Ennis sports an unwarranted high self-regard, Arvel is his inverted image, viewing himself with a contempt that he doesn't deserve, and suffering from a lack of self-esteem that is poisoning his marriage. Arvel's dilemma illustrates how the exhortation of labour to be flexible—one of the clarion calls of neo-liberal ideology—is, as Bauman astutely argues, disingenuously contradictory. It masks how "flexibility" is defined largely by the interests of capital: "to meet the standards of flexibility set for them by those who make and unmake the rules ... the plight of the 'suppliers of labour' must be as rigid and *inflexible* as possible—indeed, the very contrary of 'flexible'; their freedom to choose, to accept or refuse, let alone to impose their own rules on the game, must be cut to the bare bone" (Bauman 1998, 105).

Such exhortations are part of an atmosphere of strategic intolerance that also informs the tensions in McKay's novel. Thom Workman characterizes globalization as "a tooth and nail strategy to depress wages" (2003, 9), and part of that strategy is the orchestration of a climate of instability and desperation. "It is about creating large pools of underemployed people so that wages will remain low. It is about ruthlessly attacking social programs that are seen to prop up minimum wages. It is about callously attacking the poor themselves for fear that they might pass on a rotten job" (9). In *Twenty-Six*, Ziv recounts overhearing two older men complaining that people should have to work for welfare. "'Give them a job cleaning up the streets or the beaches. Just until something better comes along.' I felt like saying, 'This is the eighties, you shitheads, not the forties. Something better is *not* coming along. Something *worse* is coming along'" (L. McKay 2003, 153; italics in original). As Ziv's reaction highlights, the neo-liberal consensus "cultivates a severely judgmental outlook on people struggling with poverty," perversely "intensif[ying] poverty at the same time that it promotes a social outlook that harshly judges the poor" (Workman 2003, 104).

Such dire straits make getting on at Eastyard look like an opportunity and compel Arvel to keep working there in the face of hazardous conditions. When an acquaintance proposes to use his political pull to get the three of them jobs at the mine, Ziv displays little enthusiasm, and when he is teased about his job at Zellers, he retorts that at least "Zellers has never blown up" (L. McKay 2003, 252). He recognizes all too well that in Albion Mines "he had no other option than to choose between a shitty job and a deadly one" (258). Whereas Ziv quits on his first day in the mine, Arvel sticks it out, although it is not long before the utter disregard for safety at Eastyard compels him to question his decision. Reflecting the conditions at Westray prior to the explosion, the mine at Eastyard is littered with volatile trash, hazardous levels of coal dust and methane are allowed to build up inside the mine, and the miners are compelled to keep digging deeper without taking the requisite care to shore up the roof of the mineshaft. These concerns are belligerently dismissed by the mine manager, Fred Brennan, a profane and overbearing ogre clearly modelled on Gerald Phillips. Brennan's contemptuous and menacing managerial style creates a censorious atmosphere in the mine, compelling the men to keep their silence, despite the palpable dangers of their working conditions:

> When a sparking engine or a miner whose methane detectors had been disconnected flared blue momentarily in a pocket of gas, or when several men were trudging through fuel-soaked explosive dust that was halfway up their shins, or when a foreman or manager ordered them to continue using damaged equipment, the men no longer spoke about these things. They clamped their jaws and shook their heads. (81)

Glasbeek and Tucker argue that in such a climate working people "are so dependent for their welfare on private investors that they seem almost oblivious to risk. They are likely to develop rationalizations for their actions, creating a culture which inures them to daily fears" (1995, 427).

However, the men on Arvel's shift are sufficiently unnerved by the powder keg in which they work to arrange a meeting with Gavin Fraser, who had quit after a confrontation with management over conditions in the mine. Reflecting how the tendency to regard unionization warily is intensified within "the neoliberal culture of austerity" (Workman 2003, 47) because of the fear of repercussions, Arvel's colleagues, most of whom failed to support the union drive he spearheaded, are too divided and disorganized to respond coherently to Gavin's ultimatum—"You either do what I did and get out, or you wait to die" (L. McKay 2003, 77)—and his suggestion that they "all quit together, in which case management has to act" (78). Recognizing that "every day we don't make that choice is a day closer to the other option" (80), Arvel implores Gavin that when something happens to them, "Just tell people.... Just tell them what it was like. Just tell them what happened" (80).

In a replay of events at Westray, just before the explosion, the men are forced to use a miner (a piece of heavy equipment) with a disconnected methanometer even though the "methane levels are so high, the fucking thing keeps gassing out" (85), and Arvel is compelled to confront Brennan over such a homicidal disregard for safety. Apoplectically dismissing the miners' concerns about the methanometer, Brennan uses the threat of unemployment to berate them into getting back to work: "why don't you just sign on for pogey, like you've done all your worthless lives, and sit in your fucking living rooms doing nothing" (89). Arvel's half-compliant, half-defiant rejoinder proves all too prophetic, "If we get killed down here ... [d]on't expect me back next shift" (90).[7]

If the scenes leading up to the explosion provide a detailed sense of the context in which Arvel and the other miners have come to put their lives on the line, the sections of the novel set after the explosion are a study in lives interrupted, as the explosion and the deaths of twenty-six miners, including Arvel, reverberate throughout the community. McKay focuses particularly on Ennis, who goes on a drunken rampage, trashes the family home, and is put in hospital by his infuriated wife, Dunya. Holding Ennis accountable for encouraging their sons to go into the mine, she batters his skull with a cast-iron kettle before retreating into a stoic, mournful silence. The loss of Arvel and Dunya's violent outburst prompt in Ennis a complete reversal of his priorities. Although secretly proud of Arvel's involvement in the unionizing drive at the mine, he had driven his son away. Indeed, in Ennis's last exchange with Arvel, he threatened to run him out of the house with his .30-30, to which Arvel had defiantly responded, "You ever point a gun at me, old man, it better be loaded and you'd better pull the trigger" (L. McKay 2003, 32). In the wake of the explosion, that is exactly what Ennis feels he has done: "He had told his son he was happy to see him go into the pit. And his son had died there" (339). Ennis tries to convince himself that "he would have apologized when Arvel had gotten home that morning" but realizes that "[h]e'd never apologized to anyone in his life" (201).

Wrapped up in his self-recrimination and mourning for his son, Ennis at first neglects that Arvel's death is part of a larger cause, one currently taking shape in response to the judicial inquiry being held to examine the disaster. He finds himself unable to attend the inquiry and to contribute his wealth of experience to the families' group organizing a response to the disaster, because Arvel "is dead. Nothing is going to make his death right. Nothing can justify it, nothing can explain it, nothing can make it hurt less" (342). That such a staunch advocate of workers' rights is reduced to fatalistic passivity in the face of such a preventable calamity is, of course, an implicit victory for capital. However, partly through his relationship with his surviving son, from whom he has been no less estranged, Ennis moves toward a healthier balance between the personal and the political, giving the ending of the novel a muted sense of reconciliation and renewal.

This reconciliation unfolds against the backdrop of debate over how best to respond to the deaths of the miners. In the case of Westray, as Susan Dodd has argued, this involved resistance to corporate and government attempts to dictate how the miners' deaths were to be framed and memorialized, much as they dictated the terms of their working lives (1995, 226), a dynamic which is reflected in *Twenty-Six*. Both Ennis and Ziv are initially ambivalent about being involved, reflecting that nothing can undo the implacable fact of Arvel's death. As they become more absorbed by the inquiry, however, they chastise each other for being apathetic, and their frank exchanges ultimately lead to reconciliation. Ennis's rejoinder to Ziv, "[m]aybe I've made mistakes with my life and maybe I've got regrets, but you have to do something before you can make a mistake" (L. McKay 2003, 379), gives Ziv pause for thought. He "wonders if it has taken Arvel's dying for him to see that maybe his father is right" (380) and subsequently he commits himself to the cause of transforming Eastyard into a memorial for the miners. This suggests implicitly that Ennis has passed on, however uneasily, the legacy of his advocacy for workers' rights to his son. This sense of healing is consolidated by the final scene in the novel, in which Ennis takes Ziv out cross-country skiing in a scene redolent with symbolism of reconciliation and renewal: "Two white spruces, squared off on opposite sides of the trail, appear to be bowing to each other. The tips of their branches reach out across a lifetime's distance toward the other, ready to shake hands or embrace" (385).

As Workman points out, one of the more insidious accomplishments of neo-liberal ideology over the last few decades has been a reprogramming of attitudes toward the inequitable distribution of wealth and opportunity.

What has been cultivated is an implicit consensus that the underemployed, the unemployed, and the poor are effectively responsible for their own plight. The proliferation of such an attitude, of course, furthers the ends of capital, because it serves to discipline labour, keeping its ranks pliable and acquiescent to low wages, poor working conditions, and marginal unemployment. As a fictional rendering of the Westray disaster, *Twenty-Six* dramatizes the logical terminus of such a trade-off—that endangering the lives of workers is an acceptable risk in the pursuit of necessary profits—and presents a powerful rejoinder to such self-serving, ideological brow-beating. As a textual testament to the fallen miners, furthermore, *Twenty-Six* cautions against lapsing into a passive silence, which would effectively exonerate capital for its deadly pursuit of profit at the expense of the safety of labour.

"Consider the overall public good": Lisa Moore's *February*

For all its allure, the offshore oil and gas industry has exhibited a similarly troubling trade-off. In the blush of offshore exploration in the early 1980s in Newfoundland, Sean T. Cadigan notes, the provincial government "focused almost entirely on which jurisdiction would control the benefits of development, and, like the federal government, it paid little attention to the regulation of offshore workers' safety" (2009, 269). The importance of regulation, though, has been highlighted by significant disasters, including the March 2009 crash of a Sikorsky S-92 helicopter ferrying workers to oil rigs off the coast of Newfoundland, killing fifteen (with only one survivor), and, more dramatically, by the capsizing and sinking of the semi-submersible offshore oil rig *Ocean Ranger* in the Hibernia oil field in 1982, killing all eighty-four men on the rig, including fifty-three Newfoundlanders. In his epilogue to *Rig: An Oral History of the Ocean Ranger Disaster*, Mike Heffernan describes how he was prompted to pursue his project because of the repetition, decades after the disaster, of a familiar atmosphere of hubris, with Newfoundlanders "still leaving in droves to head out West to the Promised Land, to Alberta, in the hopes of making a life for themselves, while the government puffed its proverbial chest about how oil, about how Hibernia, Hebron and White Rose, was our economic salvation. The old political rhetoric of 'have not will be no more' was chic yet again" (2009, 199).

This hubris is put into stark perspective in Lisa Moore's novel *February* (2009), a moving account of a woman who loses her husband in the *Ocean Ranger* disaster. In *February*, Moore develops a portrait of what Sigmund Freud describes as "the work of mourning" in the wake of the disaster within a larger political economy that distinctly shapes the "economics" of loss. Moving back and forth in time, extending from the couple's courtship and

Section 1: I'se the B'y That Leaves the Boats

FIGURE 4 Drill platform of *Ocean Ranger*, lost 15 February 1982.

marriage a decade before the disaster to the immediate present, *February* charts the reverberations caused by the loss of Cal O'Mara in the life of his wife Helen, from her struggles to raise four children to her remarriage as a middle-aged woman, as well as the impact his death had on their son John. The novel is framed by turning points in the lives of Helen and John in late 2008, and from there Moore ranges back into the past, to their lives before, during, and in the wake of the *Ocean Ranger* disaster. In the 2008 frame narrative, Helen is on the cusp of a new relationship with the man who has been renovating her house, while John has been apprised, by cell phone, that a week-long fling in Iceland half a year earlier has resulted in a pregnancy. These moments are the culmination of a decades-long process of trauma, mourning, and recovery that Moore explores over the course of *February*.

In his influential essay "Mourning and Melancholia," Freud outlines the similar symptoms of mourning and melancholia, characterizing mourning as a destabilizing and alienating fixation on the lost one (1957, 244). *February* pulsates with this psychic anomie, with Moore depicting Helen as a beleaguered but stoic amputee, preoccupied for two and a half decades with processing the sensations emanating from her phantom limb. When Cal is lost in the sinking of *Ocean Ranger*, Helen feels not just robbed but banished, living her life in a state of suspended animation. She is exiled to the outside while pretending, for the sake of stability and appearances, to be on the inside, and Moore's chronicling of her life is a study in this psychic duality.

On the one hand, she is distracted and consumed by an obsessive longing for her lost one; much of the narrative is taken up with Helen's retrospective reveries about the past, her melancholy inventorying of her life with Cal, over which hovers, implacably, the spectre of his death. On the other hand, Helen displays a fierce determination to sustain a facade of normality and order for her family.

Perhaps her greatest challenge in pretending to "be inside" is coping with her son, who is also displaying unmistakable signs of the trauma of loss and grief. While John dutifully takes on a paper route to contribute to the family income and accompanies Helen to the hospital when she goes into labour, his trauma manifests itself in visibly eccentric symptoms such as chewing pencils and eating with his mouth open. But it also conspicuously takes the form of a fear of water and dreams about the hag, a nightmarish staple of traditional outport culture. John manages to overcome these early symptoms to succeed in school and go on to a successful career in the oil patch. However, the trauma of the loss of his father continues to manifest itself in John's uncharitable, eccentric perspective on his parents' marriage, a reaction to loss that has substantial implications for his own relationships with women. Tracy Whalen argues that "love—especially hard, dangerous love—constitutes the ethical centre of Lisa Moore's fiction" (2008, 5), and *February* offers an interesting variation on that preoccupation. Here Moore intertwines the concepts of risk as a central factor in a major marine disaster and risk as a central factor in romantic and emotional relationships. Through both John and Helen's perspectives, she portrays Helen and Cal's marriage as an embrace of risk, not just the calculated risk of Cal's taking a job on *Ocean Ranger* but also the emotional risk of unequivocal, mutual commitment. For John in retrospect, his parents' intense attachment seems reckless and irrational— "Why did you love each other so very much? It destroyed you" (Moore 2009, 107)—and he frames their commitment to each other in the then-emerging discourse of risk assessment: "They had believed that there was a new science devoted to the assessment of it. Risk could be calculated and quantified. The risk, they had believed, was worth it" (108). In turn, the trauma of the outcome of his parents' marriage fuels his own resistance to emotional commitment and the prospect of fatherhood.

When he receives Jane Downey's call out of the blue while vacationing in Tasmania, John responds to the news of her pregnancy by impulsively and callously asking if she has considered an abortion, prompting her to hang up. He assesses the situation in the language of neo-liberal economic globalization—ease of movement, minimizing of complications, contractual over moral obligations: "There'd been a tacit understanding ... that nobody would come out of a seriously fun and even deeply affecting week of fucking and eating and drinking fabulous wine and bombing around glaciers on Ski-Doos ... with anything but fond memories" (33). He realizes, however, that Helen is "going to make him take responsibility" (41) and—with various echoes of her own history, such as being left pregnant at the time of Cal's death—she convinces him to take an interest in the baby. Thus when Jane comes to the realization that she does not want to bring the baby up without a father and eventually calls John back, he is both alarmed and relieved. By the end of the novel they are effectively living together in St. John's after Jane has had the baby, and John's clear commitment suggests that he has finally worked through his trauma.

For Helen, such a recovery entails a more troubling process of replacement. A central contention of "Mourning and Melancholia" is that "mourning impels the ego to give up the object by declaring the object to be dead and offering the ego the inducement of continuing to live" (1957, 257). As is the case with John, Helen's regeneration requires a reconfiguration of her attachment to Cal, a process that is both turbulent and protracted. "For a long time nobody dared" (Moore 2009, 22) to suggest the possibility of Helen seeing someone else. When her sister's daughter-in-law recommends Barry as a carpenter, Helen defensively intuits her ulterior motive: "Sherry had imagined her to be lonely. Helen was flooded with shame.... She would not be pitied" (59). As Tammy Clewell emphasizes, Freud's model gives the process of mourning a disturbing finality (2004, 44); in this light, Helen's reluctance can be attributed to her anxiety that, as Freud's model suggests, "we must sever one attachment to make another possible" (Clewell 2004, 47). With Barry's protracted presence while renovating her house, however, Helen rediscovers her dormant desire for physical intimacy and finds the courage to risk offering herself to somebody else, which involves a readjustment of the place of Cal in her life. As Clewell stresses, Freud revisited his earlier model of mourning and melancholia later on in *The Ego and the Id* (1917), depicting the substitution of the lost object as less final and complete. In this revised view of mourning, "working through depends on taking the lost other into the structure of one's own identity, a form of preserving the lost object in and as the self" (2004, 61). This distinction can be seen in Helen's accommodation to the loss of Cal. She is finally able to set aside her obsession with the sinking of *Ocean Ranger* at the same time as she comes to understand an implicit part of the pact she made with Cal: "If Cal died out there on the rig, Helen would never forget him. That was the promise" (Moore 2009, 302). For Clewell, Freud's revision of his model of mourning "raises the possibility for thinking about mourning as an affirmative and loving internalization of the lost other" (2004, 64), a conclusion that *February* very much seems to echo.

If this trajectory of mourning and regeneration still seems to emphasize the importance of moving on after a loss, Moore's presentation of the disaster itself and her portrait of what can be characterized as a broader neo-liberal sensibility suggest a much more complicated politics in the novel. Moore locates the "economics" of mourning within the larger political economy shaping both the response to loss and the loss itself. While Moore's strategy of chronicling the experience of a woman widowed by the disaster puts the calamity at a distance, at the same time she resists effacing the economic and occupational circumstances of the disaster and, indeed, engages with the wider economic and political climate that has prevailed since it occurred.

Moore's eschewing of a more direct and mimetic representation of the disaster seems appropriate in light of the uncertainty surrounding the capsizing of the rig. Her presentation of the disaster reflects the findings of the joint federal-provincial royal commission into the disaster, which concluded, as Cadigan summarizes, that

> a critical ballast control room had been located too close to the water in a support column, including a porthole with glass insufficiently thick to withstand severe pounding; the rig also had a ballast control system that was difficult to use in emergency conditions. Worst of all, the workers who operated the Ocean Ranger did not fully understand how to operate the ballast controls during an emergency such as the storm that developed that February night. Having to abandon the rig, workers were without survival suits and found its lifeboats almost impossible to launch in the prevailing sea conditions. (2009, 269)

The commission findings point to a regime of lax regulatory oversight and inadequate safety provisions (a combination that arguably has been encouraged by proponents of the idea that industry self-regulation is much more efficient and cost-effective than government oversight). As the commission highlighted, though, communications from the rig on the night of the disaster conveyed little sense of urgency almost up until the moment of evacuation (Royal Commission 1984, 89–90, 105), and thus what happened during the evacuation is largely a matter of speculation. "How the crew left the rig is not known" (1984, 122), the report concluded, but "[w]hatever the means of evacuation adopted, it is evident that none was practicable or safe under the prevailing wind and sea conditions" (123).

The focus on Helen's experience arguably conveys, in part, Moore's recognition of the paradox of comprehending the disaster—the excruciating desire to know, and the impossibility of knowing what it must have been like for the men—and her keeping the disaster itself at a speculative distance. While Helen knows the rough chain of events and "lives through the disaster every night of her life," what she wants is "to be in Cal's skin when the rig is sinking. She wants to be there with him" (Moore 2009, 70). Helen, who has followed the proceedings of the commission, recites the chain of misfortunes that led to the sinking of the rig, "has memorized the ifs and she can rhyme them off like the rosary. If the men had the information they needed, if they lowered the deadlight, if the water hadn't short-circuited the control panel, if Cal had had another shift, if Cal had never gotten the job in the first place, if they hadn't fallen in love. If she hadn't had the children. If" (293–94). However, while "Helen wants to know exactly what happened because she can't stand the idea of not knowing" (294), ultimately she confronts the brute fact of its impossibility and accepts that Cal is gone and, furthermore, that they had agreed upon that possibility, sharing his "panic of facing death" (301).

The distance at which the event is held in *February* thus can be seen as a sign of Moore's reluctance to impose a spurious certainty on what remains in many ways a substantially enigmatic event. By exploring the disaster as it registers on the lives of the family of one of the men, Moore is able to preserve a sense of distance necessitated by the relatively enigmatic circumstances of the disaster itself, particularly the evacuation, given that there were no survivors to describe what happened. At the same time, Helen's obsession with the fate of her husband offers the opportunity to meditate on, rather than erase, the experience of the men. For instance, even though Helen subsequently questions its veracity, her imagining of the aborted rescue attempt, in which the men on board the supply ship *Seaforth Highlander* risked their lives under appalling conditions to try to reach survivors in a lifeboat, is particularly poignant. It evokes the drama, the courage, the compassion, and the peril of the moment: "These men were in the water and the men on the *Seaforth Highlander* had to untie themselves so they could reach farther, and they were in danger of going in themselves, and they threw the ropes, but the men from the lifeboat could not raise their arms. Life preservers floated within reach, but those men could not reach" (297).

Moore also underscores the role of the companies in the sinking of the rig (the company operating the rig, ODECO Canada, was working under contract for Mobil Oil Canada). Through Helen she highlights the companies' culpability not only for the disaster but also for their handling of it after the fact. Summarizing oral testimony about conditions on the rig, Douglas House describes "a picture of offshore working conditions in which productivity was always given priority over safety: accidents were frequent, safety concerns ... were given low priority, men suffering from minor injuries were expected to carry on working, and those that complained were severely dealt with by senior rig personnel" (1987, 49).[8] Moore's novel, in its preoccupation with the emotional reverberations of loss, does not neglect this crucial element of the political economy of the disaster. Instead, the corporate hubris and failure of safety regulations that contributed to the disaster, as well as the imagined distress of the men tossed into the frigid ocean, is woven into the narrative along with Helen's agonizing over her ability to raise a family single-handed and her memories of life with Cal before the disaster.

An important part of the disaster, for instance, is that there had been a recent precedent, prompting concern about the safety of the rig. A week beforehand the rig had developed a list, a perceptible tilt (Royal Commission 1984, 50), and at least some witnesses reported a disorganized attempt to muster the lifeboats (see Heffernan 2009, 17, 19–20). In *February*, Helen reflects that "[t]hey all knew they weren't safe. Those men knew. And they had decided not to tell anyone" (Moore 2009, 97). Moore's portrait of this precedent underscores the disciplinary effect of an atmosphere of economic austerity on the mindset of the crew of the rig, "There are men who would kill to have this job: that was the wisdom they worked under. And: the helicopter was a terror. But it was impossible to imagine the whole rig capsizing" (97). Their response reflects not so much a lack of courage and resolve but what Workman describes as the internalization of neo-liberal ideology, which cultivates an ambivalence in workers, who "feel frustrated and bitterly disappointed with their jobs on one hand, yet relieved that they even have a job on the other" (2003, 50). Indeed, even though Helen and Cal had formulated plans to buy a store with gas pumps, "they didn't speak of those plans. Because if they talked about Cal giving up the rig, they were admitting the risk. And it was something they had agreed never to admit" (Moore 2009, 98–99). At the end of the novel, Moore offers through Helen a clear indictment of the company: "The Royal Commission said there was a fatal chain of events that could have been avoided but for the inadequate training of personnel, lack of manuals and technical information. And that is the true story. It is the company's fault" (301). Struggling to digest the horror of the fate of the men, Helen underlines the hubris of the company that exposed them to such a fate: "The idea of men drowning in that cold darkness was staggering and nightmarish, and the company had said the bloody thing would never sink no matter what" (271).

The company's reaction to the disaster comes under even more scathing scrutiny, reflecting how, as House argues, "the aftermath of the tragedy [was] co-opted by the official class" (1985, 273). ODECO, observes House, "maintained a stony and unsympathetic silence. Mobil, which could hardly avoid the public eye, recovered from its initial shock to take on the guise of the concerned, sympathetic corporate citizen," while "industry and government officials were scrambling to avoid any appearance of having been culpable for the disaster" (1985, 275). In *February*, Helen's musings on the company's immediate response to the disaster highlight the corporate calculation involved—"the families heard on the radio that their loved ones were dead. And they didn't believe it because surely the company would have called" (Moore 2009, 270). Incredulous that the company failed to do so, Helen is inclined to believe that "they all wanted to *manage the situation*" (268; italics in original). Evoking the emergence of a corporate culture of professionalized public relations and damage control, Helen speculates, "They may not have known about spin back then ... but they were thinking spin" (269). "On her better days" (269–70), though, Helen does consider the possibility that those who worked for the company were simply overcome themselves.

In *A Brief History of Neoliberalism*, David Harvey points to neo-liberals' use of euphemistic, "wonderful-sounding words like freedom, liberty, choice, and rights, to hide the grim realities of the restoration or reconstitution of naked class power, locally as well as transnationally" (2005, 119). This linguistic dimension of neo-liberalism can be seen in a key passage in *February* as Helen meditates on a symposium held by the oil companies on risk assessment after the disaster, highlighting the companies' coercive definition of risk:

> The oil companies were all about acceptable levels of risk and they always had been. They spoke of possible faults in the system and how to avoid them. Here, here. They advised strongly against intuition when assessing risk. If you were scared shitless, they said, that was only intuition, and you should ignore it. They asked the public to consider the overall good to be achieved when we do take risks. They spoke in that back-assed way and what they meant was: If you don't do the job, we'll give it to someone who will.
> They meant: There's money to be made.
> They meant: We will develop the economy.
> They meant there isn't any risk, so shut the fuck up about it. Except they didn't say *fuck*, they said: Consider the overall public good.
> (Moore 2009, 118; italics in original)

What Moore effectively highlights here is a crucial aspect of neo-liberalism: its strategic concealment of the redistribution of risk. At the same time, even as Moore explores the culpability of the companies both before and after the disaster, ultimately Helen concedes the importance of the unprecedented and unpredictable role of the natural elements: "there is also the obdurate wall of water, and because of it Helen will finally give up her careful recital of the fatal chain of events" (301).

Moore's concentration on Helen's experience of the disaster and its aftermath, then, amounts to more than resisting a dubiously omniscient depiction of an event about which not much is known. While she distances the disaster by representing instead Helen's struggle to imagine and cope with it, she also arguably brings it closer by situating it within a web of social, economic, and emotional relationships, thus preventing its isolation as an anomalous calamity. In his introduction to *Response to Death: The Literary Work of Mourning*, Christian Riegel observes that the "psychic nature of mourning is complemented by its socio-historical context, for grief is framed, ordered, and filtered by the historical, social and cultural setting of the mourning subject" (2005, xx). This sense of context is crucial to *February*, as Moore examines how Helen's immediate sense of personal, romantic, and familial loss is complicated by the social, political, and economic context in which it occurs. The "work of mourning" is compounded not only by uncertainty about the circumstances of that loss but also by the agonizing question of culpability and by the companies' expedient, calculated approach to the disaster after the fact.

The companies' dodgy, self-serving presence in the process of mourning, though, is part of a conspicuously cosmopolitan and globalized zeitgeist that Moore sets out to diagnose in *February*. What sticks out from this cosmopolitan fabric—particularly through the movements of John, a globe-trotting oil patch consultant and engineer—is the prevalence of a characteristically neo-liberal, individualist mentality and a corporate management style stressing efficiency, austerity, and profitability. John, for instance, is interviewed for a position with Shoreline Group, a company that "worked to eliminate redundant safety procedures" (Moore 2009, 139). Describing the company, Moore foregrounds the euphemistic damage control that neo-liberal restructuring and austerity has necessitated: "They specialized in all the touchy-feely stuff from the 1980s: lateral thinking, creativity in the work-place, psychological support during downsizing or natural disaster, pink slips, sweater-vests and distressed denim, a bold new self-generating speak that boiled over and reduced to a single, perfect word: *efficiency*" (130). John clearly internalizes this ideology, as he later tactlessly opines at a family gathering that "[i]t's not good for the industry, the culture that has developed around safety. They're like a crowd of old women," only to be pointedly reprimanded by Helen, "Safety is a good thing" (178). Later, Moore parodies the seductive and manipulative emptiness of corporate marketing, as John listens to a woman at a business lunch in New York "presenting an advertising campaign to promote offshore drilling development on a global scale" (222–23):

Section 1: I'se the B'y That Leaves the Boats

> We're planning a series of ads from all over the world, specifically indigenous, acutely indigenous, showing high-powered cocktail parties on rooftops, beach parties. We're looking at Bondi Beach, and subtitles, just very, very international, speaking to that thing, that ethnic thing, that thing, connectedness.... The thingies, the derricks or whatever, the rigs on the ocean fade to silhouette, music of course. Something Wagnerian. (224)

The austerity, exploitation, and profit-consciousness underlying such glossy rhetoric are by no means restricted to the oil industry. For instance, Jane hopes that her father's response to the news that she is pregnant will be to offer her refuge. Instead, he upbraids her for her selfishness, pointing to the impact of the global financial crash that frames the contemporary action of the novel: "She could not expect others to assume the cost of her carelessness. It was that kind of thinking that had the whole world in the mess they were finding themselves in right now. Had she thought of the state of his portfolio, he wondered" (89). Here Moore points to the social toll of neo-liberalism's promotion of individualist accumulation that, taken to its extreme, is at the root of the very crisis Jane's father bemoans, even while he uses it to justify his defensive austerity. If, as Whalen contends, "Moore's work ... is a literary model for becoming more compassionate, empathetic people" (2008, 17), a crucial aspect of *February* is the way in which it conspicuously takes on an ideological framework that cultivates just the opposite.

Moore's tentativeness in approaching such a significant and traumatic moment in the history of Newfoundland and Labrador as the sinking of *Ocean Ranger*—her focus on a mourning subject grappling with the consequences—perhaps reflects her awareness of the intense emotional investment of the people of the province in the disaster. Moore's strategy of concentrating on the experience of the bereaved and treating the circumstances of the disaster somewhat obliquely is, I would argue, both respectful and politically sophisticated. Her novel does not simply avoid what might be seen as opportunistic polemicizing about the disaster. *February* also, and more importantly, situates that seemingly singular event in a broader culture of corporate austerity, lack of regulation, and manipulation of the public. Moore highlights the exploitation of economic desperation, the compromising of safety by cost calculation, and the dissipation of responsibility through euphemistic response and the strategic complexity of corporate authority. In the process, the novel resists the isolation of the capsizing and sinking of *Ocean Ranger* as an anomalous disaster and positions it within a broader political economy of risk. *February* does present the sinking of *Ocean Ranger* as a moment when things went terribly wrong, but it does so while keeping in sight how the circumstances that contributed to the disaster and informed its aftermath were not atypical but derived from a mentality that has come to be assumed as a kind of common-sense, no-alternatives ideology.

"THE OFFSHORE OIL INDUSTRY MAY BE THE ECONOMIC SAVIOR OF NEWFOUNDLAND and Labrador," writes Cadigan at the end of *Newfoundland and Labrador: A History*, "but that depends on whether the province may use the wealth generated by the industry to invest in people and communities in ways that sustain both them and the ecologies in which their fortunes are inextricably bound" (2009, 297). Moore's *February* suggests that, while resource megaprojects offer the allure of provincial self-sufficiency, the costs of reaching the Promised Land are, just like the benefits, inequitably apportioned. While working on the rigs, like working in the mines, dangles the tantalizing prospect of a well-paid job in a region generally characterized by the lack of such, Lisa Moore's novel, like Leo McKay's *Twenty-Six* and Alistair MacLeod's *No Great Mischief*, highlights how the trade-off for such an opportunity is the acceptance of considerable risk. Moreover, Moore and McKay stress how the dangers of such occupations, while to a great degree inherent to the work itself, are often exacerbated by management's less stringent and profit-driven determination of "acceptable levels of risk." In the process, Moore, like MacLeod and McKay, locates her portrait of men engaged in hazardous work in a detailed cultural, social, and economic nexus, stressing how local conditions of work are shaped by broader, even global, trends in government oversight of economic development and in relations between capital and labour.

4 |

Uncivil Servitude: The Service Sector

Along with the more fundamentally modern, industrial, and corporatized visions of physical labour in the Maritimes and Newfoundland explored in the previous two chapters, another significant element of work in the region that runs counter to traditional stereotypes is the pronounced shift of the economy toward the growing service sector. If, as Margaret Conrad and James Hiller argue, the four decades after the Second World War are a better candidate for the real golden age of the region, that prosperity came largely not from the traditional resource sectors but from "the burgeoning trade and service sectors, and [was] often tied to state spending" (2001, 199). Indeed, by the turn of the millennium, fully two-thirds of Atlantic Canadians were working in the service sector (Workman 2003, 40). This shift has obviously reshaped the social fabric of the region and is increasingly reflected in Atlantic-Canadian literature, particularly, as we will see in the next section, in the vigorous engagement with tourism as a dominant industry in the service sector. Some writers have also turned their attention to the world of public service, and their work often reflects an acute consciousness of how that sphere is being reshaped by larger political and economic forces, generally to the detriment of the quality of those services and to those in the position of providing them.

"Can I have your sin?": Sheree Fitch's "Civil Servant"

Although known and celebrated principally for her writing for children, New Brunswick poet Sheree Fitch has also written for adults, and her 1993 poem "Civil Servant" not only provides an example of these concerns with life in the service sector but also cleverly dramatizes the underlying tensions of the region's reliance on a service economy in a climate of scarce employment. Playing on the word "sin" as the acronym for "social insurance number," Fitch's speaker, who works in an unemployment insurance office, imagines herself as St. Peter, inquiring about the "sins" of the sad souls who parade by her desk. Despite the lighthearted premise, "Civil Servant" poignantly evokes the bitter humiliation of the office as a kind of bureaucratic purgatory for the unemployed, as well as the tenuous irony of the speaker's own employment, working as a manager of those who have no work. Furthermore, Fitch stresses that the tensions that characterize the unemployment office are particularly acute in economically depressed regions, as every day her speaker is "reminded of regional / despair-ity" (Fitch 1993, 72).

As Fitch highlights, the bureaucratic interaction between the employed and the unemployed staged in the unemployment office is a recipe for resentment, because "people without jobs / get desperate" (70). Running beneath the poem is a current of simmering hostility and potential violence, for which the speaker routinely arms herself: "every day I sharpen / HB pencils / my daggers / in case anyone should threaten me" (70). Underscoring not just the anger that an impersonal bureaucracy cultivates but also the social and economic oppression it embodies, she imagines to herself "the battle with pencil and paper and pen / staple gun," after which

> the floor is stained
> with ink drawn directly
> from the veins of sin-filled civilians
> and the civil servants
> whose job it is
> to smile while
> we tell lies like
>
> *it will only be a little while*
> *then someone will take care of you* (70)

She also describes the very *real* altercations that come with the position because of her literal placement at the divide between those who have work and those who don't: the time "a man / threw his record of employment / across the desk at me," and the time that, after consoling someone who told her "there were no groceries" the week before Christmas, she was spat on and verbally abused, "*what the fuck do you know / stupid bitch you got a job*" (71).

Despite the power the speaker is perceived to have and represent, however, the crisis of conscience she experiences stems from her perception of her own lack of power. Cleverly playing on the image of the civil servant as confessor, she describes how she has

> no power to give to give absolution
> or even a bit of hope that someday
> the phone will ring
> the job they have been waiting for
> is theirs (72)

Essentially seeing herself as a conspirator in the disempowerment of others, Fitch's civil servant ultimately packs it in, although she still has dreams in which "people swivel by my desk / in turnstile fashion" as she intones, "Can I have your sin? / Can I have your sin?" (72). Fitch's poem not only poignantly and humorously depicts the social costs of the lack of economic vitality in the region but also cleverly captures the essential hollowness of reliance on a service economy. "Civil Servant" gives a glimpse of how, in a sense, what the service industry is doing in an economically depressed region is catering to despair.

"The assholes with the red pencils": Wendy Lill's *Corker*

A more expansive version of this tension can be seen in Wendy Lill's 1998 play *Corker*, which chronicles the challenges of characters working both at the top and the bottom of the public service hierarchy, grappling with the impact of neo-liberal policies on the lives of public servants and those they serve. The play dramatizes how, under neo-liberalism, "[i]ndividuals' duties and obligations are trumpeted over deeper and broader citizenship rights, like social rights, to which the welfare state was committed under Keynesianism" and, furthermore, how "those who rely on the state are considered wastrels and scroungers, and those mobilizing for an active state and alternative agendas are written off as pesky 'special interests'" (Dobrowolsky 2009, 6). In *Corker*, Lill is clearly drawing on her two terms as the NDP Member of Parliament representing Dartmouth and her experience as the party's culture critic and spokeperson on disability issues. Although Lill felt that the play could have been set just as easily in Ontario as in Nova Scotia,[1] *Corker* takes place in Halifax, and its portrait of the way in which the prevailing neo-liberal consensus exacerbates the social divide between the privileged and the disadvantaged has a particular relevance to Atlantic Canada.

Corker focuses on an upwardly mobile couple, Merit and Leonard, who travel in influential circles and live in the city's affluent south end. Merit is

Section 1: I'se the B'y That Leaves the Boats

a civil servant and trusted adviser to the premier, and during the play she is promoted to the position of clerk of the cabinet. Leonard is an acquisitions lawyer hoping to leverage his association with Merit into a government contract for the American company he is representing. Their hectic, stressful lives, however, are thrown into turmoil with the arrival of Corker, a mentally challenged young man who had been taken under the wing of Merit's socially conscious hippie sister Serena before her suicide. Corker's disruption of their lives serves as the catalyst for a reassessment of their privileged (if somewhat precarious) affluence and, more generally, for Lill's dramatization of the human costs of the neo-liberal regime of privatization, austerity, and efficiency.

At the beginning of the play, Merit is depicted as being the epitome of the competitive self-absorption that Lill clearly sees as characterizing the new regime. In moving to the south end, the selfishly distracted and aloof Merit has left behind her roots and her family. As her mother points out, she failed to visit her father during the five years he was ill before his death, and she walks by her sister's coffin talking into her cell phone. Whereas her sister emphasizes community and family and lives for the moment, Merit, whose nickname is The Slasher, regards her family as a burden she needs to cut herself free from and, as the premier's trusted advisor, is overseeing a series of drastic cutbacks to social services. Overworked and stressed, she and Leonard live not for the moment but for an annual two-week getaway to Costa Rica.

The degree to which Merit and Leonard's bubble of privilege is inflated and insulated at the expense of others is underscored by the arrival of Corker. Corker associates Merit with Serena and, after his first eviction, repeatedly returns, breaking into the house to be close to her. Initially, Merit views Corker as a nuisance, "the last bad joke played on" her by Serena (Lill 1998, 29), and looks to fob him off on the proper authorities: "There are places for people like him. A whole system in place for people like him. Our taxes pay for them. And it isn't cheap" (29). Corker's persistent return to their home compels Merit and Leonard to confront the consequences of the cutbacks they so insouciantly supported. Corker's social worker Glenny observes in response to their disbelief that Corker had simply walked out of the Pit, a noisy and seedy group home, "It's not a prison. There are no locks on the door. The night staff can't be everywhere at once. They're overworked, tired out, understaffed" (37). When Corker persists in breaking into their house, Merit is increasingly forced to see in him the consequences of the regime she represents, which reflects the neo-liberal tendency "to assess only those policy outcomes that are easily captured in quantitative terms, such as dollars and cents spent or saved" and to neglect "to measure the actual success of policy measures in peoples' lives" (Braedley and Luxton 2010, 11). Confronted by Merit after a violent clash between Corker and Leonard in the middle of the night, Glenny springs to Corker's defence, arguing that his volatility is the result of inadequate care: "That's the low maintenance solution at the Pit. Drug them and let them stare at the walls. Cheaper than counselling or programs" (Lill 1998, 46). The tone for such neglect, Glenny stresses, is set at the top, where austerity is cynically and selectively applied. Glenny rightly predicts that more cuts are coming—"We'll get the news just before the Premier and his cronies go off on their winter vacations"—and will leave the elite untouched. "Cut welfare, cut social services, cut education, but he doesn't touch the corporations and the bond dealers" (47). The system, as Glenny succinctly puts it, is "at the mercy of the assholes with the red pencils" (103).

Another key plot development that foregrounds the dubious effects of neo-liberal "rationalization" and the triumph of economies of scale is that the American company for which Leonard is serving as lead consul is seeking a major health management contract with the province as "the biggest provider of health services" (68). However, Leonard's aspirations are derailed as Merit increasingly undermines his cause. She misses a crucial meeting when she takes Corker to the emergency department, where she discovers first-hand the results of her ideological handiwork. "We waited two hours at the hospital before we even saw the intake worker" (Lill 1998, 99), she explains to Leonard. Then a drunken Glenny reveals to Merit that the supposed "world leaders in human services delivery" (104) Leonard represents, Slamemshut International, are poised to take over and close the more stable group home to which Corker is waiting to be moved. Rather than specializing in medical management, Merit berates Leonard, the firm "run[s] jails in the United States! What does that have to do with the mentally handicapped!" (102). This revelation marks a turning point for Merit, who undermines the company's credibility in a subsequent meeting with company representatives. She observes to Leonard that they have no experience in what they are being contracted to do, and instead of using the term "home" use terms like "'facility,' or 'premise,' or 'installation'" (104). As Merit goes on to argue, the neo-liberal celebration of efficiency is often merely code for profitability, and applying neo-liberal arguments to the provision of public services amounts to profiteering at the expense of people's well-being: "They're making a fortune on their prisons. Warehousing humans is a very lucrative business. What does that have to do with the public interest?" (105). Although Lill can be accused of being heavy-handed here, through this subplot she gestures to what Raewyn Connell describes as neo-liberals' "astonishing success in creating markets for those things whose commodification was once almost unimaginable" (2010, 23) and suggests that the terminus of the discourse of austerity is a callousness toward human suffering straight out of Dickens.

The ending of the play offers a somewhat compromised resistance to the insidious accountant's vision of neo-liberalism. Merit salvages her idealism and embraces her sister's humane vision by prioritizing, as Serena advised in her suicide note, family and community over power and prosperity. After Merit effectively condemns the family home by refusing to subsidize it and announces her plan to shuffle her mother Florence off to Hawthorne House, a "prestige address for gracious senior living" (Lill 1998, 108), Florence, recognizing their affinity as socially marginal liabilities, absconds with Corker to Montreal. This final crisis completes Merit's change of heart. Pulling back from the precipice of complete, cynical complicity, she sabotages Leonard's ambitions by exposing Slamemshut's trail of lawsuits, and then resigns from her post as clerk of the cabinet in order to look after Frances and Corker, whom she takes into her own home. Although the play thus stages a resistance to the devastation wrought on people's lives by neo-liberal austerity and corporate profit-mongering, the ending of *Corker* signals at best a partial (though not Pyrrhic) victory. Over the course of the play, Merit, a motivated, competent, ambitious civil servant, is forced to choose between her career and being relegated to the traditional position of caregiver. This dilemma exemplifies what Pat Armstrong describes as "the privatization of responsibility" under neo-liberalism, in which "individuals or their families are expected to take responsibility for themselves and earn enough through the market to provide for their own needs. This form of privatization provides a rationalization for inequality through the assumption that we get what we deserve as a result of our efforts" (2010, 187). Although Merit's transformation is undeniably emotionally positive—unlike her job, her guardianship of Corker leaves her feeling "legitimate, useful" (Lill 1998, 100)—it is hard to overlook that, in material and aspirational terms, Merit's wings have been clipped. Indeed, *Corker* seems to provide a telling theatrical example of Janine Brodie's insight that, by off-loading the provision of social services from the state, restructuring facilitates the reassertion of patriarchal norms. The ensuing social burden, Brodie stresses, is overwhelmingly assumed by women: "Privatization and the erosion of the welfare state have the effect of forcing health, child, and elderly care back onto the family and the unpaid work of women. As a result, many women are forced to leave the paid labour force or settle for low-paying part-time employment to meet these caring needs" (1995, 53–54). The agenda of restructuring, as Brodie among others argues, is highly gendered, as government cutbacks result in the curtailing of women's freedom; in this fashion, "the state reconstitutes the domestic by fiat instead of explicit regulation" (1995, 53). While Merit's abdication from her role of support staff to the collusion between the state and the private sector is undeniably salutary, Lill nonetheless emphasizes that such a decision carries a high cost.

"Ride the privatization wave": Edward Riche's *The Nine Planets*

The shift in Atlantic-Canadian literature away from the world of the rural petty producer is perhaps most conspicuous in contemporary fiction from Newfoundland. The fictional worlds of Lisa Moore, Michael Winter, and Edward Riche, for instance, are largely urban, cosmopolitan, and middle class, built around characters working in the service and cultural industries. In Riche's latest novel, *The Nine Planets* (2004), his portrayal of the service sector—in this case, education—is consciously positioned within a larger global economy dominated by corporate players, and the novel displays an acute, if highly satiric, awareness of the economic and political machinations attendant on globalization. Riche's main protagonist in *The Nine Planets* is Marty Devereaux, the co-principal of The Red Pines, a tony private school catering to the increasingly international elite of St. John's. Dissatisfied with life, Marty becomes embroiled with (and ultimately broiled by) George Hayden, a local developer seeking to build a gated community on a pristine peninsula just outside the city. Marty's ill-fated collaboration with Hayden serves to dramatize the intensified imbalances of power within a global economy, as well as the capacity of capital, as Edward Soja argues, to reshape geography in accordance with its own interests.

Marty's position as co-principal of a private school reflects the larger context of neo-liberal restructuring. The Red Pines represents an entrepreneurial venture for Marty, as he and his friend Hank Lundrigan had the idea that, "with the government getting out of the state, why not ride the privatization wave and open their own damn school?" (Riche 2004, 19). Having purchased a leftover U.S. military hospital, Marty has adopted a "strategy of dressing and stressing the place to make it look like it had a lengthy history" and "some, albeit spurious, connection to a venerable line of English schooling" (23) (though the school's uniforms are made in Malaysia). The clientele of The Red Pines emphasizes the position of the city in a post-recovery Newfoundland. While "rural Newfoundland was dying" (20) in the wake of the moratorium, "[o]ffshore oil was buoying the urban economy and drawing itinerant petrochemical families from Texas and Norway, engineers from France and England" (20), an affluent international elite to whose children The Red Pines caters. A large part of Marty's dissatisfaction with life stems from his sense of being merely a high-end worker in the service industry, making innumerable manoeuvres and compromises to keep his eccentric staff and affluent customers happy. Marty and Hank's venture is thus a dubious success and a managerial headache.

For Marty, the association with Hayden holds out the promise of a much larger and more lucrative venture. Riche's portrait of Hayden is a wicked satire of the rootlessness and fickleness of economic globalization. Hayden is the scion of a local family firm, arrivistes "on the fringes of the St. John's merchant class" who made their fortunes through "political connections to the Smallwood autocracy" (Riche 2004, 237). The firm has graduated from such local projects as schools and airports to "the fruits of this generation's labours, a prison in Ecuador, a resort in Mexico, fish plants in Indonesia. The world was now their oyster or, more accurately, their flash-frozen farmed prawn" (238). Hayden confides to Marty that the development is small potatoes to them: "By necessity we've become international. Smaller fish, bigger pond—that's the way things are these days" (43). Instead, the development, according to Hayden, is a sop to his sentimental and dying father: "I tell him we're building six fish-processing facilities in Vietnam, it means nothing to him. But something in sight of the graves of his family ... and, truth be told, his old enemies ... it means everything" (43).

Marty is seduced by the idea that he might similarly branch out from his constrictive position as a co-principal, and through his collaboration with Hayden, Riche satirizes the penchant for privatization as a greed-driven commodification of services. Highlighting the exacerbation of disparities between the affluent and the hoi polloi in the brave new world of public austerity and privatized services, Hayden entices Marty to consider taking advantage of economies of scale in a new regime in which the public system has been hung out to dry and the private sector stands to cash in by catering to the educational needs of the rich. Hayden suggests to Marty the possibility of branching out, extending the model of The Red Pines to a line of schools, although when Marty broaches the subject to Hank he has trouble responding to Hank's concern that systematization runs counter to people's expectations of private school. Marty's hesitant response suggests a corporate vision of educational efficiency and reveals the oxymoronic deception of the very concept of a chain of private schools: "Each school would be unique ... seem unique ... appear to be a stand-alone operation ... and quality controls ... like assurances of a certain standard of instruction would be part of the deal. There would be a uniform curriculum, using the same texts and such" (55). Hayden's henchman Ken lauds the fact that in The Red Pines Marty has "created a great brand," a conclusion that Marty immediately embraces: "It was his concern that things look or seem right that created an overall effect that provided the consumer, in this case the parents, with a level of comfort with and confidence in their purchase. It kept them coming back" (140). Here Riche's satire is reminiscent of Naomi Klein's analysis of the supplanting of the product in contemporary consumer culture by the more amorphous "message" of the brand (2000, 24).

As part of his vision for the development of Perroqueet Downs, Hayden encourages Marty to draft for city council a vision of a private school for the development, one Marty envisions as the precursor for an entire chain, "the manual for operation of future outlets, a document laying it all out, from principles of design to curriculum" (Riche 2004, 141–42). As he contemplates his franchise, however, he quite consciously positions it within the impermanence and mobility engendered by economic globalization:

> The middle class of North America was, as never before, transient—following the economy from northeast to southwest. St. John's was flourishing now but in twenty years … who knew? It made sense to operate schools that could be disassembled, loaded into semis, and hauled to the next market, be it Arizona or British Columbia, or for that matter packed into a container and shipped to the U.A.E. or New Zealand. You could roll up the Astroturf playing fields and take them with you to Japan. Japan! (147)

Here Riche's satire evokes a broader trend in which neo-liberalism "accompanies and promotes a profound shift in the corporate world from the long-term planning characteristic of an earlier stage of industrial capitalism to a systemic focus on short-term profitability" (Connell 2010, 33).

Marty's collaboration with Hayden, however, is predicated on his providing aid to Hayden's envisioned development of the Perroqueet Downs, which, despite the fact that Hayden and his associates have half of council in their pocket, is threatened by opposition. Marty has been conscripted to exercise his influence on Hank, whose environmental advocacy and opposition to the development appear to be swaying the city's erratic and impressionable mayor in the wrong direction. Initially, Marty is ideologically onside; inclined by disposition toward cynical expediency, he sees development as inevitable and Hank's opposition to it as grandiose idealism. However, he is given pause for thought when he goes on a picnic to the Perroqueet Downs with his prospective lover, Jackie Spurell, and her heavily medicated husband Ted (their illicit liaison having been complicated by the cancellation of Ted's AA meeting). The downs, he discovers, are breathtaking. Although he understands how something precious will be ruined he still remains ambivalent, rationalizing that "progress came at a cost. The preservationists were advocates of doing nothing" (Riche 2004, 201). Marty thus buys into the capitalist principle of creative destruction, that progress and change are a priori preferable.

What Marty discovers, however, is that he is no match for Hayden even in his cynicism, let alone in his financial resources, as Riche engages in some wicked satire of the ruthlessness and hypocrisy of the capitalist class. What Riche most crucially foregrounds is the manipulative public relations in which Hayden engages to advance his cause. As the development progresses, Hayden and his henchmen spin the positive aspects of the development and then just as cynically cast them aside to bolster their profit margin, revealing how, for all their rhetoric, it is ultimately all about the money. For instance, they boast that the development will have "an environmentally friendly waste water plant" (135), but this later disappears from their plans. Furthermore, because the Perroquet Downs is the site of a tiny fishing community resettled during the Smallwood era, Hayden's associate Ken suggests with arch cynicism that their development, rather than being built on pristine land, is in fact an instance of "de-resettlement" (141), reflecting not a genuine concern with heritage but a creative capacity for opportunistically exploiting its cachet.

Marty likewise falls victim to this expediency, as Hayden brusquely casts him off after Hank manages to convince the mayor to oppose the development. When Marty shows up at Hayden's office to pitch his mission statement, he is summarily dismissed: "Did someone ... give you the impression that we wanted to invest in some school scheme? I'm sure we said we looked into it and decided against it.... I think we said first right of refusal or something to that effect ... and that in return you would shut your friend up" (Riche 2004, 240). For all his world-weary cynicism, Marty ultimately proves to be a gullible greenhorn, suckered into thinking that he could be a big fish in a pond in which he is but a minnow, quixotically believing himself capable of steering an enterprise that requires far more capital and political pull than he can muster. Marty realizes that "[t]hey'd played him, imagining they might employ him in some chicanery to advance their plans for the Peroquet Downs, cutting him loose when he proved useless." Furthermore, rather than tricking Marty outright, they had merely exploited his own eagerness and gullibility, "they'd sucked him in with vague blandishments, they'd seduced but never lain down with him" (251).

Initially Marty consoles himself that "[t]heir actions were without malevolence, it was just business" (251), clearly having bought into the neo-liberal characterization of competition "as a naturally occurring social good"—"an 'impersonal force' rather than structured by people's decisions" (Braedley and Luxton 2010, 8). Later, though, he comes to realize to what degree his competitive disadvantage is grounded as much in a lack of ruthlessness as in a lack of wealth. With Marty having failed to muzzle Hank, Hayden conspires to remove Hank from the picture by conjuring up charges that he has sexually assaulted the son of one of Hayden's business associates, Russell Malan, a stupid but cunning lout whom Hank had goodheartedly tutored. Hayden engineers a scenario in which Hank "was so closely associated with opposition to the Perroqueet Downs development that a gambit to stop the bulldozers now would be akin to sanctioning child abuse" (Riche 2004, 265). The end of the novel overwhelmingly underlines the power of the financial elite to silence opposition and to impose its will on the populace and, furthermore, without drawing undue attention to its capacity to do so. "It wasn't cowardly on their part to have the police do the dirty work, it was just the way they were. They always got the help to do that sort of thing. They paid more than their share of taxes, they should be afforded some special service" (265). While Riche's satiric style imparts to this portrait of capitalist development in the regime of economic globalization a somewhat hyperbolic facetiousness, *The Nine Planets* nonetheless conveys some mordant truths about the implications of the increasing concentration of political and economic power, as well as of the mobility of capital in a global economy. Although Marty is a relatively prosperous member of the upper middle class, his brush with a much bigger operator like Hayden brings home to him his almost utter lack of power and his relative inability to determine his own fate.

RICHE'S DEPICTION OF MARTY'S ILL-ADVISED VENTURE INTO THE HALLS OF POWER illustrates a dynamic at the heart of the lives of so many working-class and middle-class Atlantic Canadians today, whether they are labouring in the educational system, the civil service, the resource sectors, the hospitality industry, or any number of other occupations: the feeling of diminishing power to dictate the terms of one's employment. Whereas Folk iconography propagates the mythic image of independent petty producers contending only with the elements, contemporary Atlantic-Canadian literature provides a much more complex, in some ways more mundane, and much less rosy picture of the occupational hazards now faced by working people in the region. Here are few farmers, lumberjacks, or fishermen, insulated from the ravages of modernity and engaged in timeless, solitary toil to sustain their close-knit families and communities. Instead, so much of the writing currently being produced in the region provides a picture of people whose working lives are very much defined by forces beyond their control—indeed, the very forces of modernity, "progress," and capital from which the Folk are ostensibly insulated. Here historical change, political ideology, and commerce are potently combined in the form of a neo-liberal restructuring—a profound reconfiguration of capital's relationship with labour and with various levels of government—that has done much to deprive Atlantic Canadians of their flexibility to work and live as and where they see fit.

Conclusion to Section One

To stress the degree to which contemporary writers in the East are increasingly conscious of the impact of these economic, political, and historical forces on the lives of Atlantic Canadians is not to suggest that Atlantic-Canadian literature as a whole has tended to perpetrate Folk stereotypes in the past. Ian McKay rightly argues that writers such as Frank Parker Day, Thomas Raddall, and Hugh MacLennan made a substantial contribution to the consolidation of the Folk paradigm in Nova Scotia, and Lucy Maud Montgomery's idyllic, pastoral vision of the agricultural society of Prince Edward Island has been leveraged into a global brand with impressive staying power and vast merchandizing potential. But writers such as Al Pittman, Milton Acorn, and Alden Nowlan chronicled the hardscrabble existence and class conflict that has characterized much of the history of the region, and even Ernest Buckler's nostalgically pastoral classic, *The Mountain and the Valley*, as David Creelman notes, is consciously set against the backdrop of a crisis in the apple economy of Nova Scotia's Annapolis Valley (2003, 85). What we see in more recent writing, however, is a much more palpable—and at times even blatantly conscious—tension between the Folk paradigm and the image of the East in its literature. Contemporary writing in the region reflects its position within a larger, postmodern, global consumer culture and, more importantly, reflects the degree to which the political and economic marginality of the region has been exacerbated by a neo-liberal emphasis on competitiveness, mobility, and profitability. Although the work of some contemporary writers reflects the more affluent and mobile side of that global consumer culture—the urbane, cultured, middle-class cosmopolitans of the fiction of Edward Riche, Lisa Moore, and Michael Winter, for instance—much Atlantic-Canadian literature (including the work of the trio above) consciously speaks to the erosion of traditional social structures in an environment of economic restructuring and the reconfiguration of space within global capital. The working lives of Atlantic Canadians as depicted by writers in the region are increasingly divergent from the depictions of the working lives of the Folk, and that dissonance tells us much about the present state of the region and the preoccupations of its writers. Rather than the stable, elemental, pre-capitalist world of resource cultivation and extraction that Folk imagery perpetuates and romanticizes, contemporary Atlantic-Canadian literature increasingly reflects a more mobile, stratified, and service-oriented economy, and a much more beleaguered, dependent, and "inflexible" working population.

| Section Two

"About as Far from Disneyland as You Can Possibly Get": The Reshaping of Culture

One of the crucial achievements of representations of work in contemporary Atlantic-Canadian literature is that they often situate people working in the resource sectors or service sector within a larger, even global web of political, economic, and social relations. This distinction is likewise significant to the reconfiguration of culture in contemporary Atlantic-Canadian literature, which increasingly highlights how misconceptions about the East Coast, especially Folk stereotypes, are fostered and sustained within a thoroughly modern, and increasingly post-modern, commodity culture that has significant political and economic ramifications. In *The Quest of the Folk*, Ian McKay describes the vision of the Folk as selective, conservative, and essentialist: "The Folk were traditional, somewhat reclusive, relatively uninterested in protest or in politics, fiercely superstitious, family-centred and respectful of conventional moralities" (1994, 137). Part of the problem with such an essentialist vision is that it lends itself readily to the perception (whether critical or approving) that the Atlantic provinces have been left behind by modernity and progress and that the culture of the region is both uniform and harmonious. Furthermore, it "removes any detailed consideration of the structure of power. It leads one to a complacently organic view of society, in which there are no fundamental social contradictions and no underlying differences in perspective" (298).

Section 2: "About as Far from Disneyland as You Can Possibly Get"

The result is a reinforcement of both internal and external structures of dominance. First of all, the perpetuation of Folk stereotypes reinforces hierarchies of power within the region by suppressing the diversity and conflicted social and cultural relations that characterize, and always have characterized, life in the Atlantic provinces. Secondly, it facilitates the continuing cultural colonization of the region by the more powerful parts of the rest of the country. "In Canada," Tony Tremblay argues, "a cultural program of nostalgia, literally *homesickness*, polices and reinforces an east-coast Celtic ethnicity that is Old World, racially white and homogeneous, near-pathological in its demands for thematic integration in all the arts, from literature to music, and architecturally resistant to interrogation" (2008, 37). Indeed, in his response to a forum on *The Quest of the Folk* in Acadiensis in 2005,[1] McKay reiterated the relevance of the book's critique of anti-modernism and argued that engaging in a critique of the paradigm of the Folk is even more necessary, given what he describes as the near-totalitarian influence of neo-liberalism,

> when everything is measured as a dollars-and-cents proposition.... Under conditions of capitalist modernity and regional marginalization, Maritimers in the Canadian myth-symbol complex easily become yet another "people without history" ready to fill the part the Canadian liberal cultural producers have assigned them—that of patronized primitives, pitiable dependants and anachronistic curiosities. It causes middle-class Torontonians, those archetypal CBCites, no grief whatsoever to be mildly charmed by the quaint Folk of the East, with their colourful ways, salty vocabularies and perpetual kitchen parties.... Just do not ask these CBCites to share the wealth or critique the system that vests them with so much symbolic and political power. That would be, well, *so 20th century*. (2005, 156–57; italics in original)

The present context of cultural commodification and neo-liberal dominance, then, not only imparts a sense of urgency to the reconfiguration of the culture of Atlantic Canada in its literature but also is the informing context in which that reconfiguration must be viewed. At the end of *The Quest of the Folk*, Ian McKay argues for a more pluralistic and inclusive image of culture in Nova Scotia (1994, 308). His view that "much new cultural work in the Maritimes extends the political implications of this seminal moment in which the gaze is refused" (1994, 309) is very much a prescient one for the Atlantic region as a whole. Current literary production in the Atlantic provinces presents a view of the region that is conspicuously urbane, cosmopolitan, and diverse, reflecting what Susanne Marshall (referring to Lisa

Section 2: "About as Far from Disneyland as You Can Possibly Get"

Moore's stories) describes as "the interarticulation of the regional and the cosmopolitan" (2008, 81). The work of Moore, George Elliott Clarke, Lynn Coady, Edward Riche, Michael Winter, and others reflects a culturally and stylistically sophisticated, consciously global sensibility that constitutes in itself a substantial rejoinder to the caricature of the East Coast as rural, parochial, and culturally rudimentary. Leo McKay Jr.'s fictionalization of the Westray explosion in *Twenty-Six*, for instance, is intercut with scenes depicting the experiences of Ziv Burrows's girlfriend Meta Leblanc while teaching English in Tokyo, where she first hears of the explosion on the radio. These segments, Leo McKay observes, mirror his own experience of hearing about the disaster in his home town while halfway around the world, teaching English in Japan. But they also serve to counter the view of the East Coast as an insular, backward, Folk society, a "little world set apart," resisting the impression "that we're all here in the Maritimes, a bunch of humble fiddlers on the back porch, banging away on spoons and mumbling at the passers-by in Gaelic" (L. McKay 2009). What is important here is not just Leo McKay's recognition that the region has been left behind by history and progress is false but also his concern about how it masks the region's thorough incorporation in a global economic regime.

Beyond this sometimes conscious, sometimes unconscious cosmopolitan sensibility, literary activity in the Maritimes and Newfoundland since the publication of *The Quest of the Folk* has continued to reconfigure the culture of the Atlantic provinces in two important ways. First, it has implicitly or openly contested the idyllic, homogeneous vision of the Folk paradigm by drawing attention to the much more varied and less harmonious social realities on the East Coast or by openly critiquing the implications of a Folk vision of that society. Secondly, writers in the Maritimes and Newfoundland have openly engaged in challenging and deconstructing the stereotypical views of the region that are cherished by outsiders and often presented to visitors. This refusal of the gaze, to use Ian McKay's terms, has most conspicuously taken the form of a preoccupation with tourism itself as an economic, cultural, and political force in the region. As well as being an often intrusive material presence, tourism in Atlantic Canada routinely draws on simplistic and exclusive images of a uniform, earthy, and authentic culture (a recent tourist pitch described Newfoundland and Labrador as "about as far from Disneyland as you can possibly get"). The reality, many of these writers suggest, is a lot more complicated and, in many ways, not "as far from Disneyland" as one might think.

5 |

"The Simpler and More Colourful Way of Life"

One of the problems with the Folk paradigm, Ian McKay stresses, is that it promotes ethnically exclusive definitions of culture. McKay highlights how identifying people as members of the "Folk" "only worked if there were some who were not 'Folk.'" Those who found themselves on the wrong side of this opposition "either adapted to this uncomfortable situation by intensifying their own separate identity, or they sought, by assimilating, somehow to cancel the polarity" (I. McKay 1994, 13). With the growing assertion of their rights in the 1960s and 1970s, however, women and minority groups in Atlantic Canada began to counter such suppression and marginalization and to express their distinctive experiences and identities in more empowering terms (Conrad and Hiller 2001, 201–6). Largely excluded from overviews of literary production on the East Coast in the past, writers from racialized minority communities certainly have established a more significant presence in contemporary Atlantic-Canadian literature. Afro-Nova Scotian George Elliott Clarke is one of the region's best-known writers, and the late Rita Joe was a significant literary elder for a whole generation of younger Native writers. Although Native writers in the region conspicuously have not achieved the same stature as their counterparts in other parts of the country—think of now-canonical figures such as Thomas King, Tomson Highway, and Eden Robinson—there are signs of burgeoning literary activity, such as *The Mi'kmaq Anthology* edited by Lesley Choyce and Rita Joe (1997). While Clarke has done much—especially with his two-volume anthology *Fire on the Water* (1991/92)—to affirm the long history of writing by people of African heritage in the Maritimes, in the last few decades there has been an undeniable profusion of work by Black writers, including Charles Saunders, Maxine Tynes, and George Boyd. While

Section 2: "About as Far from Disneyland as You Can Possibly Get"

perhaps less pronounced than in the rest of Canada, there has been a growing trend since the 1970s to recognize Atlantic-Canadian literature as a multicultural literature.

The gender imbalance that historically characterized the literature of the region has undergone an even more pronounced change, likewise reflecting a broader trend across the country. Perhaps the most significant development in the literature of the Atlantic provinces over the last thirty years has been the proliferation of writing by and about women. While the region's—indeed, arguably the country's—best-known writer is a woman (L.M. Montgomery), writing by women in the region (Sophia Almon Hensley, Margaret Marshall Saunders, and Margaret Duley, among others) historically has been overshadowed by the work of male writers (Thomas Chandler Haliburton, Charles G.D. Roberts, Bliss Carman, E.J. Pratt, Ernest Buckler, and so on). In the recent explosion of writing in the region, however, women have had almost as much of a presence as their male counterparts: poets such as Anne Compton, Anne Simpson, Lynn Davies, Sheree Fitch, and Mary Dalton, along with Joe and Tynes; writers of fiction including Lynn Coady, Lisa Moore, Bernice Morgan, Donna Morrissey, M.T. Dohaney, and Linda Little; and playwrights such as Wendy Lill and Catherine Banks. While the work of these writers is stylistically and thematically diverse, from the somewhat sentimental outport realism of Morrissey's fiction to the topical and political theatre of Lill, to the cosmopolitan, urban impressionism of Lisa Moore's work, one of the central features of contemporary writing by women in the Atlantic region is that it presents a collective challenge to the patriarchal bias of Folk archetypes, grounded in a gendered division of labour and of power and mobility as well.

"Decidedly Monochromatic in Practice"

Although there has been a long tradition in the region of constructing Acadians as Folk, Black and Native people, Ian McKay notes, have tended to be excluded (1994, 230). Thus, as Maureen Moynagh archly puts it, the "'simpler' and more *colourful* way of life" associated with the Folk "tended, not surprisingly, to be decidedly monochromatic in practice" (1998, 17; italics in original). Black and Native writers, however, have presented an increasing challenge to this "monochromatic" experience in a number of important ways: by asserting the significance of their pasts in the face of colonialism's distortion or erasure of their histories; by articulating contemporary social, economic, and political concerns, including exploitative treatment by the dominant culture; by consciously critiquing the exclusivity of Folk images of life in the East; and, not least of all, by drawing on cultural and aesthetic traditions beyond those of the dominant culture, and in the process diversifying and reinvigorating Atlantic-Canadian literature.

The erasure of Native people in the Folk paradigm is fraught with all sorts of ironies, pointing to wider tensions within what is called, in post-colonial parlance, settler-invader culture. That is, the construction of the Folk as timeless, rooted to the land, and so on, evokes a sense of original belonging that is, of course, historically spurious. Although the Folk seem like they have been here forever, they have *not* been here forever. In that sense, the Folk paradigm is complicit in the colonial tactic of constructing the land as unoccupied territory, because it cultivates the impression that the Folk have always belonged there. However, as the work of Native historians and writers has helped to underscore, that is simply not the case. At the core of the history of the Maritimes, as Mi'kmaq historian Daniel Paul, for one, contends, is a systematic process of dispossession of Native peoples and expropriation of their land (2000, 181). Likewise, in looking at the work of Native writers in the East, it is important to keep in mind poet and scholar Jeannette Armstrong's reminder that, "[c]ontrary to the predominant view, Aboriginal literatures are not 'emergent' Canadian literary voices arising as a result of Aboriginal peoples' literacy in an official language and their introduction to Canadian literature" (2005, 180), but have a much longer genealogy.

One of the most prominent of these voices in the Atlantic provinces has been the poet Rita Joe, who died in 2007. A status Mi'kmaq who lived most of her life on the Eskasoni Reserve in Cape Breton, Joe, in her debut collection *Poems of Rita Joe* (1978), *Song of Eskasoni: More Poems of Rita Joe* (1988), and *Lnu and Indians We're Called* (1991), provides consistent reminders of the long presence in Atlantic Canada of Aboriginal peoples. Joe's philosophy is very much a positive, conciliatory, and healing one, stressing the need for Native peoples to assert their presence, their story, and their culture, but gently rather than radically or polemically, "we need more writers in our own culture, but please not the negative stuff, just the gentle story of what's happening today, the positive side we all experience" (1989, 28). Of Joe's numerous poems that "address the problems of Indian-white relations," Hartmut Lutz observes that "[g]ently but persistently they draw attention to conflicts of racial prejudice, cultural rejection and social marginalization, but again and again they extend to the white readers an open hand of forgiveness and even friendship" (1996, 281). Joe's poetry chronicles the near-eclipse of traditional Mi'kmaq culture, the pressures of assimilation, as well as the pain of her own turbulent life story— including her life in a series of foster homes, attendance at the Shubenacadie residential school, and her marriage to her often abusive husband Frank. But she resolutely emphasizes themes of survival, reconciliation, and the promise of future generations. The gulf between Native people and the dominant culture is not to be decried so much as bridged. "Teach me the art of communication," she requests in a characteristic gesture of invitation in "The Art of Communication," "Because, I want to tell you about me / The Indian of today / The lonely stranger to her own land" (Joe 1988, 17). This gesture is present even at the end of "I Lost My Talk," a poem that has often "been treated as if it were Joe's personal signature tune" by non-Native critics (Fuller 2004b, 178). The poem serves as an indictment of the cultural erasure effected by residential schools, thanks to which, Joe observes, "I speak like you / I think like you / I create like you" (1988, 32). For Sam McKegney, the poem is characteristic of what he terms Joe's "affirmatist" perspective, that she "affirms the positive potential of a particular colonial imposition in relation to healing and empowerment without trivializing the pain the process of imposition has caused" (2007, 129). Joe stresses the importance of cultural recovery, but again in mutually constructive rather than condemnatory terms, "gently I offer my hand and ask, / Let me find my talk / So I can teach you about me" (1988, 32). The poem, McKegney contends, "is not so much deference to non-Native authority as a call for the slackening of forces that seek to circumscribe Native agency. The speaker claims a degree of power in a non-threatening, conciliatory yet determined, position" (2007, 130).

However, while Joe tends to accentuate the positive, she does recognize the inequitable power relations within which attempts at reconciliation and mutual understanding are to be made. In "You, I, Love, Beauty, Earth," for instance, she proposes changing places as a way of highlighting the dominance of mainstream culture and the disappearance of her own:

> Let us trade places just this once
> And you listen while I go on about my culture
> Important just like yours
> But almost dead (1991, 19)

Furthermore, Joe's poetry registers historical and contemporary issues of concern in the Atlantic region and in the country as a whole. She writes, for instance, of the extinction of the Beothuk in poems such as "Shanawdithit" (1988, 43) and "Demasduit" (1991, 59), and in "I'm A Beothuk" entertains the possibility that because her husband has roots in Ktaqmkuk (Newfoundland), her own children may well have a grain of Beothuk ancestry and thus, as her son proclaims, "They didn't all die like history says" (1991, 60). In "James Bay," she employs prosopopoeia, speaking in the voice of the dead to protest the desecration of Aboriginal burial grounds as a result of hydroelectric development: "My grave you dare disturb! / Because you think me less"

"The Simpler and More Colourful Way of Life"

FIGURE 5 Donald Marshall Jr. addresses the press after his acquittal, May 1983.

(1988, 48). "The Lament of Donald Marshall Jr." evokes one of the most notorious wrongful convictions in Canadian history, and is one of a number of what Lutz describes as "honouring songs which celebrate the achievements of exemplary individuals" (1996, 285). A young Mi'kmaq living in Sydney, Cape Breton, Marshall served eleven years in prison for the 1971 murder of a Black man, Sandy Seale, before being exonerated in 1982.[1] Bob Wall concludes that "Marshall's arrest, trial, and conviction were the direct result of the incompetence of the police, lawyers, judges, and other officials of the justice system that existed in Sydney in 1971, mixed with the bigotry and racial stereotyping typical at the time" (1992, 25). Marshall's wrongful conviction was made the focus of a royal commission (completed in 1990) and became an international *cause célèbre*: "My pain it is known, it is known the world over" (Joe 1988, 70). The refrain of Joe's poem, written from the perspective of Marshall himself, stresses that the murder victim, Sandy Seale, was Marshall's friend, and Joe's repeated appeal signals the implicit message that such a miscarriage of justice was grounded in the punitive divisions of racism: "We are the same, we are the same, we are the same" (1988, 70).

In "Oka," her response to one of the most turbulent moments in the modern history of relations between Native peoples and the mainstream culture in Canada,[2] however, Joe seems to be struggling with the limits of her patient, conciliatory stance. Here, Joe empathizes with the Mohawk protesters' concerns—"I know you are angry, I am the same" (1991, 63)—but she distances herself from their methods, her "spirit vague, wanting to help," but "to help in another way, into the future" (63). Although Joe's counsel is somewhat ambiguous, what she seems to be promoting is a more passive and less obstructionist resistance, taking the long view of reform: "Let them do their thing my good people in Oka / I know it will be slow, / But it will be done" (63). For a younger generation of activists cognizant of the lack of reward that Aboriginal people's patience has garnered historically, though, such counsel is likely to seem like a recipe for sustaining the status quo.

Compared to other Aboriginal and Métis writers such as Armstrong, Lee Maracle, and Maria Campbell, Rita Joe's engagement with the legacy of colonialism in Canada seems mild and, for some, excessively forgiving. "Joe's willingness to downplay the negative," concedes McKegney, "renders her work vulnerable to attack from more aggressively anti-colonial Native critical factions" who might view such a position "as politically debilitating, socially regressive, and even historically inaccurate" (2007, 123). Danielle Fuller, though, like McKegney, sees Joe's "denial of the suffering inflicted on [her people] by their colonizers" as the very source of her strength and optimism: "Carefully emphasizing her own ability to cope with the past ... Joe refuses to be a victim and urges her community to look to its collective strengths and traditions" (2004b, 171). However conciliatory it may be, the work of Rita Joe is nonetheless a significant reminder that, even though the presence of people of European heritage goes back in Atlantic Canada much longer than in the rest of the country, it does not go back into the proverbial mists of time. The poetry and prose writing of Rita Joe keeps in view that history of conquest and articulates the persistence of the Mi'kmaq and other Native peoples into the present and the future. Even though "[y]our history tells our children / what you want them to learn" (1988, 63), Joe affirms in "Warriors," "[o]ur children learn today / our ancestors were there" (1988, 63).

A somewhat more trenchant and incisive stance is evident in the work of Chief Lindsay Marshall, leader of the Chapel Island First Nation in Cape Breton. Like the poetry of Rita Joe, Marshall's *Clay Pots and Bones / Pkáwóqq aq Waqntal*, published in 1997, evokes the experience of Mi'kmaq people both past and present, but Marshall's engagement with the consequences of colonialism is much more critical and less conciliatory, and his poetry touches on contemporary issues with a much keener edge.

Like Joe's poetry, *Clay Pots and Bones* evokes the cultural and social richness of the Mi'kmaq people, as many of the poems in the collection pay tribute to the wisdom and influence of elders, the spiritual sustenance provided by drum and dance, and sustaining ties of family and community. The collection's evocation of the past, though, is more consistently shot through with lamentation and accusation, highlighting the damage wrought by colonialism and its rapacious successor, contemporary capitalism.

"Clay Pots and Bones," for instance, interrogates the justice of the 1752 settlement between Mi'kmaq chiefs and the Crown: "Write down the reasons why / the land under our feet became / foreign soil in perpetuity" (Marshall 1997, 50). The treaty, Daniel Paul argues, implicitly recognized the Mi'kmaq as a nation and guaranteed hunting, fishing, and other rights, but was routinely violated and ignored first by the English and then by Canada (2000, 122). Stressing the inequity and cultural presumption of such a transaction, and the transition of the Mi'kmaq "from owners / to wards of the selfish state," Marshall provides a stern reminder, "The cost of keeping us does / not reflect the real cost" (1997, 50). Addressed to a grandson, "Now It's Your Turn" laments both the decimation of natural resources and the loss of autonomy; the speaker laments that "I can't walk more / than fifteen minutes" without being "reminded by a sign that this / land is no longer ours to do / with as we see fit" (62). As with many of Marshall's poems, though, the tone is, if not optimistic, at least not resigned or defeated, as the speaker exhorts his grandson, "Make me a promise that you will / not let us lose any more. / The land that is gone stays gone" (62). Likewise, the haunting emptiness of "No Match for Steel"—in the midst of which is "[a] bow with broken sinew / laid quiet, no match for steel"—is dispelled at the end of the poem, as "[a] scream of life echoes within / a new wi'kuom, bouncing off the faces / of skin and granite, dispersing to a / forest reborn" (40).

Marshall's attentiveness to contemporary concerns and injustices is similarly acute. Reminiscent of King's deconstruction of caricatures of Aboriginal peoples in popular genres such as Westerns, Marshall's "Save the Last Bullet" playfully contemplates "[t]he monosyllabic dialogue / of unionized Mediterraneans / riding against the Duke," who, affirming the untrammeled barbarity of the enemy, cautions the obligatory imperiled damsel, "[s]ave the last bullet / for yourself, in case" (1997, 55). The poem ends more seriously, though, in considering the colonial imposition of the iconic Mount Rushmore in the Black Hills, "Sacred stone cut to provide / monumental caricatures / of men" where "**Consent forms [are] required to pray**" (55). Marshall's critical wit is also in evidence in his contemplation of a more local devastation, the quarrying of Matuesuey Kmtin, located near the Canso Causeway joining Cape Breton to the Nova Scotia mainland, in "Matuesuey Kmtin (Porcupine Mountain)." Witnessing the dwindling of the mountain as "bulk carriers ... / come seeking cargo to cover / the green with slabs of grey / in cities south and west," Marshall subversively considers resisting the posted warning, "**Turn Off All Radios / Danger / Blasting Area**," to reverse the mountain's fate. The poem ends

Section 2: "About as Far from Disneyland as You Can Possibly Get"

with Marshall self-reflexively resigned to the destruction of the mountain, lamenting that it is likely to endure only in

> obscure poems by an obscure poet
> who lacked the resolve to
> play his radio and sing along
> momentarily preventing its
> determined demise. (66)

Sustaining a more serious tone are a series of poems dealing with prominent cases of miscarriages of justice. "Forth and Back," for instance, although the reference is not explicit, is unmistakably addressed to jailed American Indian Movement activist Leonard Peltier. Peltier was arrested and subsequently convicted for the murder of two FBI agents during a tense standoff near the village of Oglala on the Pine Ridge Sioux reservation in South Dakota on 26 June 1975. Widely viewed as a political prisoner, Peltier has been in prison since 1977, his conviction having been upheld through an exhaustive series of appeals.[3] Marshall certainly takes that view of the treatment of Peltier, whom he imagines pacing like Nelson Mandela in "state-issued shoes," stoically persisting and resisting the temptation of despair: "Lesser men would have / worn their last necktie or / stood with one shoelace / still tied to the state-issued / shoe while the other ..." (1997, 22; Marshall's ellipsis). Closer to home, Marshall writes of the wrongful conviction of Donald Marshall Jr. in "They Took Your Word." Much more explicitly than Rita Joe, Marshall dramatizes the case as a wilful miscarriage of justice: "For four thousand days you knew. / We knew. / And they knew" (31). Marshall pays tribute to the resolute support of Donald Marshall's parents and the quiet resilience and integrity of "Junior" in the face of coercive attempts to extract from him false confessions of guilt. But he also pays tribute to Marshall's fortitude and courage in taking the cause of Native fishing rights all the way to the Supreme Court in a landmark case that was still in progress when *Clay Pots and Bones* was published. Thus Marshall writes, "We wait / and you wait again / for truth" (31).

Perhaps the most piercing poem in the collection, though, is "Brown Shoelaces," which considers the fate of Master Corporal Clayton Matchee, a Cree soldier with the Canadian Airborne Regiment in Somalia, who, along with part-Cree Trooper Kyle Brown, was charged with murder in the brutal beating death of Somali teenager Shidane Arone in 1993. While in custody, Matchee attempted suicide by strangling himself with his bootlaces. Although the attempt was unsuccessful, Matchee was left brain-damaged and later was pronounced unfit to stand trial. In the wake of the Department of National Defence's attempts to cover up the scandal—which prompted a federal commission and eventually led to the disbanding of the regiment—many suspected, however, that Matchee had had "assistance." In "Brown Shoelaces" Marshall actively considers that possibility. He highlights the contradictions in the case, such as the "brown shoelaces / for his black combat boots,"[4] wishing he could ask the unresponsive Matchee, "Did someone help you onto a chair / so your new laces could make / you airborne forever?" (Marshall 1997, 20). Alluding to the presence of self-identified white supremacists in the regiment, he draws attention to the tenuous position of Native soldiers in a highly racialized military environment: "Didn't he know that he, a Red man, / in their Aryan eyes is the low man?" (20). Sherene Razack argues that, although Brown and especially Matchee were the central participants in the beating, they were acting in a neo-colonial atmosphere which sanctioned physical abuse against Somalis. The trials of Brown and Matchee, she contends, effectively served to construct them "as the few bad apples in an otherwise good barrel" (2004, 89) and suppressed the "systemic racial underpinnings of the encounter between Somalis and Canadian troops" (115) that fostered and condoned such abuse. Razack points to the conspicuous imbalance of blame in the scandal, noting that the "white soldiers and leaders" involved "were cast as lesser players, guilty of negligence and poor leadership, if anything but not guilty of torture and murder" (89). In a similar vein, Marshall underscores the complicity of Matchee's superiors, their silent assent to his bearing the burden of guilt:

> Silence from Master Corporal Matchee,
> a temporary reprieve for those
> higher up the totem with maroon
> hats and hands that don't come clean. (Marshall 1997, 20)

As "Brown Shoelaces" in particular underscores, colonialism is not a thing of the past. One of the significant achievements of *Clay Pots and Bones* is that it stresses not only the material and cultural devastation wrought by colonialism historically but also its continuing reverberation in and constraining of the lives of Mi'kmaq and other Aboriginal peoples across, and outside, the country.

The experience of people of African heritage on the East Coast likewise illustrates how, as Carol Talbot observes, "the term 'visible minority' is a misnomer" (quoted in Clarke 2002, 35). The overwhelming emphasis on the European heritage of the region tends to obscure the long presence of Black people, both those brought in as slaves and those who came as free men and women. The arrival of Blacks in Canada likely dates back to the early seventeenth century (Mensah 2002, 44), and waves of immigration after the American Revolution and again after the War of 1812 consolidated the presence of Black people on the East Coast, principally in Nova Scotia. As a result of broken promises, economic competition, and racism, they tended to be pushed to the margins—given poor land on the edge of or away from white communities. A "'place' had been established for blacks, and it was limited to the lowest paid and least secure fields of employment" (Walker 1986, 99). From the beginning, in other words, they were not embraced as members of the burgeoning colonies on Canada's East Coast, and their continued effacement not just in Folk archetypes of Atlantic Canada but also in the broader cultural profile of the region reflects the persistence of that divisive historical legacy. George Elliott Clarke, for instance, points to how he grew up in a culture in which the presence of African Canadians in Nova Scotia was thoroughly erased: "Official—tourist brochure—Nova Scotian culture consisted of kilted lasses doing Highland flings to ecstatic fiddle accompaniment, or of hardy, stolid fishermen—or sailors— perishing amid the heaving North Atlantic waves, or of 'folkloric' Acadians pining for exiled 'Evangeline' in their 'picturesque' villages" (2002, 3).

Over the last forty years, however, that situation has changed considerably. Beginning in the 1970s, there has been a pronounced consciousness-raising and an outpouring of cultural activity in the Black community in Nova Scotia and more broadly in the Maritimes. Central to this revival was the resettlement and razing of Africville, a Black neighbourhood on the Bedford Basin on the edge of the city of Halifax in the mid-1960s. The fate of Africville dramatized the marginality and political vulnerability of Black people in the region and galvanized them to a greater level of social, political, and artistic self-assertion. Other factors, Clarke argues, played a role in what has come to be seen as the Black Renaissance in Nova Scotia. As Alexander MacLeod has demonstrated, the indefatigable Clarke, in his multiple capacities as academic, activist, poet, dramatist, and novelist (to name a few), has almost single-handedly given a national literary presence to the imagined community he calls Africadia—a term giving a kind of territorial or state identity to "the Black populations of the Maritimes and especially of Nova Scotia" (Clarke 1992b).[5] His work is but the nationally visible edge of a flowering of literary activity that includes the work of Maxine Tynes, Walter Borden, George Boyd, and many others.

Although the concerns and interests of writers of African heritage in the Maritimes are diverse and wide-ranging, the epochal event at the heart of that body of work is unquestionably the relocation and destruction of the community of Africville. The fate of Africville is not simply one of those cultural erasures, as Clarke's comments suggest, an instance of how the experience of Black people in Nova Scotia is excluded from monolithic images of Nova Scotian cultural identity. It also represents, within the Folk paradigm, a substantial irony: the steamrolling by modernity of a community that came much closer to the Folk ideal than did the contemporary, mainstream culture from which it was excluded. In that sense, representations of the history and destruction of Africville have a doubly subversive effect, drawing attention not only to the problematic exclusiveness of Folk stereotypes of Nova Scotian culture but also to the very illusory nature of those stereotypes by exposing the hegemonic modernity that they conceal.

Analyzing the city's decision to relocate the residents of Africville and to bulldoze the community, Donald Clairmont and Dennis Magill highlight city representatives' oscillation between a development model emphasizing urban renewal and real estate concerns, and a liberal welfare model emphasizing the improvement of living conditions and social integration. They argue that the development model ultimately held sway, especially because of inadequate appreciation of the social and historical value of the community and inadequate follow-up on promises made to relocatees. City representatives and others, they contend, saw Africville as a blight to be erased and soon to be forgotten. However, precisely the opposite has happened, because Africville has become a crucial focus of Black cultural consciousness in Nova Scotia. Rather than an urban slum that was demolished to make way for progress, they note, since the early 1980s Africville has been reconceived as a source of pride "and even an heroic community since its people struggled against so much racism and neglect" (Clairmont and Magill [1974] 1999, 283).

A substantial part of that redefining has been conducted by Afro-Nova Scotian cultural producers—filmmakers, poets, playwrights, and novelists. Writers such as Clarke, Tynes, Boyd, Charles Saunders, and Frederick Ward have resurrected and consecrated Africville, Moynagh argues in "Africville: an Imagined Community" (1998), as the focal point of Black nationalist consciousness in Nova Scotia. Boyd's play *Consecrated Ground*, first produced by Eastern Front Theatre in Halifax in 1999, territorializes this redefinition in its depiction of one family's struggle in the face of relocation. Through the divergent responses of his protagonists Willem and Clarice Lyle to the pressure to relocate, Boyd stages a debate over the meaning of Africville and theatrically endows the community with a sacred status.

One of the major points of contention in *Consecrated Ground* is responsibility for conditions in Africville, the deplorable state of which whites see as a reflection of the inhabitants themselves. Clairmont and Magill observe that "Africville was a depressed community both in physical and socio-economic terms. Its dwellings were located beside the city dump, and railroad tracks

Section 2: "About as Far from Disneyland as You Can Possibly Get"

FIGURE 6 Africville houses on either side of a hillside lane, seen from the opposite side of the railroad tracks.

cut across the one dirt road leading into the area. Sewerage, lighting, and other public services were conspicuously absent. The people had little education, very low incomes, and many were underemployed" ([1974] 1999, 1–2). But they also contend that conditions were such because of prejudice, historical neglect by the city, and, later, because the looming threat of relocation and development was a disincentive to home improvement. Africville was thus a particularly acute instance of how Blacks in Nova Scotia "were not, in general, so much subject to direct economic exploitation as to a 'definition of the situation' wherein they were regarded as marginals and outsiders and their deprivation was seen as the ordinary, although perhaps unfortunate, state of affairs"([1974] 1999, 51). Indeed, one of the central ironies of the fate of Africville in the context of Folk definitions of Nova Scotian culture is that the community was characterized by "a system of social relationships that can be described as communal, familistic, informal, primary, isolated, and sacred" (Clairmont and Magill [1974] 1999, 48). In short, as a community Africville more closely approximated the touted virtues of the Folk paradigm than did the mainstream culture that effectively destroyed it in the name of modernization, at the same time—as Ian McKay's study highlights—as Nova Scotians were already vigorously engaged in promoting Folk culture as a central attraction of the province.

A key aspect of *Consecrated Ground* is the characters' divergent reactions to this "definition of the situation," as Boyd participates in what Moynagh characterizes as "the re-mapping of Africville" (1998, 26). Willem, raised on a farm in the Annapolis Valley and used to a greater measure of autonomy, leans toward the city's definition and sees the relocation as an opportunity to escape a life of deprivation and dependence in Africville. As the community matriarch Sarah Lied points out to Tom Clancy, the social worker assigned to oversee the relocation, the lives of the residents are circumscribed by a demeaning reliance on whites for employment: "Most the womens be going to the south end to clean and scrub on their knees to make a few cents. The mens goin' almost all to pier nine. They waits in lines almost never to be picked for work. While the new white man who just showed up gets hired" (Boyd 2004, 162). Clarice, however, who has deep roots in Africville, clings to it as a source of community and identity, stressing that if Africville is a social problem, it is a problem of the city's own making: "Oh, I knows we got the dump and the abattoir and the prison and the little white racists tauntin' us. But 'member Willem, the white man put all that here. Not us. It was pushed in our faces. It a white stench" (166). For Willem, that whites are responsible for the state of Africville is not sufficient grounds to accept it, "'cause this Black man wants to do somethin' too. I wanna work, I want my chile to go to a decent school and I wanna live in a decent house—not some scraggily 'ol shack" (166). Through Clarice and Willem, Boyd conveys the diversity, rather than unanimity, of reaction to the relocation, as well as the potential complicity of some of the residents in the ultimate fate of Africville.

Willem's amenability to relocation reflects his belief in the sincerity of the social worker's vision of relocation as the path to opportunity, a vision that is thoroughly compromised by the city's dubious commitment to the residents of Africville. The social worker Clancy is a key figure not only as the intermediary between the city and the community in the relocation negotiations but also because Boyd portrays him as the repository of the divergent and contradictory impulses of white authority. On the one hand, Clancy speaks the language of liberal improvement and racial reconciliation: "Now it's no longer acceptable to the City of Halifax that Negroes live in one place, Willem, and white people another" (175). As Clarice astutely argues, though, such apparent liberal idealism masks whites' arrogant presumption of the authority to tell Blacks how to live their lives even after restricting their opportunities to live otherwise. This arrogance is particularly evident after the death of the couple's infant son Tully, a victim of what Clairmont and Magill succinctly describe as the "[d]iscrimination by neglect" that characterized the city's treatment of Africville ([1974] 1999, 49); the baby dies after being attacked by the rats attracted to the dump, with no ambulance ready to come to his aid. When Clarice insists that Tully be buried in Africville, Clancy interjects to tell her bylaws require that he be buried in a cemetery in the city. While

Willem weakly acquiesces, Clarice is adamant in her resistance, highlighting the racist basis of authorities' presumptuous social engineering: "They play games and experiment with people's lives. They think they're God he's-self!! Live here! Bury them over there!! Well screw those white bastards and the train they rode in on!!" (Boyd 2004, 180).

In a rare editorial moment in their study of Africville, Clairmont and Magill observe that "the rhetoric of liberalism that accompanied the Africville relocation seemed empty, if not perverse" ([1974] 1999, 231). Boyd's portrait of the compromised social worker Tom Clancy conveys very much the same insight. Over the course of the play Clancy's liberal sympathies evaporate, and he comes to embody the expedient machinations of the city authorities. As he becomes familiar with the residents of Africville, Clancy recognizes the prejudiced views he had before being assigned to the case and questions his view of himself as heroic liberal reformer. In the wake of Tully's death and his realization that development is the city's main priority, he agonizes over the role he is playing in the demolition of Africville. Ultimately, though, Clancy's allegiance to the city proves stronger than his humanitarian impulse, signalled by the manner in which he plays divide-and-conquer with Willem and Clarice and by his callous resistance to Clarice's desire to bury her son in Africville. Clancy convinces Willem, to whom Clarice has signed over title to the house, to sell out. Then, responding to Clarice's anger at his presumption in telling her where she can bury her son, he has the gall to reveal that Willem has sold out by disingenuously accusing Clarice of hypocrisy. By the end of the play, he is the impersonal, unfeeling, racist voice of capitalist modernity. He informs Willem that they are no longer eligible to relocate to a housing project in Uniacke Square, because Tully's death means they are no longer a family according to white bureaucracy. In this fashion, he drives Willem and Clarice apart, symbolizing the social and emotional damage done to the community by the relocation.

Consecrated Ground resists this relentless and remorseless discourse of modernization, renewal, and progress. At the heart of Boyd's play is the redefinition of Africville as a sacred space, the "consecrated ground" of the title. For Reverend Miner, the spiritual leader of the community, the idea of consecrated ground is associated with the church alone, and he is ready if not happy to accede to the process of relocation as long as the church, which he sees as the spiritual emblem of the middle passage and the symbolic residue of the community, is spared demolition: "Africville will never die. In this church, our soul shall live" (Boyd 2004, 170). Clancy, though, is subsequently compelled to reverse his position after Clarice's insistence on

"The Simpler and More Colourful Way of Life"

FIGURE 7 Two Halifax city officials walking up an Africville path, with several houses beyond them and Seaview Baptist Church in the background.

burying Tully in Africville threatens to obstruct the city's industrial vision. The social worker sheepishly confesses to the Reverend that the church is to be torn down after all because the city wants the site for harbour frontage and approach ramps for the proposed bridge, and they "don't want people seeing a grave site" (183). Willem adopts the fatalistic stance that "[i]f the city wants our land, they're gonna take it and it don't matter what the nigger wants" (182). Clarice, though, incensed by such racist expediency, defies the white man's power to define. Evoking the long communal history of Africville, she expands the notion of consecrated ground to encompass the entire community:

> What is Africville if it ain't consecrated ground, Willem? (beat) This land been in my family for years, hundreds a years.... My ancestors, they consecrated this ground.... the kids laughing and playin' in Kildare Field consecrated it! The funerals, the hymns at the church, consecrated it.... All the baptisms down at the beach, Willem, they consecrated this ground. This is where they lived and died.... Surely no one, ain't nobody on this-here earth tellin' me Africville ain't no consecrated ground!! Ain't no Mister-Clancy-city-white-man tellin' me. I saw it ... I lived it ... I loved it ... Africville is consecrated ground!! (180; italics in original)

Section 2: "About as Far from Disneyland as You Can Possibly Get"

This subversive reconceptualization of Africville, which forecasts its redefinition decades later as the focal point of the Black cultural renaissance in Nova Scotia, is ritually confirmed in the final scene of *Consecrated Ground*. Willem, spurned and chastened by Clarice, returns during the memorial service for Tully. He takes the coffin outside the church, sets it on the ground, and starts to cover it with the soil of Africville. Clarice and the Reverend join him in this act of defiance, and the closing of the Reverend's eulogy symbolically reconfigures Africville itself as "consecrated ground": "I do consecrate this holy ... and sacred ground and do bless the small soul that lives herein to eternal and everlasting life in the name of Jesus Christ Our Lord, amen" (191). The play thus becomes a metaphor for the symbolic, retroactive resistance of the Black community to the demolition of Africville. In light of the artistic, political, spiritual, and cultural significance that Africville has accrued in the forty or so years since the relocation program, Boyd's play is a kind of theatrical annunciation of what Africville has become to the Black community in Nova Scotia, if not Canada as a whole.

If *Consecrated Ground* concentrates on what Clarke calls "the crucifixion of Africville" (2002, 115), Maxine Tynes celebrates the resurrection of the community signalled at the end of Boyd's play. Although Tynes's poetry routinely engages with the history, heritage, and sense of community of Black people in Nova Scotia and beyond, Marjorie Stone stresses the importance of keeping in view the multiple constituencies and identities that Tynes's poetry invokes, "the pluralities of otherness that constitute her poetic identity and the identities of her diverse communities of readers" (1997, 256)—the concerns of gender, race, class, and physical ability to which her poetry speaks. As a series of poems dealing with Africville in her 1990 collection *Woman Talking Woman* reflects, though, an important component of that multiplicity is the legacy of Africville. In these poems, Tynes reflects how Africville, far from being erased, has not only persisted in memory but has become the central focus of Black nationalist consciousness in Nova Scotia. Moreover, Tynes reconfigures the nostrum that the local is the global, linking the experience of Africville and Black Nova Scotians to the Black diaspora in North America and to Blacks around the world.

"Africville is dead! Long live Africville!" might be said to be the central message of the poems "Africville Spirit," "Africville Is My Name," and "Africville." As Tynes writes in "Africville Spirit," she grew up in Dartmouth "knowing about Africville and hearing / of Africville through the family talks / and from the Africville friends of my own folks" (Tynes 1990, 60). In "Africville," she evokes the sense of loss—"We mourn for the burial of our houses, our church, our roads" (62)—and speaks in the collective voice of the dispossessed, "creeping with pain away from our home / carrying, always carrying / Africville on our backs" (62). Similarly, "Africville Is My Name" combats the erasure of the community, employing anaphora to exhort others to preserve its memory,

> To voice its name with history and with pride.
> To map that community with a litany of community names.
> To raise the profile of that community,
> again and again. (61)

At the end of the poem, Tynes leads by example, listing the names of the founders of the community and the family names of the residents of Africville. In "Africville," she gestures to the park that now exists at the former site of the community: "I am Africville / says a woman, child, man at the homestead site" (62). All three poems contribute to Tynes's objective "To etch Africville into the Past, the Present, and relentlessly / into the Future" (61). As Moynagh observes, in representations of Africville there is a tension between a postlapsarian, idyllic vision of the community and a celebration of Africville as eternal; this tension can be seen "as a death and a rebirth, and … thereby a means not only of reclaiming the Africville that was, but of imagining its significance for future political action." She contends that "[t]he Africville that serves as the founding myth of an Africadian nationalism emerges from and contributes to the new symbolic significance Africville acquired among African-Nova Scotians *after* relocation" (1998, 28; italics in original).

A central strategy that Tynes employs in these poems is that she deterritorializes Africville, evoking it as a sense of heritage and community that, unlike its physical counterpart, cannot be demolished. Africville, Tynes suggests in "Africville," is resurrected and lives on in those who carry its memory,

> I talk Africville
> to you
> and to you
> until it is both you and me
> till it stands and lives again (Tynes 1990, 62)

Africville thus comes to transcend physical space—"No house is Africville. / No road, no tree, no well" (62)—and to represent instead a persistence of spirit, a less territorially circumscribed sense of community. In Tynes's evocation of the signal importance of Africville to the cultural consciousness of Black people, that sense of community extends beyond the local to include the experiences of Blacks worldwide. Tynes emphasizes that Africville lives on in the hearts and minds of Black Nova Scotians but also in the wider Black diaspora: "Africville is man/woman/child / in the street and heart Black Halifax, / the Prestons, Toronto" (62). "Africville Is My Name" deploys nationalist tropes as Tynes rallies her audience "To sing, to say, to shout the names of Africville like a map, / like a litany, like a hymn and a battle-cry, / like a flag and a constitution" (61). Her vision in "Africville Spirit," however, works to dispel the boundaries that such a nationalist apparatus suggests. Here Tynes insists on the need to acknowledge "Black community and to own community and all Black experience. / That there are no borders, no boundaries, no frontiers that matter / in the Diaspora" (60). Because oppression, disenfranchisement, and racism are universal experiences, "Soweto is Chicago is Toronto / is Detroit is Montreal is New York is Halifax and Dartmouth is / Africville" (60). As Fuller puts it, "Tynes not only situates Africville at the centre of her personal experience, but also, in her rejection of colonialism's geopolitical borders and maps, she relocates the personal and collective experience of Africville to the centre of her diasporic vision" (2004b, 189).

Representations of Africville by Afro-Nova Scotian writers, Moynagh argues, resist a "state-sponsored" vision of a particular and exclusive kind of imagined community, "not only by rewriting particular elements of the antimodern vision of the quest of the folk, but more generally by disrupting the conventional homogeneity of imagined communities through a foregrounding of the competition over the way a community is imagined" (1998, 30–31). In "contesting hegemonic representations of Africville," these writers run the risk of asserting an illusory homogeneity and harmony—of replicating the cultural airbrushing of Folk discourse—but, Moynagh contends, "to the extent that this unity is scripted as a political strategy in response to disenfranchisement, exclusion and dispossession, it simultaneously refuses to become fixed as an identity" (1998, 31). In "The Birth and Rebirth of Africadian Literature," Clarke likewise evokes the destruction of Africville as a kind of phoenix narrative, and points to its central role in cultivating the Black Renaissance that followed: "If all art is a cry for identity, that cry, for Africadians, became much more urgent after the martyrdom of Africville" (2002, 116). But if the fate of Africville has a central place within Afro-Nova Scotian literature in that sense, that literature nonetheless goes well beyond its boundaries, nor does it dwell solely on what Clarke describes in his introduction to *Fire on the Water* as the "apocalyptic" in the experience of Africadians, that which entails "the denial or destruction of identity" (1991, 22). Instead, Clarke stresses here the fact that "Africadian" writers are more affirmative than negative; "they treat racism as another calamity—like death, taxes, and natural disasters" and instead "are more interested in affirming Black presence, Black dignity, and Black identity against a deracinating and sometimes murdering society which seeks to deny their right to be" (25).

This balance can be seen in Clarke's own work, such as in the celebration in his debut collection *Saltwater Spirituals and Deeper Blues* (1983) of the achievement of the African United Baptist Church in Nova Scotia. One of the major problems with Black history in the Maritimes, James St. G. Walker contends, is that it "has often been presented as a story of degradation," which denies "the internal dynamics of the black communities, and ... reinforce[s] the notion that all historical trends of any significance have been established by whites," or as the story of "exceptional individuals who rarely represent the black experience generally" (1986, 102), an approach which "tends to underemphasize the community existence and collective endeavour which has characterized so much of black history" (103). That sense of collective endeavour is the animating spirit of the "Soul Songs" series of *Saltwater Spirituals*, in which Clarke, engaging in a kind of spiritual geography, maps in verse the archipelago of African Baptist churches around Nova Scotia. No sepia-toned poetic postcards, these lyrics evoke the local geography and genealogy of churches from Sydney to Amherst to Liverpool, as well as the history of slavery and the struggle against racism that they embody. This history is succinctly evoked in "Amherst African Methodist Episcopal Church," where

> under the tombstones
> and foundations
> ... worms work out a final solution
> to the problems of race. (Clarke 1983, 19)

Furthermore, in some poems Clarke also situates those churches in a contemporary social and economic context. In "Campbell Road Church," for instance, "an ancient, CN porter lusts for africville," raging in his recollection "to protest his home's slaughter / by butcher bulldozers / and city planners molesting statistics" (15). The speakers of "Liverpool United Baptist Church" are beset not so much by the raging elements as by their employer, National Sea Products Limited, which "chains bitter-keen winds to our hearts, / batters us with wrecking storms and debt" (20). To try to put their burdens

Section 2: "About as Far from Disneyland as You Can Possibly Get"

behind them, they "go to a charmless chapel / of birch benches and hard sermons" (20), but still

> national sea products limited
> shackles the deeps to our eyes
> clamps the storm-winds to our ears,
> fetters us to death by water
> or by exposure to banks and trusts. (20)

At the same time, Clarke clearly celebrates these churches as a testament to survival and cultural vitality, a signal achievement of a people pushed to the margins, starved of resources, and oppressed by a racist mainstream society ready to blame them for their state of deprivation.

A similar celebration of survival and a singular example of the exuberance and vitality of the Black Renaissance in Nova Scotia is Clarke's *Whylah Falls* ([1990] 2000), a vibrant evocation of life in a rural Black community in the Annapolis Valley during the interwar years. The world of *Whylah Falls* is a sensory cornucopia of passion, food, music, natural beauty, and fervent faith, and the rural intimacy of Clarke's characters brings to mind the elemental, communal autonomy of the Folk paradigm in many ways. This impression is reinforced by the central narrative thread of *Whylah Falls*, the pastoral romance between the returned prodigal poet Xavier Zachary (X) and the comely Shelley Clemence, and by myriad evocations of the pastoral beauty of the Annapolis Valley as an idyllic setting for romance and passion.

However, for various reasons the denizens of Whylah Falls are not the self-contained, happy peasants of the Folk paradigm. First of all, they are hardly sealed off from history and the outside world. Their link to the wider Black diaspora, for instance, is signalled by the blues, jazz, and gospel music that is evoked at every turn in the collection: Ma Rainey, Billie Holiday, Leadbelly, and so on. Pablo Gabriel, the suitor of Shelley's sister Amarantha, is a Cuban exile who has migrated to Canada seeking "a gentler imperialism, a haven for imagination" (Clarke [1990] 2000, 77), and X (Xavier) returns from exile brimming with the echoes of European modernism. Culturally, they are clearly citizens of the twentieth century. Furthermore, beyond the immediate demands of their daily lives is their awareness of looming historical events such as the rise of Fascism in Europe: "The newspaper scares me with its gossip of Mussolini and the dead of Ethiopia / The radio mutters of Spain and bullets. / Only the Devil ain't tired of history" (92).

Most importantly, they are not the autonomous, happy-go-lucky souls of the Folk paradigm because they are hemmed in by the dominant society. If Whylah Falls in many respects is a pastoral paradise, it is also "a snowy, northern Mississippi" (xxvii), where the sexual, political, and working lives of Clarke's characters are impinged upon in various ways by the presence of the Man. Hovering over them are exploitative white politicians who trade empty promises for votes, about whom Shelley's mother Cora cautions, "[t]he road to Hell is paved before elections" (165). Self-reliance is a challenge in an economy dominated by whites, where punitive labour is usually the only option. Shelley's father Saul, for instance, is ruined from spending fifty years "stooped in a damp, vicious cave, dark with smoke and tuberculosis, shovelling gypsum just for the pennies to fix one's shoes" (33). Shelley herself, if "she takes the Liberal Party leaflet" handed to her, is allowed to ride in Jack Thomson's "smelly truck" to work in a fish plant, "tough labour for one cent per pound of gutted fish. That's all they get. Where else can they go?" (81).

Indeed, the crisis of *Whylah Falls*, the murder of Shelley's brother Othello, is the result of the machinations of "Ex-MP Jack Thomson" (119), who, lusting after Amarantha, convinces Scratch Seville that Othello is "sniffing around [Seville's] little pussy, Angel" (111). Scratch blows a hole in Othello's stomach with a shotgun, though it turns out that it is Jack himself, as Othello posthumously reports, "who was screwing Seville's old lady" (121). Although the murder of Othello does not come across as explicitly racialized, it is based on the highly racialized killing of a Black man named Graham Cromwell near Digby in 1985, and the institutional prejudices that the case exposed percolate through *Whylah Falls*. Thirty-two-year-old Cromwell of Weymouth Falls was shot in the thigh by a white acquaintance and crawled into the middle of the highway, where he died. Claiming self-defence, Jeffrey Mullen was acquitted by an all-white jury, a verdict which Clarke says "has not been, and never will be, accepted popularly as having been just" (1992a, 23). Particularly because of irregularities in the conduct of the trial and because of the Nova Scotia Attorney General's dismissive response to their concerns, the decision galvanized the Black community to protest racial biases in the Nova Scotia justice system (see Clarke 2007b, 137–38). This contemporary scandal resonates throughout the interwar narrative of *Whylah Falls*; Cromwell's fate is clearly echoed as Othello, "a puckered hole / In his stomach, stops on bloodied gravel / While silence whines in the legislature" (Clarke [1990] 2000, 114). The sense that the trial of Cromwell's killer was a travesty is signalled in "This World Is Passing Away": "In court, Scratch joked, / 'Self-defence.' His white-wash jury guffawed" (122). Clarke's anger over the case is reflected in a parodic article on Othello's murder in the fictitious *Whylah Moon*, in which it is reported that "Mr. Justice Pious Cutthroat of the Nova Scotia Supreme Court" granted Seville bail, "noting the background of the case indicated the victim had been an 'evil drunk'" (118), echoing a comment made by the trial judge in the Cromwell case as

Section 2: "About as Far from Disneyland as You Can Possibly Get"

part of a pattern in which the deceased himself seemed to be the one on trial (Clarke 1992a, 18–19).

Despite the pastoral beauty of the Annapolis Valley of *Whylah Falls* and the (mostly) easygoing hedonism of Clarke's characters, then, the community does not have the luxury of the self-sufficiency of the Folk because of their situation within oppressive political, social, and economic relations. These relations not only define in a broader sense the hardscrabble lives of the people of Whylah Falls—such as the abusive behaviour of Saul Clemence to his wife and daughter—but more directly are reflected in the injustices dramatized by the murder of Othello Clemence. At the same time, the affirmative ending of *Whylah Falls* suggests that Clarke's characters are survivors, and the verbal ebullience and fragile beauty of their world serve as a testament to the resilience and vigour of the rural culture of "Africadia."

Writing of the Maritimes, David Creelman rightly argues that "commentators have spent more time attending to the groups of British origin that have historically dominated the region," that is, "the populations that have descended from English, Loyalist, Irish and Scottish ancestors" (2003, 6). The effect of this concentration on the dominant culture is that the diversity of the region has been overlooked. "If these essentialist perceptions are set aside," Creelman contends, "discrete cultural patterns gradually become evident as we examine how particular groups experience distinct changes, absences, losses, and fragmentations" (2003, 6). However, Creelman's conclusion that "diversity and change are the most distinctive marks of the Maritimes" (6), seems a bit of a leap, overstating rather than understating the cultural heterogeneity of the region. If writing in Atlantic Canada— reflecting the demographic mix in the region—is not as "monochromatic" as is often assumed, it still is more monochromatic than the literature of most, if not all, of the rest of the country. Creelman nonetheless contributes to a necessary perceptual readjustment, countering a stereotype of the East Coast as culturally and ethnically homogeneous, part of an ideological arsenal that serves to construct the region as behind the times and out of step with a multicultural, progressive, and globalizing national culture. As Fuller argues, "[t]he work of Atlantic writers challenges the perception that Atlantic Canada must be culturally homogeneous because the region's present-day immigration levels are low compared to levels in other parts of the country" (2004b, 36). At the same time, while stressing the increasing multiculturalism of Atlantic-Canadian literature, it is important to keep in view the ways in which, as Eva Mackey has argued, the embrace of multiculturalism in Canada serves to mask the construction of a hierarchy between "a dominant and supposedly unified, white, unmarked core culture" and implicitly subordinate "fragments of folk 'multicultures.'" This move cultivates "a situation in which those who share in the white unmarked core culture conceive of themselves as 'real' and 'authentic' Canadians, who tolerate and even celebrate the 'colour' and 'flavour' of multicultural 'others'" (2002, 153).

In this region are many women

Another problem with the Folk paradigm, argues Ian McKay, is that it cultivates the illusion of a harmonious social order rooted in traditional, patriarchal relations and thus is "deeply attractive to anyone with an interest in evading the twentieth century's difficult politics of gender" (1994, 264). Much of the recent writing by women in the Atlantic region contests this vision of harmony and the uneven distribution of power and mobility, both in the past and the present. In various ways, the work of writers such as Lynn Coady, Sheree Fitch, M.T. Dohaney, Wendy Lill, and many others not only defies the restrictive boundaries of the Folk paradigm's subordinating vision of women but also challenges the prerogatives of male power.

Certainly one of the key challenges has been to the notion of the "hearth" as a comfortable and natural place for women. Instead, contemporary women writers in the region have often highlighted how the home is potentially stifling, oppressive, and threatening. A good example is the series of poems titled "In this house are many women" in Sheree Fitch's collection of the same name. This opening suite of *In This House Are Many Women* (1993) consists of short, lyric pieces in the voices of those who work in, live by, or take refuge in a women's shelter. Leavened by anger, humour, and humanity, these poems explore, from a series of angles, what continues to be one of the principal social divides and "one of the worst expressions of men's abusive power over women" (Currie 1992, 216), not least in Atlantic Canada. The opening poems chronicle the fevered and agonized exodus to the shelter, "a womb / of many rooms" (Fitch 1993, 20). "What Rhoda Remembers About the First Five Minutes" describes one woman's hesitation on the threshold of refuge: "an intercom voice asking: who is there / wanting to say me just me / choking on my name" (21). "Filling Out the Form" (23) gives concrete form to the shattered, scattered state of mind encountering the unaccommodating order of bureaucracy (see Figure 8).

"Jane's Observation Notes" and "Barbara" explore the shelter from the perspective of the women who work there. In "Barbara" the speaker intervenes to stop a twelve-year-old boy from pounding his sister and lays down the law of the house when his mother slaps him for being saucy and kicking

Section 2: "About as Far from Disneyland as You Can Possibly Get"

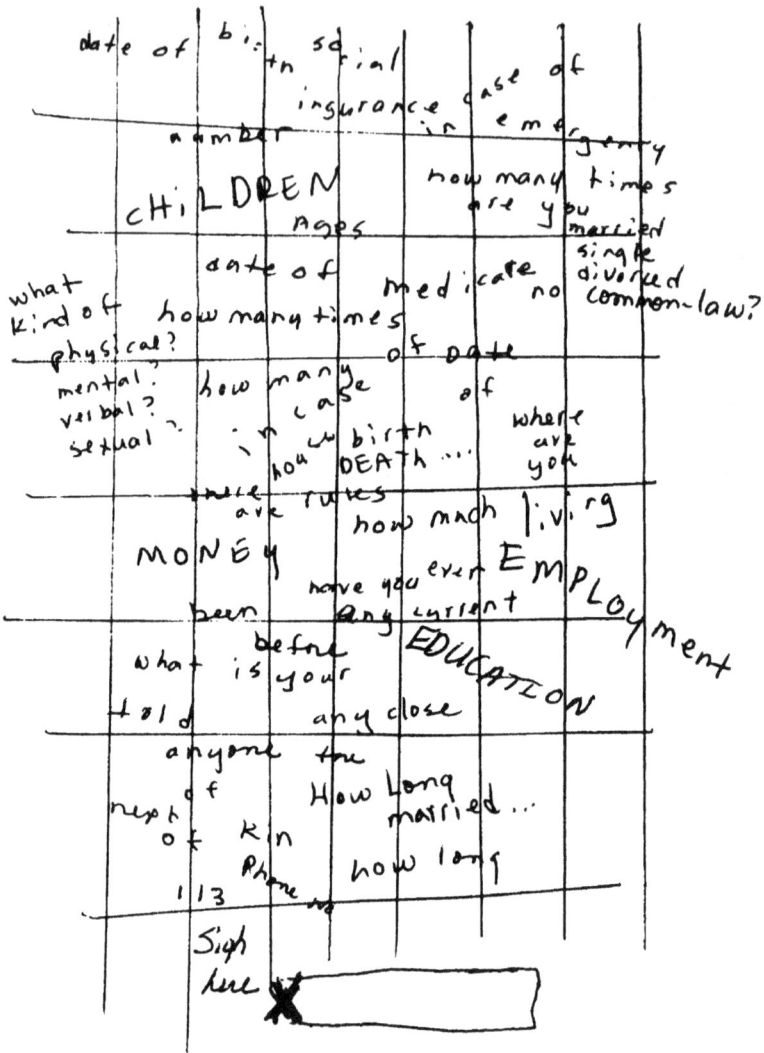

FIGURE 8 Sheree Fitch, "Filling Out the Form."

her, actions that highlight the psychic toll of living in a physically abusive environment:

> hitting and name-calling
> not allowed
> house rules
> they both looked
> relieved (31)

Here as elsewhere in these poems, the domestic crises from which these women have fled remain largely implicit, a strategy that, Fuller points out, serves to emphasize how the women are "survivors rather than victims" (2004b, 205).

According to Andrea Currie, "[f]or most residents and ex-residents, getting a job and improving their standard of living ... are their most immediate goals" (1992, 222), and *In This House Are Many Women* emphasizes the atmosphere of collective humour and support in which the women struggle to reconstruct and improve their lives. In "The Fashion Show," for instance, the women collaborate to dress up Rhoda, "whose skin is sallow / whose hair has been / tangled since she first came in" (Fitch 1993, 37–38), for a coming job interview. After her "metamorphosis," Rhoda softly intones, in a voice "filled with thistles / ... / well sir my qualifications are / fuck all" (38). After "squeals of laughter" (38), the women

> gather at the table once again
> tell their horror stories
> sometimes
> holding each other (39)

"If I do say so myself" evokes the modest hopes for recovery and independence, as the speaker bids "farewell / to / welfare" and hello to a minimum-wage job slinging "stickinlickinchicken": "soon I'll have enough / for a down payment / on a mobile home" (40). A more substantial hope—and one that underpins the whole suite of poems—is articulated at the end of the final poem, "Marie's Lullaby," in which Marie

> pray[s] that someday
> in this house of many women
> there will not be
> any women (44)

Here Fitch seems to echo Currie's contention that the "issue of battering must be viewed in the larger context of women's equality" (1992, 229) and not just as the product of "a 'deviant,' 'bad' relationship" (217).

Fitch's vision of the domestic order stands in dramatic contrast to the traditional regional image of the home place as a nurturing environment. This more positive view, as Gwendolyn Davies rightly argues, is a key trope in Maritime literature, an image emerging in the 1920s and rooted in "social, economic, and cultural realities on the east coast that distinguish it from similar images in other areas of Canada" (1991, 193). "[T]hroughout the

Section 2: "About as Far from Disneyland as You Can Possibly Get"

outmigration and declining economic and political influence" of the rest of the century, the image of the home place "has continued ... to illuminate Maritime literature with a sense of cultural continuity and psychological identification" (Davies 1991, 199). With Ian McKay's critique of the Folk paradigm in mind, Davies concedes that the pastoral and nostalgic resonances of this image render it susceptible to charges of romanticism, but argues that "to dismiss this literature as static, merely the product of middle class romanticization, is to ignore the elements of realism, irony, and economic cynicism permeating much of it" (1996, 196). In *Writing the Everyday: Women's Textual Communities in Atlantic Canada*, though, Fuller echoes Ian McKay in extending a similar skepticism about exclusionary and essentialist constructions of regional identity to the idea of the home place. Fuller argues that Atlantic women writers "tend to debunk nostalgic and romantic notions of home as the products of privilege or the reluctance to accommodate cultural change" (2004b, 34) and underlines that the home place is often the site of physical and emotional conflict (33–34). Fuller is suspicious of the implications of traditional constructions of literary regionalism for women because they "do not allow us to understand regions as differentiated spaces, and they encourage critics to select texts that fall into a narrowly defined aesthetic" (2004b, 37). Instead, Fuller adopts a "strategic regionalism" that emphasizes the networks of relationships within which women write but also articulates the "common grounds, intra-class and cross-racial alliances that are informed and made possible by subordinate (non-elite) knowledges of economic marginality, geographic isolation, and various forms of social exclusion" (2004b, 38). Fuller's notion of "strategic regionalism" nicely articulates the gendered politics of *Strange Heaven* (1998), Lynn Coady's debut novel about a Cape Breton teenager who returns from a spell in a psychiatric ward to her "cuckoo's nest" of a family after giving up her baby for adoption. Coady's *Bildungsroman* emphasizes the challenges of growing up female in a small Maritime community and dramatizes the patriarchal strictures that complicate the image of the home place as a nurturing environment for women.

To the degree that *Strange Heaven* portrays the traditional rural culture of Cape Breton, the novel emphasizes the way in which that culture is heavily gendered and affords males and females unequal degrees of agency and freedom—providing a distinct counterpoint to the predominantly male world of Alistair MacLeod's fiction. As Coady's narrator succinctly reflects about protagonist Bridget Murphy, "if she had been a boy it would have been more fun" (Coady 1998, 158). Bored by an adolescent female culture characterized by stuffed animals, talk of parties and proms, and the emotional melodrama of relationships, Bridget longs for her male cousins' culture of hunting and fishing. Bridget's physical and psychic development takes place within what

Judith Butler, in her characterization of gender as a kind of performance rather than an essential identity, describes as a tacit social agreement about what it means to be male or female, an agreement to be flouted at one's peril (Butler 1990, 140–41). In Coady's novel, the expectations that define the boundaries of gendered identity are reinforced by Bridget's father Robert and his ham-handed attempts at socialization, reflected in his choice of religious icons for his children: "Her father had this idea that girls liked Mary and boys liked Jesus just as girls liked Barbies and boys liked G.I. Joes" (1998, 117). Such rigid gender divisions frustrate Bridget's spiritual as well as social development. As a young girl, the enthusiastic and knowledgeable Bridget not only wants to become a Catholic priest but also aspires to be John the Baptist and ultimately Jesus. At a young age, she is reassured by a kindly priest that "she could do no wrong in the eyes of Jesus because she was a child." With puberty, however, comes the Fall. Seeing "her parents' horror, Gerard's disgust," Bridget realizes that "she had left the state of grace and could get away with nothing any more" (157). Reconceptualizing gendered identity as a performative effect, Butler argues, is necessary to open up "possibilities of 'agency' that are insidiously foreclosed by positions that take identity categories as foundational and fixed" (1990, 147), and Bridget's dilemma in *Strange Heaven* is rooted precisely in such a foreclosing of possibilities.

The crisis of identity around which the novel revolves comes when this fall from grace is completed by Bridget's pregnancy. She feels even more betrayed by her body and is forced by her mother to give up her baby for adoption. Having weathered the psychologically abusive and volatile behaviour of her boyfriend Mark prior to the pregnancy, Bridget afterward emotionally disengages herself from the past, and, suffering from post-partum depression, ends up in the psychiatric ward of the children's hospital because she is too young for the adult hospital. Here, Coady's hilarious but chilling portrait of an alienating, pathological, institutional culture evokes and alludes to Ken Kesey's *One Flew Over the Cuckoo's Nest*, Sylvia Plath's *The Bell Jar*, and Anthony Burgess's *A Clockwork Orange*, as Bridget struggles not only with her own ennui and her body's stubborn will to persist but also with the institution's perverse and arbitrary culture of surveillance, discipline, and rehabilitation.

One of the novel's central motifs is the implicit parallel between the bedlam of the psychiatric ward and the tumultuous atmosphere of the Murphy household. Bridget's obsessive-compulsive "retarded" uncle Rollie, her senile and demented grandmother Margaret P., and not least of all the profane and overbearing Robert combine to render *chez* Murphy a perfect "[g]oddamn cuckoo's nest"—as Robert himself mutters (Coady 1998, 133). For the traumatized and alienated Bridget, the Murphy home falls short (to say the least) of providing a nurturing, rehabilitative atmosphere. This is not, at first glance anyway, Davies's Maritime "home place," "a symbol of cultural continuity and psychological identification in the face of social fragmentation, outmigration, and a continuing hardscrabble economy" (1991, 194).

Rebellion against the mores of the family and the community has been a crucial feature of the *Bildungsroman*, and central to Bridget's development is the way in which she reaches the limits of an ostensibly rebellious adolescent culture that she ultimately finds unfulfilling and stifling. Throughout the novel, Coady develops a tension between the self-destructive inertia of Bridget's social circle and the chaotic climate of a household that drove her into the clutches of her peers in the first place. Resolving to opt out of the melodramatic, emotional politics that obsess her social circle, Bridget comes up against the conformist disapproval so familiar from other fictional portraits of Canadian small towns. As Bridget has come to realize, her peers' absorption in the personal lives of others is ultimately a question of social power and control: "People never want anything except to have power, and that's what knowledge about others gives them, or so they think" (Coady 1998, 120). Partly because it challenges their sense of self-importance and partly because Bridget's plight feeds her friends' craving for melodrama and excitement, opting out is difficult and unpopular.

The denial of Bridget's agency as a young woman gives an important twist to the familiar narrative of the sensitive protagonist's resistance to a suffocating small-town social order. Her pregnancy clearly confirms for Bridget that her attraction to Mark was merely a symptom of her own boredom. In turn, Mark's reaction to her rejection exemplifies the town's largely proprietorial and patriarchal attitude toward relationships. Already abusive and volatile before the pregnancy—he sees himself and Bridget as "the next Sid and Nancy" (159)—Mark becomes more belligerent and self-righteous upon Bridget's return from the hospital. His masculine pride has been wounded by Bridget's unilateral decision to give up the baby and by her apparent indifference to him, breaking the unwritten rule: "Everybody knew that the girl wasn't supposed to dump the guy after getting pregnant" (Coady 1998, 92). Bridget's sense of being scrutinized, assessed, and under surveillance is a crucial effect of the juxtaposing of her life inside and outside the institution. Just as Bridget was monitored, interviewed, and even videotaped in the hospital, after her release she is monitored both by her concerned family and the community at large, institutions similarly desiring to identify and regulate deviant behaviour. Such psychic discipline, distinctly grounded in patriarchal assumptions, has a potentially nasty edge in a climate where so many (including Mark and Bridget's father) are "eternally spoiling for a fight, a new enemy" (92). After friction had developed earlier in their relationship,

Mark had started essentially stalking Bridget, alternately making friendly phone calls and menacing ones, aggressively and self-righteously twisting Bridget's words in order to make her the aggrieving, and him the aggrieved, party. Bridget also describes how "sometimes she'd be on her way to bed and have almost all the lights turned out when she'd spot the double reflection of his glasses outside the front door" (44). After her return from the hospital, Bridget is keenly aware that she continues to be monitored, that her behaviour will be reported to Mark by their mutual acquaintances. The claustrophobia of such a tight circle of bored, sensation-seeking adolescents is complemented by the fishbowl quality of the town itself. Bridget is scrutinized, judged, and pitied as she eccentrically wades back and forth through the snowdrifts in the church parking lot "[j]ust for the hell of it" (137), and when she is forced to work in her family's store. She contemplates how in a small town "everybody knows your business" and keeps a mental file or "information roster" of the various inhabitants (180).

This impression of the small town as a variation on Michel Foucault's description of the panopticon—whose effect is "to induce in the inmate a state of conscious and permanent visibility that assures the automatic functioning of power" (1977, 201)—is consolidated by the staging of the climactic confrontation between Bridget and Mark during a power outage in the central and highly visible post office, temporarily illuminated by emergency lights. Mark claims to have been betrayed by Bridget and threatens to fight back, expressing his custodial rights in a patriarchal variation on the this-town-isn't-big-enough-for-the-two-of-us speech: "If Bridget thought she could live in the same town with him and do whatever she pleased and fuck around with the likes of Dan the big fat fairy Sutherland and Troy fucking Bezanson she was fucking crazy" (Coady 1998, 194). Bridget fleetingly wonders if she has underestimated Mark's commitment to the relationship, but the outcome of their altercation reveals that Mark's concern is not reconciliation but power. Infuriated by his self-righteous, patriarchal assumption that he "had a son" and that "Bridget had taken him away from him" (195), she finally and unequivocally repudiates Mark. While doing so, she ostensibly gives him the victory he is looking for by vomiting on the floor, a sign of weakness that concedes all that matters to him—her relative lack of power: "He wanted to be friends now. It had all been about winning. It had all been about making the woman puke" (196). Despite this apparent capitulation, however, the ultimate victory can be read as Bridget's. She had talked to Mark hoping that "if she could just stand there and listen for as long as it lasted, then maybe she wouldn't have to do it again" (194). Her physical punctuation of the exchange figuratively suggests that she has purged herself of him at last.

Section 2: "About as Far from Disneyland as You Can Possibly Get"

Bridget's extrication of herself from her oppressive relationship with Mark and their peer group, though, is coupled with a renewed understanding of her responsibility to and engagement with others. She realizes that her retreat from her family has been motivated by a myopic self-interest: "Wanting to be herself, wanting to be alone. That was selfish. You can't be that way when there is an old woman and her retarded son to look after" (Coady 1998, 144). The *Bildungsroman*, Franco Moretti notes, moves between "[s]elf-development and integration," which are "complementary and convergent trajectories, and at their point of encounter and equilibrium lies that full and double epiphany that is 'maturity.' When this has been reached, the narration has fulfilled its aim and can peacefully end" (1987, 18–19). In Coady's novel, the typical resolution and closure of the *Bildungsroman* come about through a rapprochement with the family. In that respect, the ending of *Strange Heaven* seems compatible with Davies's claim that an "'intensified realization' of self is what the 'home place' conveys in Maritime literature" (1991, 199). That reconciliation, however, more specifically takes the form of an identification with the resilient Margaret P., evoking Susan Fraiman's suggestion of an alternate resolution to the *Bildungsroman*, which is "to reconceive a girl's progress as the building of solidarity between women" (1993, 10). Nonetheless, in its underscoring of the patriarchal culture that limits Bridget's sense of agency, psychically and emotionally warping her, the novel reflects what Fuller describes as "a resistant regional sensibility, one that is ideologically opposed to regionalisms that represent social and cultural coherence where there is none, and that, by doing so, mask acts and articulations of protest" (2004b, 39).

Writing by women in Atlantic Canada, I have no hesitation to say, has never been more varied and robust.[6] From the formal innovation and technical prowess of poets like PEI's Anne Compton and Nova Scotia's Anne Simpson, to the charming, comic eccentricity of Newfoundlander Jessica Grant's debut novel *Come Thou, Tortoise* (2009), to the widely popular children's literature of New Brunswicker Fitch and the sophisticated young adult fiction of Nova Scotian Budge Wilson, women's writing in the region exhibits an impressive range and quality. This development reflects the broader gains achieved by women over the last forty years, but what is demonstrated by Fitch's *In This House Are Many Women* and Coady's *Strange Heaven*, as well as the work of Bernice Morgan, Lisa Moore, and Wendy Lill discussed in the previous section, is that women writers in Atlantic Canada are also aware of the continuing challenges women face not just in the region but also within the broader, neo-conservative political and economic climate in which many of those gains are increasingly coming under attack.

"The SImpler and More Colourful Way of Life"

IF ONE OF THE CULTURAL PITFALLS ON THE EAST COAST IS A TENDENCY TOWARD nostalgia, an inclination to see the past as more prosperous, less dependent, and a greater source of regional pride, contemporary writing by Native, Black, and women writers provides a timely reminder that the old days were not necessarily the good old days for everybody. There are obviously some important caveats to be attached to the contention that the twentieth century has marked a steady decline in the fortunes of those in the Atlantic provinces. While they have hardly reached the Promised Land, in many respects conditions and prospects for women and minorities have substantially improved. Indeed, this can be seen in the increasing visibility and influence of the writers themselves, which reflects changes in attitudes toward and in the material conditions of those previously disempowered, marginalized, and largely silenced groups. In other words, the recent proliferation of writing by Native people, people of African heritage, and especially by women is not the result of a belated, collective urge to pick up the proverbial pen, but the result of sustained and determined challenges to the monopolization of material opportunities and cultural power by an affluent, white, male elite. The cultural heterogeneity of the East Coast, such as it is, is not the product of recent immigration but a long-standing historical fact; thus the prevailing impression of the region as culturally homogeneous is an indication of the dominance of that elite. Likewise, the historical silence of women has not been a sign of their collective contentment to reside at the cultural, social, and political margins.

6 |

Rebuffing the Gaze

The work of Native, Black, and women writers in the Atlantic provinces increasingly serves to contest the prevailing power structures in the region, challenging the demographic and cultural hierarchy and exclusiveness of Folk stereotypes in the process. Another important strategy more and more evident in the literature of the East Coast is a conspicuously resistant, often subversive and parodic engagement with those cultural stereotypes, particularly as they are retailed by the tourism industry. Writers in the Atlantic provinces increasingly reflect a consciousness of the ways in which their region is framed through monolithic and constricting cultural stereotypes and the impact of those stereotypes on the region's self-image and on its relationship with outsiders.

Central to this cultural self-consciousness is a recognition of the implications of the growing role of tourism in an economically vulnerable region like Atlantic Canada. Although it has had its ups and downs, tourism has become "the single most important place-based industry" in Atlantic Canada (Bantjes 2004, 259), and has had a pronounced influence in various ways on cultural production in the region. As Rod Bantjes observes, all four provinces have been aggressively engaged in branding their provinces as leisure destinations:

> Newfoundland's marketing has less to do with culture than with Atlantic wilderness—icebergs, whales, and fjords. PEI, with its Anne industry and its island appeal to the Japanese, has unassailable product differentiation and access to a unique international market. Recent Nova Scotia and New Brunswick promotional campaigns focus on

ecotourism, whale watching, fine beaches, and eighteenth-century replica villages. (2004, 259)

The influence of tourism on cultural production can be seen in the conspicuous preoccupation with tourism itself in the literature of the region, which creatively dramatizes the cultural, political, social, and economic implications of the region's reliance on that industry. A central theme in the growing body of tourism theory that is particularly relevant to the Atlantic provinces is the structural relationship between tourism and economic underdevelopment. In other words, tourist destinations are more likely to develop as such not out of some ingrained sense of hospitality and instinctive inclination of host societies to share the bounty of their locale with others but out of economic necessity. Thus tourism, as Kevin Meethan points out, reconfigures "the boundaries between hospitality as a form of social obligation ... and hospitality as a commodified form" (2001, 149). Consequently, tourism (if not necessarily, then certainly commonly) is characterized by a fundamental tension: it requires a staged hospitality, an openness to visitors that, while potentially genuine, is also usually compelled to some degree. Rather than an innocent, free flow of people from one area to another, tourism involves a kind of coerced hospitality, with host societies compelled to go out of their way to cater to tourists' expectations and needs. Unsurprisingly, one result of such asymmetrical power relations is a resentment of and resistance to the material and symbolic imposition that tourism typically represents, a reaction increasingly visible in the literature of Atlantic Canada.

"The Maritime Way of Life"

If "resisting the outside gaze," as Christopher J. Armstrong maintains, is "central to the literary and cultural regionalism of Atlantic Canada" (2010, 43), a good example of the strategic and subversive engagement of regional stereotypes that this resistance entails is the subplot of Lynn Coady's *Strange Heaven*, which revolves around Bridget's relationship with Alan Voorland, an "adult" man from Guelph who works as an engineer at the local mill (Coady 1998, 32). The denizens of *Strange Heaven* are obviously a far cry from the simple, content, unreflective fisherfolk who are the staples of Folk ideology. However, Coady's depiction of an oppressive, patriarchal small town and the self-destructive adolescent histrionics its lack of opportunity breeds, lends itself to the flip side of the paradigm called Folk Innocence by Ian McKay: pervasive constructions of the East Coast as Canada's social, economic, and cultural basket case, populated by alcoholic deadbeats, welfare mothers, and rockbound trailer trash. However, Coady complicates the politics of this exposé of small-town claustrophobia through her portrait of Bridget's relationship with Alan, an outsider who wanders "around town examining and exclaiming at everything like an anthropologist" (32). The characterization of Alan highlights how Coady's strategic regionalism involves contesting the ways in which the region is constructed not only from within but also from without.

Through her portrait of Bridget and Alan's relationship, Coady turns back on itself the anthropological gaze that *Strange Heaven*'s dissection of the small town otherwise seems to invite. As a come-from-away, Alan, although working, is consciously transient, and his attitude is reminiscent of John Urry's description of the "tourist gaze": "When we 'go away' we look at the environment with interest and curiosity.... In other words, we gaze at what we encounter" ([1990] 2002, 1). Through Alan's commentary on the town, his parodic media discourse, Coady stresses his assumption of an ironic superiority to his surroundings that, for Alan, "were positively alien" (1998, 33). Although Bridget finds his posture amusing—"You sound like a newscaster" (33)—the tenor of his commentary is commensurate with negative stereotypes of the region so aptly summarized by then-Conservative leader Stephen Harper's infamous attribution of Atlantic Canada's troubles to the prevalence of a "culture of defeat" ("Negative Talk" 2002, A6). "Do not get me wrong," Alan tells Bridget. "This is a wonderful place, a fascinating people with a thriving, unique culture. And yet there is a sadness. A hopelessness about it all. The dependence on welfare, unemployment insurance. The bottle" (Coady 1998, 32).

Although Alan sees Bridget as a refreshing exception to his impression of Maritimers as evolutionary throwbacks, he nonetheless treats her as a regional novelty and employs the same commentator's voice in framing his interaction with her: "Here I am with Bridget Murphy.... A fascinating young lady" (32). Even his taking advantage of Bridget is ironically framed through, and associated with, the language of sensationalist media. "Here I am in love with pregnant teenager Bridget Murphy" (40) he intones, after he and Bridget make love in his Ford Escort. If Bridget is a novelty for Alan, however, the loquacious Alan is equally of interest to Bridget, who is used to a culture in which masculinity is consonant with monosyllabic reticence: "He talked just for the sake of talking, using words that weren't even necessary to get the meaning across. He may as well have had a horn coming out of his forehead" (34). Equally exotic are the images of an affluent, dynamic, middle-class Ontario with which Alan longingly regales Bridget, underscoring the culture of deprivation in Cape Breton: "To think of her and Alan and Deanna and all of Alan's cool buddies who worked in television and were photographers and played in rock and roll bands, real rock and roll bands, not George and Mark mangling Aerosmith in Chantal's living room" (39). Alan and Bridget's mutual attraction, in other words, is grounded in an exoticism born of both regional and class disparities.

Strange Heaven, however, provides a particularly regional variation on the old cliché that familiarity breeds contempt. The authority of Alan's reportorial stance, for instance, wavers as the "place that had once been so fascinating [loses] its rustic charm" (Coady 1998, 38) and as his distance from the subjects of his "field work" shrinks. Reporting that Mark, jealous of his friendship with Bridget, has been telephoning him as well, "Alan pursed his lips.... It was all too sordid. Tabloid news. Alan couldn't wait to go home" (40). Alan's simultaneous fascination with and revulsion toward his surroundings—his tabloid irony—is implicitly associated with the media's lurid coverage of the murder of Bridget's schoolmate Jennifer MacDonnell by her estranged boyfriend. The incident is sensationalized not just as an instance of adolescent violence—"there was a piece on the local news about violence in our schools, even though it happened outside of a donut shop" (11)—but also, in keeping with the concept of the Folk, as an instance of urban depravity migrating to the margins: "What was happening to the young people? This, according to the news, was what people of the area were asking themselves. It was because of television, and music, and videos. It was getting as bad as the city" (11). The murder further jars Alan out of his complacent anthropological detachment. Reflecting on how the murder happened near his apartment, Alan responds with mild hysteria: "'Oh, I want to go home,' he said, loudly and suddenly, not like he was reading the news" (39). Clearly, Alan's fascination with a "thriving, unique culture" imbued with a sense of disappointment and despair reflects another form of Folk Innocence, and his authoritative newscaster's tone falters when the proximity of the murder shatters that illusion and his sense of distance.

Unconsciously presuming superiority, Alan takes for granted Bridget's acquiescence to his critical perspective, and for the most part she passively demurs, mesmerized by his apparent sophistication. However, prior to his departure, the gulf between them—and, more broadly, the caricature of the East Coast as Canada's lumpenproletariat—is dramatized during a brief encounter with two stoned acquaintances of Mark and Bridget's. As the two emerge from their "basement shit-box," eyes "at half-mast" (Coady 1998, 91), Alan chirps "'How's she going?' ... stupidly imitating the local idiom," and then observes to Bridget, blithely unaware of the blanket condescension his comment entails, "I see even the Maritimes has white trash." Although Bridget says nothing in response, the insult registers all the same: "You have more or less just pissed on my flag, she might have said to him then" (92).

Nobody ever said federalism was easy, and the faltering romance at the heart of *Strange Heaven* dramatizes the undercurrent of ambivalent desire running through regional cultural politics in Canada. In "Books That Say Arse," her introduction to the anthology *Victory Meat: New Fiction from Atlantic Canada*, Coady could well be referring to Alan as she describes the fetishizing of the region by outsiders:

> every initial infatuation must inevitably mature into respect or else degrade into contempt.... It can also be called resentment, the other side of infatuation, when instead of fetishizing a culture that clearly differs from the one you inhabit, you become annoyed with it. You make fun of the accent, so to speak, as if it's not genuine but some kind of folksy contrivance affected to score personality points. Somebody told me recently of a complaint some writer made about "all these new books from the east coast that say 'arse.'" So resentment—the state of the disenchanted lover—permeates the arts community too, but to me it's like complaining about British novels for using words like "chap" and calling elevators "lifts." (2003, 3)

Indeed, Bridget had worried that Alan's friendship might simply have been infatuation, the "allure of a quiet, tortured, passive teenager" (Coady 1998, 88), and their parting of ways at the end of the novel certainly corresponds to Coady's description of regional disenchantment. When Bridget calls Alan in Guelph as she reaches a crisis of sanity, Alan starts out by making fun of her accent, implicitly assuming his southern Ontario idiom as the norm:

> "How *are* you?"
> "Good, good. It's stormin out."
> "Stahr-min, is it?" he said.
> "Ha, ha."
> "Well dat's how ya sound, lord t'underin."
> "I do not."
> "Ah doo nut." (189)

Alan's treatment of Bridget emphasizes not only his centrist presumption of superiority but also his subscribing to the same patriarchal assumptions as Mark. Like Mona, Bridget's Central Canadian friend on the psychiatric ward, whose "eternal point of reference had been herself" (81), Alan narcissistically expounds on his own problems and ultimately shuts Bridget out, oblivious to her unarticulated *cri de coeur*. Expressing the same masculinist wariness of heterosexual, platonic friendship as Mark,

Section 2: "About as Far from Disneyland as You Can Possibly Get"

he lectures Bridget about what his pregnant girlfriend will think of him getting nocturnal phone calls from another woman. Despite Alan's farewell salutation, "From my strange and wonderful Bridget Murphy" (191), it is clear that the novelty—Bridget's appeal as an anthropological curiosity—has worn off. For all his sympathy and kindness, Alan confirms his own advice to Bridget: "Guys are fucking pigs and the sooner you get that figured out the better off you'll be" (170). *Strange Heaven* thus presents us with a familiar portrait of a sensitive soul straining against the prevailing social mores of a small town, not in a pastoral, romantic, pre-modern Maritime landscape but in a "fallen" postmodern world of welfare apartments, tabloid violence, and doughnut shops—call it *Anne of Tim Hortons*. Coady's East refuses the polarized alternatives of what might be termed a homespun, Made in Canada, lower-case orientalism. It is neither the idealized, pastoral "ocean playground" of Anne Shirley nor the retrograde, underdeveloped, and parasitic "culture of defeat" of Stephen Harper. The "home place" is, as ever it was, a complex site.

A more dramatic (in both senses of the word) example of the subversive self-consciousness of contemporary Atlantic-Canadian literature is New Brunswick playwright Charlie Rhindress's play *The Maritime Way of Life*, first produced in Sackville in 1997 and, along with George Boyd's *Consecrated Ground*, published in Bruce Barton's anthology of Maritime theatre *Marigraph* in 2004. As the title suggests, Rhindress's play counters unitary and essentialist conceptions of Maritime culture. Perhaps more importantly, it highlights how such cultural straitjackets are not merely imported products but are, in part, fabricated in the Maritimes. *The Maritime Way of Life* is a parodic variation of a Maritime staple, the return of the prodigal child from going down the road to the big city.[1] Maggie McGarrity returns to her home in New Brunswick after an absence of seven years and three months, and the tension of the play hinges on Maggie's alternatives of fleeing the constricting confines of her past and her family or being true to her roots and staying to help in her family's hour of need. Rhindress, however, transforms this familiar paradigm—which hinges on a binary opposition between the tight familial and communal culture of the Maritimes and the alienating individualism of urban Central Canada—through his hyperbolic, facetious construction of the family's crisis and its solution to it. In the process, Rhindress sends up stereotype after stereotype, puncturing Folk images of the region and Maritimers' defensive adoption or internalization of monolithic images of themselves. In short, Rhindress implicitly criticizes not only the imposed cultural essentialism that oppressively pigeonholes Maritimers but also the essentialism

Maritimers themselves often resort to as a means of contending with their limited options.

One of the abiding comforts of life in the Maritimes (and, as with many stereotypes, there is much truth to it) is that, unlike in the dog-eat-dog world of the big city, people pull together to survive in hard times. This myth animates the action of *The Maritime Way of Life*, as the McGarritys weather their straitened circumstances through mutual reliance and familial pride. However, the family's state of crisis is both real and, in a sense, manufactured, as Rhindress simultaneously spoofs the stereotype of the stoic, resilient Maritimer and Maritimers' fatalism in the face of a depressed economy. Maggie has returned from Toronto, for instance, because she has discovered that her father has lost a lung from working in a coal mine. But it turns out that Pa has continued to work in the mine even though it has been closed for some time. When Maggie suggests that someone should tell him, Ma testily responds, "Your father's a proud man. What would he do if he couldn't go to work every day?" (Rhindress 2004, 9). Rhindress further spoofs the stereotype of the Maritimer's selfless endurance, as it is revealed that Pa is well aware the mine is closed but continues to go to work day after day because "all this time I didn' wanna bother you with it" (35). Maggie's brother Donnie, meanwhile, is the soul of entrepreneurial adaptation, surviving the best he can in a depressed economy. Inspired by the example of little Johnny Gallant, who won $5,000 playing the video lotto, Donnie stolidly does the same at the Kwik Way, striving to improve his family's fortunes: "Six days a week. Eight hours a day. Just like a job" (26). When Maggie reacts with understandable skepticism, Ma underlines the lack of available opportunities and the difficulty of getting enough work hours to qualify for Employment Insurance now that "[t]here ain't a cod left in the ocean." When Maggie points out that Donnie never fished, he responds, "it's got me down all the same" (13). Here Rhindress's satire suggests that pride and stoicism are perhaps a thin substitute for a vibrant economy or for more active resistance to the political and economic forces that perpetuate the region's subordinate status. Rounding out this dysfunctional family's roster—and spoofing the stereotype of the importance of extended family in Maritime culture—is Maggie's grandmother, who has become an incoherent quadriplegic in her absence. Ma, a parodic family martyr, thus spends all her time looking after Grandma, including carrying her on her back to the doctor instead of taking a cab: "Oh, sure and have everybody say I can't get my own mother to the doctor" (16). This burden, too, turns out to be a manufactured one, as Grandma reveals to Maggie that she has been playing the invalid to restore a sense of purpose to Ma's life in the wake of Maggie's departure. She now hopes that Maggie will stay home so that such a masquerade will no longer be necessary.

Maggie's resistance to this appeal to family solidarity leads to the central conspiracy of the play, itself a spoof on Maritimers' resorting to the "alternative economy" in the absence of a diversified and sustaining real one.[2] After Maggie rejects Grandma's proposal, Grandma pushes her down the stairs and incapacitates her. When Donnie discovers that Maggie has medical insurance, the McGarritys conspire to capitalize on Maggie's apparent paralysis. The family invites an insurance agent to assess the extent of her injury and are ecstatic at his estimation that her condition will likely warrant a payout of half a million dollars (while Grandma in the background manoeuvres to conceal Maggie's gradual recovery of movement). The family coaxes the elderly and blind Dr. Drury out of retirement to provide the necessary medical confirmation of Maggie's paralysis, but before he arrives Maggie revives and attempts to escape. In a convoluted bit of stage business, Donnie pulls her back down the stairs, knocking her into a coma, and is then dragooned by his mother into cross-dressing as Maggie, who, they have told the doctor, is conscious and mumbling. The farcical ruse succeeds as Maggie, in a temporary out-of-body experience, looks on unbelievingly. So much for stoic dignity and family solidarity in the face of hardship.

The McGarritys' machinations unfold against a backdrop of Folk stereotypes of Maritime culture that their self-serving behaviour thoroughly deflates. The earthiness, pride, and familial cohesion so often upheld as compensation for regional underdevelopment are here hyperbolized, parodied, and ultimately undone by the McGarritys' get-rich-quick scheme. Folk motifs are conspicuously trotted out throughout the play; it opens and closes, for instance, with the McGarritys singing regional folk songs that serve as a coda to the arduous rhythms of their lives. Pa (in an unmistakable gesture to Sheldon Currie's seminal 1979 story "The Glace Bay Miner's Museum") is repeatedly moved to get out his bagpipes, even though he only has one lung (the other is kept in a jar on top of the fridge) and doesn't even know how to play them: "My father played bagpipes and his father before him. And I'll play the bagpipes too. Ya can't fight what's in the blood" (Rhindress 2004, 17). On a couple of occasions in the play, Pa punctuates the action with earthy but wooden lyricism; when Ma says of Maggie's paralysis, "We can handle this. We're Maritimers. We're strong," Pa adds, "Strong like the wind and the waves that beat against the shore" (20). A parody of folk wisdom, Pa also routinely mangles aphorisms: "You know what they say, where there's smoke there's a gun" (25). The McGarritys, furthermore, are hyperbolic naïfs, unfamiliar with the rudiments of

FIGURE 9 "The McGarritys watching TV," from *The Maritime Way of Life*

technological consumer society; they are depicted as *very* simple folk, so simple that Donnie, as he prepares to contact the insurance company, asks, "Do you dial one for 1-800 or do you call the operator?" (24). Bourgeois affluence is so foreign to them that Donnie, rifling through Maggie's wallet, is agog at her collection of credit cards, "Sears ... VISA ... Club Zed" (22).

Rhindress also parodically gestures to what Raymond Williams underlines in *The Country and the City* as a long-standing tradition of "seeing innocence in the country, vice in the city" (1973, 148). The opposition between the alienating city and the communitarian Maritimes so crucial to the anti-modernist profile of the Folk is thoroughly confounded, as Rhindress spoofs the tendency to demonize the city and Central Canada and the uncritical assumption of family and community as nurturing forces. For instance, even though the play is set in New Brunswick, Maggie is referred to as coming from the mainland; when Maggie points out that "Toronto is not the mainland," Ma retorts that it "[m]ight as well be; much as we ever see you" (Rhindress 2004, 8). Ma routinely interprets Maggie's critical stance toward her relatives as come-from-away uppitiness: "We might not know lotsa big words, and maybe we can't say all our ABC's and maybe we can't tie our shoes but that don't mean we're any less than you. 'Cause we got big hearts" (15). She says of Maggie's fall and paralysis, "I knew sooner or later something like this would happen. Big city ain't no place for a Maritime girl" (20). If the city-as-taint myth is rendered absurd, so is the heartwarming vision of the nurturing family, such as when Ma lectures

Section 2: "About as Far from Disneyland as You Can Possibly Get"

Maggie for making fun of Donnie's line of "work": "He's family, Maggie. You don't go 'round criticizing family. All them awful things your father's mother did to me over the years, I never said a word. I just let them build up inside until I hated her more and more with every passing day. That's what you do for family" (14). Finally, of course, the central situation of the play is a grotesque turn on the archetype of Maritime family solidarity and the return of the prodigal, as the McGarritys celebrate the fact that, by being paralyzed, Maggie has come back to do her part. When Maggie attempts to abscond, Pa stresses the "wonderful opportunity for the family" (36) the ruse offers and sees it as comparable to Robin Hood stealing to give to the poor—in this case, themselves.

The Maritime Way of Life further undoes the regional stereotype by ending not with the restoration of the prodigal to the bosom of the family, but with the prodigal out-scamming the scammers and beating a hasty retreat to the city. After the family returns with their ill-gotten gains, Maggie, who has been pretending to be incapacitated, has contacted her boyfriend to rescue her and makes off with the money in the dead of night. For the supposedly stoic and homespun McGarritys, this is further evidence of urban corruption. "It's all them years in the big city," laments Ma. "She just ain't our Maggie no more" (Rhindress 2004, 47). Notwithstanding the fact that she had faked her own incapacity and had pushed Maggie down the stairs in the first place, Grandma similarly laments that she "[m]usta been fakin' the whole time. What kinda person would do that to their family?" (47). The play finishes with the plucky McGarritys determined to soldier on despite this setback, Pa rallying the family to "hang on to what's left of our dignity. If we're goin' down we're goin' down with our heads up and music in our hearts. We're Maritimers" (47). And indeed, all hope is not lost, as the play ends with Grandma (taking advantage of the fact that Pa has taken out insurance on the whole family) pushing Donnie down the stairs. No culture of defeat for her.

As a farce directed at regional stereotypes, *The Maritime Way of Life* is at times rough-hewn and excessively campy. Indeed, in his stage directions Rhindress suggests that all the parts be played cross-dressed in order to leave no doubt that the play is not to be taken as a genuine, earnest representation of "the Maritime way of life." While his satire is often a blunt instrument, bludgeoning rather than skewering the stereotypes that he serves up, Rhindress nonetheless makes some telling points about stereotypical visions of the Maritimes that not only are imposed on the region but are also promoted, for various purposes, within it. He does more than puncture the monolithic image of Maritimers as honest, dignified, fiddle-playing, fiddlehead-munching Folk. He also suggests that making a virtue

FIGURE 10 "Poor Donnie."

of necessity—that is, subscribing to binary oppositions such as the corrupting city and the nurturing, homespun region—may be just as deluded and disempowering. Rhindress satirically highlights the abject position of the Maritimer, reduced to dubious entrepreneurial improvisation in the absence of a sustaining economy, and also suggests that celebrating an ersatz simplicity plays further into the subordination of the region. The ultimate effect of *The Maritime Way of Life* is to underline the mutual misrepresentation—involving both distortion and deception—ensuing from regional stereotypes, whether they are imposed or defensively deployed.

"We got a taste for tourist"

Strange Heaven and *The Maritime Way of Life* highlight how the East Coast is framed by outsiders and the impact those external perspectives have on the self-image of people in the region. That tension, of course, is central to the experience of tourism. Although it has undeniable economic, social, and cultural benefits, tourism increasingly seems to be a preoccupation of writers in Atlantic Canada, and there is a profound dissonance between the testy attitude toward tourism in Atlantic-Canadian literature and the benevolent boosterism of the tourism industry itself. This attitude is nicely captured in one of Alistair MacLeod's most powerful stories, "Clearances," set in a Cape Breton increasingly being transformed by the forces of a leisure economy. Bristling at tourists' objections to his cutting down trees to make a living, a

Section 2: "About as Far from Disneyland as You Can Possibly Get"

young man bitterly complains, "This isn't my recreational area. This is my home" (Alistair MacLeod 2000, 426). As Meethan observes, the "development of tourist space means change at the level of lived experience for those whose space of home, or of work, is the space of leisure for others" (2001, 37), and this conflict is registered in a number of ways in contemporary writing in Atlantic Canada. The preoccupation with tourism in Atlantic-Canadian literature tells us much about current economic, political, social, and cultural conditions in the region but also about tourism as an extension of an ambivalent and often imperializing globalization.

As the work of Ian McKay and James Overton has underlined, governments, cultural producers, businesses, and tourist promoters have consciously turned the region's lack of development—which much of the rest of the country otherwise holds against it—to its advantage, repackaging the region as unspoiled and culturally distinctive. For much of the twentieth century, tourist development on the East Coast, responding to the need to generate revenue and diversify economically, has promoted the region's pristine ecology, opportunities for outdoor recreation, and unique cultural atmosphere. "To the elite city dweller, seaside locales, bucolic villages, and deep forests were imbued with the power to reinvigorate mind and body" (Parenteau and Judd 2005, 233). That promotion, as McKay and Overton argue, catered to a prevailing sense of anti-modernism, a negative reaction to the homogeneity and inauthenticity associated with technological progress and mass consumption. Tourism in Nova Scotia in the interwar years, McKay argues, promoted the myth "that the province was still enchanted, unspoiled, a Folk society, natural, and traditional" (1994, 32). Likewise, Overton states that since Victorian times, Newfoundland has been promoted as "a therapeutic space" (1996, 15) where, "[f]or the sufferer of neurasthenia and the anti-modernist a period of therapeutic primitivism, through contact with nature and those living natural lives, would restore vitality and even virility" (13). A key part of the therapeutic quality of the East Coast, moreover, was the possibility of contact with ostensibly authentic and unspoiled peoples. However, in presenting such a profile to lure tourists, tourist promoters in Atlantic Canada have trafficked in very problematic stereotypes of the region's culture as pre-modern, rural, and small-m maritime, as McKay and Overton have demonstrated. In short, the culture and environment of the Atlantic provinces have been constructed for over a century as a restorative antidote to the alienating inauthenticity of a dog-eat-dog, technologized modern society, and the marketing of the region as such continues apace.

That cultural atmosphere, however, has very much been packaged (even literally "canned")[3] and thus one of the key concerns about tourism is the inequitable economic and political relationships that such packaging entails. One of the central insights of McKay's study is that the construction of this essentialist, pre-modern Folk identity was to a great degree cultivated by the state and capitalist entrepreneurs. Thus, while provincial culture was presented as an escape from capitalist modernity, "it was almost always a *commercial* antimodernism, structured by the very modern capitalism from which it seemed to provide a momentary and partial escape, and reliant upon its fast-developing technologies of persuasion" (I. McKay 1994, 35). Likewise, Overton stresses that successive "attempts at economic diversification and reconstruction" in Newfoundland "have included attempts to develop tourism *not* as an alternative to industrialization but as a key component of the modernization of the economy" (1996, 11; italics in original). Thus tourism, rather than an escape from capitalist modernity, is instead perhaps its quintessential manifestation.

In that sense, one of the main problems with tourism is the way in which it transforms local cultures in order to attract tourists and generate profits. As numerous critics have argued, tourism is a reconfiguration of place with the intent to please others and, depending on the host culture's economic circumstances, usually involves asymmetrical relations of power. Tourism, Overton contends (drawing on the work of Henri Lefebvre), is part of "the spread of industrial capitalism into the realm of leisure" (1996, 4), and tourist development thus "has proceeded, overall, in an uneven and, for the most part, unplanned fashion" (1996, 4–5). With the spread of tourism to every corner of the globe, however, critics have become more inclined to see tourism as a form of neo-colonialism, a central expression of the structural inequities of globalization. For Graham Huggan, the paradox of tourism is that tourists, while ostensibly seeking the exotic and novel, implicitly demand the familiar and predictable. In the process, tourism "contributes to the sameness of a world whose difference it needs to make its profits. Tourism thus requires the other that it repeatedly destroys" (2001, 178). While it is important not to caricature tourism either as a simplistic, harmonious sharing of the natural and cultural wealth of a particular locality with others, or (as is more likely the case) as a homogenizing, neo-colonial juggernaut, tourism is, as Urry argues ([1990] 2002, 57), often the last resort, particularly in developing countries. Tourist destinations thus feel compelled to stage a kind of spectacle of the extraordinary or the exotic in order to satisfy their tourist clientele, and that sense of compulsion has significant political, economic, and cultural implications. As Overton observes, tourism is marked by conflicts that "may arise over control of resources, access to land, and even access to affordable housing" as well as "over how

Section 2: "About as Far from Disneyland as You Can Possibly Get"

history and culture are packaged and presented" (1996, 7). Many commentaries on tourism point to how the host society may come to resent being compelled to perform their culture for visitors, to provide it in packaged, consumable, ersatz form. Thus many regions reliant on tourism as an economic mainstay, including Atlantic Canada, exhibit resistance to its influence, a resistance more and more visible in Atlantic-Canadian literature.

Tourists are often figures of fun in Western culture, and certainly one recurring response to tourism in Atlantic-Canadian literature is an inclination to satirize tourists as naïfs propelled by a kind of wilful self-delusion. Tourism, commentators such as Urry and Dean MacCannell note, is a highly overdetermined process, in which tourist expectations, often informed by essentialist cultural stereotypes, shape and distort tourism as an encounter with different places and cultures. Urry describes how places are framed within "the tourist gaze," in which "[p]laces are chosen to be gazed upon because there is anticipation, especially through daydreaming and fantasy, of intense pleasures, either on a different scale or involving different senses from those customarily encountered"; furthermore, this "anticipation is constructed through a variety of non-tourist practices" ([1990] 2002, 3), including various media. What tourists want, as Newfoundland poet Mary Dalton's poem "Lies for the Tourists" suggests, is a highly airbrushed experience: "that rug was hooked by a sweet white-haired grandmother / for love, not money" (Dalton 2006, 45) and "Those children playing in the crooked streets—so friendly / so quaint—/ are fed on the milk and honey of our simple island kindness" (45). Because of a sometimes considerate, sometimes pragmatic reluctance to disabuse tourists of their routinely unrealistic and misguided assumptions, the host society must in effect take pains to give tourists what they want.

A subversive response to this desire can be seen in Coady's portrayal of regional culture in *Strange Heaven*. While Coady's portrait of Alan Voorland rebuffs the paternalistic gaze of a Central Canadian and his self-fulfilling, derogatory stereotypes of the East, her intent is not to reinscribe a sense of an innocent, authentic Folk culture. Indeed, an important part of her subversion of the outsider's gaze is her parodic approach to the idea of an authentic Folk culture. This subversion is carried out principally through Coady's depiction of Robert as a parodic Folk artist. Disillusioned by the community's resistance to his attempts to revolutionize the town's spring festival to bring in more tourists—including doing away with "the traditional bagpipe contest that led him to refer to the festival as 'Cat Killing Days'" during a radio interview (Coady 1998, 73)—Robert retreats to his workshop. He dismisses the idea that his woodworking is art rather than a craft and declines an invitation to "be on some program about Maritime folk art. 'I'm no dope-smoking hairy-faced fruit'" (73). Although Coady makes fun of Robert's reactionary, homophobic imitation of the artist—he makes "flitting gestures with his short yellow fingers" (74)—she nonetheless employs his approach to his craft to deconstruct the concept of Folk art, "an art that supposedly inhered in materials and in people enjoying an unmediated relationship with nature and an unproblematic, 'fresh,' 'spontaneous' relation between conception and execution" (I. McKay 1994, 292). Robert playfully carves caricatures into diseased, bulbous pieces of wood, delighting "in any chunk of wood that bore a passing resemblance to parts of the human anatomy" (Coady 1998, 74). His subversive inclinations extend to his business practices, as he cannily "over-price[s] his art work outrageously for the tourists" (74–75) and exploits his reputation as "a character" by browbeating customers into making purchases if they linger too long in his shop.

Robert's other creations likewise suggest Coady's parodic presentation of regional culture. Similarly overpriced are Robert's handcrafted golf balls, to produce which "he peeled away half of the ball's pitted skin and then carved goofy faces into the hard rubber beneath. Everyone thought this was ingenious" (75). Set in contrast with Robert's decoys, such apparent kitsch suggests Coady's playful questioning of purist notions of authentic Folk art. Whereas Robert's golf balls are individualized creations crafted out of mass-produced objects, his decoys are handcrafted originals that appear to be mass-produced:

> His decoys were simply beautiful, more beautiful than any actual duck. They were completely smooth and flawless—he did not bother with feathers or any other realistic detail that might disturb the decoy's linearity. The result was a perfect, liquid platonic ideal. Perfect duckness. He stained—never painted—and then varnished them. The wood was what mattered. The acknowledgement and refinement of the wood rather than any attempt to deny it was what made the carvings very nearly sublime. People came from far and wide to purchase one of Bridget's father's ducks. They were all exactly the same. (75)

In "The Work of Art in the Age of Mechanical Reproduction" Walter Benjamin maintains that "the technique of reproduction detaches the reproduced object from the domain of tradition" and that "that which withers in the age of mechanical reproduction is the aura of the work of art" (1969, 221). Robert's production of identical decoys blurs the boundaries between the lost aura of authenticity in capitalist mass production and the erstwhile authentic individuality of the handicraft, and hence blurs the boundary between pre-modern Folk Innocence and the homogeneity of industrial modernity. His golf balls and his decoys playfully confound Benjamin's argument that the "whole sphere of authenticity is outside technical ... reproducibility" (1969, 220).

Robert's taking on his brother Rollie as an apprentice likewise reflects his canny, subversive exploitation of consumerist desire for Folk authenticity. When Rollie's school is shut down, Robert turns him loose in his workshop and retails the results as the work of "a religious artist": "Little cards in front of each announced what the wooden blobs were supposed to represent, from 'Jesus Heals the Sick' to 'Saint Paul on the Road to Damascus'" (Coady 1998, 77). Shrewdly exploiting the notion of Rollie as an idiot savant, as well as tourists' readiness to equate price with quality, Robert

> daringly set them at the same price as his carved golf-balls, a great favourite among locals and tourists alike, and in a flash of inspired business savvy put up a bigger sign above them all which read:
> *Religious Wooden Statues.*
> *Done by Retarded Man.*
> *Twenty-five dollars a piece.* (78)

Coady's depiction of Robert as a happily cynical cultural entrepreneur provides a playful indictment of the tourist industry in Nova Scotia, which represents a paradoxical commodification of Folk Innocence and authenticity, "simultaneously celebrating the pre-modern, unspoiled 'essence' of the province and seeking ways in which that essence could be turned into marketable commodities within a liberal political and economic order" (I. McKay 1994, 35).

A final element of Coady's parodic commentary on folk culture is the popularity of "The Ballad of Jenny Mac," reflecting with arch irony the community's morbid fascination with the death of Jennifer MacDonell. Here, a murder outside a doughnut shop—an emblem of postmodern consumer culture—takes the form of a traditional ballad:

> *A sweeter girl you never saw,*
> *Her parents' special pride,*
> *She had a smile for all she knew*
> *Until the day she died* (Coady 1998, 161)

The ballad continues "on and on, actually going into lurid detail about Jenny meeting Archie and Archie chasing her with a gun and pointing it in her face and saying: '*If you'll not be my love, / You'll be the love of none*'" (161). Cleverly synthesizing the tabloid's obsession with murder victims and the narrative lyricism of the traditional Folk ballad, Coady underscores the sentimentality and idealization behind the memorializing of Jennifer. As if cryogenically frozen in a state of innocence, Jennifer is transmogrified and commodified: "Jennifer MacDonnell, who had never been called Jenny in her life, had sunk entirely beneath the horizon. Something else being erected in her place. She was queen of the prom, on her parent's mantelpiece forever, now" (162–63). Thus Coady dramatizes the dangers of proprietorial patriarchal attitudes toward women while simultaneously spoofing what McKay sees as the preoccupation in constructions of the Folk "with essence—with locating the genuine wisdom, the true and original ballads, the cultural bloodstream uncontaminated by the virus of modernity, the fixed and final forms of culture" (1994, 275).

In a similar vein, in her poem "Markings" Jeanette Lynes highlights tourists' pursuit of an illusory, mythical culture, a central construction of tourist promotion, especially in Atlantic Canada. Urry describes how tourism is a prime example of what Daniel Boorstin calls 'pseudo-events': "Isolated from the host environment and the local people, the mass tourist travels in guided groups and finds pleasure in inauthentic contrived attractions, gullibly enjoying 'pseudo-events' and disregarding the 'real' world outside" ([1990] 2002, 7). Evoking tourists' desire for the idyllic pastoral society of *Anne of Green Gables* or the imaginary happy fisherfolk Ian McKay describes—two staples of tourism in Atlantic Canada—Lynes likewise suggests that what matters is the anticipation rather than the consummation:

> There's an island where
> lives, much of the world believes, an orphan
> with red hair. She has never been home.
> There's a regal shore where fishermen dance,
> women gather moss in contentment. No one
> has ever found it. Perhaps no one
> wants to. (Lynes 2001, 6–12)

She likens tourists in Cape Breton to the disappointed Vikings who, while searching for the mythical Vinland, "a land where you could hump and / eat grapes all day long" (13–14), instead discovered Newfoundland's Great Northern Peninsula, where "they beat their fists / against the barely thawed ground, wept bitterly" (15–16). In their giant RVs, "not so different from Viking ships" (19), these tourists—parodic, latter-day adventurers with "tanned skin, plastic cards"—"have no idea how lost they are" (20, 21). Lynes

Section 2: "About as Far from Disneyland as You Can Possibly Get"

suggests that what tourists consume is a preconceived image rather than the reality, highlighting how, as Overton nicely puts it, "[i]t may be that people are perpetually cheated of that which they are offered and forced to consume the menu rather than the meal" (1996, 110).

However, Overton adds that "to see people as dupes who are manipulated by the advertising industry does not get us very far" (110) and emphasizes that the myths retailed to tourists work because they cater to their needs and desires (1996, 111). Meethan more strenuously resists what he sees as the "arrogant and patronizing" belief "that people are simply passive consumers or even cultural dupes, in particular that 'the masses' are easily fooled into accepting contrivance as the 'real thing'" (2001, 112). He furthermore objects to the view of tourism as a form of neo-colonialism, especially in the developing world, arguing that "the notion that other cultures need preserving from the onslaught of a totalising modernity and that their authenticity is under threat" is a potentially disempowering form of essentialist Folk romanticism (2001, 65). While there is merit to Meethan's stance, he arguably underestimates the degree to which tourism constitutes a serious political, economic, and spatial imposition on the lives of local inhabitants, a concern highly visible in recent Atlantic-Canadian literature.

One of the potential problems with tourism, as Mike Robinson asserts, is that it usually involves sharing, and even vying for control of, places: "Tourists at various times occupy the places which 'belong' to others and which carry cultural meanings for the host community" (2001, 48). This competition for space is central to Alistair MacLeod's "Clearances," in which his aging protagonist sees his Cape Breton homestead increasingly encroached upon by the forces of a leisure society. In this powerful story, the decline of the resource sector, increasing out-migration, and outsiders' view of Cape Breton as leisure real estate combine to create conditions that replicate the earlier Highland clearances that led to the migration of the protagonist's Scottish ancestors to Cape Breton in the first place.

The story dramatizes the disruption of familial and occupational continuity that has been a central consequence of the East Coast's economic plight from the late nineteenth century through to the present. Near the end of a life that he has lived much as his forefathers did, the protagonist has witnessed one son go off to fish in Lake Erie after the decline of the local fisheries, fishing being the principal livelihood of his family for generations. After the accidental death of his other son, his daughter-in-law has unexpectedly sold off the part of his homestead to which he, in a "fit of delayed guilt" (Alistair MacLeod 2000, 422), had given her title. The new owners are "a surly summer couple who erected a seven-foot privacy fence and kept a sullen pit bull who paced relentlessly behind it" (423).

Furthermore, the government has curtailed salmon fishing by locals "for the benefit of the summer anglers" (426)—reflecting the way fish and game have been "transformed into forms of property controlled by alien state agents in the interest of nonresident recreations" at the expense of the rural working class (Parenteau and Judd 2005, 246).

Meanwhile, a nearby park increasingly encroaches on their lives, travelling "like a slow-moving glacier, claiming more and more land to be used as hiking trails and wilderness areas, while the families in its path worried about eviction notices" (Alistair MacLeod 2000, 426). The looming threat of displacement is underscored by the protagonist's young cousin, "one of a series of 'clear-cutters' who yearned for the spruce trees that had gradually reclaimed the field he had once cleared as a younger man" (425). Although the protagonist is skeptical about the greed of these men and the havoc that they wreak, he is also sympathetic to his young cousin in his bitterness about the tourists, who "slept late and often complained about the whine of the clear-cutters' saws" (425) and some of whom "had taken pictures of the carnage left behind by the clear-cutters and had them published in environmental magazines" (425–26).

The sense of rupture and dispossession that these developments cultivate is reinforced for the protagonist by the arrival of a real estate agent, trying to broker the purchase of his land by a pair of German visitors "looking for land with ocean frontage" (427). The visitors fail to appreciate the irony that the area is "[n]ice and quiet" because, as the protagonist muses, people have had to migrate to the U.S., "Halifax or southern Ontario" (429). While the protagonist is immediately resistant, his son, who has temporarily returned from economic exile in Central Canada, encourages him to sell in order to stall what seems to be inevitable displacement: "Maybe if this worked out I could stay here with my wife and children for a while" (429). Thus "Clearances" serves as a succinct allegory for the politics of transition from a resource economy to a leisure one, highlighting the vulnerability and aggrieved dignity of those who find themselves effectively being evicted in the process. As the protagonist's young cousin complains, "People like you and me … are no match for the Government and the tourists" (Alistair MacLeod 2000, 426). The story ends on a note of resistance to such encroachment, with the protagonist and his faithful sheepdog (an emblem of Gaelic heritage characteristic of MacLeod's work) confronting the neighbours' pit bull, which has escaped and bears down on them wearing "a collar covered with pointed studs" and "mov[ing] with deliberate, measured steps" (430). The outcome of their resistance—which borders on uncharacteristically melodramatic anti-modernism—remains uncertain, however, and the tone of the conclusion is profoundly ambivalent, suggesting the immanent end of an era of generational continuity in the face of overwhelming economic and political forces. Nonetheless, through its portrait of the external pressures eroding the foundations of a long-standing way of life built around natural resources, "Clearances" succinctly dramatizes how tourism so often is a literal contest over territory and over how physical spaces are to be configured and used.

Another recurring response to tourism in Atlantic-Canadian literature is the depiction of tourism as not just a physical imposition. While recognizing that tourism entails a certain level of self-deception, most writers also appreciate the power exerted by such preconceptions and thus the need to counter the symbolic imposition that they involve. One strategy for doing so is the reassertion of the complexity of place in the face of its reconfiguration for consumption by tourists. As Overton maintains, "Space is transformed by tourism, but so is the meaning and representation of space" (1996, 7). With the tourist industry "skewing the built environment to meet the expectations and preferences of the tourist," Robinson argues, "the cultural elements of placeness—continuation, evolution, stability and familiarity—are eroded" (2001, 50–51). Part of the response to tourism in Atlantic-Canadian literature is a contesting of touristic definitions of space and place and a reassertion of what are regarded as prior and/or local definitions. In PEI poet Brent MacLaine's "North Shore Park," for instance, the Island is poetically reclaimed from its dominant summertime image as MacLaine's speaker contemplates a frozen seaside vista after a winter storm. Highlighting the seasonal selectivity of touristic perceptions of the island, the speaker underscores the incongruity of a summer-oriented leisure apparatus, as "the seaward-facing benches / look ironic" (MacLaine 2002, 5–6) and "uncomprehending cottages / close their plywood eyes" (11–12). In what might be seen as a chilly reversal of Charles G.D. Roberts's famous late-nineteenth-century poem "Tantramar Revisited" (in which Roberts's speaker prefers the imagined, remembered version of the landscape spread out before him and sustains the illusion by staying at a distance), MacLaine's speaker considers that "the truth / of it may be clearer now" (31–32), in contrast to the perception imposed by "those others ... , / dreamy for sleep-inducing surf, / hot for magic castles" (25–27) who "will reconfigure all this ice / to sand, make an oasis here / beneath the tilting pines" (29–31). This contrast suggests a distinction between what MacCannell, reworking Erving Goffman's model of social interaction, calls back regions and front regions of tourism, "the putative 'intimate and real' as against 'show'" ([1976] 1999, 94).

As MacCannell also rightly suggests, however, the distinction between back region and front region is difficult to sustain, and one of the paradoxes that both McKay and Overton highlight is the way that host societies are complicit in the perpetration of, and often internalize, touristic constructions of their own cultures. Meethan goes farther, arguing that characterizations of tourism as an agent of alienated modernity soiling ostensibly unitary and authentic cultures are both erroneous and patronizing, based on false dichotomies between the authentic and the inauthentic, the traditional and the modern (2001, 90–91). In this light, MacLaine might be seen as trying to assert an illusory and potentially essentialist "real" sense of place in response to the tourist's "artificial" one, reflecting how, as Tracy Whalen cautions in considering literary representations of Newfoundland, essentialist constructions of place are "beloved by tourist operations and those whom one might term cultural nationalists" alike (2004, 67). However, resisting dominant touristic definitions of space is not necessarily the same thing as reasserting a geographically essentialist identity. Instead, "North Shore Park" can be read as foregrounding the one-dimensionality of the tourist version of PEI, perpetually frozen in summertime. In the process, MacLaine emphasizes the problematic transience of the leisure economy, its limited existential investment in a place that has not one season, but four.

Perhaps the most significant strategy for confronting tourism in contemporary Atlantic-Canadian literature is a kind of resistant reading that stresses the coercive conditions behind the performance of culture for tourist consumption. Such a strategy is evident, for instance, in Kenneth J. Harvey's *The Town That Forgot How to Breathe*. As Robinson observes, tourism can cultivate cultural conflicts that are manifested in a range of ways, "from a rather intangible sense of disgruntlement and embarrassment on the part of the host to (in extreme cases) violence against tourists and the component elements of the industry as symbols of external influence and cultural change" (2001, 38). In Harvey's novel, a central part of the conflicted response to the calamity in Bareneed is an aggrieved resentment of the role of outsiders in bringing it about, including tourists. As Urry argues, a key consideration in tourism is the "extent to which *tourists can be identified and blamed* for supposedly undesirable economic and social developments" ([1990] 2002, 53; italics in original). Such an impulse, furthermore, is usually more evident when there are significant economic, cultural, and ethnic differences between tourists and visitors and "when the host population is experiencing rapid economic and social change" (53), as is the rural Newfoundland of Harvey's novel. Thus the resentment of the residents is directed in part at tourists, because they are seen as exploiting the vulnerability of a beleaguered society. As contemptuous of tourists as he is of bureaucrats, displaced fisherman Doug Blackwood depicts tourism as

Section 2: "About as Far from Disneyland as You Can Possibly Get"

a kind of cultural prostitution and predation, with outsiders picking the bones of a once vital community:

> Put the people of Bareneed on display like they were museum pieces, the last of the fisherfolk done up in period costumes for some arse-backward reenactment. Have a good look, ladies and gentlemen. Step right up. See how they wiggle like fish on the ends of a hook, gasping their final breath. Bait for you to nip at. See how their boats are rotting and their children don't have a clue what a codfish even looks like. (K. Harvey 2003, 149)

Here Harvey, like Ian McKay, stresses the irony of performing a seafaring way of life that has been eradicated by history, so that tourism becomes a kind of cultural necrophilia—getting off on the corpse of the departed, as it were. Harvey's novel dramatically underscores how trafficking in such anti-modern cultural essentialism, as McKay argues, "is ethically troubling because it exemplifies the transformation of living people (and their customs and beliefs) into articles of exchange" (1994, 41). It also brings to mind Guy Debord's characterization of life under "modern conditions of production" as "an immense accumulation of *spectacles*. All that once was directly lived has become mere representation" ([1967] 1995, 12; italics in original).

As Debord's observation suggests, what tourism entails is a paradoxical process in which the host society caters to the desires of tourists so much that they experience not an authentic Other but a performance of culture tailored to the tourists' expectations and needs. In that sense, tourism is an instance of what Jean Baudrillard describes as the hyper-real, the displacement of the real by the simulacrum, "substituting signs of the real for the real" (1994, 2). This aspect of tourism, as Paul Chafe has nicely illustrated, is deftly spoofed in Edward Riche's first novel, *Rare Birds* (1997). The novel revolves around the concocted sighting of a rare duck near the restaurant of protagonist Dave Purcell in order to restore the restaurant's flagging fortunes. As Dave's co-conspirator Alphonse Murphy presciently argues, what matters is the spectacle rather than the substance, the perception of authentic experience rather than the experience itself. "One will catch a gull or a kittiwake out the corner of his eye," Phonse reassures Dave, "and say 'Did you see that?' and another one will say 'Yeah! I saw something!' and they'll go wild for it. Psychology of the mob, Dave, mass hysteria!" (Riche 1997, 80). Such deception, Chafe observes, is facilitated by tourism's reliance less on authentic experience than on tourists' perceived consummation of their preconceptions: "These birders do not need to see the duck so much as they need to be in the presence of its mystique" (2008, 182), and, in staging that presence as a lure, "Dave and Phonse commit the central deception of the tourist industry" (180).

In *Rare Birds*, Riche satirically highlights the performance of culture, in which, as Chafe nicely puts it, "the culture marketed to tourists is more act than actual" (2008, 184). While his anti-hero Dave contemplates tourism as literally the last resort for a desperate province, Riche underscores how Newfoundland culture is reduced to a humiliating pantomime: "Tourism. It was the last hope for Newfoundland, to become some kind of vast park, its people zoo pieces, playing either famished yokels or bit parts in a costume drama, a nation of amateur actors dressed up like murderous Elizabethan explorers, thrilling to the touch of their tights and tunics as they danced for spare change" (Riche 1997,148). This desperation is reinforced with the appearance of the Minister of Tourism Heber Turpin and his entourage at Dave's restaurant. Turpin confides to Dave that "Newfoundland has come to a fork in the road" in which the choices for economic development are either playing host to tourists or playing host to toxic waste disposal (152). Turpin congratulates Dave on having had the acuity to open a restaurant in Push Cove and thus be poised to capitalize on the frenzy over the rare bird. He even proposes conspiring to stage the phenomenon if necessary: "if the birds weren't here I'd say you would be wise to say they were anyway. I could talk to some people in Wildlife" (154). When Hans Spiedel, an internationally respected German ornithologist, arrives and dismisses the presence of a *Tasker's Sulphureous* as a myth, Turpin—oblivious to the irony of his comments—denounces "foreign experts" as a "plague on Newfoundland" and reassures Dave, "We'll get our own fucking experts on the case. I have friends down at Wildlife, Dave, I can send them around" (202).

The chilling effect of Spiedel's intervention on Dave's restaurant points to how a crucial aspect of the tourist experience is the pursuit of authenticity. As many commentators on tourism have observed, however, tourism seems subject to a variation of the Heisenberg Uncertainty Principle, which posits that objects under scrutiny change their behaviour: that is, tourism tends to compromise, often quite substantially, the very encounter with authenticity that tourists ostensibly seek, and what they consume instead is a commodified version. Tourism, Robinson contends, routinely entails an imperialistic

> commodification process whereby traditions, rituals, and "ways of life" are packaged, imaged and transformed into saleable products for tourists. Culture(s), as a living and learning form, together with the idea of culture and its shared meanings, become a superficial subjugate of consumerism and lose their social role, social and political function, and authenticity. (2001, 43)

Section 2: "About as Far from Disneyland as You Can Possibly Get"

Although Robinson concedes that "commodification, in itself, need not generate conflict if it carries the consent of the host culture and the latter can reap the benefits of acceptable commercialization," he nonetheless exhibits a wariness of the culturally corrosive effects of tourist commodification (2001, 43).

Likewise, in *Rare Birds* Riche satirizes the commodification of the spectacle by the tourist industry, the transformation of nature and culture into consumable products. Dave reflects that the site most eagerly sought after by tourists (referring to the notorious sexual abuse scandal at Mount Cashel) "was 'that orphanage where all the little boys were abused by those priests, like in that miniseries'" (Riche 1997, 149), bringing to mind Urry's surmise that "the worse the previous historical experience, the more authentic and appealing the resulting tourist attraction" ([1990] 2002, 118). In a scorching bit of satire of the cynicism of tourist development and the prurient voyeurism of tourism, Dave considers that, in light of the tourists' disappointment, "[w]hat Newfoundland tourism needed, much more than a decent restaurant, was a ghastly wax-works of hiked black cassocks and splayed ivory limbs, a national bum-fucking museum" (Riche 1997, 149). Similarly, when Phonse carves an exact replica of the *Tasker's Sulphureous*, which makes an elusive appearance and revives the excitement—and tourist traffic—Riche spoofs tourism as a kind of gratuitous manufacturing and franchising of the spectacle. After it reappears, Dave with some dismay reflects on the possibility that the elusive and mysterious duck, like the Loch Ness monster, could inspire "a loyal following of quacks. Dave supposed there was a sister restaurant to the Auk in Scotland, on the shores of that famous murky lake. The Auk could possibly survive by hawking trinkets and novelties, duck key chains and T-shirts, candy duck eggs and whatnot" (204).

Here Riche seems to be depicting tourism as a double alienation, in which tourists and hosts conspire in the undermining of authenticity and genuine cultural meaning, a vision of tourism as modernist alienation that Meethan vigorously opposes:

> The notion of a loss of meaning for both the "natives" and the tourists is problematic. The former are either criticised for commodifying and selling their heritage, or for being the passive victims of modernity, while the latter are either being deluded by the "natives" or are deluding themselves if they think that what they get is the real thing. Both positions run the risk of falling into a patronising elitism which views other cultures as possessing essential authentic attributes which need to be preserved simply for the gaze of tourists, which also assumes that such cultures are locked in the past and "going nowhere."
> (2001, 92–93)

For Meethan, tourism is much more interactive, and the tourist, rather than "simply being a passive recipient at the end of a commodity chain [is] an active agent capable of reflexively organising experiences into forms of self-identity" (2001, 86). Indeed, he sees tourism as a process of formation of cultural capital (88). While Meethan's critique of patronizing views of tourists is persuasive, he is arguably guilty of defusing valid critiques of tourism by associating them with an essentialist tendency to romanticize pre-modern cultures. In doing so, he underestimates the dynamics of tourism as an infernal machine that transforms culturally complex and meaningful phenomena into decontextualized, culturally empty commodities, something that Riche's portrait of tourism stresses.

At the heart of Riche's satire of tourism, not only in *Rare Birds* but also in *The Nine Planets*, is a sense of dismay at the desperate dependency that tourism reflects. Responding to overly economic prescriptions for tourist development in Nova Scotia, a *New Maritimes* editorial highlights tourism as a doubly objectifying capitalist process: "We want [tourists] because they bring money. The tourist exists for us, not as a person in his or her own right, but merely as a means to an end—our economic survival; and we exist, in turn, for the tourists, as a series of sights, thrills, and sensations—a means to the end of regenerating their shattered nerves" ("Limits of Tourism" 1987, 5). As a way of earning a living, then, it is potentially mutually demeaning. Riche makes this point in a diatribe delivered by George Hayden in *The Nine Planets*, while spoofing the commodification of Folk stereotypes of Newfoundland's cultural heritage built around anti-modernist, romantic images of the hardy, independent petty producer of the outport. The real heritage of Newfoundland, Hayden rails, is

> commerce. They didn't cross the pond in leaky boats for a theatre festival or to watch whales, they came to this place to make money, to kill whales and sell their fat. North America is about capitalism, and it got its start here, right here. Money means vitality, money means movement. That's our lost tradition ... not running the fucking goat. (Riche 2004, 141)

Riche's satire humorously highlights the simplistic and anti-modern stereotypes that permeate touristic attitudes toward Atlantic Canada, and exposes the exploitative machinery of tourist development. Nonetheless, that satire is underpinned by a more sobering awareness of the economic conditions that make tourism the last resort that it is, as well as of the social and cultural implications of that state of affairs. At the end of his cynically expedient free-market tirade, Hayden underscores the problems with Newfoundland's increasing dependence on a service economy: "Men have been doing business in Newfoundland for five hundred years. We've traded with Lisbon and London and Havana and Genoa from the get-go, and there are those that would have us all gamekeepers and actors. Build, baby, or wait tables" (141). The point here, essentially, is that tourism expands to fill a vacuum—the economic void left by Newfoundland's failed industrial development and the collapse of the fisheries that Riche, for all his wicked satire of tourism, recognizes as the source of a profound crisis of identity for Newfoundland.

For Riche, Hayden, unsavoury as he may be, is nonetheless giving voice to a crucial imperative for Newfoundland: the need to redefine itself culturally and economically rather than continuing to retail a culture that has expired (see Riche 2008, 218). Indeed, in *Rare Birds*, Dave mournfully contemplates the legacy of remote and abandoned roads, soccer pitches, and softball diamonds, the relics of Sisyphean efforts to develop Newfoundland, and likens them to "the wooden planes built by the cargo cults, ghostly activity undertaken to attract somebody with a real purpose, industrial decoys" (Riche 1997, 86–87). This palpable evidence of failure then prompts him to consider Newfoundland reverting to its pre-contact state: "The Norse had failed. The Basques had failed. And now the British Empire and its Canadian water boys were failing. The island belonged to the black bears and caribou and lynx and crows. And they would soon have it back" (87). Despite the satiric hyperbole of Dave's gloomy meditations, however, the underlying message is an earnest one: "if we don't change, that is our future. We can hand the keys to the crows" (Riche 2008, 218).

This apocalyptic tone, muted in Riche's work, gets the full treatment in Newfoundland playwright Frank Barry's *Wreckhouse*, an especially mordant satire of tourism that premiered at the Resource Centre for the Arts in St. John's in 2002. In an economically exhausted, allegorical landscape, Thomas O'Steinway finds himself stranded at an abandoned mine site because of a flat tire. An Irish doctor living in Newfoundland and suffering from a mental breakdown, O'Steinway has developed a pathological contempt for Newfoundlanders because of their incessant promotion of their commodified culture, their "accordion screeching, nasal hymning, tribal bewilderments" (Barry 2003, 47). Reflecting back on "[t]he night they screeched me in" and the "cod kissing ceremony" (47)—rituals bonding visitors with hosts that Overton argues are social constructions, invented "traditions" (1996, 146–47)—he thinks "I could have submachine gunned the whole rubber booted, sou'westered, tourist-dollar grasping lot of them" (Barry 2003, 47–48). The play serves as a kind of surreal chastening of O'Steinway's condescension, as he falls prey to a ragged band of locals conspiring to lure and tranquilize outsiders, who are then literally consumed in ritualistic fashion. Although the central action is framed as a hallucinatory, cautionary nightmare—"'A Midsummer Night's Dream' meets 'Deliverance,'" to borrow an apt phrase from the play (95)—Barry's satire is nonetheless pointed and trenchant. The premise of the play is that competition between communities for tourists to feed off of has (as with the cod fishery) exhausted the stocks. Consequently, in a clever, parodic reversal of tourism as the consumption of a performance of culture, in which locals have to transform themselves in order to meet tourists' expectations, Barry's locals have to attract and transform others in order to consume them to survive. In the process, Barry underscores not only the colonial context of Newfoundland's economic dependency and desperation but also the colonial dynamics of the relationship between host and tourist.

Barry positions such desperation in the larger context of Newfoundland's infantilizing relationships with England and Canada. Larky, one of the locals whose job it is to recruit fresh "tourists"—mainlanders or come-from-aways—describes the locals as being "[s]tunted," "[p]assed from one withered milkless tit to another nursemaid younger but even more austere." In a scathing indictment of the condescension with which they are viewed by the rest of the country, Newfoundlanders are likened to "[a]ged children sent to the basement without any supper whenever they act up. A basement they'll never be allowed to leave" (Barry 2003, 69). This colonial debasement is then linked to tourist promotion, as these "aged children" consequently must "strive so hard to please. Dressed up in little costumes to dance little dances and sing little songs" (69). In a kind of ritualistic retribution that, Larky contends, is a response to a crisis of identity, Barry's locals torture their "tourists" into performing for them: "Because *we* have become *unreal*. That's what it *is*. *Having* to force *them* to acknowledge that *we* are real so that we can become real again" (70; italics in original). As Larky goes on to underscore, essentialist images of a Folk culture have more than a whiff of dangerous nativism to them, and they cultivate a loathing of the tourists such images are designed to attract and satisfy. But they also cultivate a self-loathing on the part of the host culture:

> Don't those TV ads depicting the bright-eyed lassies and their Menschfolk dancing in circles beneath the perfect sky to the music of *accordions* give off a faint whiff of Bavarian Uberjoy. Just add some lederhosen and steins of Lowenbrau and you got a perfect picture of Aryan Folk Himmel. And all this self promotion can only stem from one thing. A grimacing mask of hospitality covering a cringing clock of desperation. Besides, everybody hates tourists. It's natural. They create

Section 2: "About as Far from Disneyland as You Can Possibly Get"

> so much envy. They're always on holiday. They turn everyone into servants. Excuse me. Service industry workers. *(Bitterly.)* Our pudgy, pink masters. (70–71; italics in original)

The centrepiece of Barry's Swiftian vision of tourism is a disquisition on the roots of the tradition behind "the Annual Wreckhouse Folk Festival and Boil-up" (75), the ritual of consumption that provides the climax to the play. Old Crow, a shaman who is not so much the master of ceremonies as the dominatrix-in-residence, begins her dissertation with a withering vision of tourist commodification of Newfoundland's oral culture:

> Many years ago, as any folklore professor worth his tenure, is forever telling us, we people used to entertain ourselves. As they would have it, we'd gather in kitchens when the day's labour was over, to regale each other with stories and song.... These festivals are an attempt, be it ever so vapid and Paddy-fied, to relive those bygone days and sell a lot of beer at the beer tent. (Barry 2003, 76)

She then describes the tradition as a kind of outgrowth of the custom of marine salvage, as, during the "good ol' days" (77), a splinter group began to light fires to lure ships to their destruction, and then would keep the survivors for sexual pleasure and eventual consumption: "well we'd just slit their throats boil 'em up and have a grand big scoff. Oh God, I loved a feed of tongues. Words are funny that way. Well it became a tradition" (78). After the advent of steam threatened a way of life built around the perils of sailing, the building of the highway across the province brought new bounty: "And soon to our delight and amazement these huge road yachts full of plump tourists started showin' up lookin' for, would you believe it, a bit of culture. Well we had little else" (79).

Here Barry makes an ingenious allegorical link between the depletion of natural resources—more specifically, the cod stocks—and reliance on tourism, as Old Crow describes how increasingly desperate competition for tourists eventually exhausted the stocks: "But like everything else here. Too many got in on it. Too many actor-persons chasing too many gawpfish. Whole towns perverted over to it." Ultimately, "[t]he bottom went right out of her" (79). This allegorical "resource crisis" thus leads to a parodic reversal of roles in which, rather than locals having to transform themselves in order to meet tourists' expectations, they have to train outsiders to be tourists: "Now we've got to the point where we got to get people down and train *them* to be tourists instead of training *us* to be *we*. So that we can keep up our culture, see bye's. We got a taste for tourist and it's like a heroin addiction in the blood" (Barry 2003, 79; italics in original). In a hyper-real turn that Baudrillard and Ian McKay would appreciate, attracting tourists itself becomes the folk tradition.

In the ritual of consumption that provides the climax to *Wreckhouse*, Barry deftly spoofs stereotypes of Newfoundlanders as primitives by subversively deploying colonial tropes, in the process highlighting tourism as a form of neo-colonialism. Fiercely satirizing heritage culture as a kind of commodified nativism and touristic behaviour as a dance of automatons, Barry presents the consumption of tourists as a parody of the Newfoundland tradition of the "boil-up," playing on colonial caricatures of native savagery. The "tourists" "*are dressed in beige khaki safari outfits with shorts, white socks with hiking boots, and Tilley hats*" while locals Sydney and Larky are "*dressed in full oilskins and Cape Anns battened down*" (73). Their behaviour makes a mockery of what MacCannell describes as the ritualized, collective aspect of tourist experience: "An authentic tourist experience involves not merely connecting a marker to a sight, but a participation in a collective ritual, in connecting one's own marker to a sight already marked by others" ([1976] 1999, 137). In synchronized fashion, Barry's tourists, with cameras strung around their necks, ritualistically shuffle along, stopping while one points out an attraction to the others, who "*nod their heads in unison. Then in unison they all smile at each other, take each other's picture, sigh and return to their places and proceed with the 'tour'*" (Barry 2003, 74). The tourists then are verbally and physically abused (including being beaten with oars) and forced to put on a show for the locals in order to appreciate the pain of performing one's culture: "Finds it hard to dance a jig with your balls crushed in a vise, do ya?" Old Crow berates one of them. "Now ya know how it feels" (85). The "tourists" then have lobster claws attached to their arms and are thrown into a pot, where one of the locals serves them "*a round of umbrella drinks on a tray*" and they sit "*like they're in a Jacuzzi at some weird Club Med*" (97) as they are slowly brought to a boil. Just as this parodic barbarism reaches its crescendo, with the victims turning on O'Steinway, the action seems to return—à la *A Midsummer Night's Dream*—to where it began, with O'Steinway seeking help from Sydney to fix a flat tire. However, the ambiguous status of the ending (which raises doubts about whether the whole thing has been just a dream) reinforces the cautionary effect of the nightmarish vision at the core of the play, as Sydney, who shows up with a fixed tire, says to the Doctor, "remember.... Heal thyself" (103). *Wreckhouse* thus hilariously, if grimly, points to the strains caused by the fundamentally neo-colonial relations underpinning tourism as a consumption of culture.

Section 2: "About as Far from Disneyland as You Can Possibly Get"

LIKE BARRY'S *WRECKHOUSE,* MUCH OF THE LITERATURE CURRENTLY COMING OUT of Atlantic Canada conveys an underlying sense of loss, but as the works discussed above reflect, that loss is articulated in various ways from the elegiac to the angry to the satirically defiant. It permeates depictions of tourism in the literature of the region, depictions that are ambivalent at best and, more importantly, that reflect a broader resistance to the reconfiguration of the region in a neo-liberal climate obsessed with globalization. These works powerfully convey that tourism—or at least tourism in its more exploitative and intrusive forms—is a force to be reckoned with, because what is on the line in catering to tourists is not just economic survival but also dignity, cultural integrity, and a sense of identity. What these works do in their respective fashions is to engage in a form of counter-colonial resistance, defusing the power of tourism by identifying and deconstructing the neo-colonial relations it so often inscribes, resisting complicity with their own subordination by refusing in various ways the more demeaning roles that tourism thrusts upon the inhabitants of the region.

Conclusion to Section Two

In an economically struggling region like Atlantic Canada, satiric critiques of tourism may seem like kicking the goose that lays the golden eggs. Moreover, it must be stressed that some forms of tourism are more benign and locally beneficial than others and that these writers are not necessarily resisting tourism in and of itself. The resistance in these texts is grounded in a consciousness of the ultimately pernicious economic, social and cultural effects of much tourism, or at least of certain forms of tourism. What contemporary Atlantic-Canadian literature like Frank Barry's *Wreckhouse*, Lynn Coady's *Strange Heaven* and Edward Riche's novels is resisting is a kind of cultural ossification, a fixing in amber of the Folk stereotype, suggestive as it is of a perennial, immutable, home-grown culture. Not only is the stereotype inaccurate, hierarchical, and exclusive, as the work of Native, Black, and women writers dramatizes but it is also static and disempowering, effacing the profound social, economic, and cultural changes that the region has undergone and continues to undergo. The predominance of such Folk motifs mitigates against viewing culture and literature in Atlantic Canada as dynamic and evolving, reflecting these changes and wider social and cultural influences, rather than arthritically persisting in spite of them, shielded from the ravages of history. Furthermore, the fact that challenges to the Folk paradigm have come not just from those excluded by it or subordinated within it reflects the degree to which Atlantic-Canadian writers are recognizing Folk apparel for the cultural straitjacket it is.

It is important to recognize that the Atlantic provinces remain perhaps the most demographically homogeneous part of the country, largely because of an inability to attract immigrants. This inability can be attributed to a great degree to the historical underdevelopment of the region (immigrants typically gravitating to the more densely populated and prosperous parts of the country) but also, no doubt, to that demographic homogeneity itself. Nonetheless, the region has always been more heterogeneous than the stereotype suggests, and a key dimension of the cultural reconfiguration of the region in contemporary Atlantic-Canadian literature—subverting the stereotype that the region is still stuck in the past—is the increasing visibility of writing by women and racialized minorities. Rather than being perpetually stalled in a monochromatic, patriarchal past, the region is, like other parts of the country, evolving in response to important demographic, political, and social developments, including the pressures on employment options in a neo-liberal era. At the same time, that reconfiguration has also entailed a confrontation with the internal hierarchies and conflicts within the region, particularly the continuing presence of racism and sexism. But while Atlantic-Canadian writers have been engaged, if perhaps to a more limited degree, in the pronounced demographic and cultural diversification that has characterized the literature of the rest of the country for the last forty years, it is also clear that for many of the region's writers that process has been framed within the broader imperatives of countering the cultural and political marginalization of the region within Confederation and countering the commodification of culture that has been one of the hallmarks of neo-liberalism. This has given a very different inflection to that cultural reconfiguration on the East Coast, most conspicuously taking the form of a sustained and self-conscious shucking off of the attire of the Folk.

| **Section Three**

The Age of Sale: History, Globalization, and Commodification

Historical fiction, as many commentators have observed, tends to be characterized by a double vision: while it looks to the past, its representation of that past is necessarily refracted through, and often consciously energized by, concerns of the present. This insight is particularly salient in appreciating the current surge of historical fiction in Atlantic-Canadian literature, part of a worldwide trend. In tracking significant developments in the contemporary literature of the region, and their implications for the current position of the region, then, historical fiction is a crucial genre to consider. Atlantic-Canadian writers' preoccupation with the past, for one thing, says much about the present situation of the region. Historical fiction also provides an important alternative mode for engaging with many of the same concerns that we have seen thus far in this study: the region's tenuous place in Confederation, the impact of economic trends and the restructuring of work, the experience of marginalized groups, and the commodification of culture and heritage.

Atlantic-Canadian writers' conspicuous turn to history, furthermore, must be situated within the larger trend under neo-liberalism toward the commodification of history and heritage. As the discussion of tourism in the previous chapter suggests, an important consequence of the growing reliance on tourism in Atlantic Canada is a troubling attitude toward the region's past. In the lead editorial of "Bury My Heart at Peggy's Cove," a special issue of *New Maritimes* that appeared in 1987, the editors highlighted the problems of state-sponsored tourism's retailing of "easily digested stereotypes and clichés," particularly for the representation and understanding of history:

> What happens when these stereotypes gain currency as a truthful depiction of history? As these stereotypes come to influence more and more community events, will we become, in some strange postmodern sense, tourists in our own region, unable to digest more than bland, cardboard images of ourselves and our history? What happens to our sense of the past, when the state is given the authority to rewrite and package history to suit the tastes of the travelling public?... Is there not something vaguely Orwellian about a situation in which the state directly organizes and determines the experience of the past, giving us its own interpretation of "our story" and "our history" in the form of massive and expensive public spectacles? ("Limits of Tourism" 1987, 5)

As the part of Canada first explored and settled by Europeans, the Atlantic provinces have a long and rich history that in many ways is a source of pride in the region. Unfortunately, historical "richness" is not always grounds for celebration, because recognizing the complexity of the past in the Atlantic provinces, as elsewhere, entails recognizing the violence, exploitation, and other forms of conflict that characterized much of the region's history. Thus, as the *New Maritimes* editorial suggests, in the context of an economy in which it has become increasingly necessary to celebrate the region's history and its cultural heritage in order to generate revenue, there is a tendency to distort that heritage into a simplified and sanitized version fit for consumption by tourists. The recourse to tourism as a response to crises in the traditional resource sectors on the East Coast is not a recent phenomenon but goes back at least to the early twentieth century. However, tourism's centrality to the regional economy has been intensified during the era of neo-liberal restructuring, characterized by the industrialization of tourism in the region and by growing pressure to market the region's culture and history, to exploit less tangible resources than its traditional natural ones.

One of the principal problems with such a stylizing and airbrushing of history is that it amounts to a packaging of the past for consumption, rather than cultivating a constructive engagement with history as a continuing and evolving process. "The danger of heritage tourism for people living within its ambit," D.A. Muise rightly cautions, "is palpable. If they come to accept a history cleansed from any taint of social conflict, their own lived pasts will thus be neutralized, making it difficult if not impossible for their history to form a vital part of continuing political processes that redefine their lives" (1998, 132). This tension is particularly important when it comes to writing creative literature about the past, which constitutes a significant proportion of contemporary Atlantic-Canadian writing. The vogue for historical fiction, of course, is not limited to the Atlantic provinces; as part of an international trend, the historical novel has become one of the dominant literary genres in Canada. However, creative representations of the history of the Atlantic region arguably have a different set of preoccupations and resonances from their counterparts in the rest of the country, preoccupations that are very much related to the effects of restructuring and the political and economic marginality of the region. The historical fiction of the region, particularly of Newfoundland and Labrador, is thoroughly rooted in this economic and cultural reconfiguration and in the challenge to prevailing Folk stereotypes of Atlantic Canada. Thus it is a central part of the literary response to the current economic, political, and cultural tensions in the region.

David Creelman's thesis about the hesitancy of Maritime fiction—poised between an imagined communal heritage and an uncertain future—is a useful starting point for appreciating the relative distinctiveness of the historical fiction of Atlantic Canada. Both in the Maritimes and even more so in post-moratorium Newfoundland, there is a palpable sense of having crossed a distinct threshold, that a way of life built around the resource sectors is undergoing profound change. That sense of the end of an era (a cumulative impression rather than an overnight revelation, it should be said) is compounded, furthermore, by an uncertainty about what the future holds and much more doubt that it will be a prosperous one than might be the case in other regions of the country. In short, there is a pronounced sense of loss, of rupture, informing the turn to history in the literature of the region.

Given Muise's reservations about the effects of heritage tourism, this context of rupture and loss compounds a number of the occupational hazards of writing historical fiction in a postmodern consumer society with a strong impulse toward commodification. "Modern society," Dean MacCannell argues, "is especially vulnerable to overthrow from within, through nostalgia, sentimentality and other tendencies to regress to a previous state, a 'Golden Age,' which retrospectively always appears to have been more orderly or normal" ([1976] 1999, 82). Thus one danger is that the tenuous present and uncertain future of the Atlantic provinces make people in the region, including its writers, particularly susceptible to wallowing in and romanticizing its more storied past, in the process potentially reinforcing the disempowering Folk stereotypes through which the region continues to be perceived. Furthermore, in becoming preoccupied with the past, writers may be engaging, consciously or unconsciously, in a retreat from the present and the future.

Although it does not manage to avoid all of these pitfalls, contemporary historical fiction in Atlantic Canada reflects an awareness of their presence and is characterized by various strategies that resist the packaging of the region's past in sanitized Folk form. First of all, writers of historical fiction in the region, like their counterparts in the rest of the country, are less inclined to provide heroic, celebratory tales of a homogeneous and harmonious past than they are to highlight the divisions and conflicts that such celebratory narratives suppress. Secondly, rather than retreating from the present and the future into the past, many of these writers, like their counterparts elsewhere, exploit the possibilities of creative representations of the past for commenting directly or indirectly on concerns of the present. Finally, at least some of the literary renditions of the region's history recognize the vulnerability of the genre to commodification, and through various self-conscious textual strategies foreground and resist the passive attitude toward history as a dynamic and evolving process that such commodification encourages.

7 |

"A 'Sea-Change' of Sorts": Newfoundland and Labrador

The fact that the political, economic, and cultural developments described in previous chapters—especially the crisis in the fisheries and a growing concern about Atlantic Canada's place in Confederation—have resonated more clearly in Newfoundland and Labrador than in the Maritimes is arguably reflected in the striking volume of historical fiction that has come out of the province in the last twenty years. From the pronounced focus on history in the work of the province's best-known writer, Wayne Johnston, to Bernice Morgan's popular historical romance *Random Passage*, to forays into history by writers such as John Steffler, Michael Winter, Kevin Major, and Michael Crummey, the preoccupation with the past in the literature of the province is palpable. That preoccupation, furthermore, is imbued with a sense of loss that, Paul Chafe contends, "is a fundamental part of Newfoundland identity and heritage." The theme of loss, Chafe underscores, runs throughout Newfoundland's history, the "signposts of [which] include moments of bereavement, dispossession, or deprivation: the eradication of the Beothuk, the loss of independence, the loss of a generation of men at Beaumont Hamel in the First World War, the moratorium on the cod fishery" (2010, 168). In a contemporary climate of pronounced cultural, economic, and political turbulence, that sense of loss is perhaps stronger than ever, and it is easy to see the recent wave of historical fiction in Newfoundland as having been fostered and shaped by this climate of change and uncertainty.

"The river that might have been": Wayne Johnston

Perhaps the most sustained engagement with the past in the literature of Atlantic Canada can be found in the work of Wayne Johnston, who has gained an international reputation on the basis of three novels engaging with history, *The Colony of Unrequited Dreams* (1998), *The Navigator of New York* (2002), and *The Custodian of Paradise* (2006), as well as his memoir, *Baltimore's Mansion* (1999). Written at a time of increasing reflection on Newfoundland's position in Confederation, Johnston's *The Colony of Unrequited Dreams*, a fictionalized biography of Joey Smallwood, the man who steered Newfoundland into Confederation and presided over the province for four decades, and *Baltimore's Mansion*, which chronicles the tensions within Johnston's own family over the future course of Newfoundland, serve as companion pieces, providing a macrocosmic and a microcosmic view of Newfoundland's thwarted destiny. As Jeff Webb suggests, the *fin de siècle* obsession with the referendum reflects a sense that Newfoundlanders are at a crossroads: "This is a time in which economic forces, such as global competitiveness, and the closure of the seal fishery, the cod fishery and now the salmon fishery, threaten the extinction of rural Newfoundland" (1998, 183). Both of Johnston's books look back at an earlier crossroads in Newfoundland's history from an era of soul-searching in which Newfoundlanders have come to offer more vocal reservations about the wisdom of joining Canada and to give earnest (and not merely maudlin) consideration to what might have been.

"What might have been," Johnston stresses, is indeed a major theme in all his work, and not just in his historical novels (2007, 111). *The Colony of Unrequited Dreams* and *Baltimore's Mansion* are preoccupied with what Johnston has described as "the ghost history" of Newfoundland, the spectre of what might have been, and they are imbued with an elegiac recognition that the decision to join Canada marked a profound existential threshold for Newfoundlanders. But they also reflect a broader tendency to question the legitimacy of that decision and even to see it as the product of a conspiracy. Personalizing the outcome of historical forces, Webb argues, offers a sense of comfort and the illusion of control: "If we believe that some individuals were responsible for the confederate victory, then we can fantasize that Newfoundlanders did not really reject the Newfoundland nation in 1948. We are still a nation, the argument runs, but it is a secret because the truth has been hidden from us" (1998, 183). To a degree, this inclination characterizes Johnston's novel and memoir, in which the outcome of the 1948 referendum on Newfoundland's future is portrayed as a definitive, watershed moment. Not only is it a divisive and narrowly won decision to forego independence; it also signals the twilight of a distinctive, largely pre-industrial, and independent culture.

The momentousness of the referendum decision is conveyed in *Baltimore's Mansion* principally through the contrast and tension between Johnston's father Arthur, and Arthur's father Charlie. To Johnston, Charlie, a fisherman and blacksmith, clearly represents the pre-industrial rural autonomy of pre-Confederation Newfoundland; whereas Arthur, a former fisherman who after Confederation works as an inspector for the federal fisheries department, is in a position emblematic of Newfoundland's transition to subordinate modernity within the Canadian nation. The contrast of occupations, however, is highly ironic, given that over the course of *Baltimore's Mansion* Arthur emerges as a quixotic standard-bearer for the cause of independence, while Charlie, it is suggested, may well have voted for Confederation. As Johnston struggles to penetrate this central enigma of his family's history, *Baltimore's Mansion* takes shape as an elegy for a lost way of life and the lost possibility of an independent Newfoundland.

Although Charlie Johnston died a decade before Wayne Johnston was born, through the eyes of Arthur, *Baltimore's Mansion* evocatively renders the predominantly pre-modern milieu of Charlie's life in Ferryland at the southern tip of the Avalon Peninsula. In a series of scenes focalized through a younger Arthur, Johnston captures the rhythms of a way of life sustained over centuries and eclipsed almost overnight. As a blacksmith, Charlie is mythologized as "Ferryland's Hephaestus" (Johnston 1999, 29). While Johnston gives to Charlie's forge almost mythical proportions, he also underscores the arduousness and perils of his rural existence, particularly in a stirring scene in which Charlie and Arthur, returning with a cartload of ice cut from the sea shore, are almost marooned in a blizzard. What is most pronounced in Johnston's portrait of Charlie, though, is the sense that he represents a bygone era. Returning from a trip by horse and cart to a foundry in St. John's, Charlie forecasts to Arthur the replacement of blacksmiths like himself by the foundries they have just visited: "Everything I make they'll make it there but ten times faster" (1999, 37).

If Charlie is thus associated with a social and economic order rapidly being eclipsed by the forces of industrial modernity, he is also associated with a political order that is in a similar position: Newfoundland's almost century-long status as "a self-governing colony of Britain"—"a fancy phrase for country" (43), as Arthur sees it. Charlie is a confidant of Major Peter Cashin, the leader of the anti-confederate cause, and the Johnstons are passionate opponents of Confederation and its principal advocate, Joey Smallwood. Indeed, Arthur remains a staunch and bitter anti-confederate well into the 1970s, decades after Newfoundland's fate is decided in favour of Confederation. Arthur's stance is fuelled by what Johnston describes as "the animating myth of many Newfoundlanders, the myth that the true king was always in exile or in rags while some pretender held the throne" (178). Johnston somewhat parodically portrays his father's quixotic role as standard-bearer for the anti-confederates, riffing off the Arthurian resonances of his name, Arthur Reginald (King Arthur), to give a certain heroism to his role. What emerges over the course of the memoir, though, is the degree to which Arthur's singular adherence to the cause—he still sees himself as "a man without a country" in the 1970s—is bound up with his conflicted feelings about his own father (176). Arthur is away on the mainland at the time of Charlie's death, which occurs in the hiatus between the 1948 referendum and Newfoundland's becoming the tenth province on the eve of April Fool's Day, 1949. Thus Arthur returns to an island that has been profoundly transformed during his absence, and Charlie's passing is irrevocably associated with the passing of "the old Newfoundland": "His death divided the century and ... kept his children rooted in both time and space, imposed on them an obligation to continue, however pointlessly or tokenly, to resist Confederation" (202). For decades after, Arthur remains obsessed with the "ghost history" of Newfoundland, in which "the independents had won the referendum, the members of the national parliament of Newfoundland had been meeting since 1949, and it was Joey's and not Cashin's name whom no one under forty could remember" (242). He does so, moreover, as a former fisherman "who used to be an anti-confederate now walking around in what he still thinks of as his country with the badge of the federal Fisheries of Canada plastered on both shoulders" (155).

At the same time, however, central to the memoir is Johnston's suspicion that Arthur and Charlie had a falling out before Arthur left for the mainland because one or the other may have belonged to that most despised of species, "the closet confederates," those "who had outwardly opposed Confederation and, indeed, opposed it in their heart of hearts but in the secrecy of the ballot box had voted for it" (Johnston 1999, 58). When Arthur affirms to Wayne late in the memoir that he did vote for independence, Johnston concludes that the closet confederate must have been Charlie. This possibility is subsequently rendered in a speculative scene, in which Johnston depicts an agonized Charlie in the voting booth being moved "to do what to him seemed and always will seem wrong" (245). This conclusion, though, is not confirmed by Arthur himself, who instead encourages his son to let go of the past, compelling him to realize that "a shift, a swing, a fall took place that would have taken place no matter which side won" and that to try to reanimate the past is futile: "No path leads back from here to there" (239).

Arthur's concession to the irrevocability of a decision that he has spent most of his life resisting captures the central paradox of *Baltimore's Mansion*, a memoir, after all, that is obsessed with going "from here to there." The book strives to capture the pre-Confederation world of Charlie's work and his father's youth, and at the same time self-consciously foregrounds such reconstruction as closer to mythology than mimesis. *Baltimore's Mansion* evokes a lost world of mythical proportions, an impression consolidated in the final scene, in which Charlie is depicted at the moment of his death crossing over into (the mythological) Avalon, the geography around him "fixed in a moment that for him will never pass" (272). This sense of temporal suspension arguably applies to most of Johnston's memoir, the ultimate effect of which is a sense of historical discontinuity. Pre-Confederation Newfoundland is consistently positioned on the other side of a profound ontological divide, as remote and inaccessible as that other Avalon. Furthermore, the passionately anti-confederate Johnstons "had followed the river of what should have been, knowing it led nowhere" (186), and in *Baltimore's Mansion* this preoccupation with Newfoundland's "ghost history" overshadows its post-Confederation history as a province within Canada, what might be termed "the river that was and is." Thus, Johnston in his memoir clearly ignores his father's advice to accept the irrevocability of history and to forget the past, imbued as *Baltimore's Mansion* is with an overwhelming sense of loss. Although the suggestion is made that this loss would have occurred no matter which side won the referendum, the elegiac quality of Johnston's memoir leaves little room to convey that anything has been gained. It also gives no sense that, as James Hiller argues, "whatever their individual reasons may have been, the majority of Newfoundland voters made a wise decision in 1948" (1993, 380) and that almost a century "of responsible government had demonstrated, it seemed, that Newfoundland did not after all have the resources with which to build a viable independence" (380–81). This is reinforced by the impression Johnston creates of the confederate cause as pragmatic, half-hearted, and even counter-instinctive. Indeed, *Baltimore's Mansion* offers a vision of Newfoundland after Confederation as very much the fallen world of his father's anti-confederate mythology.

The Colony of Unrequited Dreams is just as preoccupied with what might have been, particularly because Johnston's concern with the "ghost history" of Newfoundland is mirrored by and figured through an unrequited romance between the protagonist Smallwood and his nemesis, Sheilagh Fielding. As a fictional representation of the most central and controversial figure in the history of Newfoundland, *The Colony of Unrequited Dreams* stirred a great deal of controversy when it was published, with critics objecting to the appearance of the novel so soon after Smallwood's death, to Johnston's playing around with the historical record, to his invention of a fictional lover for Smallwood, and to the representation of Smallwood himself. Such a stance was typified by a high-profile review in *The Globe and Mail* by columnist and notable Newfoundlander Rex Murphy, who argued that the novel "drains and diminishes the Smallwood that so many Newfoundlanders still remember,

Section 3: The Age of Sale

producing a pasteboard substitute" (1998b, D15). Johnston responded to such criticism by pointing out that he was being "criticized for failing to do something it was never [his] intention to do—namely, to portray the 'real' Joe Smallwood" (D1) and emphasizing the long tradition of historical fiction in which he was working. To expect "accuracy of this sort in a novel," Johnston argued, was beside the point, and he stressed instead his hope that "readers everywhere would see reflected their own attempts to crawl out from underneath the avalanche of history with their human individuality intact" (1998b, D1). Stan Dragland rightly argues that the complex and protean Joey Smallwood has spawned a wide array of fictional and non-fictional interpretations and that, accepting "reality as plastic," it is important to assess Johnston's moulding of history as "a new sort of whole whose value depends on the depth and intensity of the vision it serves" (2004, 204). That vision, however, dealing as it does with the history of Newfoundland and a pivotal moment in its political destiny, necessarily has political resonances. While it may speak to readers around the world, it is also quite clearly a novel of Newfoundland, presenting that history and destiny in a particular light. Like numerous other contemporary Canadian novels, *The Colony of Unrequited Dreams* is self-consciously historiographic and post-colonial, emphasizing England's baleful influence on the fortunes of Newfoundland. But it is also characterized by a nationalist nostalgia and an ambivalence about Newfoundland's post-Confederation fate. It suggests the inevitability of Newfoundland's present liminality—disenchanted with Confederation and tantalized by independence—while lamenting the loss of that independence all the same.

This trajectory is an effect of the two principal parts of the novel, Smallwood's fictional autobiography and Fielding's parodic version of his career and of the history of pre-Confederation Newfoundland. In the former, Johnston depicts Smallwood not as the demonic leader of the Confederation side but as a much more complex and conflicted figure. The history that Johnston's Smallwood is "trying to crawl out from underneath" is that of Newfoundland's centuries-long mistreatment by England, which very much shapes Smallwood's apprenticeship in politics, his advocacy of the cause of Confederation, and his dictatorial and disastrously spendthrift behaviour as premier.

A key thread running through Smallwood's apprenticeship is his subversive, if somewhat hamstrung, resistance to colonial attitudes toward Newfoundland. At Bishop Feild College, where "[m]ost of the masters were wittily scornful of Newfoundland" (Johnston 1998a, 34), Smallwood conducts a running battle with Headmaster Reeves, who relishes digressing from his history lessons to heap abuse on Newfoundland. When Smallwood mentions that D.W. Prowse, the grandfather of Smallwood's fictional classmate Prowse, has written a history of Newfoundland, for instance, Reeves has "no doubt that it is a well-researched, competently written chronicle of misery and savagery, full of half-educated politicians and failures-in-exile like myself and their attempts to oversee and educate a population descended from the dregs of the mother country" (38). Smallwood responds to Reeves's condescension by humorously and subversively coming to Newfoundland's defence. Despite Smallwood's arguably post-colonial resistance, Reeves's presumption of Newfoundland's inferiority leaves its stamp on him all the same. Smallwood reprises this role as quixotic critic of colonialism decades later, after Britain's suspension of Newfoundland's autonomy during the Depression. "We live in an occupied country," a drunken Smallwood proclaims at a reception for journalists at Government House, "and that it has been occupied at our request only makes it that much worse" (366). Cutting a comical figure, Smallwood is then ejected after confronting Hope Simpson, the effective head of the commission government, over his callous and condescending attitude toward Newfoundland and its heritage. As Smallwood's erratic political career develops and Newfoundland is faced with a referendum on its political future, Smallwood comes to see Confederation as the best way to challenge the dominance of the merchant elite of St. John's and to improve the lives of the impoverished inhabitants of rural Newfoundland. When he becomes the most prominent representative of the cause, Smallwood is requested for a private audience with Governor MacDonald, who tacitly expresses Britain's support for having Confederation put on the referendum ballot. Rather than reacting with outrage, Smallwood defers to this breach of Britain's neutrality, not just out of political ambition and expediency but also because he sees it as a necessary step for getting out from under colonial control: "A mutual good riddance" (442).

If Smallwood's political apprenticeship is depicted as being shaped in resistance to colonial control and the hegemony of the merchant elite, the longer history of the impact of colonialism on the development of Newfoundland is provided by Fielding's *Condensed History of Newfoundland*. Fielding's topsy-turvy history satirically excoriates England's centuries-long alternation between malign neglect and malign exploitation of Newfoundland, underscoring the class and sectarian divisions that have marked its turbulent history. Fielding's *History* serves as an ingenious solution to a major dilemma Johnston faced in writing the novel, the question of how to "include in the book the mass of knowledge a reader would need about the history of Newfoundland" (Johnston 2003, n.p.). Although Fielding's history "is barely thirty pages long," Johnston observes, "the reader, by the end of the book, knows as much about Newfoundland history as most Newfoundlanders do"

FIGURE 11 Daniel Woodley Prowse, ca. 1900.

(2003, n.p.) At the same time, Fielding's parodic history gives to the novel a crucial historiographical self-consciousness. Fielding routinely inverts and spoofs colonial perspectives on episodes in Newfoundland's history, encouraging readers to consider how history tends to be written by the victors and undermining the impression of Olympian objectivity present in so much colonial historiography. Fielding's succinct and thoroughly ironic account is a seeming rejoinder to other histories of Newfoundland that have criticized England's treatment of Newfoundland through the centuries, especially D.W. Prowse's monumental *A History of Newfoundland* (1895). Nonetheless, it reinforces by implication what Jerry Bannister sees as Prowse's romantic nationalist view of the history of Newfoundland as "a narrative of the long struggle for control over the island between the tyrannical West Country merchants along with their allies in the British government, on the one hand, and the humble settlers and their political champions, on the other" (2003, 125).[1]

Fielding's history, for instance, highlights how the settlement and development of Newfoundland was actively discouraged by England, because of the influence of West Country merchants resistant to permanent inhabitants who would disturb the monopolizing of the fishing grounds by their migratory fleets. For instance, what Prowse describes as a brutal punitive expedition by the fishing admirals in 1675, the result of a "decision to destroy a whole population of Englishmen, to condemn them to ruin, extermination, and exile from their cherished homes and all the accumulated wealth of several generations" (1895, 190), Fielding presents as a botched census, the result of a misunderstanding ensuing from their having lost their orders from the king. Her description of Newfoundland's achievement of autonomy through ironic understatement stresses England's capricious and abusive government of Newfoundland. Fielding writes of the "dark days" of agitation for responsible government in the mid-nineteenth century, observing that one of "the darkest is March 26, 1857, when the infamous Labouchere

Despatch is issued, in which the colonial secretary instructs Governor Darling to tell the Newfoundland people that henceforth, if they want their territorial rights arbitrarily amended, they will have to do it themselves" (Johnston 1998a, 336).[2] As Fielding's history itself suggests, any account of the past is necessarily a rhetorical construct, "an extended metaphor," as Hayden White argues, assembling historical detail in a narrative form that imparts to it a particular rhetorical slant (1978, 91). Fielding's *Condensed History* ultimately contributes to the novel a particularly post-colonial perspective on Newfoundland's history that dovetails with the narrative of Smallwood's political career. That is, Fielding portrays England's treatment of Newfoundland as having had a crippling effect on its destiny, undermining its prosperity and autonomy, and propelling it toward a humiliating subordination within Confederation.

The thwarted romance between Smallwood and Fielding allegorically reinforces the emphasis on the detrimental impact of the legacy of colonialism evident in Smallwood's career and in the thwarted destiny of Newfoundland. Despite his immediate attraction to Fielding, Smallwood is acutely aware that while she belongs to the "quality," the St. John's elite, he is an interloper, one of the great unwashed. Her erratic, hesitant behaviour (which Smallwood interprets as signalling her affection for his nemesis Prowse) recurrently poses another obstacle to their coming together. What gradually emerges over the course of the novel is that Fielding's enigmatic, vacillating behaviour reflects her attempt to hide the secret that as a teenager she had been made pregnant by Prowse and bore twins who have been raised in New York as her mother's children. This subplot symbolically underscores the impact of Newfoundland's colonial history and class divisions on the lives of individuals, as the letter that she forges implicating Smallwood, whom she knows she will not be forced to marry, is a collage of letters cut from the title page of Prowse's *History*. The protracted, convoluted revelation of this secret takes place over the course of the whole novel, during which Smallwood and Fielding repeatedly come together and part acrimoniously, like mutually repelling magnetic particles. The key moment comes when Smallwood impulsively proposes marriage and then interprets Fielding's hesitation as rejection, pretending he had been joking to save face and mask his vulnerability. In response to Fielding's perplexing hesitation, a spurned and resentful Smallwood finds release in his political ambitions, the suggestion being that if he cannot tie his fortunes to Fielding's, he can at least tie them to Newfoundland's.

While Smallwood succeeds in championing the cause of Confederation, he is ultimately unable to crawl out from beneath the weight of the past completely. Once in power, the historical Joey Smallwood embarked on an ambitious program to modernize and develop Newfoundland and to wean it off its dependency on the fisheries, efforts Harold Horwood (echoing Smallwood himself) described as being intended to "drag Newfoundland kicking and screaming into the nineteenth century" (1989, 217). The results were spectacularly disastrous, as Smallwood frittered away Newfoundland's pre-Confederation surplus, at a total cost of "$30 million. Had Smallwood literally taken $10–15 million and burnt it in a bonfire atop Signal Hill, the end result, in terms of Newfoundland's progress, would not have been greatly different" (Gwyn 1968, 168). Johnston's Smallwood describes how all sorts of dodgy opportunists "proposed, and were given government grants for, the most unlikely, far-fetched, bizarre schemes for the economic development of Newfoundland, almost all of which flopped or never got off the ground" (1998a, 523–24). What Johnston emphasizes in Smallwood's gullibility when dealing with investors and his own shady director of industrial development, Alfred Valdmanis, is that the premier's blind trust is part of a colonial cringe, a deference to those he sees as his social superiors: "I was infatuated, not so much with Valdmanis, as with the man he was impersonating, who had all those qualities that I felt the lack of in myself—worldliness, sophistication, business savvy, education, culture, taste, refinement" (514). Thus Johnston suggests that Smallwood's shortcomings in office are in part the consequence of an inferiority complex that political success does little to mitigate.

At this juncture in his career, Smallwood's ambivalent, oscillating relationship with Fielding comes to a head, and the resolution of their misunderstanding reinforces the elegiac overtones of Smallwood's political failure. During this time, Smallwood's fiercest and most brazen critic is Fielding, whose hyperbolically satirical column "Field Days" does for Smallwood's political career what her *Condensed History* does for the history of Newfoundland, and Smallwood's desire to defuse her criticism leads, paradoxically, to the solving of the enigma of their relationship. After Valdmanis is arrested for fraud and tries to use Fielding's purloined journals to blackmail Smallwood, Smallwood returns the journals to Fielding. She finally discloses the full details of her secret history, and *The Colony of Unrequited Dreams* ends with a somewhat improbable reconciliation between the acerbic Fielding and Smallwood at the height of his dictatorial control of Newfoundland. After finally grasping the lack of affection between Fielding and Prowse and hearing her full story, Smallwood consoles her and "[f]orty years of love were consummated with one hug" (Johnston 1998a, 541). Smallwood realizes that in this Platonic embrace, "[o]ur one moment, our one point of intersection, had just come and gone. We had for years been moving closer together and from now on we would move apart" (542). When Fielding subsequently asks Smallwood whether knowing the truth would have made a difference when he proposed to her in New York, he recognizes the truth, thinking, "I would have done what I wound up doing anyway, would have tried to convince myself that I had never really loved her and that it therefore did not matter that she was not what I had imagined her to be" (550). Realizing the consequences of his vanity and political ambition, Smallwood takes solace in the possibility that Fielding loves him now and that "I had at least once in my life been capable of that, able to escape my self long enough to love." At the same time, he is overcome with emotion: "Suddenly, the unacknowledged sorrows and blunders of my life surged up in me all at once" (550). The allegorical romance between Smallwood and Fielding, then, underscores Smallwood's inability to throw off the shackles of history, his sacrificing of emotional commitment for the sake of political advancement and success, and the colonial cringe that ultimately derails that success.

As various critics have recognized, the failure of their romance reflects, in turn, Smallwood's failure to truly embrace the potential of Newfoundland. Consequently, the belated reconciliation between Smallwood and Fielding and their joint mourning over what might have been have their parallel in the reaction to the outcome of Newfoundland's turbulent political fortunes. Although Johnston's Smallwood may not be an attempt "to portray the 'real' Joe Smallwood," *Colony* is certainly engaging in a complex dialogue with that historical figure and the historical events in which he played a crucial role. In a similar fashion, the novel develops a particular perspective on the referendum as a Pyrrhic victory at best and as a joint loss. Johnston depicts Newfoundlanders' attitudes toward Confederation as profoundly ambivalent, and in that ambivalence effects a retrospective reconciliation between confederate and anti-confederate. The bitter acrimony over Newfoundland joining Confederation is depicted not so much as a profound political division but as a kind of shared, repressed ambivalence in the face of the inevitable. "We confederates," Smallwood says of the campaign, "took out on the independents the shame and guilt we could not admit, even to ourselves, to feeling, and the independents were all the more fanatically for independence the more they doubted, the more tempted to join our side, they felt" (Johnston 1998a, 477). "Spouses, brothers, sisters, parents, children, churches, unions were divided," Smallwood asserts, "not along religious lines and not, though they would have told you otherwise, because their politics were different" (478). The principal resonance Johnston gives to the referendum, finally, is the sense that it marks an inevitable, collective loss. In an entry to her

Section 3: The Age of Sale

journal addressed to Smallwood and written at the time of Newfoundland's entry into Canada, Fielding laments Newfoundland's surrender of autonomy, recognizing at the same time its inevitability:

> *Nationality, for Newfoundlanders a nebulous attribute at best, will become obsolete, and the word* country *will be even more meaningless than it was before. The question that has been there from the start, unasked, unanswered, unacknowledged, will still be there.*
> *We have lost something we would have lost no matter which side won.* (493–94)

Although Fielding, in her almost impenetrable irony, cannot be explicitly identified with the anti-confederate cause, the parallels between her own life and the fate of Newfoundland clearly put the symbolic weight of the novel on Newfoundland's thwarted destiny, on what might have been and therefore must be collectively mourned. At the end of the novel, in a "Field Day" column written a decade after Confederation, Fielding's reflections clearly signal the parallels between her own life and the fate of Newfoundland,

> We have joined a nation that we do not know, a nation that does not know us.
> The river of what might have been still runs and there will never come a time when we do not hear it.
> My life for forty years was a pair of rivers, the river that might have been beside the one that was. (560)

This ambivalence, moreover, persists after the victory of the confederates. Fielding reflects in her journal that "*even the winners, knowing that nothing new can happen now, will think about the past. And though they will deny it, even to themselves, and though they will not understand it, they will feel guilty, as I do*" (Johnston 1998a, 493). Likewise, Smallwood, at his moment of triumph, muses on the silence that falls over the city: "There lay over everything the guilt that accompanies the doing of a terrible but necessary thing" (495). While Fielding's decision to reunite with her daughter suggests a reorientation to the future, there is little sense in the novel of looking ahead to what Newfoundland might be within Confederation. Instead, the emphasis firmly resides on what might have been. This is even the case for Smallwood. If, for Fielding, Confederation marks a moment of perhaps inevitable loss, much the same can be said of the erstwhile victor, whose obsession with "what might have been" between him and Fielding by extension condemns him to a melancholy political retrospection as well, one quite clearly demarcated, as

FIGURE 12 J.R. Smallwood campaigning for Confederation.

Dragland rightly argues, from the confident and forward-looking Smallwood of his memoir *I Chose Canada* (2004, 196). Ultimately, Smallwood's relationship with Newfoundland, as with Fielding, is a disappointment, an unrequited romance: "I did not solve the paradox of Newfoundland or fathom the effect on me of its particular beauty. It stirred in me, as all great things did, a longing to accomplish or create something commensurate with it. I thought Confederation might be it, but I was wrong" (Johnston 1998a, 552).

The end result of Johnston's tactic of developing a fictional, unrequited love affair that serves allegorically as a figure for Newfoundland's thwarted independence is a narrative, like *Baltimore's Mansion*, obsessed with "what might have been" and imbued with a profound sense of loss. If *The Colony of Unrequited Dreams* can be read as a fictional comment on the referendum, the ultimate effect of the novel is a collapsing of the distinction between confederate and anti-confederate, and the reunion and reconciliation of the two sides in shared melancholy, loss, and regret. "*We have lost something we would have lost no matter which side won*"—this note, sounded in both *Colony* and *Baltimore's Mansion*, arguably defuses the tensions between the two sides by suggesting the inevitability of loss and, arguably, the historical irrelevance of the referendum. Thus Johnston seems to be participating in what Bannister characterizes as Newfoundland nationalists' drive to cultivate a questionable sense of unity, "creating the cultural means through which diverse peoples can unite behind a single political goal," which "necessarily entailed the masking of social cleavages" (2003, 151).

The explanation for this reduction may well be found in the geography of Newfoundland itself. As Alexander MacLeod has persuasively argued, if Johnston's treatment of history is heterogeneous, postmodern, and self-consciously historiographic, his treatment of geography is naturalistic and essentialist (2006, 74). Reading Confederation as a triumph of rural Newfoundland over "the entrenched urban power of the St. John's merchants," MacLeod argues that if "the landscape is 'permanently imminent,'" as Smallwood perceives it to be, a potential waiting to be grasped, "then it is always in the process of arriving at its destiny, always *nearly* here"(80). But that imminence can also be read as "always *never* here." The suggestion in *Colony* is that Newfoundland, not so much because of its history as because of its geography—its tantalizing insularity, suggesting cohesion and autonomy while denying the resources to achieve it—is doomed to a perpetual kind of limbo. In the run-up to the referendum, Smallwood wonders "if independence really was a luxury that Newfoundland could not afford, a prideful dream, a vain delusion impossible to sustain if you lived anywhere in Newfoundland except St. John's" (Johnston 1998a, 433). More pointedly, just as Newfoundland enters Confederation, Fielding writes in her journal that "We have been in limbo for the past nine months, neither country nor province. Only a few would understand that this is just the old abiding limbo made manifest, that we have always been in limbo and perhaps always will" (493). Chafe contends that *Colony* lends itself to "hybrid and multi-faceted" post-colonial readings through which "the present does not become the latest chapter in a narrative of loss and failure, but a possibility among infinite possibilities" and "inspires its audience to become postcolonial readers who refuse to lament, valorize, or dismiss the idea of a successful Newfoundland as another unrequited dream" (2003, 344). While there is some truth to this, there is little sense that *Colony* is looking to the present, let alone the future.

"Just out of the frame": Michael Crummey

The work of another Newfoundland writer, Michael Crummey, is likewise permeated by a sense of loss, a loss grounded in both the history of the province and in the history of Crummey's own family. As Crummey describes in an interview, his 1998 collection of poems and prose pieces *Hard Light* came out of his desire to write about his father's life, "growing up in an outport in Newfoundland, taking part in the fishery" (2007, 296). In *Hard*

Light, Crummey writes of the culture and labour of the salt fish economy, as well as of the perils of the seafaring life associated with it, striving to capture a milieu that "was exactly the way people had lived in Newfoundland for almost 250 years" but that had "in the span of [his father's] lifetime ... disappeared completely" (2007, 296). But the sense of loss in Crummey's work also has post-industrial resonances, in that Crummey attributes it at least in part to growing up in the dying mining town of Buchans in central Newfoundland—a milieu he captures in the stories in his 1998 collection *Flesh and Blood*. In "Journey to a Lost Nation," Crummey describes Buchans as a kind of post-industrial ghost town: "Since the closing of the mine in the early 1980s, the population of permanent residents has shrunk to about one-tenth of its heyday when nearly three thousand people called it home" (2004, 14–15).

Buchans, though, is also proximate to another, perhaps more foundational, loss, as it is close to Red Indian Lake, where the capture of Demasduit, one of the last remaining Beothuk (the only Aboriginal group to be completely wiped out during the history of colonialism in North America), took place in 1819. This incident is the centrepiece of Crummey's celebrated historical novel *River Thieves* (2001), in which he develops a complex romantic and political intrigue among a group of settlers involved in the capture of Demasduit, dubbed Mary March. Like many other Canadian novelists writing about the history of colonialism (John Steffler, Jane Urquhart, and Margaret Sweatman, for instance), Crummey evokes the settler subject's destabilized sense of belonging as a result of the death or displacement of the country's original inhabitants, but he does so against the backdrop of a more contemporary sense of loss, giving *River Thieves* a distinctly post-colonial resonance.

The fate of the Beothuk has inspired a vast body of both scholarly and literary treatments, dating well back into the nineteenth century. As both Mary Dalton and Richard Budgel have argued, though, writing about the Beothuk by the settlers who have supplanted them is plagued with problems. Budgel sees in writing about the Beothuk a series of propensities, all of which tend to polarize or simplify the portrait of Beothuk-settler relations. Whereas some works idealize the Beothuk "as primitives/exotics, of an essentially benign nature," others portray "the Beothuks and/or their fellow aborigines, the Micmacs, as savages." Conversely, some works present "early Newfoundland settlers as savages." A final and more ambivalent trend is the construction of "parallels and relationships between Beothuks and Newfoundlanders" (Budgel 1992, 17). Especially given the irrevocable absence of the Beothuk and thus the challenge of assessing the accuracy of these varying propensities, what tends to unify the array of writing about the Beothuk for Mary Dalton is that it represents a figurative effacement of the Beothuk themselves, who stand instead as symbolic projections of the writers' desires, anxieties, and fantasies:

> The literary works about the Beothuks, full of expressions of empathy and sympathy and awe and guilt, nonetheless exclude and deny them.... While some works struggle against it, the Newfoundland literature about the Beothuks treats the Indian as emblem: the Noble Savage, the spirit of Nature, the past, the timeless, death, the source of wound for the European colonizers. Variations on these motifs constitute much of our writing on the Beothuks, a writing preoccupied with guilt and death and the land, for which the vanished Beothuk, especially the Beothuk woman, serves as figure. We write shadow Indians, who serve us beyond the grave. (1992, 144)

Crummey approached the writing of *River Thieves* acutely aware of these propensities and sensitive to the presumptuousness of attempting to portray the Beothuk from the perspective of an eradicated and ultimately enigmatic Aboriginal population: "that attempt to recreate the Beothuk on the page ... to me has always felt completely wrong-headed and beside the point" (2007, 300). In contrast, Crummey's strategy is to structure the narrative so that the elusiveness and marginality of the Beothuk to the lives of the settlers is the very point. "The Beothuk," Crummey observes, "are largely off-stage throughout the book, a shadowy presence just out of the frame" (2001, 42), a lack of visibility which indeed, "in the end, made their extinction possible" (2007, 336). Instead, the hostilities between the two groups and the settlers' growing awareness of the decimation of the Beothuk serve as a catalyst and, in a way, as an analogue to the relationships between the settler characters, particularly the romantic intrigue between John Peyton Sr., his son John Peyton (two historical figures prominent in the history of the Bay of Exploits area), and their housekeeper Cassandra Jure.

River Thieves thus stands in stark contrast with other representations of the Beothuk that do attempt an imaginative projection of their milieu and world view, such as Bernice Morgan's recent *Cloud of Bone* (2007). Although Morgan's novel consists of a triptych of stories, the principal narrative, wedged between a mid-century wartime account of an AWOL Newfoundland sailor and the story of a contemporary forensic anthropologist, is an extended tale of the embattled Beothuk's extinction from the perspective of Shanawdithit (the erstwhile last of the Beothuks). One of the principal tensions in her narrative is a dubious love triangle between Shanawdithit, Demasduit, and Demasduit's husband Nonosabusut, replete with sexual manipulation and simmering jealousy. Reviewing the novel, Fiona Polack rightly cautions that "Morgan's desire to approach Beothuk history with empathy is clear, but her textual choices make what is intended as a commemorative gesture appear appropriative" (2008, 150). To write about the Beothuk from their perspective, Cynthia Sugars suggests, is to "risk reproducing an imperialist dynamic by colonizing the Beothuk all over again" (2005, 149), and in *River Thieves* Crummey is consciously determined to avoid such an outcome.

FIGURE 13   John Peyton Jr., Justice of the Peace, Twillingate

Like Johnston's *The Colony of Unrequited Dreams* and Steffler's *The Afterlife of George Cartwright* (1992)—and, indeed, other Canadian writers' revisionist versions of settler history that reverse the trajectory of celebratory accounts of colonization—*River Thieves* depicts the history of Newfoundland and Labrador as being far from a heroic narrative of European explorers and settlers triumphing over adversity. At the same time, Crummey resists the simplistic reversal that Budgel describes, in which the fate of the Beothuk is romantically sentimentalized and the settler becomes the barbarian, perhaps as a strategy for contemporary writers to "distance themselves from earlier Newfoundlanders and demonstrate the success of social evolution. See, we're well-educated middle class Newfoundlanders, look how far we've come from our savage ancestors" (1992, 26). Instead, Crummey depicts colonial society in Newfoundland not as a homogeneous, unified invading force but as internally divided, particularly along class lines. He accomplishes this by situating the capture and eventual death of Mary March in a complicated web of tensions and allegiances involving not just the settlers and the Beothuk but also the colonial authorities, the Mi'kmaq, and the unforgiving European pecking order from which the settlers have escaped to Newfoundland.

Section 3: The Age of Sale

The epicentre of these divisions in the novel is the Oedipal clash between John Peyton Senior—who responds to Beothuk raids on his fishing posts with indiscriminate brutality—and Peyton, his son, who is poised to take over his father's trapline. Peyton adopts a more conciliatory and less belligerent attitude toward the Beothuk, supporting English naval officer David Buchan's efforts to establish friendly contact with them. While this contrast in part reflects a distinction between the historical John Peyton Sr. and John Peyton Jr. (see Crummey 2007, 304), it also reflects a sexualized Oedipal tension ensuing from their shared desire for Cassie, a historical figure whose role in the novel is largely fictionalized. Initially, John Senior hopes she may one day be a wife for his son, but after stumbling upon her in the process of taking a bath, he is smitten with the possibility that "he might have her himself" (Crummey [2001] 2002, 191). His son's subsequent discovery that Cassie has been forced to resort to a backwoods abortion confirms his lingering suspicion that his father has taken her as his mistress.

These tensions simmer beneath the expedition to Red Indian Lake, during which Mary is captured, and they shape its fateful outcome. Indeed, the expedition is a kind of reverse image of a previous journey into the interior headed by Buchan, during which two marines, left with the Beothuk as a gesture of trust and goodwill, were murdered and beheaded. Whereas the first expedition (despite the disastrous outcome) was an attempt to establish friendly relations with the Beothuk, the second expedition is driven by a desire for retribution, after the Peytons' fishing boat is stolen and vandalized by the Beothuk. His belligerent stance seemingly vindicated by the outcome of the first expedition, John Senior has little patience for his son's pacifist inclinations and his reluctance to take part in the proposed expedition to the interior to recoup their losses. Fearful that the expedition will spin out of control, Peyton obtains the blessing of the colonial authorities to capture a Beothuk, for which they have posted a substantial reward. However, this strategy ultimately fails to stem the violence he fears. Approaching Red Indian Lake, the Peytons and their men surprise and give chase to a group of Beothuk, and Peyton, throwing down his arms, manages to catch hold of Mary. One of the fleeing Beothuk then approaches the party brandishing a birch branch and attempts to free her from their clutches. When the man grapples with John Senior, Peyton is forced to order his men to fire, after their efforts to beat him off with their muskets prove ineffectual, and the man is killed. Although Peyton's attempt to impose restraint on the expedition is undone, the outcome results not in the reassertion of his father's authority but its erosion. The authorities react to the news of the death of the Beothuk man by establishing an inquiry and calling upon Peyton to testify. The jury's conclusion that the "obstinance of the deceased [who turns out to

"A 'Sea-Change' of Sorts"

FIGURE 14 Artist's rendering of the murder of Nonosabusut and the capture of Demasduit, March 1819. Mark Ferguson of The Rooms notes that the painting was "generated as a prop in the 1960s/70s for our regional museum in Grand Falls" by one of the museum's artistically inclined technicians.

have been Mary's husband] warranted the Peytons acting on the defensive" (258) seems to vindicate Peyton's claim of self-defence and to reinforce the automatic priority given to settler interests. However, their verdict is not unequivocal, as they also request that other members of the party be interviewed at a later date, suggesting lingering suspicions about the veracity of Peyton's account.

Such suspicions (which were clearly harboured by the historical jury) turn out to be warranted. Buchan, put in charge of the investigation, discovers by questioning Mary that a second killing had taken place, one less amenable to a claim of self-defence. What Peyton withheld from the inquiry was that a second man had been shot by John Senior while attempting to escape and then was mercifully dispatched by Joseph Reilly, the Peytons' Irish head man. Peyton suppressed the details of this murder to protect his friend Reilly, whose history as a thief, along with the fact that he is Irish, practically guarantees he will be hanged. Peyton defuses the situation essentially by blackmailing Buchan (who he discovers was the real father of Cassie's aborted child), which consolidates a transfer of authority from father to son. The need to suppress the second murder thus compromises the Peytons in a fashion that signals a broader discrediting of the uncompromising belligerence toward the Beothuk that John Senior represents.

Revisionist versions of the past in contemporary Canadian historical novels often question the authority of colonial accounts of significant episodes, and part of Crummey's project in *River Thieves* is to interrogate and even adjust the historical record around the capture of Mary March. In depicting a second, less justifiable murder, Crummey is not merely taking liberties but rather is developing an interpretation of the episode that he feels is justified by the gaps and tensions in the historical record. The historical John Peyton Jr.'s account of the incident in a deposition to Governor Hamilton portrays the Beothuk man as the aggressor and the violence of his own party as necessary but regrettable:

> could we have intimidated him or persuaded him to leave us, or even have seen the others go off, we should have been most happy to have spared using violence, but when it is remembered that our small party were in the heart of Indian country, one hundred miles from any European settlement, and that there were in our sight at times as many Indians as our party amounted to, and we could not ascertain how many were in the woods that we did not see, it could not be avoided with safety to ourselves. (1819, 135)

In his seminal history of the Beothuk, J.P. Howley, though aware of the possibility of a second killing, clearly subscribes to the belief that only one occurred, and defers to John Peyton himself, in a passage that Crummey repeats in the prologue to *River Thieves*: "Various versions of this event have appeared from time to time in our histories and other publications, but as numerous discrepancies characterize these accounts, I prefer to give the story as I had it from the lips of the late John Peyton, J.P. of Twillingate, himself the actual captor of the Beothuck woman" (Howley [1915] 1974, 91).[3] Howley's account thus unsurprisingly makes no mention of a second murder and makes short shrift of the scuffle, downplaying the violence of the encounter ([1915] 1974, 93). In her biography of the Peytons, Amy Louise Peyton describes just the one killing, shifting the responsibility to Demasduit's husband Nonosabusut for launching himself at John Senior: "If his main intent had been to rescue his mate why didn't he attack the younger John, who was holding her captive? Apparently he was more intent on seeking revenge of the older Peyton for his mistreatment of natives in previous years" (1987, 44). In her comprehensive study of the Beothuk, however, Ingeborg Marshall, after summarizing John Peyton Jr.'s account, notes that in a version told by Shanawdithit, who witnessed the scene, she described a second killing, that of Nonosabasut's brother (1996, 164), and this alternative, a muted if not absent possibility in the historical record on the Beothuk, is the position that Crummey adopts. "It is my conclusion," Crummey observes in an interview, "that there were two men killed there and that the version that Peyton tells is a truncated or a modified or a biased version that is designed to protect somebody or some people" (2007, 310). Sugars suggests that Crummey's emphasis on "the settlers' complicity and ambivalence might be doing a certain kind of cultural cathartic work, enabling Canadians to speak the crime that has no name" (2005, 162). This effect is redoubled by his unearthing of a potentially suppressed crime within the larger calamity of settler responsibility for the extinction of the Beothuk.

However, while Crummey's revisionist version of the capture of Demasduit serves as an indictment of settler violence, it is situated in a more nuanced and less polarized political context than tends to be the case with literary treatments of Beothuk-settler relations. Not only does the relationship between the two Peytons illustrate divergent views toward the Beothuk but Crummey also highlights the hierarchical politics within colonial Newfoundland itself, qualifying the picture of the settler populace as a monolithic, invasive force. Indeed, he effects something of a political reversal in the novel between the settlers and the colonial authorities. Whereas the settlers appear initially to be the colonizing aggressors, their forced expulsion from the French Shore by English soldiers later in the novel—long a source of grievance toward England among Newfoundlanders—positions them as the aggrieved victims of the expedient politics of the colonial centre. Furthermore, Crummey takes pains to highlight the way in which these characters' relocation to Newfoundland, while undeniably an extension of a larger process of colonial expansion and expropriation, was fuelled by a desire to escape the oppression and poverty of an unforgiving, class-bound society in Britain. In contrast, whereas Buchan early in the novel comes across as the benevolent champion of pacifist relations with the Beothuk, when he returns to conduct the investigation into the murder he is much more the embodiment of an arrogant, authoritarian colonial order.

Despite this more nuanced and ambivalent picture of the politics of colonial Newfoundland, the ultimate effect of *River Thieves* is a destabilizing of the settler's sense of belonging—a central theme of post-colonial, revisionist historical fiction. In light of their role in the extinction of the Beothuk, the "Peytons and the other characters," as Chafe puts it, "can never be comfortably at home on this island because they always exist where someone else *was supposed to have existed*" (2004, 97; italics in original). This realization is conveyed in refracted form in the resolution of the Oedipal triangle between father, son, and Cassie, whose discovery of the suppressed murder

Section 3: The Age of Sale

at Red Indian Lake irrevocably alienates her from both Peytons. Earlier in the novel, Peyton articulates a sense of belonging that mirrors his desire for Cassie, reflecting that his intimate knowledge of the backcountry "made him feel he was closest here to belonging, to loving something that might, in some unconscious way, love him in return" (Crummey [2001] 2002, 207). However, at the end of the novel, after making a final, unrequited overture to Cassie, Peyton mournfully expresses a sense of loss and alienation that applies as much to Newfoundland itself as it does to Cassie: "All my life I've loved what didn't belong to me" (408). In this fashion, as Anke Uebel contends, the novel "eschews the mystification of the natural world that is a precondition for the symbolic union of true Newfoundlanders with their land" (2010, 146). Peyton and his father, in that sense, can be seen as the main contenders for the title of "river thieves."

River Thieves thus resonates with the sense that the extinction of the Beothuk, as Chafe argues, is "the fundamental loss in Newfoundland's history—the originary moment when *what could have been* was separated from *what is*." At the same time, that originary loss informs a literature that is permeated by loss, "loss of independence, the loss of the cod fishery, the loss of countless lives to the sea, and the loss of opportunity" (2004, 93; italics in original). Thus underlying Crummey's representation of this originary loss is a contemporary sense of loss, the sense that Newfoundland has crossed a definite cultural and historical threshold into an uncertain future, leaving behind a way of life that defined the province for centuries. This is reflected in a kind of dual temporality in the novel, a retrospective anxiety about the ethical responsibilities entailed in representing the past. In a passage reminiscent of Muise's skepticism about heritage tourism, in "Journey into a Lost Nation" Crummey expresses his wariness of the commodified nostalgia that is proving to be a prevalent response to the profound historical and cultural shift the province is undergoing:

> "The Past" is big business in Newfoundland these days. *St. John's: City of Legends* is awash in tourist kitsch: "Newfie" stores selling Viking memorabilia and plastic sou'wester hats, faux screech-ins at George Street bars, fiddle music blaring from storefronts. People have to eat, I guess, and you give tourists what they want or they stop coming. But there's something about the undertaking that feels unhealthy and dishonest to me. Even the subtitle of this book—*Journey into a Lost Nation*—slants the contents towards the past in a way that makes me slightly uncomfortable. It was meant to point to a way of life in the midst of an unprecedented upheaval, a "sea change" of sorts, which will permanently alter what it means to live here. If it also suggests

that there's nothing to Newfoundland but nostalgia, however, it does a disservice to the people and the place itself. (2004, 32)

In *River Thieves*, Crummey's strategy for avoiding this kind of commodifying heritage impulse— that is, the impulse to turn the novel into a kind of textual guided tour—is to break the mimetic illusion, the seductive appearance of historical verisimilitude. Doing so reminds readers that history is always a selective reconstruction from the perspective of the present and thus it should not be uncritically and passively taken as a mirror of the past. This strategy is most palpable in a key passage in *River Thieves* in which Peyton pauses before opening Buchan's journal, which he has asked Reilly to steal after witnessing Cassie writing in its margins:

> He would find himself in there, and his father and Mary, and all the men who made up the party to the lake, but not, he was sure, in the fashion they had conspired to present themselves. The start of their undoing, that little book, now or some time beyond their time. There were things he'd seen and heard in his days he vowed to take to his grave, as if that was a safe place for the truth. But two hundred years from now, he knew, some stranger could raise his bones from the earth and put whatever words they liked in his mouth. It was a broken, helpless feeling. (Crummey [2001] 2002, 347)

As this self-reflexive *mea culpa* suggests, Crummey wants his readers to keep in view that the novel is a speculative, retrospective fiction; the author is putting words in the mouths of his fictional creations. As Crummey stresses, "[t]he 'stranger' that John Peyton points his sadly accusing finger at is me, sitting on the other side of the computer screen. I thought I owed him that much at least" (2001, 42). While any resemblance to persons living or dead may be more than coincidental, Crummey stresses, there is a fundamental distinction to be made: these are not the same people.

River Thieves is certainly susceptible to the suspicion that it may be another compensatory, consolatory meditation on the impact of colonialism, "yet another tale of European angst in the face of imperialist atrocity, a tale about the survivors, rather than about those who were extinguished" (Sugars 2005, 149). Nonetheless, the novel stages a significant resistance to the inclination toward stylized, nostalgic, and commodified representations of the province's history. Not only does the novel highlight a key episode in the history of Beothuk–settler relations through its revisionist representation, pointing to the eradication of the Beothuk as a profoundly destabilizing "original sin." It also does so in a carefully qualified and nuanced fashion that challenges simplistic polarities without resorting to equally troubling equations between the two sides. Crummey undeniably asserts a revisionist interrogation of the historical record, compelling readers to consider that two murders took place during the capture of Demasduit. But he frames that project within a much more tentative historiographical self-consciousness, encouraging readers not to passively accept this version as a given but to consider this possibility within the context of a larger awareness of the process of constructing history. Crummey is conscious that he is writing at a time when Newfoundland is at a kind of threshold, experiencing a profound sense of loss. But he is also clearly aware of how the settler society whose culture he chronicles not just in *River Thieves* but in *Hard Light*, and his second novel, *The Wreckage* (2005), is founded on another, originary loss, which—as Uebel argues, is not Newfoundlanders' loss but the Beothuks' (2010, 142)—troubles the very authority of that culture and thus any tendency to nostalgically celebrate its passing.

"The ship goes away and they're there": Bernice Morgan

Published just before the 1992 moratorium, Bernice Morgan's popular novel *Random Passage* (1992) offers another good example of how the tensions and uncertainties of the present have shaped Newfoundland writers' concern with the past. As Morgan notes in an interview, *Random Passage* is to a degree based on the experience of her relatives in the outport salt fish economy (Morgan 1995, 17), and the novel has been celebrated as an imaginative engagement with that outport heritage, breathing life into the rural origins of many Newfoundlanders. The appeal to Newfoundland readers of Morgan's depiction of this long-standing fixture of Newfoundland's culture, Tracy Whalen argues, "points to a similar desire for routine and predictability at a time when the future seems uncertain" (2001, 38). At the same time, it arguably represents that heritage in a revisionist or corrective fashion. Marilyn Porter asserts that images of the fishing industry tend to be highly gendered, focusing "on the harvesting sector of the fishing industry, sometimes to the complete exclusion of the processing sector (in which, of course, many women are found)" (1987, 50). In contrast, *Random Passage* emphasizes the contribution of women to the fisheries and to survival in the harsh and demanding environment of the outports. Furthermore, Morgan locates her depiction of the intertwined lives of the Andrews and the Vincent families in the larger political and economic contexts of England's colonial power and the hegemony of the fishing merchants both in England's West Country and in St. John's. The feminist and post-colonial energies of the novel, however, do not always sit easily with the machinery of romance. While ultimately

Morgan avoids the romanticizing impulse of heritage tourism, instead highlighting the brutal rigours of outport existence, the novel certainly runs the risk of idealizing the past as a simpler, more cohesive, and more heroic time. As a result, *Random Passage* provides an interesting study not only of the tensions in representations of the maritime heritage of Atlantic Canada but also of the tension between the empirical, documentary impulse of the historical novel and the emotional architecture of the historical romance.

One of the central accomplishments of *Random Passage* is Morgan's ability to imagine the particular experience of the outport settler and the social dynamics of tiny, primitive, and isolated communities, without succumbing either to nostalgic idealization or to an alienating litany of hardship. *Random Passage* had its genesis in part in Morgan's fascination with "what happens to a family who sets their bags down on a Newfoundland coast—the ship goes away and they're there" (1995, 17). Although by the start of *Random Passage* the Vincents and Thomas Hutchings are already established on Cape Random, the arrival of the Andrews family at the onset of winter highlights the precariousness of the community's foothold on the harsh and unforgiving French Shore. Morgan depicts with unflinching directness the starvation and illness that ravages the community: "Endless buckets of water have to be lugged from the pond and heated before bodies and bedding can be washed. Buckets of vomit and excretum must be disposed of. Thomas and Frank dig a pit into which the terrible waste is thrown and covered with layers of lime, sand and gravel" (Morgan 1992, 163). Morgan also emphasizes the dangers of the work that contributes to the survival of the community—fishing and sealing. When the boys of Cape Random are entranced by visions of how each will one day "sign on under one of the great sealing captains, will sail north to walk over ice floes among herds thick as sand on the beach, will come home with real money in his pocket" (107), Josh Vincent launches into an uncharacteristic diatribe, emphasizing the brutality and dangers of the industry: "Famished, with a blizzard blowin', your feet and face frozen and you half-blind jumpin' across open water. I seen times we put our hands inside the seal carcass just to thaw out, yes, and to get a bit of heart or liver—eatin' it raw, we're that hungry.... And in the end you gets fifteen pounds or so" (108). Indeed, Josh's caution proves to be prophetic when, in St. John's at the end of the novel, Thomas Hutchings witnesses "the black frozen bodies of two men—men standing, hunched together, their arms wrapped around each other" and looking "like a huge hacked piece of coal" being lifted out of the hold of a sealing ship, and then realizes that he is "staring into the frozen faces of Peter and Joe Vincent" (261).

One of the important developments in the recent boom in historical fiction in Canada, reflecting the influence of social history and feminist history, is an emphasis on women's experiences, addressing the suppression of those experiences in the overwhelmingly masculine world of traditional historiography.[4] Like Urquhart's *Away* (1993), Margaret Atwood's *Alias Grace* (1996), and Sweatman's *When Alice Lay Down with Peter* (2001), *Random Passage* concerns itself with the magnitude and fabric of women's experiences, in this instance in the claustrophobic and demanding world of the outport. The revisionist energies of such feminist history and historical novels, however, have often produced a critical reaction on the part of historians and reviewers, with one frequent charge being that to emphasize women's experiences is to distort history. Morgan's response to such a charge in a review of *Random Passage* throws light on her aims in the novel, whose emphasis on women she sees as more corrective than revisionist. Resisting the suggestion that she "was downplaying the men's role" and emphasizing conflict between the genders, Morgan argued that the male characters were modelled on her uncles, for whom she had a great deal of respect (1995, 19), and that all the characters "were working cooperatively to a great extent" (20). Nonetheless her aim was "to show that the women did just as much, perhaps more because they probably worked longer hours, God knows, if it's possible" (19) and in the process "to add another layer to what had been reflected in a lot of the community histories" (20). Morgan describes the separate but interdependent rhythms of men's and women's work in the salt fish economy, as "[e]ach day the men make three or four trips to the fishing ground ... and the women must spend every waking minute down on the flakes gutting and splitting fish" (1992, 61). While Morgan hardly ignores the offshore activities of the men, most of the narrative is focused on onshore activity, which is principally the domain of women. Their work, *Random Passage* dramatizes, is both punishing and crucial to the survival of the community. Various passages in the novel capture the rhythms of women's work in the fishery, such as the reflections of Jennie Andrews, "the oldest person on the Cape":

> As she works, she thinks of what she has learned in the past eight months: how to clear rocks from the ground, how to slide a knife through a cod, flicking its guts into the barrel at the end of the table, how much salt to spread on fish, when to turn them. She has learned that the food they will have next winter will depend upon these things, upon the credit they can build with Caleb Gosse, upon how much fish the men catch and how much the women make. (61)

The women must also tend the children, care for the health of the community, and see to feeding it. This includes establishing and tending to gardens, a particularly arduous task in such rocky soil: "Their faces become ingrained with smoke and soot, their fingernails tear and split, blisters rise, break and bleed until their hands grow as hard and calloused as the men's" (58). Life in outport Newfoundland, suggests *Random Passage*, is no pastoral idyll, and the arduous labour it takes to survive is required at least as much of women as of men.

At the same time, Morgan's portrait of life in Cape Random emphasizes the particular closeness and mutual reliance of women's relationships in isolated outport communities, the appreciation of the particular abilities of individual women—Meg Andrews's regal bearing and leadership, Mary Bundle's healing abilities, Lavinia Andrews's education and imagination. Furthermore, Morgan highlights the shared intimacy and communion that results from women's collective labour. Despite the exhausting work in the garden, the women find it "exhilarating to be outside." Sitting down on the ground for their midday meal and "[t]aking time to look around at what they have done, they talk quietly, become female again, tidying their hair, rubbing aching limbs" (58). About halfway through the novel, Lavinia, who is considered almost childlike and remains aloof from the rest of the women, has a kind of epiphany in which she becomes attuned to the distinct rhythms of the women's lives:

> All the minute details of everyday life suddenly leap into focus for Lavinia. For the first time she begins to hear the quiet conversations women have—talk of a child's fever, what their mothers had said about this or that, how to prevent miscarrying, what they pray for, the pain in their backs, the timing of their periods, how the berries are coming, ruminations about the question of sin, what is cooking over their fires. She catches glimpses of lives as varied as the grains of sand. (Morgan 1992, 123)

Within the contemporary context of destabilization, deracination, and increasingly mobility in Newfoundland, however, it is easy to fall into a nostalgic, anti-modernist celebration of community. Although at times Morgan seems to succumb to this temptation, largely she resists cultivating a false impression of feminine harmony. Instead, she chronicles the strains, disputes, and conflicts that necessarily ensue from such claustrophobic proximity and mutual reliance for survival. Lavinia's aloof bearing and childish self-absorption is often interpreted as laziness, and Mary Bundle remains somewhat at odds with most of the rest of the community throughout the novel, sparking tensions with the rest of the women when she secretly cultivates and stakes off a garden in a fertile bog up the hill from the community. A key subplot in the novel involves Annie Vincent's affair with the married Frank Norris, whose wife Ida, assumed to be insane, finally puts an end to it by launching into a very public tirade and running Annie out of the house.

If Folk archetypes of the fisheries have tended to cultivate an idealized and insulated image of the petty producer as independent, hardy, and self-reliant, one of the key achievements of *Random Passage*, in contrast, is the way in which it qualifies the image of the isolation of a community like Cape Random, stressing instead the larger political and economic contexts that give rise to such communities and shape life in them. "Stereotypes of hardy fisherfolk and popular nostalgic images of Newfoundland," Danielle Fuller maintains, "are disrupted by Morgan's attention to the inequalities that shaped her ancestors' daily lives" (2004b, 141). These inequalities stem principally from English colonial power and the hegemonic control of the economic elite, not only in St. John's but in England and Ireland as well. The Andrews family, for instance, is forced to leave Weymouth after Ned's employer discovers that he has been selling fish on the side during his trips to Newfoundland and is enraged by his impertinence. Meg Andrews underscores how they are at the mercy of the fishing merchant's monopolistic power: "even if he didn't have Ned arrested, who'd give him work, or have dealings with any of us if it meant bein' bad friends with the Ellsworths?" (Morgan 1992, 25). Sarah Vincent mentions that her grandfather, too, was a refugee from the abuses of English power; press-ganged into serving on an English man o' war, he jumped ship in Newfoundland. Thomas Hutchings' exodus to Newfoundland is prompted by his failed attempt to form a land league to improve the lives of the overworked, impoverished, and starving Irish peasantry. The naive and idealistic Thomas convinced his more pragmatic and cautious mentor Mike Tracey that they should interrupt a gathering of powerful landowners to present their concerns in person, precipitating a melee in which one of the landowners and a couple of Thomas's associates are killed. Thomas is forced to flee to Newfoundland, where he adopts a false name and agrees to take a position in remote Cape Random, keeping his troubled past a secret. Whereas the English historical romance, as Helen Hughes argues, tends to reinforce the natural authority of the aristocracy (1993, 15) and of England as the model liberal nation-state (91), *Random Passage* questions this natural order by portraying the exercise of authority as capricious and oppressing to the protagonists of the novel.

If the inhabitants of Cape Random thus can be seen as refugees from political and economic exploitation, *Random Passage* also emphasizes the degree to which such oppression makes the transatlantic voyage with them. Indeed, the very presence of the two families on Cape Random is transgressive, a defiance of the authorities. Sarah Vincent observes that "none of we crowd, except for Thomas, got any rights livin' in this place" and remarks that, only a generation before, the English navy "used to come down this way burnin' every house that had a chimney" (Morgan 1992, 43). Their presence is also in defiance of Thomas's employer, Caleb Gosse, who "holds the power of life and death" (43) over Cape Random and other remote outports. A key part of *Random Passage* is Morgan's portrayal of what amounts to the settlers' servitude within the economy of the salt fish trade. Gosse sees those in his employ merely as commodities, expendable if they threaten his profit. Thus, Thomas reflects, when the community survives the first winter after the Andrews family improvidently arrives without the resources to sustain them, a man like Gosse "will not be pleased to discover he has housed and fed a dozen strangers all winter" (43). What matters, ultimately, is the settlers' ability to provide for themselves by earning their keep through catching and making (i.e., cleaning and salting) fish. As Mary Bundle discovers after driving herself all summer and introducing innovations to increase the community's output, however, the settlers' labour is framed within a system of exchange that is heavily weighted against them. Mary realizes as Thomas tallies up their totals that neither she nor anybody else will see any money, "just little marks scratched in after their names, marks that show how much flour, sugar, potatoes ... how much molasses, kerosene, cloth, needles, tea and salt, how many pairs of boots, and how much fishing gear they will get from Caleb Gosse in exchange for their work" (Morgan 1992, 67). *Random Passage*, then, makes it hard to sustain a nostalgic, idealized vision of outport life and the salt fish economy not just because of its depiction of the rigours of the labour itself and the challenge of surviving but also because of Morgan's emphasis on the class, gender, ethnic, and religious inequities and conflict that characterized colonial Newfoundland.

For all its post-colonial and quasi-feminist orientation, however, the narrative of *Random Passage* is to a great degree driven by the machinery of the romance, which is arguably somewhat contradictory to the political overtones of the novel. Hughes argues that the element of social criticism in the historical romance is routinely at odds with its more stylized and mythical romantic elements (1993, 11), and this tension can be detected in *Random Passage* as well. Morgan's characters are more rounded and realistic than the stylized, archetypal stock characters of romance. Still, the narrative arc of what is otherwise a fairly episodic story is provided by a thread of romantic intrigue that runs through the fabric of the everyday lives of the community, heightening readers' emotional engagement with the characters. At the centre of this intrigue are Lavinia and Thomas, two reserved and repressed people who find expression for their reflections and sentiments only in Lavinia's journal, and whose inability to reveal themselves to each other contributes to the crisis of *Random Passage*. "Abductions, escapes, rescues, disguises and unknown identities," Hughes notes, "have been the mainstay of romantic plots since the days of the first Greek romances" (1993, 3), and the story of Lavinia and Thomas greatly relies on stock situations built around such narrative elements, the "disguises and concealments arising from the hero's mission, the subsequent misunderstandings, conflicts and reconciliations between heroes and heroines, the rescues which reveal that a hero cares for the heroine after all" (Hughes 1993, 15). From the beginning, the inhabitants of Cape Random find Thomas to be aloof and enigmatic, but given the slim pickings in the isolated community, he nonetheless becomes the object of desire of both Lavinia and Mary. Mary's attraction to Thomas is largely fuelled by a desire for prosperity and power, and when her advances are unrequited, she settles for the impecunious but affable Ned. The romance between Thomas and Lavinia, who secretly records her attraction to him in her diary, is sparked during an excursion to gather seabirds' eggs, and after they return to Cape Random Thomas starts making daily appearances during the lessons Lavinia gives to the children. However, as we learn from Thomas's journal, this unarticulated courtship abruptly comes to a halt after he stumbles across Mary's daughter Fanny lying naked in a secret hollow behind the community, and leaps to the conclusion that Ned has been dallying with his stepdaughter. Overcome with a mixture of lust and shame, he reverts to his reserved and enigmatic behaviour, much to the perplexity of Lavinia. These mistaken assumptions lead to one yet more crucial. When Thomas, after shunning the Andrews family, suddenly appears at the schoolroom door urgently looking for Fanny, his curious request provides the seed of an explanation for his odd withdrawal and also for Lavinia's ultimate though inadvertent betrayal of Thomas. Announcing that Fanny is pregnant, Mary confronts Lavinia and predicts that she likely knows who the father is, and a paralyzed Lavinia merely emits the name "Thomas" (Morgan 1992, 179). Mary then opportunistically corrals Thomas into marrying Fanny, a platonic union of convenience that puzzles the entire community and enrages Peter Vincent, who is enamoured of Fanny, when he returns to Cape Random. The pot reaches a full boil when the enigma of Fanny's pregnancy is explained with the appearance of the Beothuk man, Toma, who for some time has been shadowing the inhabitants of the cape. Striding onto the beach, he takes hold of Fanny, who pliantly heads toward the woods with him. He is then attacked by Peter Vincent, who grapples away the iron bar the man is carrying and subsequently kills him, after which "no one on the Cape ever again felt innocent" (190).

When Fanny dies in childbirth shortly thereafter, ending the first part of *Random Passage*, Thomas leaves Cape Random for St. John's, with the intention of going to Ireland to face the consequences of his crime. But on the boat he is given Lavinia's journal—as a kind of explanation and apology on her part—and begins to write his own account in it as he awaits the Church's decision on his case in St. John's. His attempt to put Cape Random behind him is thwarted, though, as chance once again intervenes. After the frozen bodies of Peter and Joe Vincent are returned to St. John's, Thomas arranges for Peter's destitute wife Emma and her children to return to Cape Random. At the last moment, Emma jumps ship, leaving Thomas with the children. He heads back to Cape Random (and, as readers discover only in *Waiting for Time*, to a happy reconciliation with Lavinia), "seeing more clearly than I had ever seen, or may ever see again, that all creatures ... moved in great swirling patterns which God alone understands and over which He alone has control" (Morgan 1992, 269).

Thus, through a series of coincidences and contrivances, Morgan steers Thomas back toward the reunion and reconciliation of the romantic protagonists typical of the historical romance. Fuller argues that Morgan's use of this emotional orchestration typical of the historical romance extends organically from her portrait of life in an isolated outport community: "Morgan brings melodrama into her 'fictional social history' to dramatize the intensity of the cape women's emotional lives and their resilience in the face of personal tragedy" (2004b, 138). Morgan employs melodrama, Fuller contends, "not so much for the 'thrills' it brings to the narrative as for its ability to render ordinary aspects of the characters' existences within the context of extraordinary circumstances" (2004b, 126). While that may be true, it also arguably mitigates the force of Morgan's otherwise gritty portrait of outport life and thus renders it more susceptible to a nostalgic recuperation. This is especially likely, as Whalen argues, in the context of "the demographic upheaval and economic shifts in the province," when there is a heightened inclination to "feel nostalgic for a Newfoundland left behind or for a Newfoundland that no longer exists (if it ever did)" (2001, 39).

"When there's a choice in the matter": Michael Winter

In contrast with Morgan's mimetic (if somewhat romantic) portrayal of outport culture, Michael Winter's historical novel *The Big Why* (2004) sets its picture of the bygone world of rural Newfoundland at a couple of removes, first of all by presenting that picture from the perspective of an outsider and secondly through its self-consciously anachronistic perspective. Winter's

Section 3: The Age of Sail

The Big Why presents a view of Newfoundland at the twilight of the age of sail from the perspective of an artist, and moreover, an artist "from away." *The Big Why* takes the form of the private journal of the mercurial American painter Rockwell Kent, who came to stay in Newfoundland on the eve of the First World War and was expelled sixteen months later, after his provocative behaviour fuelled suspicions among the citizens of Brigus that he was a German spy. An innovative variation on the conventional historical novel, *The Big Why* is a faux confessional, providing Kent's private musings on his failure to establish himself among the people of Newfoundland. Kent laments near the end of *The Big Why* that "there are events in youth that form you so strongly that a mere year can live within you for the rest of your life. Part of me has always regretted the failure of my Newfoundland plans. That is the reason for this book. To discuss openly the very events that caused my will to be rebuked" (Winter 2004, 360–61). This premise thus imparts to the book a very different ontological status than that of the traditional historical novel. It not only provides a picture of Newfoundland refracted through the perspective of a foreigner failing to embrace and be embraced by it but also an anachronistic meditation on the challenges of being an artist and the challenges of writing about the past.

In *An American Saga: The Life and Times of Rockwell Kent*, David Traxel comments that despite "his vitality and charm" Kent was an abrasive and aggressive person who made life difficult for himself and those close to him: "Hard-driving, impatient, critical and domineering, he felt a need to always be considered right. He, and those around him, suffered from his inability to tolerate opposition" (1980, 185). *The Big Why* chronicles the impact of such a personality on two of Kent's romances: his love for his first wife Kathleen, and his attachment to Newfoundland. The populist and socialist Kent's aim is to make Newfoundland his permanent home: he and his family will "blend into Newfoundland life. I'd be a people's painter. Yes, I wanted to raise a brood of Newfoundlanders and honour my wife" (Winter 2004, 17).[5] In both cases, however, Kent's narcissistic and uncompromising joie de vivre undermines his objectives, as Winter takes Kent's stillborn residence in Newfoundland as the opportunity for a meditation on the price of being true to oneself and living life to the fullest. At the same time, while Kent is naturally the centre of his own retrospective, his ambivalent relationship with Brigus says almost as much about Brigus and Newfoundland as it does about him. The bemusement, wariness, and ultimately suspicion of the people toward Kent suggest to him a narrow provincialism and limited imagination, but it also reflects a spirit of pragmatism and mutual reliance, a sensibility with which the self-righteously exuberant Kent inevitably clashes.

"A 'Sea-Change' of Sorts"

FIGURE 15 Rockwell Kent in studio.

What Winter emphasizes in Kent's apprenticeship in the rural culture of Newfoundland is the fact that this sensibility has been shaped by a brutal and demanding climate. In many ways the archetypal outsider finding in Newfoundland a therapeutic retreat from modernity described in James Overton's *A World of Difference*, Kent is initially charmed by the quaintly picturesque atmosphere of Brigus and finds much to inspire his art in the surrounding landscape and rhythms of the men's and women's work. As the novel progresses, though, he is increasingly exposed to the profound hardship and peril that defines their lives. For instance, Kent learns the story of the suicide of Robert Dobie, the father of his young friend Tom during a desperate winter which reduced Tom's father to begging for food from his equally destitute neighbours. After he and Tom survive a fall through the ice while hunting, Robert bludgeons his twin girls with an axe and turns a rifle on himself, in an act of pragmatic desperation to save his wife and son: "He would have done it in the woods, but they needed the rifle and he did not want to risk their not finding it" (Winter 2004, 89). During Kent's sojourn in Brigus, Tom's friend Stan Pomeroy dies while fishing for cod when he falls into a trap brimming with fish. "None of us can swim," explains Tom afterwards. "So he just sank beneath the fish" (186). Perhaps the most poignant and dramatic illustration, however, is an account given by none other than Judge Prowse, whom Kent befriends during a trip to the Labrador, of a case he has heard involving a salt banker being essentially cannibalized by the residents of a remote Labrador community. After the boat foundered on the rocks offshore, while the crew "drowned and perished of hypothermia, a small gang from the town had rowed out in a chain of dories and stripped the banker of plates and silver and manila rope and tobacco.... They had pushed survivors aside for the booty" (220). When Judge Prowse questions one of the accused about the accuracy of the charge, her bitter lament underscores the barbaric imperative of survival: "Why did they have to go up on the rocks. And tempt us like that?" (223). As Kent becomes more intimate with the vicissitudes of his neighbours' lives, *The Big Why*, even more so than Morgan's *Random Passage*, discourages a dewy-eyed view of the fishing and sealing culture of bygone days.

The imperatives of this culture, furthermore, are brought into relief through Kent's inability to recognize or accept them. An artist from a relatively affluent background, Kent imposes hardship and discomfort on himself, whereas for the Newfoundlanders around him it is a given, the cost of survival. Although after the death of Kent's father his family "lived as though we had money because that was the only way we knew how to behave," Kent has thrived on an ethic of entitlement that is utterly foreign to those he encounters in Newfoundland: "I've always felt money is my right, even though I had no cause to expect it. But I've learned that much comes to those who expect it should" (Winter 2004, 153). In this sense, he is far from a man of the people, since his immersion in deprivation is calculated: "I get up early, Tom. Because I want to lie in bed. And I work because I'm lazy."[6] Tom's reaction is that it's "a queer thing.... When there's a choice in the matter" (154).

Attracted to such an elemental existence, Kent is eager to integrate himself into the community, but in the process he commits a series of faux pas that highlight, and indeed increase, his distance from it. For instance, when Kent complains that Brigus "does not take advantage of the seascape" because of the small, northwesterly facing windows of most of the houses, Tom retorts, "Why would we want to look at the salt water? When we're out on it all day long and that's enough of it" (92). In a more egregious instance of his lack of attunement to the priorities of the community, when a ferocious storm blows up, Kent is oblivious to the fact that the "*Southern Cross*, full of men from Conception Bay," is caught out at sea: "I had forgotten that things happened beyond the skirt of vision laid before me" (122). Kent publicizes this disparity of priorities when, after the storm, he suggests that the captain, "beholden to the merchants here in Brigus and in St. John's" (136), endangered the sealers by trying to be first home with a heavy load. The bad impression created by this untimely attempt to promote the unionization of the sealers (Kent has met and been impressed by William Coaker, the head of the Fisherman's Protective Union) by blaming a man who has gone down with his ship is compounded when Kent kicks up a fuss in the wireless office about the loss of his father's tools during the storm while those in line behind him, as the shipping agent points out, "are looking for fresh word" (138) about the men lost at sea. In his own eyes, Kent's socialist populism represents a refreshingly maverick bucking of convention and an admirable promotion of social justice, but such incidents reflect his fundamental self-absorption and obliviousness to things that the rest of the community takes for granted.

This uncompromising self-righteousness prompts the turning point of Kent's stay in Brigus, a confrontation with his neighbour Jim Hearn, who reneges on an oral agreement to let Kent use his field for a tennis court. Word of Kent's planned revenge leaks out, so a crowd is on hand to witness Kent grab Hearn in a headlock, wrestle him into the train station, and dramatically if facetiously threaten his life: "When you have an audience you must perform" (Winter 2004, 211). Although his triumph over the unpopular Hearn wins Kent some initial accolades, it also starts to turn the community against him: "They felt Hearn a fool, but still what right did I have to make a public fool of him. I was an outsider" (214). After Judge Prowse is indulgently sympathetic and gives him the choice of a five-dollar fine or thirty days in jail, Kent further alienates the community by paying the fine on the spot: "I made a show of it to the crowd. They were silent from the sight of so much money so easily handed over" (247–48).[7]

Kent's eccentric, impractical behaviour as an artist and his provocative grandstanding lay the grounds for a more substantial rupture upon the outbreak of the First World War. Dismissing the conflict as the antics of capitalist imperialism and encouraging Newfoundlanders to have no truck with it, Kent displays an uncompromising lack of empathy in his defence of German culture and his contempt for Newfoundlanders' allegiance to England. After his singing of Schubert in German in church prompts suspicion that he may be a spy, Kent reacts with outrage and inflammatory satire of the gullibility of the locals. Accused of subversion, Kent responds by writing "rich letters to the New York papers," letters "larded ... with provocative claims. I wanted a German submarine to blow this tiny British enclave to smithereens" (282). His hope "that all this would make them cower" and "lick their wounds, see how mistaken they were, and retract and apologize" (284) proves to be thoroughly naive. His subsequent behaviour is histrionically self-aggrandizing as much as it is facetious. He writes to the newspaper in St. John's, for

Section 3: The Age of Sale

FIGURE 16   Kent dressed as German spy.

instance, requesting "to be exonerated from all charges. Either that or put up against a wall and shot" (309). Rather than moving to quell suspicion, Kent provocatively writes BOMB SHOP on his studio door and addresses some prisoners in an internment camp in German, reassuring them, "The kaiser is winning the war! It will not be long now!" (317). Ultimately, Kent's dream to stay for the rest of his life and "live with a rural people, to love them and be loved" (46) founders on the rocks of his extravagant self-righteousness, when his antics lead the government to order him and his family to depart. Even though Kent is invited to return to Newfoundland decades later by Premier Joey Smallwood in a public gesture of apology and reconciliation, he depicts the failure of his initial stay as a formative one: "It came down to a small chunk of time that broke me. It formed me. It pried apart my backbone and left me beached. It shucked me" (46).

If Kent's falling out with the people of Brigus dramatizes the fine line between standing on principle and inconsiderate self-righteousness, this is even more so the case with the unravelling of his marriage to Kathleen, likewise a casualty of their stay in Newfoundland. Traxel writes of the historical Rockwell Kent that "one of the attractions of marriage seems to have been that it set boundaries to be transcended; it also served as a refuge from which he could sally forth to explore new territory" (1980, 156). In *The Big Why*, Winter links this narcissistic attitude toward sexual relationships to Kent's relationship to Newfoundland by piling a fictional affair onto a fictionalized one. As Gemey Kelly notes, shortly after marrying Kathleen Whiting, Rockwell Kent had an affair with a woman he had met in Monhegan, Maine (1987, 14), and her subsequent pregnancy nearly ended Kent's marriage (18). Kent's affair with Jenny Starling in *The Big Why* mirrors the development of this affair. Preceding his family to Newfoundland, Kent by chance meets Jenny in New York, first resisting, then giving in to the temptation to sleep with her. He returns from Newfoundland to find Kathleen holding a letter apprising him that Jenny is pregnant, and he is subsequently forced to compromise by agreeing not to see them while providing child support. Secretly, though, he resents Kathleen's forgiving nature: "I accepted it like a punch to the ribs to protect the face" but "hated the way my wife's face remained steady" (Winter 2004, 61). In his portrait of Kent's infidelities, Winter explores the contested frontier between self-realization and consideration for others:

> I am not a great man. I have fucked over those I love. I hurt Jenny and did very badly by Kathleen. I am a man of appetites and an inability to refrain from the most intimate act a man and a woman can do.... I am not religious, except for sex and art. They are my king and queen, and I do not mind lying to honour them. There is a greater honesty at work, or at least to hell with telling the truth. To lie does not betray integrity. At least, my definition of integrity. (57)

Kent's frank rationalization of his infidelity is a good illustration of the paradox of *The Big Why* as a faux confessional: at once more honest than the memoir written for public consumption (as Winter mentions in his acknowledgements), and still disingenuous, as Winter portrays Kent recognizing the limits of his integrity and yet not quite confronting the implications.

That adhering to "my definition of integrity" is hard to distinguish from being self-serving is demonstrated in Kent's affair with Emily Edwards, a Brigus teenager who comes to help while the pregnant Kathleen is in hospital in St. John's. Kelly mentions that during the pregnancy the historical Kent "stayed in the house in Brigus, assisted in the housekeeping and tending of the children by a young Newfoundland woman" (1987, 35), and Winter (playing the odds) portrays Kent taking advantage of Kathleen's absence. Kent's far from spontaneous gravitation toward Emily (the figurehead that he has restored and mounted over his front door bears a striking resemblance to her) constitutes a betrayal not just of Kathleen but also of the very people to whom he seeks to belong, particularly Emily's sweetheart Tom Dobie. In the context of Kent's "sense of integrity," though, it seems the right thing to do: "Sleeping with Emily would douse the spirit to sleep with her.... I could be better to Kathleen after sleeping with Emily.... I am not advocating this to all—there is no blanket for all—I am just warning you against those who would repress desire" (Winter 2004, 307). With an elastic sense of integrity, Kent convinces Emily in part by reassuring her that he has an understanding with Kathleen about his infidelities: "It isn't something dreadful." Emily's reaction, "It sounds dreadful" (313), turns out to be a better prediction of

Kathleen's response when she returns to Brigus. Witnessing a fleeting intimate gesture by Emily, she jumps to the correct conclusion and fiercely upbraids Kent for his boundless rapacity: "You want everything and yet you know you can't have everything. For to have it all excludes a deepening of anything" (324). When Kent pleads with her to keep the affair secret from the town, she is stunned at his hypocrisy, his inability to take responsibility for the consequences of his actions captured in a characteristically striking Wintery image: "You remind me of a man in a towel who is staring as his house burns down. I was having a bath—that's what he says" (326).

The repercussions of this affair also involve irreparable damage to the lives of those "rural people" with whom he aspired to harmonize. Kent discovers from Tom much later that the young man returned from his overseas tour as a soldier to marry Emily, who was pregnant presumably with Kent's child. Tom recounts how the schooner Emily boarded to join him in St. John's was blown out into the Atlantic, all the way to Scotland, an ordeal that brought the young woman close to death. Emily then took up with an older Scottish widower instead, because, as Tom observes, "She loved me, but she'd gone and done something" (352). Kent's affair with Emily—the "something" in question—can be seen as an extension of his relationship with Brigus in which, despite his idealism, his "motives were not true," in that, as Kent admits, "I was using the culture. I was exploiting it. And what I was creating is not what happened here" (271). Kathleen says to Kent before her death from cancer years later, "In the end ... it's all about repercussions. The sum of your acts, and your concern for or indifference towards those who have loved you. The question is not have you been loved, but have you loved" (359).

If *The Big Why* is a meditation on the perennial tensions between self-actualization and consideration for others and between the extravagance of art and the pragmatism of survival, a central innovation in Winter's novel is the portrait of Bob Bartlett. Regarded as one of the most prominent figures in Newfoundland history, Bartlett serves as a kind of counterpart to and philosophical intimate of Kent. In his foreword to *Bartlett: The Great Canadian Explorer*, Horwood laments that "[m]any readers today ... refuse to believe in greatness" and heralds Captain Bob Bartlett as "indeed a great man, with extraordinary courage and tenacity wedded to exceptional gentleness and generosity, as all who knew him attest. He went through life with an heroic self-image, doing what he could to live up to it" (1977, x). In *The Big Why*, Winter paints a different and less heroic portrait of Bartlett, who is the catalyst of Kent's coming to Newfoundland and one of his closest allies during his turbulent stay. Winter offers an image of a man whose quest for

FIGURE 17 Captain Bob Bartlett using a sextant.

integrity is equally troubled but who manages to maintain a dignity that the flamboyant and self-indulgent Kent lacks.

If Winter is interested in exploring through Kent the limits of the questing artistic spirit, Bartlett serves as both foil and complement to Kent. The historical Rockwell Kent was as much an adventurer as an artist, his travels taking him to the wilds of Alaska, Tierra del Fuego, and Greenland, and Winter's Kent is depicted as a man obsessed with discomfort, "Or it may be that I hated discomfort so that I got a kind of exultation from the effort of overcoming it" (Winter 2004, 45). Conversely, Bartlett, whose epic exploits as an adventurer and an explorer in the Arctic (including piloting Richard Peary on his quest for the North Pole) perhaps represent the pinnacle of discomfort, can also be seen as an artist. In the days of his youth, Kent reflects, "we were all interested in the Arctic. It was a novelty, going to empty, dangerous places. We loved hearing about men starving or freezing to death for the sake of a technical achievement" (7). Responding to Bartlett's bemusement at Kent's "love for beautiful things," Kent considers this man "who had driven a wooden boat through ice into the Arctic Ocean for nothing more than the illusion of being at the geographic top of the world," and suggests to Bartlett, "Deep down ... youre an artist too" (113).

Section 3: The Age of Sale

At the same time, Bartlett serves to reinforce the pragmatism cultivated by necessity that Kent fails to truly appreciate in Newfoundlanders. "Deep down," Bartlett responds to Kent's characterization, "I'm a survivalist. Nothing matches sailing out of Brigus in a sealer" because "a sealer is going to decide if his wife and babies will have molasses with their fish. Deep down, Kent, we're all for survival—even you" (113). During Kent's turbulent stay in Brigus, Bartlett tries to steer Kent clear of trouble, pointing out the recklessness of paying his fine in court: "You want to be a man of the people.... But scenes like that divorce you from them. High-learnt and full of money. They cannot help looking at you as different" (260). At the same time, the view of Bartlett that comes through is double-edged. While he is portrayed as legendary in his exploits, he also almost gratuitously sinks a collier carrying seven tons of coal for Kent by impatiently trying to ram it through pack ice to reach Brigus, and a fisherman Kent meets during his trip to Labrador calls Bartlett a "cunt" and suggests that he swindled him out of a fair price for his fish.

When Kent meets Bartlett years after his expulsion from Newfoundland, he presents a view of a legendary man fallen on hard times: "For twenty years he wiggled the arses of vessels through pack ice. At thirty-three he got to stand eighty miles from the north pole. And that was it. From then on, it's been downhill" (371). In his own memoir, *The Log of "Bob" Bartlett*, the historical Bartlett describes himself during the lean postwar years as "a mangy lion, a has-been who was being carted around to a free dinner here and there in hopes that he would break out into some rich sea tale and stage a freak monologue free of charge" (1928, 20). Winter's Rockwell Kent provides a similar view of Bartlett being forced to prostitute himself by retailing stories of his exploits: "It's one thing to lecture and another to find yourself holding a glass of whisky, realizing you are the embodiment of the word *regaling*" (Winter 2004, 348). "He did it and the worst part was the agreeing," Kent observes. "A man retains the structure of integrity, even after he has sold off the shelves of goods that integrity insisted should never be sold" (349). When Kent first meets Bartlett, the latter is critical of Peary for sending him back on the cusp of reaching the North Pole—"It has humiliated me. It's dampened my passion for other people's witnessing my deeds" (68)—but changes his tune when Peary finds him work during the lean thirties. If Kent is presented as too uncompromising, Bartlett is presented, to some degree, as too compromised.

If this portrait of Bartlett is not dramatically demythologizing (or perhaps remythologizing), the final view of Bartlett in *The Big Why* certainly is. Playing on the historical captain's conspicuous celibacy (the first chapter of his memoir is titled "The Trouble with Women"), Winter has Bartlett embark on a very different kind of exploration at the end of the novel. When Kent meets Bartlett in New York decades later, shortly before the latter's death, Bartlett confides in Kent about having recently visited a nightclub "where a man was aloft, his legs in straps," ready for the taking (371), and about how Bartlett's companion, a younger married man, took him back to Bartlett's hotel where they "got into it," Bartlett fisting the man until he "could feel the man's heart beat" (371). This confession serves as the prelude to the central philosophical question from which the novel takes its title, as Bartlett, contrasting Kathleen's emphasis on consideration and reciprocity, puts self-actualization first and foremost:

> The question is not, he said, were you loved. Or did you love. Or did you love yourself. Or did you allow love to move you, though that's a big one. Move you. The question, Rockwell, is did you get to be who you are. And if not, then why. That, my friend, is the big why. (Winter 2004, 372)

In the wake of Bartlett's confession, this question seems to apply as much to himself as to Kent. Empathizing with "a man who was in a very macho world and couldn't yet be who he really was" (2010, 128), Winter decided to represent Bartlett "as a gay man trapped in a time when he couldn't express himself in that way, and yet that won't diminish his greatness" (127–28). Thus, Bartlett seems to be engaging in a retrospective self-assessment similar to Kent's, highlighting the principle of being true to oneself and perhaps suggesting—at the end of a narrative that underscores the consequences when, as Kathleen puts it, "people must be so relentlessly themselves" (Winter 2004, 359)—that there is a certain kind of integrity to such a heedless pursuit of self as Kent's.

Winter's portrait of Bartlett in *The Big Why*, in which the captain engages more in sexual and existential exploration than the kind which made him legendary, is another signal of Winter's lack of interest in writing a traditional historical novel mythologizing the epic stature of Newfoundland's days of sail. While readers may balk at the transformation of the hardy, salty skipper almost into a sensitive, new age-type of guy, that sense of anachronism is a central, conscious feature of *The Big Why*. The memoir format, Winter confesses in an interview, freed him from a couple of problems that plagued a more conventional initial draft of *The Big Why*. Given that Kent died in the 1970s, Winter observes, presenting the tale as the first person retrospective of a come-from-away who "can have very modern thoughts" freed Winter from the perils of anachronism and the tyrannical demands of

Section 3: The Age of Sale

historical accuracy: "if he somehow gets it wrong which sail goes up first on a schooner or what the things were on the fish flakes, he can get those things wrong because he's no expert" (2010, 127).

Thus Kent is looking back on his experiences at a point after his invitation to revisit Newfoundland late in life, and his portrait of both Brigus and Newfoundland is imbued with a sense of what is to come after Kent's expulsion. Kent describes Brigus early on as "a merchant town that had been the headquarters for the annual seal hunt. A rich town on the decline" (Winter 2004, 16), and Bartlett reminisces about how "[t]here used to be forty vessels in line.... Sixteen thousand men in parade. You could walk across the harbour from your house to Tom Dobie's and not get your feet wet" (111). But if Brigus is in the twilight of its role as the centre of the sealing industry at the time of Kent's sojourn there, his portrait of the town and the rural culture of Newfoundland is written after its further decline in importance and after the profound changes to that culture in the Smallwood years. That is, by the time Kent is escorted by Smallwood on a visit to Brigus, the resettlement program is already well underway, as is Smallwood's campaign to modernize and industrialize the province: "We've got to get the people off fishing, Smallwood said. That's stone age. We have mining and hydro, paper mills and shipbuilding. There's chemicals and oil refining and agriculture and logging" (362). But the anachronistic quality of the narrative extends not just from the fact that it is the retrospective of a man who died in 1971 looking back to the First World War. It also reflects how Winter is looking back from beyond the turn of the century, so that the scene in which Smallwood describes his attempt to industrialize the province and wean it off the fishery is redolent with irony, not only because of the program's spectacular failure but also because of the subsequent moratorium on cod in 1992.

The conspicuous sense of retrospection and anachronism in *The Big Why* undermines the sense of temporal unity and historiographical empiricism on which the historical novel traditionally relies, a subversion fortified by Winter's embellishments on the historical record. The ultimate effect is to suggest a kind of anxiety parallel to Kent's recognition of his own failure to merge with the rural culture of Newfoundland. Witnessing the modernization of St. John's during his tour with Smallwood, Kent observes that the city "was not picturesque, but can you expect people to live in squalor just so you can have good material for paintings?" (Winter 2004, 362). Implicit here is that a similar question might be asked of writing historical novels, and Winter's solution is to eschew an ostensibly transparent, mimetic recreation of the harsh realities of the rural culture of yore. Instead, *The Big Why* is a self-consciously anachronistic exploration of an artist's ambivalent ambition to blend in with, and to paint, people of a fundamentally different culture, and the contrast of extravagance and pragmatism, of solipsism and sociability, that aspiration involves. This contrast is developed through the focus on Kent's courtship and betrayal of both Kathleen and Newfoundland, a result of his unstinting solipsism and the distance between his staged, comfortable embrace of discomfort and the profound, taken-for-granted discomfort of Newfoundlanders. It is also developed through the relationship between Kent and Bartlett, who becomes Kent's philosophical and existential counterpart in *The Big Why*, and who suggests that a true definition of survival may be getting to be who you really are. Referring to his 2007 novel, *The Architects Are Here*, Winter observes that "part of my worry about writing about Newfoundland is making it appear to be isolated or quaint or somehow fitting the stereotype of Newfoundland when in fact it's not like that at all" (2010, 133), and that resistance can be seen in his approach to historical fiction in *The Big Why*. Winter's faux confessional, then, is a consciously anachronistic and historiographically subversive strategy for evading the commodification of the past and for dramatizing the struggle of the artist both to live and to create art.

IT WOULD BE HARD TO DISPUTE THAT THE THREAD OF LOSS RUNS THROUGH THE representations of Newfoundland's past explored above; indeed, at times it is as thick as a rope. Nevertheless, in these historical novels (and Johnston's memoir) there is a surprising diversity of response to loss. While there is much to lament, this is no Greek chorus bewailing misfortune in unison. If Morgan's novel is at times a somewhat wistful farewell to the traditional fishing culture of the outports, she also readjusts the emphasis on masculine activity in established visions of outport life. Crummey's emphasis on the role of the vanishing Beothuk in Newfoundland's settler history gives a much more conflicted inflection to the idea of loss and Newfoundland identity than is the case with Johnston's laments for a lost independence. In turn, Winter looks upon the pre-industrial culture celebrated in Johnston's *Baltimore's Mansion* through the eyes of an outsider, perhaps reflecting his own status, as he describes in an interview, as "a 'permanent visitor' to the island" (quoted in Wilkshire 2003, 18). Winter was born in England and moved at the age of three to Newfoundland where, Claire Wilkshire notes, "there's a firm divide between Newfoundlanders and CFAS (Come-from-Aways). To be a Newfoundlander means born and bred, with family dotted around the island: living here for almost your entire life does not make you a Newfoundlander" (2003, 17–18). It is hard not to speculate that, in chronicling Rockwell Kent's truncated assimilation into the community of Brigus, Winter is drawing on his own liminal position, pointing to a fairly fundamental division running through the whole Atlantic region. Perhaps only in Quebec—as captured in the notion of the pure laine Québécois—is the distinction between insider and outsider so socially and culturally charged, and Winter's concern with that distinction in *The Big Why* gives an inkling of what may well become a significant concern in Atlantic-Canadian literature. Thus, while these works do collectively reflect a sense of loss, most of them reflect rather than suppress the significant divisions that run through Newfoundland society, past and present.

8 |

"A Place That Didn't Count Any More": The Maritimes

Given the substantial tradition of historical fiction in the region, it is curious that there has not been a profusion of historical fiction in the Maritimes equivalent to that in Newfoundland and Labrador over the last few decades. The writing of historical fiction in the Maritimes goes back at least to what is considered to be the first novel published by a native-born writer in Canada, Fredericton-born Julia Catherine Beckwith Hart's *St. Ursula's Convent, or the Nun of Canada* (1824). At the turn of the century, the influential New Brunswick poet and critic Charles G.D. Roberts wrote historical fiction among his many other works, as did his brother Theodore Goodridge Roberts and numerous others. Nova Scotia's Thomas Raddall was widely known in the middle of the twentieth century for historical novels such as *His Majesty's Yankees* (1942) and *Roger Sudden* (1944). While historical fiction has undergone a revival and redefinition at the end of the twentieth century, that trend has yet to register as much in the Maritimes as it has elsewhere in the country. This is not to say that concern with the past is absent in contemporary Maritime literature. David Adams Richards's *River of the Brokenhearted* (2003), for instance, is modelled on his grandmother's experiences as a pioneer in the early-twentieth-century motion picture industry in Eastern Canada, and his *The Friends of Meager Fortune* (2006) is set during the era of the lumber barons on the Miramichi. Nevertheless, Maritime writers have yet to exhibit the same preoccupation, often revisionist in spirit, with key figures and episodes in the region's history as is the case in Newfoundland. There are signs, though, that this is starting to change, and the work of Harry Thurston and George Elliott Clarke offers a glimpse of what is likely to grow into a substantial literary engagement with the past in the Maritimes.

Section 3: The Age of Sale

"A long looking back": Harry Thurston

Perhaps the best example of the dual vision of historical fiction—its simultaneous preoccupation with the present and the past—is a long poem, Nova Scotian poet Harry Thurston's *A Ship Portrait: A Novella in Verse* (2005). In part the fictional autobiography of nineteenth-century Nova Scotian ship painter John O'Brien, *A Ship Portrait* is as much a meditation on the present as it is a glimpse into the erstwhile "golden age of sail" in the Maritimes. O'Brien's career as a painter corresponds with the rise and decline of the global economy of the sailing ships, but the significance of Thurston's choice is that O'Brien, like Thurston and his contemporaries, is land-bound, moored to the shore rather than loosed upon the unbounded sea. In that sense, O'Brien is an ideal vehicle not only for reminding us of the region's more storied past but also for contemplating its present state within Confederation and within the larger global economy. Thurston's principal strategy for conveying such a dual vision is his use of contrapuntal voices in the novella. O'Brien's fictionalized first-person musings alternate with responses and reflections by the clearly modern voice of the narrator or poet, whose interventions juxtapose the present with the past and defuse any tendency to present the age of sail with rose-coloured wistfulness. Instead, their conversation—less a dialogue than a call-and-response across the decades—makes for a more nuanced and critical assessment of both the past and present.

Thurston remarks in an interview that *A Ship Portrait* reflects his ambivalence about his own culture: "In one sense I am very proud of what we accomplished as a culture. In another way, I'm ashamed that we're very nostalgic about it, or forgetful about it, that we can't see ourselves in a sense in a better light." He describes how, growing up in the 1950s and early 1960s, he had the sense that the Maritimes were "a kind of backwater, that this was a place that didn't count any more," and part of the motivation behind *A Ship Portrait* was his "feeling that we had lost a sense of ourselves" (Thurston 2008). Certainly, one effect of *A Ship Portrait* is to remind people of the vibrant and storied past of the East Coast, perhaps to restore a sense of pride to a much-denigrated populace. In the poem "1830s," O'Brien describes the bustling maritime economy of his youth with a romanticizing tinge, emphasizing their orientation to the sea and to the future:

> There seemed no end to the cut of sails
> for ship, barque, brigantine, schooner, anchored
> at the docks. They carried molasses and tea
> from Caribe and China. (Thurston 2005, 12)

"A Place That Didn't Count Any More"

Later in the poem, after an inventory of the exotic destinations of the tall ships and artifacts brought back from distant parts of the globe, Thurston's narrator underscores the expansive vision and reach of the age of sail:

> Once we were cosmopolitan,
> once we set our hopes like our sails,
> seaward, to all points of the compass.
>
> Once we were at home in Bombay
> or Rangoon,
> familiar in Melbourne
> or Hong Kong,
> masters wherever
> our keels
> cut water. (15)

In much of *A Ship Portrait*, Thurston arguably can be seen as participating in what historian Phillip Buckner describes as "an invented tradition" of Maritimers having "a seaward destiny," a view that emerged "after the age of wooden ships had ended" and that is belied by the popularity of "landward programs of development" in the Maritime colonies before Confederation (1994, 362). What seems more important to Thurston, though, is not the glory of the past but the contrast with the present. As the phrase "once we were cosmopolitan" suggests, "1830s," like the novella as a whole, is characterized by a sense of regret that the Maritimes are, in a way, in a fallen state:

> We still have our Water Streets
> with their harping gulls, their raw smells,
> but the ships are long gone.
> Only the hulls of derelict draggers
> litter the shore.
> Wharves teeter on rotten piles
> where the tall ships once berthed. (Thurston 2005, 14)

O'Brien, who fell on hard times with the advent of the steamship and who died in poverty and obscurity, thus provides a reminder of a more expansive and optimistic era and, more importantly, becomes a kind of symbol of the region. In the opening sequence of the novella, Thurston's persona, underscoring the decline of the region that has marked the intervening years, describes O'Brien dying

Section 3: The Age of Sale

> in the Poor House, still waiting for your ship
> to come in. That's the way it's been,
> ever since you left us, O'Brien,
> a long looking back. The ships are gone
> but for the ones your brushes christened. (7)

Nostalgia is a doubly dangerous impulse, inclining us simultaneously to neglect the present and overlook the problems of the past, but Thurston, particularly through the contrapuntal structure of *A Ship Portrait*, avoids both perils. First of all, O'Brien's status as an Irish immigrant who sailed to Canada on one of the famine ships serves as a reminder that the age of sail was also the age of virulent Orange bigotry toward Catholics. "Historical novels," Jerome de Groot observes, "have often been used to reinsert communities into the past, rescuing them from the marginal positions to which they have consciously been consigned" (2010, 148), a strategy evident in Thurston's long poem. In "Micmac, Ship, 1853" Thurston's narrator responds to a purely commercial description of the ship in a contemporary newspaper, unearthing its suppressed history of transporting the famine Irish, "What of the trade in human cargo? / Her Irish goods were not so well / received as the wares of Auld Scotia" (Thurston 2005, 31). He goes on to deliver a diatribe in response to the patronizing bigotry shown toward the Irish by Nova Scotia Attorney General John Uniacke, who argued against efforts to improve conditions on British ships transporting Irish immigrants across the Atlantic (MacKay 1990, 203).[1] Instead, Thurston dramatizes the privation and hardship they suffered:

> Fuck Uniacke!
> None of his kin ate the herbs of the field,
> crammed their starved mouths
> with wild mustard, dock, nettletops,
> died with grasses on their lips. (Thurston 2005, 32)

Furthermore, O'Brien's status as a commercial artist largely reliant on commissions from ship owners sets up a tension between art and commerce. The artist underscores how ship portraiture is a kind of palimpsest, a concealment of the hardships and dangers of maritime trade. The key poem in this regard is "Portrait of a Ship, 1855" in which O'Brien highlights the vanity of his patrons—"I always gave them / what they wanted—'under full sail'— / as if I were painting their own portraits" (46)—and the naïveté of their desire for (at least aesthetic) reassurance: "Show them the certainty of pay-off / the promise of good passage" (46). Later in the poem, Thurston plays

"A Place That Didn't Count Any More"

FIGURE 18 *Portrait of the MIC MAC*, 1853. Painting by John O'Brien.

up curator Patrick Condon Laurette's conclusion that O'Brien's ship portraits are marked by a shadow of menace that quietly subverts the reassuring flattering of the ship's owner. In his essay on O'Brien, Laurette highlights the menacing edge of the painter's portraiture: "His pictures had always thrived on the poetic spirit of the impending storm. If the ship had to be a portrait for a merchant, the ominous sky that brought it to life would be the spirit of O'Brien himself" (1984, 57). "In my art," Thurston's O'Brien observes, "the winds were always propitious, / the way clear, the owners' fortune assured." However, he invites the reader to

> Look closely at these pictures of perfection—
> you may see the vanity of commerce,
> but always the sky is making weather,
> the sea's cruel undercurrent is pulling
> the enterprise toward the patient rocks. (Thurston 2005, 47)

Furthermore, whereas misfortune for the ships' owners is merely financial, for those who work on the ships such peril is immediate and dire. In "The Saxon, the Stag and the Omar Pacha, Barques, 1854–55," Thurston emphasizes the contrast between the stasis of O'Brien's ship portraits and the turbulence of the ships' careers at sea through a series of entries in the ship's log—a kind of found poetry—that provide a chronicle of harrowing hardship, mortality, and inevitable doom: "4 p.m. James Pollack fell from fore top gallant yard to deck" (40).

If historical fiction is a way of writing about the present by other means, Thurston's focus on O'Brien is clearly shaped by his concerns about the region's embattled marginality and powerlessness in our present globalized era. The poem is in some ways an angry requiem, as Thurston's speaker echoes the bitterness with which he endows the underappreciated O'Brien and points to the eclipse of the region's prosperity and status. O'Brien "gave us / what we now need, ... / an image of a better time, outward- / looking, not close-hauled against the shore, / insular" (48). This physical and economic orientation is contrasted to the political and economic orientation westward and inward, in a passage that articulates the widespread view in the region of Confederation as a kind of lapsarian moment, a turning away from the source of the region's prosperity; Thurston's speaker responds to O'Brien's lament in "The Plymouth, Barque, 1881" that he is "bound / for the Poor House" (79),

> And we right along with you, O'Brien,
> now that we were turning inland,
> our fortunes run out of town on rails
> into the dry-footed confederation—
> the ships run aground to rot
> up muddy creeks. (80)

This lapsed state is also an aesthetic decline into utilitarian ugliness, as the narrator, gesturing to offshore oil as the new frontier of resource exploitation in the region, apostrophizes O'Brien to see "Oil rigs jacked / above the waves / like daddy-long-legs" and, "instead of unseeable wind, the flare, / effluvia, the slick of oil in air and water" (27).

> Instead of clippers
> dressed in tiers of canvas,
> like floating wedding cakes,
> container ships, ungraceful bulks
> with boxes as big as rail cars,
> piled impossibly high— (Thurston 2005, 27–28)

The context for this fallen world, furthermore, is a global one, as Thurston's speaker laments that in place of the Irish immigrant O'Brien's colonial masters, "Now our masters / have no borders. There is no New World /where we might start over" (61). Here Thurston echoes a recurrent concern in debates over globalization, that fundamentally globalization constitutes a reconfigured, ubiquitous imperialism, a more dispersed but no less inequitable distribution of power fuelled by the increasing mobility of capital. Zygmunt Bauman, citing Paul Virilio, argues that under globalization, rather than speak of "the end of history," it might be more appropriate to speak of "the end of geography"; for an increasingly nimble, transnational elite, "distances do not matter any more, while the idea of a geophysical border is increasingly difficult to sustain in the 'real world'" (1998, 13).

Reviewing *A Ship Portrait*, David Balzer contends that in his portrait of O'Brien, Thurston is "using everything in his literary arsenal to forge an extraordinary paragon out of what might be considered a flimsy failure" and considers the possibility that "O'Brien, in his real-life haplessness, was irreparably unheroic and, consequently, a better, more gripping subject than Thurston ever allows him to be" (2006, 32). But for Thurston, O'Brien, although in many respects an anti-heroic figure, nonetheless "stands out in that artistic community in the nineteenth century." He counters that critique with the observation that "for great art to happen, you need a lot of people working in the field," and not just towering figures such as O'Brien's contemporary, the painter J.M.W. Turner (Thurston 2008). Indeed, for Thurston, O'Brien is a gripping subject *precisely* because he is not a paragon and *precisely* because of his failure. This perspective is signalled particularly at the end of the book, in a highly elegiac passage that makes O'Brien's symbolic significance crystal clear:

> In the end, you became all of us,
> watching the ships sail away,
> not, as we thought, into the future
> but forever into the past.
> We disparage you, O'Brien,
> because your failure
> is our own,
> the whole culture
> turned in
> upon itself,
> peninsular,
> forsaking the wide oceans
> where our fortunes
> were made and lost. (Thurston 2005, 85)

This passage is an ambiguous and potentially ambivalent one, seeming to echo Stephen Harper's notorious reference to the "culture of defeat" in the East; however, the more compelling reading is that it constitutes a verdict on Confederation, on the wisdom of that inward turn. Although *A Ship Portrait* is not without its tensions, ultimately Thurston manages to steer around the perils of romanticizing the days of the sailing ship while suggesting that such a maritime orientation—however much unduly mythologized—provided a source of pride that "landward development" has failed to match. His aim, then, is complex and challenging: to restore Maritimers' pride in their past accomplishments without succumbing to a disempowering and unwarranted nostalgia about that bygone era.

"No such white luck": George Elliott Clarke

Thurston's *A Ship Portrait* qualifies its meditation on the more prosperous era of wood, wind, and sail in the Maritimes by reminding us of the ethnic and religious divides and hierarchical social order that characterized the era. The work of George Elliott Clarke reminds us that if there was a golden age in the Maritimes, it definitely wasn't that colour for Black people. With his consistent evocation of the long historical presence of people of African heritage in the Maritimes and his reminders about the suppressed history of slavery in the region, Clarke provides an important counterbalance both to Eurocentric versions of the history of the region as a beneficiary of imperial power, and to post-colonial revisions of that history that see the region as the victim of a neglectful or actively repressive imperial centre. Clarke's work suggests that any nostalgia for the region's glory days is not likely shared by those of African heritage, for whom the past was marked by slavery, marginality, poverty, and suffering, and for whom the present cannot help but be a considerable improvement. What Clarke highlights, in other words, is that while the history of the region may have been shaped by at times oppressive, at times malignantly neglectful control by England, its history was also shaped by internal colonization and ethnic and racial hierarchies that continue to reverberate in the Maritimes of today.

This longer historical context is crucial for assessing Clarke's *Execution Poems* (2001) and his first novel, *George & Rue* (2005), both based on the brutal murder of a white Fredericton taxi driver in 1949 by George and Rufus Hamilton, two of Clarke's cousins. Clarke has described how the murder, for which the brothers were hanged in July of 1949, was a suppressed story in his family, related to him by his mother only in 1994. He decided immediately to write about the story, convinced that it would serve a necessary cathartic purpose for his family. However, writing about such an actively repressed and

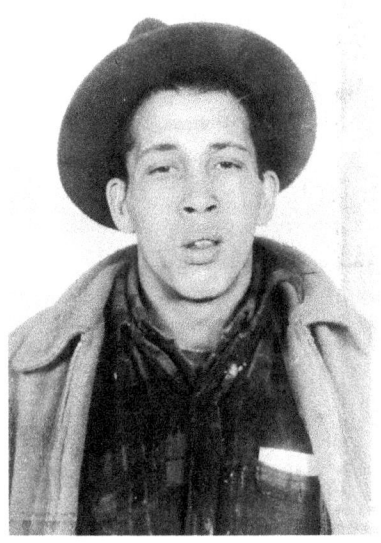 

FIGURE 19 Police photo of George Hamilton. **FIGURE 20** Police photo of Rufus Hamilton.

brutal incident, even half a century later, proved to be controversial. In 2000, while Clarke was in the process of writing *George & Rue*, he was contacted by the eldest daughter of Norman Burgoyne, the murder victim, who requested that he refrain from writing about the murder. Clarke's response was that, "given that my late cousins' crimes harmed *two* families—hers and mine—I had to try to understand why they did what they did, that I had to reclaim their bodies for us (meaning my family)" (2007b, 148; emphasis in original). The family of the victim "still deplored my desire to write a novel about the crime, but acquiesced to my interest in reuniting, so to speak, a portion of my family" (Clarke 2007a, 868). However, when *George & Rue* appeared in 2005, the eldest daughter of the victim publicly criticized Clarke and campaigned against the book, using "radio call-in programs and letters to newspapers to try to discourage people from purchasing the book" (Clarke 2007a, 868). Although Clarke proffered an apology for the pain caused to the victim's family by the actions of his cousins, he remained determined to write about the murder, and his arguments in his own defence throw light on the context in which he sees the troubled history of the Hamilton brothers. First of all, while recognizing the brutality of his cousins' crime, Clarke argued that "there remained sociopolitical attitudes, respecting 'Coloureds' in the Maritimes, in the 1940s and earlier, that merited examination, especially given that these attitudes helped to imprison black people in illiteracy, poverty, and unemployment (all excellent conditions for creating criminals and killers)" (2007a, 868–69). Furthermore, Clarke contended that these conditions were the residue of a long history of

Section 3: The Age of Sale

imperialism that, in some ways, destabilizes any easy dichotomy of perpetrator/victim. Recognizing the good character of the victim and the cowardliness of the attack, Clarke qualified this view by arguing that probably, "somewhere along the line, Burgoyne was an innocent beneficiary of the invasion of North America by his ancestors and the creation of vast wealth ... sapped from South American gold mines and the blood of Aboriginal and African slaves" (2007b, 147–48). Thus, while Clarke is careful to stress the brutality of the act and to place blame for it squarely on the Hamiltons, recognizing that there was nothing inevitable about their decision to commit such a gruesome assault, at the heart of both *Execution Poems* and *George & Rue* is the understanding that "the brothers' attack ... was a continuum of the violence that they had both imbibed" (Clarke, 2007a, 867).

In *Execution Poems*, and subsequently in more detail in *George & Rue*, Clarke depicts the brothers as being hardened at a young age by an atmosphere of brutal domestic violence and racialized psychological abuse, the legacy of a much longer history of slavery and social marginalization. In "The Killing," the poem which describes the murder in *Execution Poems*, Rue justifies his actions by framing the assault as a kind of time-lapse, delayed-reaction slave revolt: "The blow that slew Silver came from two centuries back. / It took that much time and agony to turn a white man's whip / into a black man's hammer" (Clarke 2001, 35). That equation is fleshed out in *George & Rue*, in which Clarke portrays the boys' childhood in Nova Scotia's Three Mile Plains, "a hillbilly Hell" (Clarke 2005a, 17), as an apprenticeship in abjection. The family lives in a porous, rundown shack, and the boys' parents, Asa and Cynthy, are in the process of a turbulent, "slow-motion divorce" (34), with the boys caught in the crossfire. Asa and Cynthy have little sense of "how much their personal destinies were rooted in ancestral history—troubles. Their own dreams and choices were the passed-down desolations of slavery" (14). Like most of the residents of Three Mile Plains, they "come from black slaves freed by redcoats down in Maryland and Virginia, then transported, like convicts, to 'New Scarcity' during the War of 1812.... They was so poor, they supposedly didn't even have history" (14). In an overview of the community's past, succinctly rendered in the "Blackened English" that gives the novel its distinctive feel, Clarke emphasizes the arduousness, poverty, and lack of opportunity that is their lot: "Some died broken, but everybody died broke. The people had to make their history with their sweat" (16). This turbulent legacy has left its mark on Asa, who, belittled by his job at the slaughterhouse, beats into his sons his own sense of subservience and social marginality: "They had to learn they were worth zilch.... The boys had to be abused like beasts, just whipped and slapped and kicked and punched and beaten, so they'd knuckle under and be quiet niggers" (28).

While Clarke is unflinching in depicting Asa's brutality, his portrait of the man also stresses the social and historical circumstances that contribute to such poverty and violence. Clarke explains that "Asa was one more study ... of the unskilled, marginalized, primary producer, who is useless to the economy and no good to his family" (2007a, 866). An important detail behind the characterization of Asa was Clarke's discovery from relatives that the Hamilton brothers had been beaten by their father with a bullwhip (866), as was his subsequent discovery that "the Hamilton clan had come to Nova Scotia from a vicious plantation in Georgia during the War of 1812" (867). What these discoveries consolidated for Clarke was the sense that the actions of the Hamilton brothers needed to be viewed as "rooted, perhaps, in the violence of slavery itself, carried forward in the family." Clarke theorizes that, "because their slave ancestors were abused by their white masters and overseers, the Hamilton parents extended this oppression to their own flesh and blood. They had learned only too well the lesson that blackness is evil and black people worth nothing" (867). As Geo formulates the inheritance of violence in "Original Pain," "Pops planted two twisted, crooked canes. / See: they flowered into two crooked oaks" (Clarke 2001, 15).

If the influence of white society on the incubation of the two embryonic crooks is in this sense indirect, their experiences outside the home reinforce Asa's message that they are worthless. In *George & Rue*, school is depicted as an abbreviated apprenticeship in alienation and persecution. Rufus quits at age ten after being strapped for slapping a visiting white teacher who calls him "a sly little nigger boy" (2005a, 30) and George, for whom "school composed a boxing ring" where "[w]hite kids would throw chalk dust in his face 'to make ya white'" (30), lasts but a year longer. The brothers' attempts to find respectable employment after the deaths of their parents meet with similarly discouraging results. George joins the army only to discover that all the menial jobs are reserved for minorities. When his comrades are shipped off to combat in Italy, George is left behind, where "his weapons would be a mop, a broom, a paring knife" (75); deserting to the merchant marine, he is arrested and given a critical psychological assessment that interprets imposed social marginality as an inherent flaw in his character. After a brief criminal career in Montreal, George returns to Halifax, where he hopes to redeem himself, only to be confronted by the most marginal and menial options: "Yes, he could shine shoes—again; he could carry bags—again; he could wash dishes—again. But he craved better. He tried to get on Haligonian docks stevedoring, but nothing doin for a Negro" (83). By the time he returns to the Annapolis Valley to marry his beloved Blondola, his prospects are as dim as ever. Even though being a veteran of the army earns him some respect, he is also a veteran of prison, a detail he keeps to himself.

Section 3: The Age of Sale

Rue's pursuit of income and social respectability reaps an even more bitter harvest. Smart enough to realize that in the army he will be relegated to KP duty, Rue works for a time playing the piano in a brothel in Halifax. The past catches up to him, however, when he is thrown out for assaulting his lover Purity, who reveals that she had once been Asa's whore. As with George, poverty and desperation lead to bad decisions when Rue relocates to Fredericton. Finding himself too strapped to properly court his lover India, he attempts a smash-and-grab on a store clerk and is given two years in Dorchester, "the Alcatraz of the Tantramar" (Clarke 2005a, 95). This harrowing experience consolidates his sense of criminalized alienation: "by now, he was accustomed to solo failure and solitary confinement—even outside jail" (97). What the background of both brothers suggests, ultimately, is not a trajectory of innate criminality but of increasing social marginality and decreasing options.

In a similar fashion, both *Execution Poems* and *George & Rue* emphasize the context of deprivation and desperation shaping the scheme that leads to the murder, particularly on the part of the reluctant George, married and trying to make a respectable name for himself in Fredericton. Those aspirations are undermined by the arrival of Rue, who takes up residence in George's shack and "sure didn't feel like slavin for anyone: doin Asa-type jobs for stupid, break-ass nothing. That was for Georgie" (2005a, 90). It is Rue's suggestion that the brothers knock over a taxi driver to fix what ails them financially—George needing money to pay Blondola's way out of hospital, where she has just given birth to their third child, and Rue needing money to pay his clothes' way out of the dry cleaners. This context is likewise foregrounded in *Execution Poems*, as Geo argues in "Ballad of a Hanged Man,"

> Have you ever gone in your life, going
> two days without eating, and whenever
> you get money, you're gonna eat and eat
> regardless of all the bastards in Fredericton
>
> was bust in the head, skull jimmied open? (2001, 13)[2]

At the same time, however, Clarke is careful not to sentimentalize the killing as an act of desperation, especially in *George & Rue*. Instead, the novel presents the crime as gruesomely comic, a brutal robbery gone wrong in which the brothers are both callous and inept. Having agreed to "stun and rob" (2005a, 104) a taxi driver, George gets cold feet when the taxi that arrives is driven by Silver, an affable fellow veteran—"a good man among very few good men" (118)—who had delivered George's wife to the hospital.

Disgusted by his brother's craven indecisiveness, Rue delivers the fatal blows with a hammer while George temporarily vacates the taxi to knock at the door of an acquaintance. The two then rifle the pockets of the murdered man, "cannibalizing" Silver's belongings (129), and throw his body into the trunk of his own taxi. Rue then concocts a plan to cover up the murder, which entails George leaving the taxi in Saint John, to deflect suspicion onto the locals. After squandering the proceeds of the crime at a brothel, however, George returns to Fredericton and ditches the taxi on a side road, where it is soon discovered. The brothers' loose spending and loose-lipped behaviour is quickly brought to the attention of the police, and George, believing that it will save his own skin, confesses to his role in the crime, while pinning the murder on his brother.

If the circumstances of the murder—a brutal, cowardly attack, after which the brothers squander the proceeds of the crime—undermine any sympathy the rest of the narrative might have cultivated for the brothers, their trial and execution are a different matter. Clarke's treatment of both in *Execution Poems* and *George & Rue* stresses the degree to which the punishment of the Hamiltons was informed by a highly racialized and racist context, and presents the brothers as subversive critics of a biased and vindictive justice system. This subversion is perhaps more stylized and dichotomous in *Execution Poems*, in which the figure of Rue is often imbued with a counter-canonical inflection that runs throughout Clarke's poetry, highlighting how, "for the colonized, the language of the colonizers is a double-edged sword, for while it displaces indigenous languages and cultures, and so is an agent of colonization, it is also a weapon that must be seized upon and used" (Knutson 2007, 40).[3] In the poem "Malignant English," for instance, Rue, informed by the Crown that "for a Negro, you speak our English well," plays Caliban to the Crown's Prospero: "your alabaster, marble English isn't mine: I hurl / insolent daggers at it like an assassin assaulting a statue" (2001, 38).[4] As Jennifer Andrews observes, the brothers' "resistance to and fragmentation of a standard English are important acts of self-definition and resistance against a city and a legal system that do not want to hear voices ... that deviate from the dominant white Loyalist heritage of Fredericton, of New Brunswick, and of the Maritimes more generally" (2008, 125). Facing the prospect of being hanged in "Famous Last," Geo concludes that "[t]he laws preach Christ, but teach crucifixion" and notes that the brothers will be "*disjecta membra* of Loyalist New Brunswick" (Clarke 2001, 41).

In *George & Rue*, the climate around the trials is highly charged and racialized, with the white public "feelin shaky now round their Coloured cleaners and cooks and maids" and the newspapers engaging in racial sensationalism: "'Negro thugs with hammers'; 'Coloured crooks with blonde

Section 3: The Age of Sale

tarts'" (2005a, 172). The trials are presided over by Justice Chaud,[5] who is depicted as a thoroughly anglicized Acadian, a colonized mimic man imposing imperial authority on the benighted subjects of the realm: "as a soul who was now sycophantically subordinate to the remnants of the original Anglo-Saxon empire, he felt it was his duty to ensure that the poor—and all those who were not purely white and English—stayed in their fetid stations: the Mi'kmak, the Acadians, the Negroes" (174). For Chaud, "the killers' colour was not immaterial: it made a black crime even blacker" (174). Clarke's portrait of the Crown Prosecutor Alphaeus Boyd likewise amplifies the Eurocentric undertones of the case, a subterranean racial hysteria: "Boyd heard a scintilla of Africa, of bush, in the boys' talk; also a hint of red men's hatchets, from before Europe's guns and cannons thrust Christ and Shakespeare upon the savages" (175–76). If this gives the trials a certain allegorical quality, Clarke's depiction of the exchanges in the courtroom steer closer to the tenor of the original trials, intertextually reworking the Hamilton brothers' answers and emphasizing in the process a certain subversive resistance to their inquisitors' righteous condescension. Responding to Rufus's lawyer Carl Waley's question, "Which is worse, to swat a fly or hammer a man?" George observes philosophically, "Fly ain't a man, a man ain't a fly, but both like to live" (179).[6] When Waley challenges George's suggestion that Silver would have been worried by the sight of George holding a hammer, asking "Isn't that prejudiced, a prejudiced view?" George sardonically retorts, "Depends on your colour" (180).

George's hopes of avoiding the gallows by pinning the blame on Rufus in *George & Rue*, however, prove to be misguided, undermined by Section 69 of the *Criminal Code of Canada*, according to which "Silver wouldn't've come to harm later if the boys hadn't planned on robbery initially, regardless of whether they'd wanted violence" (Clarke 2005a, 175). Clarke somewhat facetiously describes the law as grounded in "a domino theory of crime," in which intention to commit one crime was extended to any other crimes committed in the process (2007b, 157). Thus, as Justice Chaud underlines after both are sentenced to hang, "If Rufus is the physical killer, you, George Hamilton, are guilty of making murder possible" (2005a, 187). This palpably inequitable verdict renders ironic the self-righteous pontification of Chaud when he prepares to hand down the verdict. He patronizingly lectures the brothers,

> Your ancestors were forced from their native homes, brought here to this land, no doubt against their own will. You are not to blame; you may be pitied for your colour and your race, but you and we have this satisfaction, that the Coloured man, the Negro, has precisely the same

rights in a British, a Canadian, court to Justice that the purest white man could have. (186)⁷

The spuriousness of such pronouncements is demonstrated, first of all, by the lynch-mob atmosphere surrounding the execution, as thousands crowd the streets, reacting orgasmically as the brothers plummet to their deaths: "The masses in the hot, choking streets felt a collective spasm, a frisson, that made them gasp, quiver, vibrate in their genitals when they heard the trap violently clap, clatter, open. They felt emotionally alive now, but spent" (207). More tellingly, the judge's paean to British justice is thoroughly contradicted in the "Crypt" section of the novel, which describes a parallel case of two white Montreal youths convicted of bludgeoning a taxi driver to death and using his money to buy shells for an armed robbery. "They were sentenced to die," but "[n]inety minutes before their hangings, word came their sentences'd been commuted to life in prison. George and Rue—black—had no such white luck" (214). Justice, Clarke suggests, is not so colour-blind after all.⁸

As with Michael Crummey's *River Thieves*, Clarke's *Execution Poems* and *George & Rue* highlight the perilous duality of fictional reworkings of history. All three texts clearly present a particular take on a historical verdict, highlighting considerations of race and presenting the crime and punishment in such a way as to destabilize Eurocentric binaries of white innocence and righteousness and the innate criminality or culpability of the racialized Other. At the same time, all three must be seen as allegorical rather than documentary renderings of the history they represent. The inability to make that distinction, Clarke has argued, has clearly fuelled the controversy over *George & Rue*: "it forces a collision between real flesh-and-blood beings and events and the imaginary. Some readers cannot—cannot—separate the two" (2007b, 149). Pilar Cuder-Domínguez rightly argues that Clarke here uses the characteristically postmodern tactic of juxtaposing "'real' documents and fiction" only "in moderation, mostly in order to anchor his narrative in a specific historical context and thus to support his account rather than to undermine it." However, she adds that Clarke sees himself "as an interpreter and creator of 'truth'" (2010, 124). While the second half of *George & Rue* steers close to the details of the historical crime and trials, drawing heavily on the transcripts of the trials not just for details but occasionally for dialogue, Clarke treats his historical material with much greater leeway in *Execution Poems* and in the first half of *George & Rue*.⁹ As with *River Thieves*, it must be kept in mind that in a fundamental sense, these are not the same people.

Section 3: The Age of Sale

While it would be disingenuous to think that the two texts bear no relation to the historical case, it is important to remember that the primary consideration in assessing the amalgam of historical detail, speculation, and outright invention that is historical fiction is the ultimate effect of that alchemy. What both *Execution Poems* and *George & Rue* suggest is that for Clarke, the story of the Hamilton brothers is an opportunity to "recover their bodies" (2007b, 149), to consider not "how screwed up our clan is," but "how people did screwy things because of a history of very screwed-up interpretations of what their place in society should be" (2007b, 146). In other words, both *Execution Poems* and *George & Rue*, while clearly grounded in the history of George and Rufus Hamilton, are not to be taken as traditional, documentary fictionalizations of history but rather as allegorical meditations on the past and continuing impact of colonialism, slavery, and Eurocentrism in the Maritimes. Like Crummey's novel, Clarke's *Execution Poems* and *George & Rue* discomfit any impulse to look back fondly on the past from a turbulent present. They suggest that the past was turbulent too, but highlight that it was particularly turbulent for the racially marginalized, on whose labour and deprivation that sense of past glory was substantially built. "As the voices of Rufus and George so powerfully suggest," Andrews writes of *Execution Poems*, "there needs to be a wider reconsideration of the history—and legacy—of racism in the Maritimes and New Brunswick in particular" (2008, 129), an observation that applies equally to *George & Rue*.

TUMULTUOUS EVENTS SUCH AS THE EXPULSION OF THE ACADIANS AND THE 1917 Halifax Explosion have long been a source of fascination for writers of historical fiction. As Thurston's *A Ship Portrait* and Clarke's *Execution Poems* and *George & Rue* demonstrate, though, beyond these signal moments the Maritime provinces have a rich and complex history that is bound to fuel some engaging and innovative historical fiction in the decades to come. Whether it is the history of absentee landlords on Prince Edward Island, the history of the turbulent coal industry in Cape Breton, or even regional economic development in New Brunswick (a highly popular musical which debuted in Fredericton in the summer of 2010, *The Bricklin*, was based on Premier Richard Hatfield's ill-fated promotion of the mass production of a luxury sports car in the early 1970s), there is certainly ample material for the kind of rich revisionings of the past that have become a staple of Canadian literature over the last four decades. As more and more writers come to resist the vision of the Maritimes as "a place that didn't count any more," we are likely to see in the literature of the region an increasingly varied, sophisticated, and inventive engagement with the past.

Conclusion to Section Three

One of the possible reasons for the growing preoccupation with history, in Canada as elsewhere, is the anxiety occasioned by the mobility, deracination, and sense of placelessness that characterize our highly technological, globalized consumer society. Such anxiety is only intensified by neo-liberalism's reframing of human identity within a highly "financialized" vision of the social order. This inclination arguably is more pronounced in a region like Atlantic Canada that is undergoing profound economic and cultural change, even crisis—especially in Newfoundland and Labrador. Insulated and stylized, like a scenic tableau in a plastic snow globe, the vision of the past presented by heritage tourism is doubly dangerous, offering a seductive retreat from the complex turbulence of the present and providing the raw material for the transformation of the region's history into just one more cluster of products. In contrast, the achievement of contemporary historical fiction in Atlantic Canada is a dual one. It largely resists that airbrushed, sepia-toned vision but also frames that history within the context of contemporary concerns, making us think about the present and the future, as well as the past. While these works, like much recent Canadian historical fiction, reflect "the ways in which the contemporary literary historical novel has folded various tropes of formal, historiographical and theoretical radicalism into a newly popular, relatively sanitised blend" (de Groot 2010, 93), they nonetheless remind us that the past, too, was complex and turbulent, especially for those who—by virtue of their gender, race, ethnicity, or class, for instance—were low in the social, political, and economic hierarchies of the region. They also remind us of how any tendency to look to the past for a more communal, intimate, self-reliant society, in contrast to our postmodern, global, restructured present, must be qualified by a recognition of how

Section 3: The Age of Sale

most people during "the good old days" or any erstwhile "golden age" were also subject to the whims of larger, often global, political, and economic powers. Indeed, the work of Clarke, Crummey, Thurston, Morgan, and others reminds us of how the very possibility of such an era was predicated on the displacement, subjugation, and exploitation of subaltern subjects, be they the eradicated Beothuk, emancipated slaves, or impoverished Irish immigrants. Ursula Kelly's exhortation to recognize those marginalized in accounts of Newfoundland history thus can be extended to the region as a whole:

> Until, as a society and culture, we are aware of the ways in which we define and declare our own privilege as White and Christian and identify how, historically, we have exerted pressures on "others" to conform to what is dominant, ... our efforts to address our marginalization as subjects of a Canadian state will always be unduly compromised and insincere. As well, until a reference to "Newfoundland books" includes *all* our histories and cultures, and until references to "our heritage" and "our culture" include this diversity, our stories, as an increasingly differentiated and diverse culture, are only partially told. (1993, 75; italics in original)

This is not to say that the lesson of contemporary historical fiction in the region is that Atlantic Canadians, rather than celebrating their past, should be ashamed of it. Indeed, visions of the region's past such as Thurston's, Crummey's, and Morgan's reflect how the region (in contrast to the widespread view of it as the preserve of shiftless deadbeats), for all its present, postlapsarian deprivation, was built on centuries of entrepreneurial acumen and, more importantly, hard, hard work. But their writing also emphasizes the dangers of forgetting the imbalance of opportunity and privilege running through that heritage—the fact that not everyone had the option to be entrepreneurial or even to work, except perhaps in the most menial, degrading, low-paying positions.

As the work of all these writers suggests, any consideration of the history of Atlantic Canada must be attentive to the structures of power within which the political, economic, and social achievements of the region took shape: the larger context of colonialism, the history of slavery, and the dynamics of global capital. Their achievements also compel us to look to the present and future with a similar attention. They prompt us to address the continuing presence of racism and bigotry in the region, to confront the implications of its settler-invader heritage (especially in the context of outstanding land claims), to appreciate the problems with the increasing commodification of its culture, and to take a more measured, qualified pride in the region's heritage in order to withstand the pressures of globalizing forces that increasingly wither that sense of historicity.

Conclusion: Speculative Fiction for the Rest of the Country?

It may seem curious, at the end of a book on Atlantic-Canadian literature that is trying to counter the image of Atlantic Canadians as a backward-looking people, to have a section on representations of the past. What the examination of the texts in the preceding section reflects, though, is how such writing about the past is clearly energized and framed by an engagement with, and often an anxiety about, the present—whether it is Wayne Johnston looking at the 1948 referendum as a crossroads in Newfoundland's history from a *fin de siècle* climate in which the province's place in Confederation is being vigorously reassessed; Bernice Morgan foregrounding the role of women's work in the salt fish economy of the outports from the age of what threatens to be the twilight of the fisheries; or Harry Thurston revisiting the age of sail from within the framework of a very different (if no less imperial) era of global trade. What these works suggest is the continuity between concerns with the past and concerns with the contemporary cultural and economic position of the region that characterized the first two sections of this study. Offering an alternative to a touristic, Folk stereotype of the heritage of the Maritimes and Newfoundland and Labrador is imperative for many of these writers because a more complex, less stylized, and harmonious view of the past forestalls a disabling nostalgia, a misleading assumption of regional cohesion, and a disempowering acceptance of a fallen, subordinate status. Similarly, the direct engagement with neo-liberal thinking and the exploitative dynamics of economic globalization in the work of Thurston, Leo McKay Jr., Alistair MacLeod, Wendy Lill, Lisa Moore, and Edward Riche has implications not simply for the occupational and employment options of Atlantic Canadians but also for how we view the past and the complex and conflicted cultural, social, racial, and gender hierarchies in the region. The

Conclusion

consciousness in contemporary Atlantic-Canadian literature of the relationship between capital, government, and working people lays an important foundation for a reframing of the region's relationship with the rest of the country and also for a reconsideration of its place within a broader global economy.

In a broad sense, the principal concerns of this study—the changing nature of work, the reshaping of regional culture, and a post-colonial, revisionist approach to the past—are hardly exclusive to the writing of Atlantic Canada. The impact corporatization, globalization, and neo-liberal thinking have on the conditions of work explored in works like Moore's *February*, Riche's *The Nine Planets*, Lill's *Corker*, and McKay's *Twenty-Six* has been felt across the country—in the deindustrialization of Ontario and the fragile fortunes of British Columbia's forestry industry, for instance. Likewise, reconfiguring stereotypes and underscoring the cultural heterogeneity of regional literatures has been a preoccupation of writers and critics in other regions, particularly the "Prairies," who likewise are starting to be attentive to the impact touristic practices have on the images of their regions. Finally, as noted in the previous section, the revisionist and often post-colonial stance of contemporary historical fiction in Atlantic Canada is reflective of a broader national and even international trend—the historical fiction of Jane Urquhart comes to mind as similarly imbued with concerns about the ecological and cultural impact of the predominantly corporate and consumerist sensibility of our present age. What is different about Atlantic-Canadian literature, though, is the way in which raising these concerns in Atlantic Canada amounts to a much more substantial perceptual readjustment. It requires, in other words, a more sustained collective correction to the tendency to see the region as culturally static and largely unaffected by progress. Furthermore, that collective perceptual adjustment is much more imperative for Atlantic Canada because of the region's relative lack of economic and political power, its marginal and vulnerable position within Confederation and in an increasingly global economy.

In developing such a stance in this study, I recognize that there are a couple of considerable risks to my characterization of the changing shape of Atlantic-Canadian literature. First of all, to emphasize Ian McKay's critique of Folk discourse as much as I have in this study is not without its problems. Principally, it risks over-amplifying and distorting the impact the Folk paradigm has on the cultural life of the East Coast. Like most stereotypes, that paradigm is not without foundation, and many Maritimers and Newfoundlanders would agree that life in the East *is* more elemental, laid-back, friendly, and communal than it is elsewhere. That tendency is visible in much of the region's literature, even in many of the texts in this study:

in Donna Morrissey's romanticizing of the inshore fishery; in the emphasis on physical labour and collective cultural identity in Alistair MacLeod's work; and in the pre-lapsarian longings of Kenneth J. Harvey's and Bernice Morgan's depictions of post-moratorium Newfoundland. In that sense, just as McKay cautions against the reification of the notion of Folk Innocence, it is just as important not to install a similarly inflated image of a post-Folk, ironic Archness in its place. To the degree that people in the region are aware of Folk archetypes as such, most are likely undisturbed, or perhaps even amused by such essentialist, packaged images of a contented, insular, communal, rural Folk, and by the commodification of a therapeutic, unspoiled, pre-modern culture.

But not everyone is. One of the dangers of the allure of the Folk is that, for most people outside the region—who constitute the greater part of the audience for most if not all of the writers in this study—and for many within it, that vision of the region potentially overshadows or even supplants the much more complicated, much less removed, and much less reassuring society that is contemporary Atlantic Canada. Consequently, for many cultural producers the Folk paradigm is a force to contend with in one way or another. This is amply evident in the preoccupation with it in much of the writing discussed here—visibly so in Charlie Rhindress's and Frank Barry's plays, in the novels of Edward Riche, Lynn Coady, and Kenneth J. Harvey, and in the poetry of Jeanette Lynes and Mary Dalton; but also in Leo McKay's comments on work, Clarke's concern with the marginalization of Africadia, and Michael Crummey's and Michael Winter's reflections on writing about the history of rural Newfoundland. For so many cultural producers in the region it is the proverbial elephant in the room, and it is clear that at least some feel the need first to push the beast aside in order to make the room to play. To say that life in the region is more complex than the Folk stereotypes would have it is, as I suggested at the outset of this study, less than a revelation. But those stereotypes are a big part of, to borrow a phrase from Edward Said, "the structure of attitude and reference" ([1993] 1994, 111) with which writers in the region have had to contend in order to stake out a more considerable and less tenuous niche within the broader national culture, to go beyond simply being expected to produce domestic knock-offs of *The Shipping News*. As David Creelman argues of the Maritimes, however cliché such essentialist images may be, they constitute a powerful "subtext for the region" and are "still employed as a normalized default" (2008, 67), and writers from Newfoundland and Labrador perhaps even more so must contend with similarly entrenched expectations.

More importantly, though, the influence of the Folk paradigm is a visible extension of a pattern of economic, cultural, and political marginalization,

Conclusion

even infantilization, of the region that has obviously been necessary for cultural producers to confront over the last twenty or thirty years. What is, in many of the texts explored in this study, a kind of cultural counter-offensive has been made even more imperative by the intensified marginalization of the region under neo-liberalism, with its assault on social justice and the implementation of neo-liberal principles in the restructuring of work and government services. Images of complacently weather-beaten, sweatered-and-booted peasants who would furrow their brows at a passport seem particularly inappropriate not just because of the cosmopolitan, sophisticated sensibility of the contemporary culture of the region but also because of the consequences of its implication in broader economic and political structures: resource exhaustion, continuing out-migration, tenuous employment and unemployment, and corporate servitude. While, in the austere bookkeeper's world of neo-liberal economics, or behind the imaginary firewalls of neo-conservative self-interest, the Atlantic provinces are seen as failing to pull their weight, what contemporary Atlantic-Canadian literature reflects is that the people of the region *are* pulling weight—as ever they have. To return to outsiders' Janus-faced images of the region, the people of Atlantic Canada are en masse neither the hardy, independent petty producers reliant on the bounty of land and sea—a kind of Canadian variation of Soviet realism— nor the nation's sickly dependents, welfare urchins lazily sucking the teat of the federal government. Instead, they are a varied and complex population contending with a turbulent present that has significant implications for the region's future and for the region's past as well. This means contending with the changing, restructured nature of work in an increasingly unforgiving, corporatized global context, as do books like McKay's *Twenty-Six*, Moore's *February*, Morgan's *Waiting for Time*, and Lill's *Corker*. This also means engaging in a substantial reconfiguration of the culture of the region, rejecting the homogenizing mythology and comforting nostrums of Folk discourse, as in Coady's *Strange Heaven* and Rhindress's *The Maritime Way of Life*; confronting the commodifying and even imperializing dynamics of tourism, as do MacLeod's "Clearances" and Barry's *Wreckhouse*; and recognizing the implication of tourism and the production of Folk iconography in a broader, neo-liberal regime of flexible accumulation, as does a novel like Riche's *Rare Birds*. Finally, this means promoting—as do Clarke's *Execution Poems* and *George & Rue*, Crummey's *River Thieves*, and Thurston's *A Ship Portrait*—a much more nuanced and less consoling understanding of the region's history, one that energizes and better positions Atlantic Canadians to recognize and meet the challenges of the present and the future.

If an overemphasis on the Folk paradigm is one of this book's potential shortcomings, another is that this emphasis on commodification, globalization, and the impact of neo-liberalism may contribute to a vision of contemporary Atlantic-Canadian literature that is, like the Folk paradigm itself, highly selective and ideological. This is, as I conceded at the outset, most certainly the case. This study is far from comprehensive; stresses literature that is conspicuously socially, culturally, and politically engaged; and certainly privileges writers with established national and even international reputations. A different harvesting of contemporary writing in Atlantic Canada could easily produce a crop of writers far more amenable to the Folk paradigm than are the likes of Edward Riche, Leo McKay Jr., or Lynn Coady. My point, though, is that the preoccupations of the writers studied here are widespread, conspicuous, insistent. Collectively, they strike discordant notes that are difficult to ignore. More importantly, if *Anne of Tim Hortons* is guilty of providing a selective view of contemporary Atlantic-Canadian literature, that view is, I believe, ultimately more empowering than the selective vision of Folk discourse—a passive, conservative, and static construction of the region that renders it vulnerable to continuing condescension, marginalization, and exploitation.

The anxious tone of such a stance may seem paradoxical in light of the current vitality and popularity of Atlantic-Canadian literature, but it is not so paradoxical once that popularity is situated within the context of the region's present politico-economic situation and within the larger context of commodity culture and liberal, individualist, flexible accumulation. It is hard not to see the narrator's observation in Harvey's *The Town That Forgot How to Breathe* that "when a people's identity is threatened" (2003, 358) the result is often an outpouring of imaginative creativity as a self-conscious gesture to the recent explosion in Newfoundland literary and cultural activity. In turn, it is hard to resist applying that observation more broadly to the literature of the whole of Atlantic Canada during that period. Amid the profound challenges and uncertainties the region faces, the vitality of Atlantic-Canadian literature stands out as grounds for at least some measure of optimism about the region's future. Unfortunately, although the vibrancy of the literature of the region vis-à-vis its otherwise troubled economic, political, and social circumstances might suggest that its economy's loss is its culture's gain, that may well prove to be a temporary consolation. For most of its history, the writing of Atlantic Canada has been pushed to the margins of Canadian literature, and there is no good reason to think that its current popularity is the sign of a permanent reversal of its fortunes. Thus, while one can hope that Atlantic-Canadian writers have gained a somewhat more durable attention and respect, the present notoriety of Atlantic-Canadian literature may be symptomatic of a fickle consumer culture and may well prove to be a passing fad. This prospect underscores the importance of deconstructing and

Conclusion

resisting, rather than temporarily feeding, commodity culture's insatiable appetite for the exotic and novel. Thus the work of many of these writers reflects a consciousness that, in writing as in tourism, providing escape is usually a compromised position.

Atlantic Canada, unfortunately, is a small and marginal region, fortunate when it is even an afterthought in musings over the state of the Canadian nation. But if the present condition of Atlantic Canada—its literature and beyond—is not in and of itself of interest to people outside the region, what might be of interest is the way in which the region's economic, social, and cultural fortunes may provide an important cautionary tale. Newfoundland once cherished a strong sense of prosperity and independence, and the Maritimes was once one of the most affluent regions of the country, its fortunes precipitously declining as a result of, among other things, the political and economic readjustments that Confederation entailed, as well as shifts in technology, trade patterns, and resource availability. As Michael Clow argues, given the increasing light-footedness of capital and the political and economic readjustments ensuing from international agreements such as the North American Free Trade Agreement, it is not unreasonable to speculate that it may be the ultimate fate of the rest of Canada to be "Maritimized." "The 'harmonization' of Canada's economy and policy with the neo-liberal norms of the American and global economy," Clow argues, "will undermine any internal democratic processes, and make us helpless to set an alternative course. The Canadian state will be substantially hamstrung to ameliorate the devastation of the population under de-industrialization as long as we remain part of these unions predicated on neo-liberalism" (2005, 45). Clow's prediction arguably is being borne out in the current deindustrialization of Ontario, and one can without much effort envision a similar scenario in the future of the more prosperous West. To be sure, the greater population base and far more diversified and robust economy of southern Ontario, along with the considerable political influence of the region, put it in a very different situation from that of the Maritimes a century and a half before. Still, there are at least some similarities in the shuttering of factories, the departure of capital, and the ensuing out-migration of workers, not to mention the growing anxiety about the westward shift of economic muscle and political power. Part of the current dilemma of southern Ontario can be attributed to the increasing mobility of capital under economic globalization, as many businesses close down operations and head for greener (i.e., cheaper) pastures in the "developing" world. As for the West, just as the Atlantic provinces built their wealth on the bounty of an ocean that proved to have its limits, so the present economic boom in the West has been fuelled by natural resources whose finitude few seem to bother contemplating, even after the recent global recession put the steroidal growth of the oil patch on hold. Those who see the industry as the driver of the country's economic prosperity might want to stop and consider the fact that one hundred years ago, Nova Scotia's steel and coal industry—including coal mines, "its own blast and open hearth furnaces, rolling mills, forges, foundries, and machine shops"—"represented the most fully integrated industrial complex in the country" (Acheson [1972] 1985, 19). Who knows, just as Newfoundlanders and Maritimers have packaged and staged their maritime heritage for tourist consumption, perhaps in one hundred years time we will see Albertans "performing" the epic history of the oil industry in a depopulated, desertified West. In that sense, Atlantic-Canadian literature may prove to be speculative fiction for the rest of the country, giving an advance glimpse of what life is like when one of the only things you have left to sell is your past.

Whether such speculation is credible or risible, however, is not the principal issue (although a growing number of Albertans seem to be questioning the social and environmental costs of the province's prosperity). What is more important is that the ideological shift toward neo-liberal thinking over the past thirty or so years has reconditioned people to accept such vicissitudes as the price of doing business. The prevailing wisdom seems to be that capital will come and capital will go, at an increasingly accelerated pace, and the main thing is to cash in as much as possible while the opportunity presents itself. This short-term thinking is particularly precarious given that it is principally capital that gets to dictate the terms under which economic activity unfolds (and folds up) in particular jurisdictions (despite, in so many cases, a substantial level of government subsidy). In the rhetoric of neo-liberalism, the flexibility and mobility of capital is an advantage to be admired and emulated, but, as Zygmunt Bauman emphasizes, for working people and the unemployed such "fluidity" is less readily attainable and comes at a greater social, cultural, and psychic cost (1998, 104–5). To say this is not to decry mobility and flexibility per se, but to highlight how, as Bauman stresses, they are inequitably apportioned under globalization and how they generally mean different things for labour than they do for capital. Furthermore, the glorification of mobility and flexibility within neo-liberal thinking has eroded the value of geographical and communal commitment, celebrating a quasi-nomadic, protean existence while downplaying the psychological, social, cultural, and environmental consequences of what might described as the liquidation of attachment to place.

This asymmetry has been intensified under neo-liberalism by the increasing complicity of the state not only in the reframing of economic policy and labour legislation to the benefit of capital but also in the substantial transfer of public wealth and property into private (principally corporate) hands,

Conclusion

under the expedient assumption that such operations will of necessity be run "more efficiently" by the private sector. Over the last few decades, Stephen McBride observes, "governments privatized an impressive range of Crown corporations in what can only be described as a sustained attack" ([2001] 2004, 103) resulting in the transfer of a vast amount of public wealth into the hands of the private sector. This transfer of public wealth or jurisdiction over public resources, furthermore, has a multiplying effect, as it makes governments of all stripes—federal, provincial, municipal—more desperate for revenue and therefore more vulnerable to the pressure tactics of capital in the competitive process of attracting business. It also, as novels like Morgan's *Waiting for Time* and Harvey's *The Town That Forgot How to Breathe* illustrate, has substantial implications for people's ability to engage in geographically stable occupations, because of capital's preference for maximizing and accelerating profit, often through exhaustive and ecologically unsustainable practices.

One of the many worrying aspects of this glorification of fluidity is that it cultivates the ahistorical mindset that an attachment to place is disadvantageous, inconvenient, even retrograde. In such a mindset, people's deep attachment to an economically marginal region such as Atlantic Canada may come across as a stubborn refusal or even incapacity to get with the times and be realistic. Characterizing Atlantic Canadians as Folk behind the times, as so much of the contemporary literature of the region has stressed, makes it easier to infantilize them, to see them as outside of (and therefore as potential obstacles to) progress.[1] This provides a convenient rationale for dismissing their priorities and concerns, and positions them as people to be dictated to. Transformed into action, this sort of "impatience" with an "inefficient," potentially unviable region has had devastating consequences for deep-rooted cultures all around the world, who have been subjected to the merciless calculus of corporate interests and complicit governments, whether they be Balinese locals colonized by the tourist industry or First Nations communities in the toxic neighbourhood of Alberta's tar sands. The celebration of mobility, flexibility, change, and renewal under economic globalization, as Bauman and others stress, masks a much more tumultuous and inequitable reality. The mobility of capital and the fluidity of capital relations work particularly to the benefit of a privileged elite, and while certainly improving the lot of many of the world's poor, do so, perhaps necessarily, at the expense of other underprivileged populations. More importantly, they do so in an overly vigorous and destructive way. Long-standing ways of life around the world have been summarily uprooted in the name of creating immediate wealth that may have substantial short-term (and likely inequitably apportioned) benefits, but that may also have more debilitating long-term consequences, such as cultural upheaval and alienation, environmental damage, and social unrest. Writing in 1982, Marshall Berman (somewhat ambivalently) pointed to the self-consuming energies of modernity: "So often the price of ongoing and expanding modernity is the destruction not merely of 'traditional' and 'pre-modern' institutions and environments but—and here is the real tragedy—of everything most vital and beautiful in the modern world itself" (1982, 295). If capitalism can be seen as a recurring process of "creative destruction," the three decades of economic globalization since Berman's book appeared suggest that we need a future that is a little heavier on the "creative" part of the equation and plenty lighter on the "destruction."

The cultivation of this attitude of impatience points to the broader implications of what I characterized as the collective redefinition of Atlantic Canada in the contemporary literature of the region. Running through the discussion of work, the reconfiguration of culture, and the retrospective preoccupation with the past is a profound concern with—and in many cases anxiety about—a sense of space and place. Whether the focus is the archipelago of Black communities that constitute "the little state of Africadia" in Clarke's work, the machinations of urban developers in Riche's *The Nine Planets*, the gendered labour of Morgan and Morrissey's outports, the melancholy longing of MacLeod's exiles, or Coady's and Barry's spoofing of the tourist industry, there is a sustained engagement with and understanding of the interarticulation of work, culture, and place. While the attachment of Atlantic Canadians to their region is often seen as a recalcitrant rootedness, or some kind of romantic, numinous bonding (whether to be admired or lamented as anachronistic), the work of these writers prompts us to see that attachment in all its historical, economic, political, and cultural complexity. It militates against the view that Atlantic Canadians are unimaginative, improvident relics, stubbornly tied to an emptying sea. It also points to the dangers of constructing place first and foremost as "a business solution," as neo-liberal thinking has increasingly inclined us to do. This is not to say that people should have the unmitigated right to live and work where they please no matter the cost of ensuring a relative parity with the standard of living of the rest of the country. But I am suggesting that one of the major accomplishments of contemporary Atlantic-Canadian literature is that it dramatizes the consequences of letting the pendulum swing too far in the other direction and accepting the neo-liberal premise that, in an age of mobile and flexible capital, working people have to be just as flexible and mobile, no matter what the cost to them.

Mobility, of course, is not exclusive to the current age of economic globalization. Indeed, it is a central dynamic in the history of the Atlantic provinces—that of the cosmopolitan era of international maritime trade, for

Conclusion

instance, or of successive generations emigrating to find work. Furthermore, the history of the region was largely built around the advent of waves of mercantile or capitalist operations in various sectors—the salt fish economy, the shipbuilding trade, turn-of-the-century small-scale manufacturing, and the Cape Breton coal and steel industry, for instance. Although there is a long history of independent petty production in the region (autonomous individuals and families engaging in farming, fishing, woodcutting, and so on), the long post-contact history of the region is bound up with the presence of substantial investors and entrepreneurs—from lumber barons to fishing merchants to mining companies—around whose activities that deep attachment to place in the region largely developed. In that sense, it is important not to lose sight of the fact that capital both cultivates and exploits an attachment to place just as much as it destabilizes it. Thus the fortunes of mercantile or capitalist interests (for better or worse) have long been implicated in the fabric of community life in the Atlantic region, and the decline or migration of those interests has had concomitant effects on the lives of those communities. To return to the work of Edward Soja, the activities of capital have a profound effect on the ordering of space—whether that takes the form of the building of company towns, the distribution of timber leases, the vast operating range of factory trawlers, or what have you—including the space of those communities implicated in the operation of particular capitalist interests. There has long been, in other words, a tension between capitalism, resource exploitation, and the importance of community and geographical stability.

What much contemporary Atlantic-Canadian literature emphasizes, though, is that under economic globalization and the neo-liberal imperatives that have largely driven it, that tension is intensified and accelerated, as capital ever more nimbly moves through the process of developing and severing ties to communities and as the attachment to place is seen more and more as a liability, a sign of deprivation rather than an achievement. Thus the continuing attachment to place exhibited by Atlantic Canadians and reflected in the literature of the region can instead be viewed as evoking a resistance—whether conscious or not—to the deracinating, liberal individualist logic of post-industrial capitalism. While at times that resistance may serve to reinforce Folk stereotypes or may veer toward romantic, atavistic, and even nativist definitions of community,[2] for the majority such an adherence to place is not some amorphous Folk "belonging" or pre-capitalist Innocence. For most, it is the effect of long inhabitation and occupational continuity, reinforced by the development of extended familial and communal ties, as well as, especially for many newcomers, the appeal of a place that has not been so thoroughly marked by the imperatives of development and consumerism. It is important, of course, as Raymond Williams reminds us, not to overly idealize notions of settlement and place. "Settlement is indeed easy, is positively welcome, for those who can settle in a reasonable independence," he writes. For those who cannot, as generations of Maritimers and Newfoundlanders have demonstrated, migration is eminently preferable to living "under an imposed rigidity of conditions" (Williams 1973, 85). At the same time, the legendary nostalgia and longing of so many of those who do leave Atlantic Canada—most visibly and poignantly captured in the fiction of Alistair MacLeod—point to the durable appeal of the region even for those who have left. In that sense, one of the key achievements of recent Atlantic-Canadian literature is its demonstration that the region *is* a place that continues to matter, but not just to those who, one way or another, belong to it. It also matters in a broader sense because its perilous fortunes put to the test, in a neo-liberal climate in which traditional loyalties to place are being vigorously and strategically eroded, our willingness to resist the redefinition of place in such limited—and largely financial—terms.

Notes

Acknowledgements

1 *In This House Are Many Women and Other Poems*, copyright © 1993, 2004 by Sheree Fitch.

CHAPTER 1
1 See Donald Savoie's flagship essay "New Brunswick: Let's Not Waste a Crisis" in the inaugural issue of *Journal of New Brunswick Studies/Revue d'études sur le Nouveau-Brunswick* 1 (2010): 13–23, http://w3.stu.ca/stu/sites/jnbs/.
2 My investigation of Atlantic-Canadian literature in this study is restricted to literature in English and does not, for reasons of lack of space and expertise, extend to the rich body of Acadian literature. While my sense is that my approach in this study would be to some degree applicable to Acadian literature, regretfully I have neither the room nor the acumen to put that hypothesis to the test here.
3 The latter phrase in Baker's quote refers to the Royal Commission on Renewing and Strengthening Our Place in Canada, struck by the government of Newfoundland, the findings of which were published in 2003.
4 *The Quest of the Folk* was reprinted in 2006 and republished in 2009 as part of the Carleton Library Series (vol. 212).

Section One

CHAPTER 2
1 A similar tension in the logging industry informs Catherine Banks's play *Bone Cage*, which won the 2008 Governor General's Award for Drama. Set in rural Nova Scotia, the play revolves around a young man traumatized by the environmental devastation caused by the mechanized tree processor he operates to cut wood for pulp. Banks's Jamie quixotically rescues surviving fauna after

Notes

his twelve-hour shifts, appalled at the destruction but having no other realistic options, all the while realizing that—more visibly than in the fisheries—the resource he is harvesting is rapidly being exhausted: "The woods is tapped out. In ten years, *less* even, there won't be any trees in this valley." Referring to strategically screened clear-cutting—a widespread phenomenon throughout the Atlantic provinces—Jamie laments, "All along the roads is not woods anymore. What you're seeing is a screen of trees two, three tier deep and behind that is hectares and hectares of clear cut. Everything has been chewed up and spit out" (Banks 2007, 66).

2 Here Morgan's portrait mirrors the reaction to Crosbie's announcement; see Harris 1998, 162–63, for an account of the incident.

CHAPTER 3

1 Such migration, indeed, is the subject of Donna Morrissey's 2008 novel *What They Wanted*, which traces the fortunes of the children of Adelaide and Sylvanus Now.
2 The stories from these two collections were republished in *Island: The Collected Short Stories of Alistair MacLeod* in 2000.
3 See Lepaludier 2002 for a discussion of the importance of verb tense in the story.
4 For a theatrical rendering of the story of Westray, see the play *Westray: The Long Way Home*, by Chris O'Neill and Ken Schwartz (Winnipeg: Blizzard, 1997).
5 See the account by Comish 1993, 29.
6 McCormick notes that in a county like Pictou, where "average unemployment had almost doubled," manufacturing jobs were on the decline, and jobs in the service sector on the rise, "the prospect of long-term, highly paid employment would have been quite attractive" (1999a, 22).
7 This scene echoes an incident recounted by miner Shaun Comish, in which his crew was asked to work with a miner despite the fact that its methanometer wasn't working. Reacting to his boss's lack of response, Comish joked, "If we get killed, I'll never speak to you again" (1993, 34).
8 It should be added, though, that oral testimony from the disaster is far from unanimous on the issues of working conditions and safety on the rig, as both House's oral history *But Who Cares Now? The Tragedy of the Ocean Ranger* (1987) and Heffernan's *Rig* (2009) reflect.

CHAPTER 4

1 This point is made in a National Film Board documentary about Lill's dual careers, *Wendy Lill: Playwright in Parliament* (Mahoney and Ralston 1999).

Notes

Section Two
1 The forum is in *Acadiensis* 35.1 (2005): 132–57.

CHAPTER 5
1 As Michael Harris describes in his account of the Marshall case (1986, 309–47), an RCMP investigation found that the three principal witnesses had provided perjured testimony, allegedly under pressure from Sydney Chief of Detectives John McIntyre.
2 The 1990 crisis resulted when Mohawk people from the Kanesatake reserve created a blockade to stop a planned extension of a golf course in Oka, Quebec, onto what they considered sacred land. The blockade led to a tense armed standoff between Mohawks and the Sûreté du Québec and the federal army, during which a Sûreté officer was killed.
3 Peltier's case was the subject of Peter Matthiessen's 1983 bestseller *In the Spirit of Crazy Horse*, which in turn inspired two films, the documentary *Incident at Oglala* and the feature film *Thunderheart*, both released in 1992.
4 Sherene Razack describes the skeptical response of Matchee's wife to the idea that Matchee had tried to hang himself, given the low ceiling of his cell and physical evidence of a struggle (see Razack 2004, 151).
5 See Alexander MacLeod 2008 for a detailed discussion of the concept of Africadia and also for discussion of the diversity as opposed to uniformity of the Black Renaissance.
6 For a more extended discussion of writing by women in the Maritimes and Newfoundland, see David Creelman's chapter on contemporary writing by women in *Setting in the East* (2003, 173–200) and Danielle Fuller's *Writing the Everyday* (2004b).

CHAPTER 6
1 Daniel MacIvor's play *Marion Bridge* (1999) comes to mind as a prominent example.
2 The "alternative economy," however, is typically a more serious matter. In David Adams Richards's *The Lost Highway* (2007), for instance, a tale of murder and revenge develops around a potentially winning lottery ticket, and in Richards's *The Bay of Love and Sorrows* (1998), the dabbling of a self-aggrandizing upper-middle-class scion in the drug trade leads to a brutal denouement involving murder and suicide.
3 Taking inventory of tourist practices in Newfoundland, Overton remarks that one souvenir available for purchase is a can of fresh Newfoundland air (1996, 145).

Notes

Section Three

CHAPTER 7

1. Patrick O'Flaherty sees Prowse as an unoriginal but masterful champion of the romantic nationalist tradition: "he enveloped the history of the country more thoroughly than ever in a cloud of misunderstanding, by combining his genuine scholarship with sentimental editorializing" (1979, 79).
2. Labouchere's letter is considerably more upbeat, passing on the good news that "the consent of the community of Newfoundland is regarded by Her Majesty's Government as the essential preliminary to any modification of their territorial or maritime rights" (quoted in Prowse 1895, 475).
3. Howley then proceeds to gloss Peyton's account (92–96). However, Howley also includes a more incriminating eyewitness account of the encounter in a letter published in *The Liverpool Mercury* by a member of Peyton's party, E.S. (96–101), who describes how Nonosabusut, having been disarmed, persisted in clinging to his wife, when "one of the men rushed forward and stabbed him in the back with a bayonet" (99); subsequently recriminated for his action, the man is described as being unrepentant: "it was only an Indian, and he wishes he had shot a hundred instead of one" (100).
4. For an extended discussion, see my *Speculative Fictions: Contemporary Canadian Novelists and the Writing of History* (Montreal: McGill-Queen's University Press, 2002), 65–110.
5. In *It's Me, O Lord: The Autobiography of Rockwell Kent*, Kent writes, "my course, our course, was to love the life of Newfoundland, and enter into it. It was my course to love those steep, stark hills that formed the harbor and the bay; to love them and to paint them. And to love the people, and be friends with them. Not for a season's sojourn had we come to Newfoundland and made our home there: we had come to stay" (1955, 284).
6. Here Winter echoes Kent's description of his work ethic in *Rockwellkentiana*: "I have never been quite sure that the most profound incentive of my whole life has not been overcoming that lazy slothful sensuous being that I maybe am. I suspect that I get up early in the morning because I want to lie in bed, that I exercise because I want to sleep, that I work because I am essentially lazy, that I want to accomplish something because I have profoundly a contempt for accomplishment" (1933, 11).
7. See Kent, *It's Me, O Lord*, 291–96, for Kent's version of the incident, which makes no mention of the fine being paid on the spot.

CHAPTER 8

1. "The Irish emigrant," testified Uniacke, "before he comes out, knows not what it is to lie on a bed. If you put him in a bed and give him pork and flour, you make the man sick; but when a man comes to Newfoundland he gets no more than his breadth and length upon the deck of a ship, and he has no provisions but a few herrings, and he comes out a healthy man" (quoted in D. MacKay 1990, 203).

2 Clarke's central source texts for both books were the transcripts of the trials of the two brothers, and here Clarke riffs off an exchange during George Hamilton's testimony in the trial of his brother. Asked by Rufus Hamilton's attorney John A. Warner whether "It is not going to affect your appetite at all that a man is hit on the head and sits in a car beside you—a man supposed to have been a friend of yours," George Hamilton replies, "Mr. Warner, it might offend my appetite, but have you ever went in your life two days without eating, and when you get money you are going to eat, aren't you, regardless of all the people in fredericton [sic] was hit in the head?" (*King v. Rufus Hamilton*, 1949, Part 3, R.G. 13, 1680 C.C. 677, Vol. 1, 201–2).

3 See Knutson 2007 for an extended examination of the intertextuality of *Execution Poems*, particularly the central role of Shakespeare's *Titus Andronicus*.

4 This passage likewise is an extrapolation from an exchange with Crown attorney E.B. MacLatchey during the trial of Rufus Hamilton:

    Q How far did you go in school?
    A I went to grade three.
    Q Grade three?
    A Yes sir.
    Q You speak almost perfect english, don't you?
    A I do.

(*King v. Rufus Hamilton*, 1949, Part 3, R.G. 13, 1680 C.C. 677, Vol. 1., 524)

5 The name is a pun on Michaud, the surname of the historical trial judge.

6 Here Clarke compresses an exchange in George Hamilton's cross-examination. See *King v. Rufus Hamilton*, 1949 Part 3, R.G. 13, 1680 C.C. 676, Vol. 1., 123–24.

7 Here Clarke gives a pronounced colonial inflection to the self-satisfied tone of Justice Michaud's sentencing of George Hamilton: "The case against you has been fairly presented by counsel for the Crown, and you have been ably defended. I think it must be fair to say that your counsel has done all that he might reasonably have been expected to do in your behalf, in spite of yourself" (*King v. George Hamilton* [1949], Part 3, R.G. 13, 1680 C.C. 677, Vol. 1., 272).

8 Although it does not feature in the novel, another factor raises reservations about the justice of the trial. At the same time as the Hamiltons were given the death sentence, a Mi'kmaq man was convicted of manslaughter and received three years in prison ("3 Years for Manslaughter; Hanging in Other Cases," *The Daily Gleaner*, 20 May 1949, 8). Indeed, Clarke suggests in an interview that the leniency of such a sentence compared to George Hamilton's receiving the death penalty perhaps reflected a guilty conscience on the part of the judge (2007b, 155–56).

9 In *George & Rue*, for instance, the brothers are depicted as being orphaned in adolescence, whereas both parents of the historical Hamilton brothers were still alive at the time of their trials. In a letter written to the Governor General appealing for clemency, George Hamilton relates the story of his life, which indicates that his father was in Fredericton after George had moved there. The records of George Hamilton's capital case at Library and Archives Canada

Notes

contain a letter written by his mother, living in Montreal at the time, to the Governor General pleading for the lives of her two sons (R.G. 13, Vol. 1680, C.C. 677 Pt. 1). Although the Hamiltons were not literally orphans, they were, according to George Hamilton, abandoned by their parents at an early age; in his journal George Hamilton writes "You see I never had a mother or a father to love me and bring me up like other kids, you see I brought myself up into this world" (1949, 1). In "Spree" in *Execution Poems*, Geo and Rue are depicted as going on a fictional crime spree, though in George Hamilton's letter he refers to his brother spending six months in jail for "Breaking up a Restrent" in 1945 (Hamilton 1949, 4). In an interview appended to the paperback version of *George & Rue*, Clarke notes that some of the stories from his father's impoverished upbringing in Halifax are given to George and Rufus in the novel (2005b, 5).

Conclusion
1 As a man from Hamilton says to Patrick Terri—wary of offending the physically imposing Miramichier—in David Adams Richards's *Lives of Short Duration*, "*I don't mean that you yourself are backward, but the region itself has backwards sorts of ideas*" (1981, 255, italics in original).
2 See Cynthia Sugars's argument about Kenneth J. Harvey's *The Town That Forgot How to Breathe* (2010, 22–23). Donna Morrissey's latest novel, *What They Wanted*, about Newfoundlanders migrating to work in the Alberta oil patch, is arguably also vulnerable to such a critique.

Works Cited

Acheson, T.W. [1972] 1985. "The National Policy and the Industrialization of the Maritimes, 1880–1910." In *Industrialization and Underdevelopment in the Maritimes 1880–1930*, 1–26. Introduced by David Frank. Toronto: Garamond.

Alexander, David. 1983. *Atlantic Canada and Confederation: Essays in Canadian Political Economy*. Compiled by Eric W. Sager, Lewis R. Fischer, and Stuart O. Pierson. Toronto: University of Toronto Press.

Andrews, Jennifer. 2008. "Re-Visioning Fredericton: Reading George Elliott Clarke's *Execution Poems*." *Studies in Canadian Literature* 33.2: 115–32.

Armstrong, Christopher J. 2010. "The Rock Observed: Art and Surveillance in Michael Winter's *This All Happened*." *Newfoundland and Labrador Studies* 25.1: 37–53.

Armstrong, Jeannette. 2005. "Aboriginal Literatures: A Distinctive Genre within Canadian Literature." In *Hidden in Plain Sight: Contributions of Aboriginal Peoples to Canadian Identity and Culture*, edited by David R. Newhouse, Cora Voyageur, and Dan Beavon, 180–86. Toronto: University of Toronto Press.

Armstrong, Pat. 2010. "Neoliberalism in Action: Canadian Perspectives." In Braedley and Luxton, *Neoliberalism and Everyday Life*, 184–201.

Baker, Melvin. 2003. "Falling into the Canadian Lap: The Confederation of Newfoundland and Canada, 1945–1949." In the Government of Newfoundland, vol. 1 of *Collected Research Papers*, 29–88.

Balzer, David. 2006. "Capsizing Vessels." Review of *A Ship Portrait*, by Harry Thurston. *Books in Canada* 35.4: 31–32.

Banks, Catherine. 2007. *Bone Cage*. Toronto: Playwrights Canada.

Bannister, Jerry. 2003. "The Politics of Cultural Memory: Themes in the History of Newfoundland and Labrador in Canada, 1972–2003." In the Government of Newfoundland, vol. 1 of *Collected Research Papers*, 117–55.

Bantjes, Rod. 2004. "Regionalization and Environmental Governance in Atlantic Canada." In Tomblin and Colgan, *Regionalism in a Global Society*, 245–70.

Barry, Frank. 2003. *Wreckhouse*. St. John's: Killick.

Bartlett, Captain Robert A. 1928. *The Log of "Bob" Bartlett: The True Story of Forty Years of Seafaring and Exploration*. New York: G.P. Putnam's Sons.

Barton, Bruce, ed. 2004. *Marigraph: Gauging the Tides of Drama from New Brunswick, Nova Scotia, Prince Edward Island*. Toronto: Playwrights Canada.

Baudrillard, Jean. 1994. *Simulacra and Simulation*. Translated by Sheila Faria Glaser. Ann Arbor: University of Michigan Press.

Bauman, Zygmunt. 1998. *Globalization: The Human Consequences*. New York: Columbia University Press.

Benjamin, Walter. 1969. "The Work of Art in the Age of Mechanical Reproduction." In *Illuminations: Essays and Reflections*, edited by Hannah Arendt, 217–51. New York: Schocken.

Berman, Marshall. 1982. *All That Is Solid Melts into Air: The Experience of Modernity*. New York: Simon and Schuster.

Bitterman, Rusty. 1994. "Farm Households and Wage Labour in the Northeastern Maritimes in the Early 19th Century." In *Contested Countryside: Rural Workers and Modern Society in Atlantic Canada, 1800–1950*, edited by Daniel Samson, 34–69. Fredericton: Acadiensis.

Blades, Kent. 1995. *Net Destruction: The Death of Atlantic Canada's Fishery*. Halifax: Nimbus.

Bourdieu, Pierre. 1998. *Acts of Resistance: Against the Tyranny of the Market*. New York: New Press.

Boyd, George. 2004. "Consecrated Ground." In Barton, *Marigraph*, 145–91.

Braedley, Susan, and Meg Luxton, eds. 2010. *Neoliberalism and Everyday Life*. Montreal: McGill-Queen's University Press.

Brodie, Janine. 1995. *Politics on the Margins: Restructuring and the Canadian Women's Movement*. Halifax: Fernwood.

Buckner, Phillip A. 1990. "The Maritimes and Confederation: A Reassessment." In Vol. 1 of *Atlantic Canada Before Confederation. The Acadiensis Reader*, 2nd ed., edited by P.A. Buckner and David Frank, 370–95. Fredericton: Acadiensis.

———. 1994. "The 1860s: An End and a Beginning." In Buckner and Reid, *The Atlantic Region to Confederation*, 360–86.

Buckner, Phillip A., and John G. Reid, eds. 1994. *The Atlantic Region to Confederation: A History*. Toronto and Fredericton: University of Toronto Press and Acadiensis.

Budgel, Richard. 1992. "The Beothuks and the Newfoundland Mind." *Newfoundland Studies* 8.1: 15–33.

Butler, Judith. 1990. *Gender Trouble: Feminism and the Subversion of Identity*. London: Routledge.

Cabajsky, Andrea, and Brett Josef Grubisic, eds. 2010. *National Plots: Historical Fiction and Changing Ideas of Canada*. Waterloo, ON: Wilfrid Laurier University Press.

Cadigan, Sean T. 2009. *Newfoundland and Labrador: A History*. Toronto: University of Toronto Press.

Chafe, Paul. 2003. "'The scuttlework of empire': A Postcolonial Reading of Wayne Johnston's *The Colony of Unrequited Dreams*." *Newfoundland Studies* 19.2: 322–46.

———. 2004. "Lament for a Notion: Loss and the Beothuk in Michael Crummey's *River Thieves*." *Essays on Canadian Writing* 82: 93–117.

———. 2008. "Living the Authentic Life at 'The Far East of the Western World': Edward Riche's *Rare Birds*." *Studies in Canadian Literature* 33.2: 171–90.

———. 2010. "'Old Lost Land': Loss in Newfoundland Historical Fiction." In Cabajsky and Grubisic, *National Plots: Historical Fiction*, 167–81.

Clairmont, Donald H., and Dennis William Magill. [1974] 1999. *Africville: The Life and Death of a Canadian Black Community*. 3rd ed. Toronto: Canadian Scholars' Press.

Clarke, George Elliott. 1983. *Saltwater Spirituals and Deeper Blues*. Porters Lake, NS: Pottersfield.

———. [1990] 2000. *Whylah Falls*. Tenth anniversary edition. Vancouver: Polestar.

———. 1991. Introduction to vol. 1 of *Fire on the Water: An Anthology of Black Nova Scotian Writing*, edited by George Elliott Clarke, 11–29. Porters Lake, NS: Pottersfield.

———. 1992a. "The Birmingham of Nova Scotia: The Weymouth Falls Justice Committee vs. the Attorney General of Nova Scotia." In McKay and Milsom, *Toward a New Maritimes*, 16–24.

———. 1992b. "Confession." In vol. 2 of *Fire on the Water: An Anthology of Black Nova Scotian Writing*, edited by George Elliott Clarke, n.p. Lawrencetown Beach, NS: Pottersfield.

———. 2001. *Execution Poems*. Kentville, NS: Gaspereau.

———. 2002. *Odysseys Home: Mapping African-Canadian Literature*. Toronto: University of Toronto Press.

———. 2005a. *George & Rue*. Toronto: HarperCollins.
———. 2005b. "An Interview with George Elliott Clarke." In *George & Rue*, 3–11. Toronto: Harper Perennial.
———. 2007a. "George and Ruth: An Interview with George Elliott Clarke about Writing and Ethics." Interview with Kristina Kyser. *University of Toronto Quarterly* 76.3: 860–73.
———. 2007b. "We Have to Recover Their Bodies." Interview with Herb Wyile. In Wyile, *Speaking in the Past Tense*, 133–64.
Clewell, Tammy. 2004. "Mourning Beyond Melancholia: Freud's Psychoanalysis of Loss." *Journal of the American Psychoanalytic Association* 52: 43–67.
Clow, Michael. 2005. "Just More of the Same? Confederation and Globalization." In *From the Net to the Net: Atlantic Canada and the Global Economy*, edited by James R. Sacouman and Henry Veltmeyer, 25–50. Aurora, ON: Garamond.
Coady, Lynn. 1998. *Strange Heaven*. Fredericton: Goose Lane.
———. 2003. "Introduction: Books that say Arse." In *Victory Meat: New Fiction from Atlantic Canada*, edited by Lynn Coady, 1–6. Toronto: Anchor Canada.
Colas, Alejandro. 2005. "Neoliberalism, Globalisation and International Relations." In Saad-Filho and Johnston, *Neoliberalism: A Critical Reader*, 70–79.
Comish, Shaun. 1993. *The Westray Tragedy: A Miner's Story*. Halifax: Fernwood.
Connell, Raewyn. 2010. "Understanding Neoliberalism." In Braedley and Luxton, *Neoliberalism in Everyday Life*, 22–36.
Conrad, Margaret. 2002. "Mistaken Identities? Newfoundland and Labrador in the Atlantic Region." *Newfoundland Studies* 18.2: 159–74.
Conrad, Margaret, and James K. Hiller. 2001. *Atlantic Canada: A Region in the Making*. Toronto: Oxford University Press.
Cooper, Brenda. 1998. *Realism in West African Fiction: Seeing with a Third Eye*. London: Routledge.
Courchene, Thomas. 2001. *A State of Minds: Toward a Human Capital Future for Canadians*. Montreal: Institute for Research on Public Policy.
Creelman, David. 2003. *Setting in the East: Maritime Realist Fiction*. Montreal: McGill-Queen's University Press.
———. 2008. "Swept Under: Reading the Stories of Two Undervalued Maritime Writers. *Studies in Canadian Literature* 33.2: 60–79.
Crummey, Michael. 2001. "Changing History." *Quill & Quire* 67.11: 42, 40.
———. [2001] 2002. *River Thieves*. Toronto: Anchor Canada.

———. 2004. "Journey into a Lost Nation." Introduction to *Newfoundland: Journey into a Lost Nation*, by Michael Crummey and Greg Locke, 8–39. Toronto: McClelland.

———. 2007. "The Living Haunt the Dead." Interview with Herb Wyile. In Wyile, *Speaking in the Past Tense*, 295–319.

Cuder-Domínguez, Pilar. 2010. "The Racialization of Canadian History: African-Canadian Fiction, 1990–2005." In Cabajsky and Grubisic, *National Plots: Historical Fiction*, 113–29.

Currie, Andrea. 1992. "A Roof is not Enough: Feminism, Transition Houses and the Battle Against Abuse." In McKay and Milsom, *Toward a New Maritimes*, 215–35.

Dalton, Mary. 1992. "Shadow Indians: The Beothuk Motif in Newfoundland Literature." *Newfoundland Studies* 8.2: 135–46.

———. 2006. *Red Ledger*. Montreal: Véhicule.

Davies, Gwendolyn. 1991. "The 'Home Place' in Modern Maritime Literature." In *Studies in Maritime Literary History 1760–1930*, edited by Gwendolyn Davies, 192–99. Fredericton: Acadiensis.

de Groot, Jerome. 2010. *The Historical Novel*. London: Routledge.

Debord, Guy. [1967] 1995. *The Society of the Spectacle*. Translated by Donald Nicholson Smith. New York: Zone.

DeLottinville, Paul. 1994. *Shifting to the New Economy: Call Centers and Beyond*. Toronto: Copp Clark Longman.

Dobrowolsky, Alexandra. 2009. "Introduction: Neo-liberalism and After?" In *Women and Public Policy in Canada: Neoliberalism and After?* edited by Alexandra Dobrowolsky, 1–24. Toronto: Oxford University Press.

Dodd, Susan. 1999. "Unsettled Accounts after Westray." In McCormick, *The Westray Chronicles*, 218–49.

Dragland, Stan. 2004. "*The Colony of Unrequited Dreams*: Romancing History?" *Essays on Canadian Writing* 82: 187–213.

Durix, Jean-Pierre. 1998. *Mimesis, Genres, and Post-colonial Discourse: Deconstructing Magic Realism*. Houndmills, UK: Palgrave Macmillan.

Finbow, Robert. 1995. "Atlantic Canada: Forgotten Periphery in an Endangered Confederation?" In *Beyond Quebec: Taking Stock of Canada*, edited by Kenneth McRoberts, 61–80. Montreal: McGill-Queen's University Press.

———. 2004. "Atlantic Canada in the Twenty-First Century: Prospects for Regional Integration." In Tomblin and Colgan, *Regionalism in a Global Society*, 149–70.

Fitch, Sheree. 1993. *In This House Are Many Women and Other Poems*. Fredericton: Goose Lane.

Forbes, E.R. 1989. *Challenging the Regional Stereotype: Essays on the 20th Century Maritimes*. Fredericton: Acadiensis.
Forbes, E.R., and D.A. Muise, eds. 1993. *The Atlantic Provinces in Confederation*. Toronto: University of Toronto Press.
Foucault, Michel. 1977. *Discipline and Punish: The Birth of the Prison*. Translated by Alan Sheridan. New York: Pantheon.
Fraiman, Susan. 1993. *Unbecoming Women: British Women Writers and the Novel of Development*. New York: Columbia University Press.
Freud, Sigmund. 1957. "Mourning and Melancholia." Vol. 24 of *The Standard Edition of the Complete Psychological Works of Sigmund Freud*, edited and translated by James Strachey, 243–58. London: Hogarth.
Friedman, Thomas L. [1999] 2000. *The Lexus and the Olive Tree*. Revised edition. New York: Farrar, Straus and Giroux.
Fuller, Danielle. 2004a. "Strange Terrain: Reproducing and Resisting Place-Myths in Two Contemporary Fictions of Newfoundland." *Essays on Canadian Writing* 82: 21–50.
———. 2004b. *Writing the Everyday: Women's Textual Communities in Atlantic Canada*. Montreal: McGill-Queen's University Press.
———. 2008. "The Crest of the Wave: Reading the Success Story of Bestsellers." *Studies in Canadian Literature* 33.2: 40–59.
Glasbeek, Harry, and Eric Tucker. 1995. "Death by Consensus: The Westray Mine Story." In *Labour & Working-Class History in Atlantic Canada: A Reader*, edited by David Frank and Gregory S. Kealey, 399–439. St. John's: ISER.
Government of Newfoundland, ed. 2003. Vol. 1 of *Collected Research Papers of the Royal Commission on Renewing and Strengthening Our Place in Canada*. St. John's: Government of Newfoundland.
Gwyn, Richard. 1968. *Smallwood: The Unlikely Revolutionary*. Toronto: McClelland.
Hamilton, George. 1949a. "The Journal of George Hamilton." 16 June. Provincial Archives of New Brunswick, Fredericton, NB.
———. 1949b. Letter to the Governor General. 28 May. Library and Archives Canada, Ottawa, ON.
Harris, Michael. 1986. *Justice Denied: The Law versus Donald Marshall*. Toronto: Macmillan Canada.
———. 1993. *Rare Ambition: The Crosbies of Newfoundland*. Toronto: Penguin Canada.
———. 1998. *Lament for an Ocean. The Collapse of the Atlantic Cod Fishery: A True Crime Story*. Toronto: McClelland.
Harvey, David. 2005. *A Brief History of Neoliberalism*. Oxford: Oxford University Press.

———. 2006. *Spaces of Global Capitalism: Towards a Theory of Uneven Geographical Development*. London: Verso.
Harvey, Kenneth J. 2003. *The Town That Forgot How to Breathe*. Vancouver: Raincoast.
Heffernan, Mike. 2009. *Rig: An Oral History of the Ocean Ranger Disaster*. St. John's: Creative.
Hiller, James K. 1993. "Newfoundland Confronts Canada, 1867–1949." In Forbes and Muise, *The Atlantic Provinces in Confederation*, 349–81.
Hiscock, Andrew. 2000. "'This Inherited Life': Alistair MacLeod and the Ends of History." *Journal of Commonwealth Literature* 35.2: 51–70.
Holton, Robert J. 2005. *Making Globalization*. Houndmills, UK: Palgrave Macmillan.
Horwood, Harold. 1977. *Bartlett: The Great Canadian Explorer*. Toronto: Doubleday Canada.
———. 1989. *Joey*. Toronto: Stoddart.
House, Douglas. 1987. *But Who Cares Now? The Tragedy of the Ocean Ranger*. St. John's: Ocean Ranger Foundation/Breakwater.
House, J.D. 1985. *The Challenge of Oil: Newfoundland's Quest for Controlled Development*. St. John's: Institute of Social and Economic Research, 1985.
Howley, J.P. [1915] 1974. *The Beothucks or Red Indians*. Facsimile edition. Toronto: Coles.
Huggan, Graham. 2001. *The Post-Colonial Exotic: Marketing the Margins*. London: Routledge.
Hughes, Helen. 1993. *The Historical Romance*. London: Routledge.
Inwood, Kris E. 1993. "Maritime Industrialization from 1870 to 1910: A Review of the Evidence and its Interpretation." In *Farm, Factory and Fortune: New Studies in the Economic History of the Maritime Provinces*, edited by Kris Inwood, 149–70. Fredericton: Acadiensis.
Jackson, F.L. 1986. *Surviving Confederation*. St. John's: Harry Cuff.
Jobb, Dean. 1994. *Calculated Risk: Greed, Politics, and the Westray Tragedy*. Halifax: Nimbus.
Joe, Rita. 1988. *Song of Eskasoni: More Poems of Rita Joe*. Charlottetown, PE: Ragweed.
———. 1989. "The Gentle War." *Canadian Woman Studies* 10.2–3: 27–29.
———. 1991. *Lnu and Indians We're Called*. Charlottetown, PE: Ragweed.
Johnston, Wayne. 1998a. *The Colony of Unrequited Dreams*. Toronto: Knopf Canada.
———. 1998b. "Truth vs. fiction: no, it ain't so, Joey." *The Globe and Mail*, 23 November, D1.
———. 1999. *Baltimore's Mansion*. Toronto: Knopf Canada.

———. 2003. "My Treatment of History in *The Colony of Unrequited Dreams*." *boldtype: an online literary magazine* 6.12. Accessed 21 May 2003, http://www.randomhouse.com/boldtype/0699/johnston/essay.html

———. 2007. "An Afterlife Endlessly Revised." Interview with Herb Wyile. In Wyile, *Speaking in the Past Tense*, 105–31.

Keefer, Janice Kulyk. 1985. *Under Eastern Eyes: A Critical Reading of Maritime Fiction*. Toronto: University of Toronto Press.

———. 2001. "Loved Labour Lost: Alistair MacLeod's Elegiac Ethos." In *Alistair MacLeod: Essays on His Works*, edited by Irene Guilford, 72–83. Toronto: Guernica.

Kelly, Gemey. 1987. *Rockwell Kent: The Newfoundland Work*. Halifax: Dalhousie Art Gallery.

Kelly, Ursula. 1993. *Marketing Place: Cultural Politics, Regionalism and Reading*. Halifax: Fernwood.

Kenny, James. 1999. "Political Culture in Fin-de-Siècle Atlantic Canada." *Acadiensis* 29.1: 122–37.

Kent, Rockwell. 1933. *Rockwellkentiana*. New York: Harcourt, Brace.

———. 1955. *It's Me, O Lord: The Autobiography of Rockwell Kent*. New York: Dodd, Mead.

The King v. George Hamilton. 1949. Supreme Court of New Brunswick, King's Bench Division. Library and Archives Canada. R.G. 13, 1680 C.C. 677, Vol. 1.

The King v. Rufus Hamilton. 1949. Supreme Court of New Brunswick, King's Bench Division. Library and Archives Canada. R.G. 13, 1680 C.C. 676, Vol. 1.

Klein, Naomi. 2000. *No Logo: Taking Aim at the Brand Bullies*. Toronto: Vintage Canada.

Knutson, Susan. 2007. "'I am become Aaron': George Elliott Clarke's *Execution Poems* and William Shakespeare's *Titus Andronicus*." In *Canadian Cultural Exchange: Translation and Transculturation*, edited by Norman Cheadle and Lucien Pelletier, 29–56. Waterloo, ON: Wilfrid Laurier University Press.

Laurette, Patrick Condon. 1984. *John O'Brien 1831–1891*. Halifax: Art Gallery of Nova Scotia.

Lefebvre, Henri. [1974] 1991. *The Production of Space*. Translated by Donald Nicholson-Smith. Oxford: Blackwell.

Lepaludier, Laurent. 2002. "The Everyday in 'The Closing Down of Summer' by Alistair MacLeod." *Journal of the Short Story in English* 38: 39–55.

Lill, Wendy. 1998. *Corker*. Burnaby: Talonbooks.

"The Limits of Tourism." 1987. "Bury My Heart at Peggy's Cove: A Special Summer Issue on Tourism." *New Maritimes* 5.11–12: 3–5.

Lutz, Hartmut. 1996. "'Talking at the Kitchen Table': A Personal Homage to Rita Joe of Reserve, Cape Breton Island, Nova Scotia." In *Down East: Critical Essays on Contemporary Maritime Literature*, edited by Wolfgang Hochbruck and James O. Taylor, 278–88. Trier, Germany: Wissenschäftlicher Verlag Trier.

Lynes, Jeanette. 2001. "Markings." In *Landmarks: An Anthology of New Atlantic Canadian Poetry of the Land*, edited by Hugh MacDonald and Brent MacLaine, 86. Charlottetown, PE: Acorn.

MacCannell, Dean. [1976] 1999. *The Tourist: A New Theory of the Leisure Class*. Berkeley: University of California Press.

MacGillivray, William D., dir. 2005. *Reading Alistair MacLeod*. Picture Plant/National Film Board of Canada. DVD, 88 min.

MacKay, Donald. 1990. *Flight from Famine: The Coming of the Irish to Canada*. Toronto: McClelland.

Mackey, Eva. 2002. *The House of Difference: Cultural Politics and National Identity in Canada*. Toronto: University of Toronto Press.

MacLaine, Brent. 2002. "North Shore Park." In *Coastlines: The Poetry of Atlantic Canada*, edited by Anne Compton, Laurence Hutchman, Ross Leckie, and Robin McGrath, 212–13. Fredericton: Goose Lane.

MacLeod, Alexander. 2006. "History versus Geography in Wayne Johnston's *The Colony of Unrequited Dreams*." *Canadian Literature* 189: 69–83.

———. 2008. "'The Little State of Africadia Is a Community of Believers': Replacing the Regional and Remaking the Real in the Work of George Elliott Clarke." *Studies in Canadian Literature* 33.2: 96–114.

MacLeod, Alistair. 1999. *No Great Mischief*. Toronto: McClelland.

———. 2000. *Island: The Collected Short Stories of Alistair MacLeod*. Toronto: McClelland.

Mahoney, Mike, and Meredith Ralston, dirs. 1999. *Wendy Lill: Playwright in Parliament*. National Film Board of Canada. DVD, 50 min., 14 s.

Mandle, Jay R. 2003. *Globalization and the Poor*. Cambridge: Cambridge University Press.

Marshall, Chief Lindsay. 1997. *Clay Pots and Bones / Pkáwóqq aq Waqntal*. Sydney, NS: Solus.

Marshall, Ingeborg. 1996. *A History and Ethnography of the Beothuk*. Montreal: McGill-Queen's University Press.

Marshall, Susanne. 2008. "'As if there were just the two choices': Region and Cosmopolis in Lisa Moore's Short Fiction." *Studies in Canadian Literature* 33.2: 80–95.

McBride, Stephen. [2001] 2004. *Paradigm Shift: Globalization and the Canadian State.* 2nd ed. Halifax: Fernwood.

McCormick, Chris. 1999a. "Preface to Disaster." In *The Westray Chronicles: A Case Study in Corporate Crime,* 12–39. Halifax: Fernwood.

———, ed. 1999b. *The Westray Chronicles: A Case Study in Corporate Crime.* Halifax: Fernwood.

McKay, Ian. 1994. *The Quest of the Folk: Antimodernism and Cultural Selection in Twentieth-Century Nova Scotia.* Montreal: McGill-Queen's University Press.

———. 2005. "The Quest @ 2006." *Acadiensis* 35.1: 152–57.

McKay, Ian, and Scott Milsom, eds. 1992. *Toward a New Maritimes.* Charlottetown, PE: Ragweed.

McKay, Leo Jr. 2003. *Twenty-Six.* Toronto: McClelland.

———. 2009. "The Global Context of the Novel." *Waterfront Views: Contemporary Writing of Atlantic Canada.* Accessed 20 October 2009, http://waterfrontviews.acadiau.ca/flash\mckay\ mckay_global_lg.htm.

McKegney, Sam. 2007. *Magic Weapons: Aboriginal Writers Remaking Community after Residential School.* Winnipeg: University of Manitoba Press.

Meethan, Kevin. 2001. *Tourism in Global Society: Place, Culture, Consumption.* Houndmills, UK: Palgrave Macmillan.

Mensah, Joseph. 2002. *Black Canadians: History, Experiences, Social Conditions.* Halifax: Fernwood.

Moore, Lisa. 2009. *February.* Toronto: Anansi.

Moretti, Franco. 1987. *The Way of the World: The* Bildungsroman *in European Culture.* London: Verso.

Morgan, Bernice. 1992. *Random Passage.* St. John's: Breakwater.

———. 1994. *Waiting for Time.* St. John's: Breakwater.

———. 1995. "Playing around with Time." Interview with Bruce Porter. *TickleAce* 30: 13–30.

———. 2007. *Cloud of Bone.* Toronto: Knopf Canada.

Morrissey, Donna. 2005. *Sylvanus Now.* Toronto: Penguin Canada.

Moynagh, Maureen. 1998. "Africville, an Imagined Community." *Canadian Literature* 157: 14–34.

Muise, D.A. 1998. "Who Owns History Anyway? Reinventing Atlantic Canada for Pleasure and Profit." *Acadiensis* 27.2: 124–34.

Murphy, Rex. 1998. "Alas, Joey Smallwood was larger than fiction." Review of *The Colony of Unrequited Dreams,* by Wayne Johnston. *The Globe and Mail,* 3 October, D15.

"Negative talk helps no one: Harper plays up stereotype of dependent Atlantic Region." 2002. *Cape Breton Post,* 30 May, A6.

O'Flaherty, Patrick. 1979. *The Rock Observed: Studies in the Literature of Newfoundland*. Toronto: University of Toronto Press.

Overton, James. 1996. *Making a World of Difference: Essays on Tourism, Culture, and Development in Newfoundland*. St. John's: ISER.

Palmer, Bryan D. 1992. *Working-Class Experience: Rethinking the History of Canadian Labour, 1800–1991*. Toronto: McClelland.

Parenteau, Bill, and Richard W. Judd. 2005. "More Buck for the Bang: Sporting and the Ideology of Fish and Game Management in Northern New England and the Maritime Provinces, 1870–1900." In *New England and the Maritime Provinces: Connections and Comparisons*, edited by Stephen J. Hornsby and John G. Reid, 232–51. Montreal: McGill-Queen's University Press.

Paul, Daniel L. 2000. *We Were Not the Savages: A Mi'kmaq Perspective on the Collision between European and Native American Civilizations*. New 21st-century edition. Halifax: Fernwood.

Peck, Jamie, and Adam Tickell. 2002. "Neoliberalizing Space." *Antipode* 34.3: 380–404.

Peyton, Amy Louise. 1987. *River Lords: Father and Son*. St. John's: Jesperson.

Peyton, John Jr. 1819. Letter to Governor Hamilton. 25 May. Public Archives of Newfoundland and Labrador, St. John's, NL.

Polack, Fiona. 2008. "Whose Bones?" Review of *Cloud of Bone*, by Bernice Morgan. *Canadian Literature* 198: 149–51.

Porter, Marilyn. 1987. "Peripheral Women: Towards a Feminist Analysis of the Atlantic Region." *Studies in Political Economy* 23: 41–72.

Power, Nicole Gerarda. 2005. *What Do They Call a Fisherman? Men, Gender, and Restructuring in the Newfoundland Fishery*. St. John's: ISER.

Prowse, D.W. 1895. *A History of Newfoundland from the English, Colonial, and Foreign Records*. London: Macmillan.

Razack, Sherene H. 2004. *Dark Threats & White Knights: The Somalia Affair, Peacekeeping, and the New Imperialism*. Toronto: University of Toronto Press.

Rhindress, Charlie. 2004. "The Maritime Way of Life." In Barton, *Marigraph*, 1–49.

Richards, David Adams. 1981. *Lives of Short Duration*. Ottawa, ON: Oberon.

Riche, Edward. 1997. *Rare Birds*. Toronto: Doubleday.

———. 2004. *The Nine Planets*. Toronto: Penguin Canada.

———. 2008. "An Equal Opportunity Satirist." Interview with Herb Wyile. *Studies in Canadian Literature* 33.2: 210–28.

Riegel, Christian. 2005. Introduction to *Response to Death: The Literary Work of Mourning*, edited by Christian Riegel, XVII–XXIX. Edmonton: *Canadian Review of Comparative Literature*/University of Alberta Press.

Rieti, Barbara. 1991. *Strange Terrain: The Fairy World in Newfoundland*. St. John's: ISER.
Robinson, Mike. 2001. "Tourism Encounters: Inter- and Intra-Cultural Conflicts and the World's Largest Industry." In *Consuming Tradition, Manufacturing Heritage: Global Norms and Urban Forms in the Age of Tourism*, edited by Nezar AlSayyad, 34–67. London: Routledge.
Royal Commission on the Ocean Ranger Marine Disaster. 1984. *Report, Vol. I. The Loss of the Semisubmersible Drill Rig Ocean Ranger and Its Crew*. Ottawa: Government of Canada/ Government of Newfoundland.
Saad-Filho, Alfredo, and Deborah Johnston. 2005. Introduction to *Neoliberalism: A Critical Reader*, edited by Alfredo Saad-Filho and Deborah Johnston, 1–6. London: Pluto.
Said, Edward W. [1993] 1994. *Culture and Imperialism*. New York: Vintage.
Savoie, Donald. 2006. *Visiting Grandchildren: Economic Development in the Maritimes*. Toronto: University of Toronto Press.
Smith, Jennifer. 2002. "Atlantic Canada at the Start of the New Millennium." In *Canadian Political Culture(s) in Transition*, edited by Hamish Telford and Harvey Lazar, 141–62. Montreal: McGill-Queen's University Press /Institute of Intergovernmental Relations.
Soja, Edward. 1989. *Postmodern Geographies: The Reassertion of Space in Critical Social Theory*. London: Verso.
Stone, Marjorie. 1997. "'The Poet as Whole-Body Camera': Maxine Tynes and the Pluralities of Otherness." *Dalhousie Review* 77.2: 227–57.
Sugars, Cynthia. 2005. "Original Sin, or, The Last of the First Ancestors: Michael Crummey's *River Thieves*." *English Studies in Canada* 31.4: 147–75.
———. 2008. "Repetition with a Difference: The Paradox of Origins in Alistair MacLeod's *No Great Mischief*." *Studies in Canadian Literature* 33.2: 133–50.
———. 2010. "Genetic Phantoms: Geography, History, and Ancestral Inheritance in Kenneth Harvey's *The Town That Forgot How to Breathe* and Michael Crummey's *Galore*." *Newfoundland and Labrador Studies* 25.1: 7–36.
Thurston, Harry. 2005. *A Ship Portrait: A Novella in Verse*. Kentville, NS: Gaspereau.
———. 2008. "The Genesis of *A Ship Portrait*." *Waterfront Views: Contemporary Writing of Atlantic Canada*. Accessed 12 November, 2008, http://waterfrontviews.acadiau.ca/flash/thurston/thurston_genesis_lg.htm.

Tomblin, Stephen. 2004. "Introduction and Overview: Comparative New England-Atlantic Policy Lessons." In Tomblin and Colgan, *Regionalism in a Global Society*, 7–35.

Tomblin, Stephen, and Charles S. Colgan, eds. 2004. *Regionalism in a Global Society: Persistence and Change in Atlantic Canada and New England*. Peterborough, ON: Broadview.

Traxel, David. 1980. *An American Saga: The Life and Times of Rockwell Kent*. New York: Harper & Row.

Tremblay, Tony. 2008. "'Lest on too close sight I miss the darling illusion': The Politics of the Centre in 'Reading Maritime.'" *Studies in Canadian Literature* 33.2: 23–39.

———. 2010. *David Adams Richards of the Miramichi*. Toronto: University of Toronto Press.

Tynes, Maxine. 1990. *Woman Talking Woman*. Lawrencetown Beach, NS: Pottersfield.

Uebel, Anke. 2010. "Imaginary Restraints: Michael Crummey's *River Thieves* and the Beothuk of Newfoundland." In *Local Natures, Global Responsibilities: Ecocritical Perspectives on the New English Literatures*, edited by Laurenz Volkmann, Nancy Grimm, Ines Detmers, and Katrin Thomson, 137–50. Amsterdam: Rodopi.

Urry, John. *The Tourist Gaze*. [1990] 2002. 2nd ed. London: Sage.

Walker, James St. G. 1986. "Black History in the Maritimes: Major Themes and Teaching Strategies." In *Teaching Maritime Studies*, edited by Phillip Buckner, 96–107. Fredericton: Acadiensis.

Wall, Bob. 1992. "Analyzing the Marshall Commission: Why It Was Established and How It Functioned." In *Elusive Justice: Beyond the Marshall Inquiry*, edited by Joy Mannette, 13–33. Halifax: Fernwood.

Watson, William. 1998. *Globalization and the Meaning of Canadian Life*. Toronto: University of Toronto Press.

Webb, Jeff A. 1998. "Confederation, Conspiracy and Choice: A Discussion." *Newfoundland Studies* 14.2: 169–87.

Westray Mine Inquiry. 1997. *The Westray Story: A Predictable Path to Disaster*. 4 vols. Halifax: Province of Nova Scotia.

Whalen, Tracy. 2001. "Stylizing the Mundane: Bernice Morgan's *Random Passage*." *Ethnologies* 23.1: 23–43.

———. 2004. "'Camping' with Annie Proulx: *The Shipping News* and Tourist Desire." *Essays on Canadian Writing* 82: 51–70.

———. 2008. "An Aesthetics of Intensity: Lisa Moore's Sublime Worlds." *Newfoundland and Labrador Studies* 23.1: 1–20.

White, Hayden. 1978. *Tropics of Discourse: Essays in Cultural Criticism*. Baltimore: Johns Hopkins University Press.

Williams, Raymond. 1973. *The Country and the City*. Oxford: Oxford University Press.

Winter, Michael. 2003. "The Force of Mystery." Interview with Claire Wilkshire. In *Writers Talking*, edited by John Metcalf and Claire Wilkshire, 10–26. Erin, ON: Porcupine's Quill.

———. 2004. *The Big Why*. Toronto: Anansi.

———. 2010. "This All Was Said." Interview with Herb Wyile. *The Antigonish Review* 161: 117–34.

Woodcock, George. 1981. *The Meeting of Time and Space: Regionalism in Canadian Literature*. Edmonton: NeWest.

Workman, Thom. 2003. *Social Torment: Globalization in Atlantic Canada*. Halifax: Fernwood.

Wright, Miriam. 2001. *A Fishery for Modern Times: The State and the Industrialization of the Newfoundland Fishery, 1934–1968*. Toronto: Oxford University Press.

———. 2003. "Newfoundland and Labrador History in Canada, 1949–1972." In the Government of Newfoundland, vol. 1 of *Collected Research Papers*, 88–116.

Wyile, Herb. 2007. *Speaking in the Past Tense: Canadian Novelists on Writing Historical Fiction*. Waterloo, ON: Wilfrid Laurier University Press.

Photo Credits

39 Reproduced with the permission of the Minister of Public Works and Government Services Canada (2010). From Library and Archives Canada, B. Brooks, National Film Board of Canada, Photothèque collection / PA-154122.
42 Photo courtesy of the Canadian Press, 3211935 / *The Telegram* / Keith Gosse.
68 From *The Westray Story: A Predictable Path to Disaster*, Vol. 3. Reference photograph 11. Exhibit 59, photo 1 (RCMP photo 15).
76 From the Rooms Provincial Archives Division, A 41-36 / Mobil Oil Canada and G & C Associates.
109 Photo courtesy of the Canadian Press, 880126 / Albert Lee.
116 From Nova Scotia Archives and Records Management, Bob Brooks Fonds, Accession no. 1989-468, box 16, neg. sheet 4, image 29.
119 From Nova Scotia Archives and Records Management, Bob Brooks Fonds, Accession no. 1989-468, box 16, neg. sheet 6, image 23.
128 Reprinted with permission from Goose Lane Editions.
145 Scene from the 1997 Live Bait premiere of *The Maritime Way of Life*. Courtesy of Live Bait Theatre.
147 Scene from the 1999 Live Bait Theatre/Mulgrave Road Theatre co-production. Courtesy of Live Bait Theatre.
180 Courtesy of The Rooms (Provincial Archives of Newfoundland and Labrador) Photograph Collection, Division B16-17.
185 Courtesy of the Centre for Newfoundland Studies Archives (J.R. Smallwood Collection 075, Photo 5.05.321), Memorial University of Newfoundland Library, St. John's, Newfoundland.
189 Courtesy of The Rooms (Provincial Archives of Newfoundland and Labrador), J. Vey [187–?], John Peyton, and Thomas Peyton Fonds, A 17-105.
191 Courtesy of The Rooms, Provincial Archives of Newfoundland and Labrador.
205 Courtesy of the Plattsburgh State Art Museum–Plattsburgh College Foundation. Rockwell Kent Gallery and Collection, bequest of Sally Kent Gorton.

Photo Credits

208 Courtesy of the Plattsburgh State Art Museum–Plattsburgh College Foundation. Rockwell Kent Gallery and Collection, Bequest of Sally Kent Gorton.

211 The Rooms Provincial Archives Division, A 49-57; Jack Angel [ca. 1930].

221 From the collection of the Art Gallery of Nova Scotia, gift of the Estate of Arthur D. Stairs. 1993.180.

225 Reproduced with permission from the Minister of Public Works and the Government of Canada. From Library and Archives Canada/ Justice RG 13, Vol. 1680 File cc 677, Pt. 1/ C-131147.

225 Reproduced with permission from the Minister of Public Works and the Government of Canada. From Library and Archives Canada/ Justice RG 13, Vol. 1680 File cc 676, Pt. 1C-147473.

Index

Acadians, 7, 106, 114, 230, 232, 249n2
Acheson, T.W., 11, 243
Acorn, Milton, 5, 99
Africadia, 114, 121, 122–23, 126, 239, 245
Africville, 114–23; in *Consecrated Ground*, 114–20; in Tynes's poetry, 120–22
Alexander, David, 10
Andrews, Jennifer, 229, 232
anti-modernism, 33, 122, 145, 148–49, 161, 199; in MacLeod's fiction, 62, 64, 155; in *Sylvanus Now*, 34, 38, 39; *The Town That Forgot How to Breathe* and, 51–53, 158
Armstrong, Christopher, 138
Armstrong, Jeannette, 107, 110
Armstrong, Pat, 92
Atlantic Canada, 7, 21, 53–54; as backward, 6, 13, 21, 23, 26, 101, 126, 144–45, 218, 237, 238, 244, 254n1; culture(s) of, 22, 101–3, 126–27, 215–16, 240; history of, 170, 240, 245–46; as leisure space, 1, 2, 6, 22, 148–49; outsiders' views of, 1, 2, 3, 28, 103, 138, 139–40; sense of crisis in, 2, 4, 26, 171, 233, 241; sense of place in, 7, 20–21, 243–47; subordinate status of, 2, 3, 7, 9, 12–13, 18, 22, 23, 26, 27, 146–47, 169, 237, 238, 239–40, 242, 244. *See also* Atlantic-Canadian literature; Maritime provinces; New Brunswick; Newfoundland and Labrador; Nova Scotia, Prince Edward Island
Atlantic-Canadian literature, 1, 2, 4–5, 6–7, 23–28, 237–38, 240, 244, 245, 246, 247; as speculative fiction, 242–43; culture and, 102–3, 126–27, 137–38; globalization and, 1, 6, 25, 28, 99–100, 102–3, 233, 237–38, 246; sense of place in, 245–47; tourism and, 2, 4, 22, 137–38, 167, 170–71; work and, 30–31, 99–100. *See also* historical fiction; Maritime provinces, literature; Newfoundland and Labrador, literature
Atlantic Groundfish Strategy, 50
Atwood, Margaret, 198

Baker, Melvin, 12
Baltimore's Mansion (Johnston), 174–77, 185, 215; Newfoundland's "ghost history" and, 174, 176, 177; pre-Confederation Newfoundland and, 174–77; referendum in, 174–77
Balzer, David, 223

Index

Banks, Catherine, 54, 106, 249n1
Bannister, Jerry, 180, 185–86
Bantjes, Rod, 137–38
Barry, Frank, **162–65**, 166, 239, 245; *Wreckhouse*, 162–65, 166, 167, 240
Bartlett, Captain Robert A., 210, 211, 212, 213; in *The Big Why*, 210–15
Baudrillard, Jean, 158
Bauman, Zygmunt, 20, 63, 71, 223, 243, 244
Benjamin, Walter, 151, 152
Beothuk, 108, 187–96, 202, 234; in Newfoundland literature, 187–88; in *River Thieves*, 188–94, 195–96, 215
Berman, Marshall, 16–17, 245
The Big Why (Winter), 203–15, 216, 252n6; anachronism in, 213–15; come-from-away in, 203–208, 213, 215–16; rural Newfoundland in, 204–8, 209–10; self-actualization in, 204–10, 212, 214–15
Bitterman, Rusty, 33
Black Renaissance, 114, 122, 124, 251n5
Black writers, 105–6, 114–27, 135, 137, 167, 168
Blades, Kent, 36, 37, 40, 42, 46, 48
Borden, Walter, 114
Bourdieu, Pierre, 16
Boyd, George, 105, 114, **115–20**; *Consecrated Ground*, 115–20, 142
Braedley, Susan, and Meg Luxton, 62, 90–91, 96
The Bricklin, 232
Brodie, Janine, 92
Buchan, David, 190, 191
Buckler, Ernest, 27, 99, 106
Buckner, Phillip, 10, 219
Budgel, Richard, 187, 189
Burgoyne, Norman, 224–25, 226
Butler, Judith, 131

Cadigan, Sean, 13, 75, 79, 85
Campbell, Maria, 110
capitalism, 64–65, 69, 71, 75, 97, 238; as creative destruction, 16–17, 24,
96, 245; globalization and, 16, 21, 61–63, 93–97, 99–100; mobility and, 20–21, 42, 61–63, 95, 97, 99–100, 223, 242, 243–47; space and, 8–9, 20–21, 93, 246; tourism and, 148, 161–62
Carman, Bliss, 106
Cashin, Peter, 175, 176
Central Canada, 9, 11, 13, 14, 23; in *The Maritime Way of Life*, 142–46; in *Strange Heaven*, 139–42, 150
Chafe, Paul, 158–59, 173, 186, 193, 194
Clairmont, Donald H., and Dennis Magill, 115–16, 117, 118
Clarke, George Elliott, 5, 25, 103, 105, 114, 115, 120, **122–26**, 217, **224–32**, 234, 239, 245, 252n2, 253n7, 253n8; *Execution Poems*, 224–29, 231–32, 240, 253n9; *George & Rue*, 224–32, 240, 253n9; *Saltwater Spirituals and Deeper Blues*, 123–24; *Whylah Falls*, 124–26, class, 5, 18, 33, 43–44, 63–65, 139–40, 181, 233
Clewell, Tammy, 78–79
"The Closing Down of Summer" (MacLeod), 58–61; Gaelic culture in, 58–59, 60; globalization in 59–60, 66; mining in, 58–61; tribal identity in, 58–59, 66
Clow, Michael, 11, 17, 242
Coady, Lynn, 5, 25, 103, 106, 127, **130–34, 138–42, 150–53**, 239, 241, 245; *Strange Heaven*, 130–34, 138–42, 147, 150–53, 167, 240
Coaker, William, 206
Colas, Alejandro, 4
colonialism, 163, 165, 200–1, 224, 229, 232, 234; *The Colony of Unrequited Dreams* and, 178–81; Native writers and, 106, 107–8, 110–11, 113; *River Thieves* and, 187, 193–94, 195. *See also* post-colonialism
The Colony of Unrequited Dreams (Johnston), 177–86, 189; allegorical romance in, 181, 182–83, 185; as historiographic metafiction,

272

178, 179–81, 186; colonialism and, 178–81; geography in, 186; Newfoundland's "ghost history" and, 177, 183–86; referendum in, 179, 183–86
Comish, Shaun, 67, 250n7
Compton, Anne, 5, 106, 134
Confederation, 9, 10; attitudes toward, 3, 7, 10, 11–12, 13, 173, 174–77, 178, 183–86, 218, 222, 237; history of in the Maritime provinces, 10–11, 13, 242; history of in Newfoundland, 10, 11–12
Connell, Raewyn, 15, 71, 91–92, 95
Conrad, Margaret, 7, 10, 20, 21, 30, 87, 105
Consecrated Ground (Boyd), 115–20, 142; demolition of Africville in, 115–20; development in, 116, 118–19; Folk paradigm and, 116; racism in, 117–19
Cooper, Brenda, 52
Corker (Lill), 17, 89–93, 238, 240; neoliberalism in, 89–93; privatization in, 91–92; social services in, 90–92
cosmopolitanism, 6, 25–26, 83, 99, 102–3, 240. *See also* globalization
Courchene, Thomas, 18
Creelman, David, 23, 26, 99, 126, 171, 239
Cromwell, Graham, 125–26
Crosbie, John, 41–42
Crummey, Michael, 5, 173, **186–96**, 234, 239; *Hard Light*, 186–87, 196; *River Thieves*, 187–96, 215, 231, 232, 240
Cuder-Domínguez, Pilar, 231
culture, 101–62, 215–16, 240; in Atlantic-Canadian literature, 101–3, 245. *See also* Folk paradigm
Currie, Andrea, 127, 129
Currie, Sheldon, 55, 144

Dalton, Mary, 106, 150, 187–88, 239
Davies, Gwendolyn, 129–30, 132, 134

Davies, Lynn, 106
Day, Frank Parker, 34, 99
de Groot, Jerome, 220, 233
Debord, Guy, 158
DeLottinville, Paul, 20
Demasduit (Mary March), 108, 187, 189, 190–93, 196; in *River Thieves*, 190–93
development, 146–47, 182; in *Consecrated Ground*, 115, 119; in *The Nine Planets*, 93, 95–97, 161, 245
Dobrowolsky, Alexandra, 4, 14–15, 89
Dodd, Susan, 74
Dohaney, M.T., 106, 127
Dragland, Stan, 178, 184–85
Duley, Margaret, 106
Duncan, Norman, 31, 34
Durix, Jean-Pierre, 53

Execution Poems (Clarke), 224–29, 231–32, 240, 253n3, 253n9

February (Moore), 75–85, 238, 240; mourning in, 75–83, 84–85; neoliberalism and, 77–78, 79, 81, 82–85; *Ocean Ranger* disaster and, 75–85
Finbow, Robert, 7, 14
fisheries, 33–34, 55, 246; crisis in, 4, 11, 34, 35, 36, 37, 162, 174; in *Random Passage*, 198–99, 200; in *Sylvanus Now*, 34–39; in *The Town That Forgot How to Breathe*, 48–53; in *Waiting for Time*, 40–47; in *Wreckhouse*, 164–65. *See also* moratorium
Fitch, Sheree, **87–89**, 106, **127–29**, 134; "Barbara," 127–29; "Civil Servant," 87–89; "The Fashion Show," 129; "Filling Out the Form," 127, 128; "If I do say so myself," 129; "Jane's Observation Notes," 127; "Marie's Lullaby," 129; "What Rhoda Remembers About the First Five Minutes," 127

Index

Folk paradigm, 2, 4, 22–28, 29–30, 33–34, 97, 99–100; 101–3, 105, 161, 200, 237, 238–40, 241, 244, 246; Black people and, 106, 114, 115, 122; *Consecrated Ground* and, 116; gender and, 127; MacLeod's fiction and, 56, 66; Native peoples and, 106, 107; tourism and, 137, 148–49, 167; *Whylah Falls* and, 124, 126; in *The Maritime Way of Life*, 142–44, 146–47; in *Strange Heaven*, 138, 140, 150–53; in *Sylvanus Now*, 34–35; in *Wreckhouse*, 162–65. See also regional stereotypes
Forbes, E.R., 11, 14
Fordism, 14, 59, 62, 70
Foucault, Michel, 133
Fraiman, Susan, 134
Fraser, Dawn, 55
Freud, Sigmund, 75–76, 78
Friedman, Thomas, 15, 16, 17, 20
Fuller, Danielle, 24, 126, 130, 134; on Maxine Tynes, 122; on Rita Joe, 108, 110; on *Random Passage*, 200, 203; on Sheree Fitch, 129

gender issues, 92–93, 127–34, 168, 197–200, 233. See also women, writing by *George & Rue* (Clarke), 224–32, 240, 253n9; campaign against, 224–25; depiction of murder in, 228–29; portrayal of justice system in, 229–31; social marginality in, 226–28
Glasbeek, Harry, and Eric Tucker, 69, 72–73
globalization, 4, 13–21, 71–72, 241, 242, 243, 244–45; Atlantic Canada and, 1, 19, 22–23; Atlantic-Canadian literature and, 1, 6, 25, 28, 99–100, 102–3, 233, 237–38, 246; the nation-state and, 17–18; tourism and, 148, 149, 167; in MacLeod's fiction, 56, 59–60, 61–63, 66; in *The Nine Planets*, 93–97; in *A Ship Portrait*, 222–23; in *Sylvanus Now*, 36–37; in *Waiting for Time*, 42–43. See also cosmopolitanism
Grant, Jessica, 134
Gwyn, Richard, 182

Haliburton, Thomas Chandler, 27, 31, 106
Hamilton, George, 224–26, 227, 229, 252n2, 253n7, 253n8, 253n9; in *Execution Poems*, 226, 227, 228, 229, 232; in *George & Rue*, 226–31
Hamilton, Rufus, 224–26, 227, 229, 232, 252n2, 253n4, 253n8, 253n9; in *Execution Poems*, 226, 227, 229; in *George & Rue*, 226, 228–31
Harper, Stephen, 139, 142, 224
Harris, Michael, 37, 40, 41–42, 251n1
Hart, Julia Catherine Beckwith, 217
Harvey, David, 3–4, 9, 14, 18, 82
Harvey, Kenneth J., 40, **48–53, 157–58**, 239; *The Town That Forgot How to Breathe*, 48–53, 54, 157–58, 241, 244
Hatfield, Richard, 232
Heffernan, Mike, 75, 81, 250n8
Hensley, Sophia Almon, 106
Highway, Tomson, 105
Hiller, James, 7, 10, 20, 21, 30, 87, 105, 177
Hiscock, Andrew, 57
historical fiction, 27–28, 169–72, 233, 245; commenting on the present, 169, 172, 214–15, 222, 233, 237; commodification and, 171–72, 194–96; in the Maritime provinces, 217–32, 233–35; in Newfoundland, 173–216, 233–35. See also historical romance
historical novel. See historical fiction
historical romance, 44, 197, 200, 201–3. See also historical fiction
Holton, Robert, 15–16
Horwood, Harold, 182, 210
House, Douglas, 80–81, 250n8. See also House, J.D.
House, J.D., 81–82. See also House, Douglas

274

Howley, J.P., 192, 252n3
Huggan, Graham, 24, 149
Hughes, Helen, 200, 201, 202
Intercolonial Railway, 11
Inwood, Kris E, 13

Jackson, F.L., 10, 13
Jobb, Dean, 67
Joe, Rita, 105, 106, **107–10**, 112; "The Art of Communication," 108; "Demasduit," 108; "I Lost My Talk," 108; "I'm a Beothuk," 108; "James Bay," 108–9; "Lament of Donald Marshall Jr.," 109; "Oka," 109–10; "Shanawdithit," 108; "Warriors," 110; "You, I, Love, Beauty, Earth," 108
Johnston, Wayne, 5, 9, 11, 25, **173–86**, 237; *Baltimore's Mansion*, 174–77, 185, 215; *The Colony of Unrequited Dreams*, 177–86, 189

Keefer, Janice Kulyk, 23, 63
Kelly, Gemey, 208, 209
Kelly, Ursula, 3, 37–38, 234
Kenny, James, 19
Kent, Rockwell, 203–4, 205, 208, 209, 211, 213, 252n5, 252n6; in *The Big Why*, 203–15
King, Thomas, 105, 111
Klein, Naomi, 95
Knutson, Susan, 229

labour, 16, 17, 20, 55–56, 57, 62, 68–71, 75, 85, 97, 238, 243, 245. *See also* work
Laurette, Patrick Condon, 221
Lefebvre, Henri, 8, 149
Lepaludier, Laurent, 60
Lill, Wendy, **89–93**, 106, 127, 134, 237; *Corker*, 17, 89–93, 238, 240
Little, Linda, 106
Lutz, Hartmut, 107, 109
Lynes, Jeanette, 1, **153–54**, 239

MacCannell, Dean, 150, 156–57, 165, 171
Mackey, Eva, 126–27

MacIvor, Daniel, 5
MacLaine, Brent, **156–57**
MacLennan, Hugh, 5, 99
MacLeod, Alexander, 114, 186, 251n5
MacLeod, Alistair, 5, 25, 54, **56–66**, 130, **154–56**, 237, 239, 245, 247; "Clearances," 147–48, 154–56, 240; "The Closing Down of Summer," 58–61; *No Great Mischief*, 56, 57, 61–66, 85
magic realism, 48, 49, 50–51, 52, 53
Major, Kevin, 173
Mandle, Jay, 16, 20
Maracle, Lee, 110
Maritime provinces, culture(s) of, 22, 26, 102; historical fiction of, 217–32; history of, 9, 10–11, 12, 232, 242; literature of, 23, 102, 129–30, 171. *See also* Atlantic Canada, New Brunswick; Nova Scotia, Prince Edward Island
The Maritime Way of Life (Rhindress), 142–47, 240; alternative economy in, 144, 147; Central Canada in, 142–46; family in, 143–46; Folk paradigm in, 142–44, 146–47; regional stereotypes in, 142–47
Marshall, Chief Lindsay, **110–13**; "Brown Shoelaces," 112–13; "Clay Pots and Bones," 111; "Forth and Back," 112; "Matuesuey Kmtin (Porcupine Mountain)," 111–12; "No Match for Steel," 111; "Now It's Your Turn," 111; "Save the Last Bullet," 111; "They Took Your Word," 112
Marshall, Donald, 109, 112, 251n1
Marshall, Ingeborg, 192–93
Marshall, Susanne, 102–3
Matchee, Clayton, 112–13, 251n4
McBride, Stephen, 17, 18, 244
McCormick, Chris, 67, 68
McKay, Ian, 29, 33–34, 55, 57, 99, 116, 127, 130; on Folk Innocence, 58, 138, 239; on the Folk paradigm and culture, 25, 27, 101, 102, 105, 106,

151, 153, 238–39; on tourism, 22, 148, 149, 152, 157, 158. *See also* Folk paradigm
McKay, Leo, Jr., **66–75**, 103, 237, 239, 241; *Twenty-Six*, 66–75, 85, 103, 238, 240
McKegney, Sam, 108, 110
McKenna, Frank, 20
Meethan, Kevin, 138, 148, 154, 157, 160–61
Mensah, Joseph, 113–14
Mi'kmaq, 105, 107–13, 187, 189, 230
mining, 4, 55, 56–75, 246; in "The Closing Down of Summer," 58–61; in *The Maritime Way of Life*, 143; in *No Great Mischief*, 61–62, 65; in *Twenty-Six*, 66–69, 72–75
Mobil Oil Canada, 80, 82
Montgomery, L.M., 99, 106; *Anne of Green Gables*, 1, 31, 153
Moore, Lisa, 5, 56, **75–85**, 93, 99, 102–3, 106, 134, 237; *February*, 75–85, 238, 240
moratorium, 34, 40–43, 46, 48–49, 53–54, 173, 214. *See also* fisheries
Moretti, Franco, 134
Morgan, Bernice, **40–47**, 106, 134, 188–89, **196–203**, 234, 237, 239, 245; *Cloud of Bone*, 188–89; *Random Passage*, 40–41, 47, 173, 196–203, 206, 215; *Waiting for Time*, 40–47, 48, 49, 53, 240, 244
Morrissey, Donna, **34–39**, 106, 239, 245; *Sylvanus Now*, 34–39, 40, 48, 53
mourning, 73–74, 75–79, 83
Moynagh, Maureen, 106, 115, 116–17, 121, 122
Muise, D.A., 170–71, 194
multiculturalism, 7, 106–7, 113–14, 126–27, 135, 167–68; Atlantic-Canadian literature and, 105–27, 135, 167–68
Murphy, Rex, 177–78

National Policy, 10–11, 18
Native writing, 105, 106–13, 135, 137, 168

neo-liberalism, 13–21, 62; Atlantic Canada and, 18–21, 26, 46, 98, 168, 239–40, 241–42, 244–45; globalization and, 4, 9, 14–17, 26, 27, 28; history of, 4, 7, 14–15; ideology of, 3–4, 14–15, 18–20, 21–22, 233, 243–45, 246, 247; in Atlantic-Canadian literature: 28, 99, 169, 237; in *Corker*, 89–93; in *February*, 77–78, 79, 81, 82–84; in *The Nine Planets*, 93–97; in *Twenty-Six*, 71–72
New Brunswick, 20, 137–38, 232. *See also* Atlantic Canada, Maritime provinces Newfoundland and Labrador, 137, 148, 149; culture of, 22, 30, 51–52, 53, 159, 215–16; historical fiction of, 173–216; history of, 9, 10, 11–12, 179–80, 242; literature of, 24, 27, 173–216, 241; neo-nationalism in, 12, 13, 185–86; referendum in, 11–12. *See also* Atlantic Canada
The Nine Planets (Riche), 17, 93–97, 161–62, 238; development in, 93, 95–97, 245; globalization in, 17, 93–97; neoliberalism in, 93–97; privatization in, 93–95
No Great Mischief (MacLeod), 56, 57, 61–66, 85; globalization and, 61–63, 66; Gaelic culture in, 56–57, 66; mining in, 57, 61–63; tribal identity in, 57, 63–64, 65–66
Nonosabusut, 189, 191, 192–93, 252n3
Nova Scotia, 27, 57, 66, 102, 114, 125, 137–38, 148, 152, 243. *See also* Atlantic Canada, Maritime provinces
Nowlan, Alden, 5, 99

O'Brien, John, 218–23; in *A Ship Portrait*, 218–23
Ocean Ranger disaster, 75, 79–83, 84–85, 250n8; in *February*, 75–85; Royal Commission on, 79–80, 81
ODECO Canada, 80, 82

oil and gas industry, 2, 4, 55–56; in *February*, 75–85; in *The Nine Planets*, 93; in *A Ship Portrait*, 222
Oka crisis, 109–10, 251n2
out-migration, 2, 11, 75, 240, 242, 247; in MacLeod's fiction, 55, 56, 63–64, 154, 155; in *Waiting for Time*, 46–47
Overton, James, 162, 204–5; on the Folk paradigm, 29, 30, 55; on tourism, 22, 148, 149–50, 154, 156, 157

Palmer, Bryan D., 14
Parenteau, Bill, and Richard W. Judd, 33, 148, 155
Paul, Daniel L., 107, 111
Peary, Richard, 211, 212
Peck, Jamie, and Adam Tickell, 4, 14, 19–20
Peltier, Leonard, 112, 251n3
petty producer, 27, 29–30, 33, 54, 55, 97, 161, 200, 240, 246; in *Sylvanus Now*, 34–35, 38–39
Peyton, Amy Louise, 192
Peyton, John Jr., 188, 189, 190, 192–93; in *River Thieves*, 190–92, 193–94, 195
Peyton, John Sr., 188, 190, 192; in *River Thieves*, 190–92, 193–94
Phillips, Gerald, 67, 72
Pittman, Al, 99
Polack, Fiona, 189
Porter, Marilyn, 196
post-colonialism, 52, 53, 66, 178–79, 181, 186, 193, 196, 224, 238. *See also* colonialism
post-Fordism, 59–60, 61–62
Power, Nicole Gerarda, 46, 50
Pratt, E.J., 106
Prince Edward Island, 1, 137, 156–57, 232. *See also* Atlantic Canada; Maritime provinces
privatization, 16, 244; in *Corker*, 90–93; in *The Nine Planets*, 93–95
Proulx, Annie, 24
Prowse, D.W., 180, 252n1; in *The Colony of Unrequited Dreams*, 179; in *The Big Why*, 205–6, 207

racism, 109, 113, 114, 122, 123–24, 168; in *Consecrated Ground*, 116–19; in *George & Rue*, 227, 229–31; in *Whylah Falls*, 125–26
Raddall, Thomas Head, 34, 99, 217
Random Passage (Morgan), 40–41, 47, 173, 196–203, 206, 215; colonialism in, 200–1; outport life in, 196–203; romantic intrigue in, 201–3; salt-fish economy in, 198–99, 201; women's lives in, 196–200
Rare Birds (Riche), 158–62, 240; culture and commodification in, 159–61; tourism in, 158–61
Razack, Sherene, 113, 251n4
redistribution policies, 3, 4, 12–13, 14, 18–19
region, 7–9. *See also* regionalism
regional stereotypes, 3, 5, 22, 24–25, 26, 27, 28, 103, 137, 138, 169–70, 171–72, 238; in *The Maritime Way of Life*, 142–47. *See also* Folk paradigm
regionalism, 3, 7–9, 12–13, 130, 134, 138–39, 141. *See also* region
resettlement, 37–39, 46–47, 96, 214
resource sectors, 2, 4, 22, 23, 26, 30, 87, 97, 170, 171, 246; in Atlantic-Canadian literature, 33–85, 101. *See also* fisheries; mining; oil and gas
restructuring, 9, 13–21, 42, 92, 98, 169, 170, 240; in *February*, 83; in *Waiting for Time*, 44–45, 46–47
Rhindress, Charlie, **142–47**, 239; *The Maritime Way of Life*, 142–47, 240
Richard, Justice K. Peter, 67
Richards, David Adams, 5–6, 217, 251n2, 254n1
Riche, Edward, 17, **93–97**, 99, 103, **158–62**, 167, 237, 239, 241; *The Nine Planets*, 17, 93–97, 161–62, 238, 245; *Rare Birds*, 158–62, 240
Riegel, Christian, 83
Rieti, Barbara, 51
River Thieves (Crummey), 187–96, 215, 231, 232, 240; capture of Demasduit in, 190–93, 196; historiographical

Index

self-consciousness of, 195–96; Oedipal tensions in, 190–92, 193–94; portrait of Beothuk in, 188–89, 195–96, 215; revisionist history in, 192–93, 196; settler identity in, 193–94, 195–96
Roberts, Charles G.D., 106, 156, 217
Roberts, Theodore Goodridge, 217
Robinson, Eden, 105
Robinson, Mike, 154, 156, 157, 159–60

Saad-Filho, Alfredo, and Deborah Johnston, 16
Said, Edward, 239
Saltwater Spirituals and Deeper Blues (Clarke), 123–24
Saunders, Charles, 105, 115
Saunders, Margaret Marshall, 106
Savoie, Donald, 9, 10–11, 12–13, 23, 249n1
service sector, 22, 30, 87–97, 100, 101; in "Civil Servant," 87–89; in *Corker*, 89–93; in *The Nine Planets*, 93–96
Shanawdithit, 108, 188–89, 192–93
A Ship Portrait (Thurston), 11, 21, 218–24, 232, 240; age of sail in, 218–24; Confederation and, 222; globalization in, 219, 222–23
Simpson, Anne, 5, 106, 134
slavery, 224, 225–27, 232, 234
Smallwood, Joseph, 37–38; in *Baltimore's Mansion*, 175–76; in *The Colony of Unrequited Dreams*, 177–79, 181–86; in *The Big Why*, 208, 214
Smith, Jennifer, 20
Soja, Edward, 8, 9, 12, 93, 246
Steffler, John, 173, 187, 189
Stone, Marjorie, 120
Strange Heaven (Coady), 130–34, 138–42, 147, 150–53, 167, 240; Folk paradigm and, 138, 140, 150–53; as *Bildungsroman*, 130, 132, 134; gender expectations in, 130–31, 132–34, 141–42; home place in, 131–32, 134; outsiders' views in, 138–42, 150; regionalism in, 138–39, 141; tourism and, 150–52
Sugars, Cynthia, 49, 53, 64, 189, 193, 195
Sweatman, Margaret, 187, 198
Sylvanus Now (Morrissey), 34–39, 40, 48, 53; overfishing in, 35–37; petty producer in, 34–35, 38–39; resettlement in, 37–39

Talbot, Carol, 113
Thurston, Harry, 9, 217, **218–24**, 234, 237; *A Ship Portrait*, 11, 21, 218–24, 232, 240
Tomblin, Stephen, 19
tourism, 23, 147–66; in Atlantic Canada, 1, 2, 4, 137–38, 167, 170–71; in Atlantic-Canadian literature, 27, 28, 87, 103, 137–38, 147–66, 167, 240, 245; in Lynes, "Markings," 1, 152–53; in MacLaine, "North Shore Park," 156–57; in MacLeod, "Clearances," 147–48, 154–56; in *Rare Birds*, 158–62; in *Strange Heaven*, 150–52; in *The Town That Forgot How to Breathe*, 157–58; in *Wreckhouse*, 162–65; theories of, 138, 148–50
The Town That Forgot How to Breathe (Harvey), 48–53, 54, 157–58, 241, 244; anti-modernism of, 51–53; as magic realism, 48, 49, 50–51, 52, 53; moratorium in, 48–51; oral culture in, 50–53; tourism and, 157–58
Traxel, David, 204, 208
Tremblay, Tony, 5, 6, 23, 102
Twenty-Six (McKay), 66–75, 85, 103, 238, 240; mining in, 72–73; mourning in, 73–75; neoliberalism and, 71–72, Westray disaster and, 66–69, 72–75
Tynes, Maxine, 105, 106, 114, 115, **120–22**; "Africville," 120–21, 121–22;

"Africville Is My Name," 120, 121, 122; "Africville Spirit," 120, 122
Uebel, Anke, 194, 196
underdevelopment, 23, 167–68. *See also* uneven development
uneven development, 2–3, 8–9, 14, 22, 138, 148. *See also* underdevelopment
unemployment, 71, 75, 88–89, 240
Uniacke, John, 220, 252n1
Urquhart, Jane, 187, 198, 238
Urry, John, 139, 149, 150, 153, 157, 160

Waiting for Time (Morgan), 40–47, 48, 49, 53, 240, 244; globalization in, 42–43; moratorium in, 40; overfishing in, 41–43; restructuring in, 44–45, 46–47
Walker, James St. G., 114, 123
Wall, Bob, 109
Wallace, Joe, 55
Ward, Frederick, 115
Watson, William, 17, 19
Webb, Jeff, 12, 174
welfare state, 4, 17, 19; in *Corker*, 88–93
Westray disaster, 66–68, 74, 75, 103, 250n4

Whalen, Tracy, 77, 84, 157, 196, 203
White, Hayden, 181
Whylah Falls (Clarke), 124–26; Folk paradigm and, 124, 126; murder of Graham Cromwell and, 125–26; racism in, 124–26; work in, 125
Wilkshire, Claire, 215
Williams, Raymond, 30, 145, 247
Wilson, Budge, 134
Winter, Michael, 5, 93, 99, 103, 173, **203–15**, 239; *The Big Why*, 203–15, 216, 252n6
women, writing by, 106, 127–34, 135, 137, 167, 168, 251n6. *See also* gender issues
Woodcock, George, 8
work, 27, 29–30, 125; in Atlantic-Canadian literature, 29–100, 101, 125, 240. *See also* labour
Workman, Thom, 15, 19, 71–72, 73, 75, 81, 87
Wreckhouse (Barry), 162–65, 166, 167, 240; colonialism in, 163, 165; tourism in, 162–65
Wright, Miriam, 11, 38, 39

www.ingramcontent.com/pod-product-compliance
Lightning Source LLC
Chambersburg PA
CBHW052015070526
44584CB00016B/1757